DANIEL MORGAN

DANIEL MORGAN

A Revolutionary Life

Albert Louis Zambone

WESTHOLME
Yardley

Facing the title page: "Daniel Morgan at the Cowpens" bronze medal, designed in France by Augustin Dupre and struck at the US Mint in 1839. (*National Museum of American History*)

First Westholme Paperback 2021
©2018 Albert Louis Zambone
Maps by Tracy Dungan ©2018 Westholme Publishing

Westholme Publishing, LLC
904 Edgewood Road
Yardley, Pennsylvania 19067
Visit our Web site at www.westholmepublishing.com

ISBN: 978-1-59416-370-8
Also available as an eBook

Printed in the United States of America.

Edgar: What, in ill thoughts again?
Men must endure
Their going hence, even as their coming hither:
Ripeness is all. Come on.
Gloucester: And that's true too. (*Exeunt.*)
—*King Lear,* act 5, scene 2

CONTENTS

List of Maps

A gallery of illustrations follows page 130.

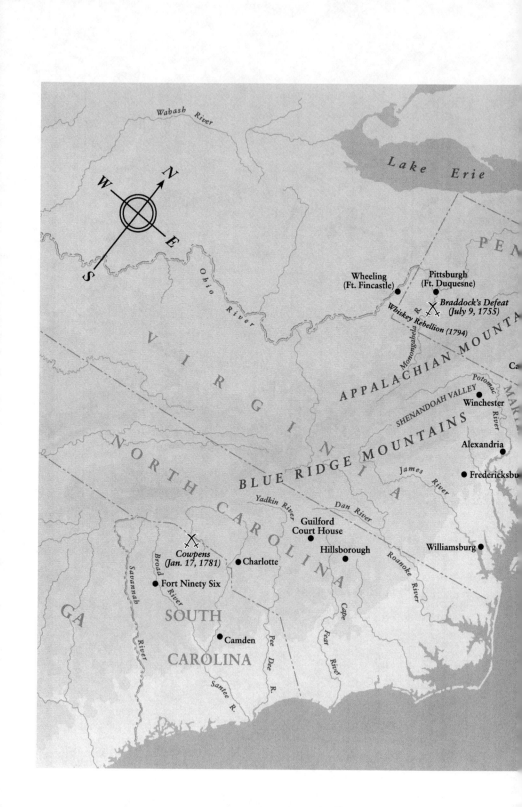

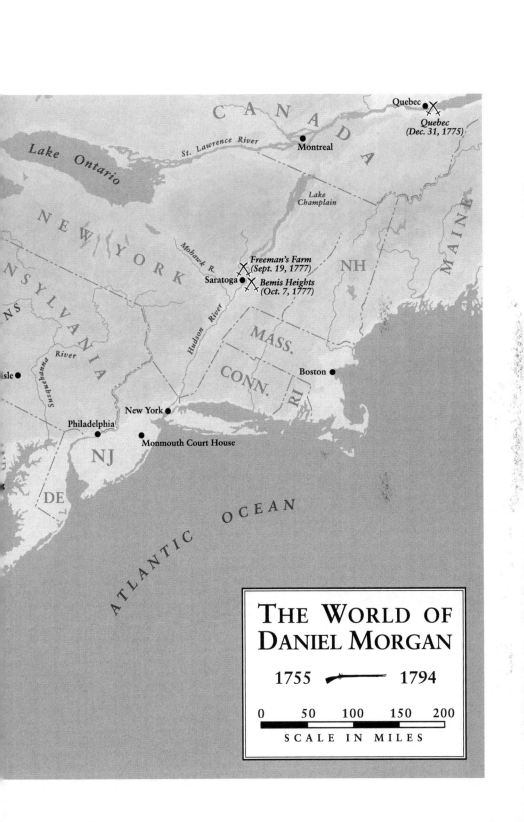

CANADA

Quebec ✕
Quebec
(Dec. 31, 1775)

Lake Ontario

St. Lawrence River

Montreal ●

Lake
Champlain

NEW YORK

MAINE

Mohawk R.

Freeman's Farm
✕ *(Sept. 19, 1777)*

NH

Saratoga ● ✕ *Bemis Heights*
(Oct. 7, 1777)

PENNSYLVANIA

Hudson River

MASS.

River

CONN.

Boston ●

Susquehanna

RI

isle ●

New York ●

Philadelphia ●

NJ

● Monmouth Court House

DE

ATLANTIC OCEAN

THE WORLD OF DANIEL MORGAN

1755 ⟋————— 1794

0   50   100   150   200

SCALE IN MILES

PROLOGUE

Let not Ambition mock their useful toil,
Their homely joys, and destiny obscure;
Nor Grandeur hear with a disdainful smile
The short and simple annals of the poor.
—Thomas Gray, *Elegy Written in a Country Churchyard*

I T was the darkness before dawn on January 17, 1781, at a crossroads in the backcountry of South Carolina, a savannah where cattle were overnighted during their amble to the coast. It was called, like other such pastures throughout the Carolinas, a cowpens, and soon it would acquire an honorific capital C. It was a series of open pastures of the Inner Piedmont, featuring long, meandering crests with occasional rolling dips and streams; a savannah of switch grass grazed by countless herds, enclosed and dotted by large trees. A mist blanketed the undulated countryside. Joining the mist was the smoke of campfires for almost two thousand men camped at the northern end of the Cowpens. Recumbent forms stretched out around the campfires, the experienced ones with their heads closest to the embers. Men who could not sleep stared into the flames, tossing occasional kindling to stoke the fire and offset the bite of the winter air.

All night the old wagoner meandered between the groups of men huddled around the flames, chatting, joking, telling them exactly what he expected of them. Some later claimed he had lifted his shirt to show them his back: the white-scarred wreckage left behind by 499 lashes, well laid on by a drummer boy back in 1756. It was one of his favorite stories: how there had been a miscount—showing that he had been conscious throughout the punishment and been keeping count—and that rather than the required five hundred he had been shortchanged one but chose not to argue the point. King George, he would say with a twinkle, mustn't have the opportunity to correct the oversight.

He was done now. Like everyone else on that field, he was waiting for dawn.

This was not the place where he had wanted to fight. He had meant to cross the Broad River and wait for the approaching British force on the slopes of Thickety Mountain, or on some other ground of his own choosing. But Banastre Tarleton was coming on hard and fast, as he always did. Now the old wagoner was caught in open country, six miles from the Broad. Now he had to fight.

He had been fighting his whole life, in one way or another. His body was a palimpsest of violence. Some kind of fight or quarrel had made him leave his home and parents. When he arrived in the Valley of Virginia, he fought to clear land, then fought to make his way as a wagoner. As wagoner, he fought other wagoners to establish his place in life. He fought Indians, and they left their mark on him. He struck an officer and got those 499 lashes in exchange. When there were no more wars to fight, he brawled and fought just for the hell of it. The Revolution meant more fighting, more damage to his suffering body. Now on that cold January morning, all the wounds and scars marked upon his body ached terribly as he waited for yet another fight.

A brawl was what he could expect from Tarleton, a straight-ahead, head-down fight. So he had put his plans down on paper—or rather his educated aides from Maryland had done so, so that everyone could read the handwriting—and shown it to all his officers. They all knew what they were to do. Now, after his nighttime rounds, his soldiers also knew what to do. There would be no ignorance or uncertainty breeding fear and anxiety, not this morning.

Daylight glimmered beneath the horizon. As men stirred and awoke, hoofbeats came hurriedly up the road from the south. A scout dashed up to the old wagoner to report. Tarleton was five miles away with his one thousand men, moving fast. Runners began to scatter with the news and with orders. A body servant held his horse, and the old wagoner, Brigadier General Daniel Morgan, mounted. Dressed in his Continental uniform, Morgan lightly spurred his horse through the camp. He began to shout, "Boys, get up, Benny's coming!"

DANIEL MORGAN was one of the unique personalities of the American Revolution. In addition to engineering the victory of January 17, 1781, at the Cowpens—the most tactically perfect American victory of the war—he was an architect of the victory at Saratoga, which remains one of the most decisive and genuinely consequential military victories in all of American history. He was thus in part or fully responsible for two of the truly decisive victories of the Continental army during the American Revolution.

It was the Revolution that revealed that whatever his other abilities and gifts, Daniel Morgan was a tactical genius. He knew how to lead his men—what to ask them to do and how to get them to do it. He also understood how to place those men on any given bit of ground. At Saratoga he used his chosen band of riflemen and sharpshooters from the Shenandoah Valley as if they were themselves one great sniper rifle under his personal control. He aimed them at the heart of the British army, killing its officers, its artillerymen, and their horses; breaking apart key formations; and allowing other Continental army regiments the opportunity to exploit the chaos he had created.

Yet, Revolution or no, Morgan was also a man of humble origins who wished to be recognized as a gentleman. When he was passed over for command of the new light infantry wing of the Continental army in 1779, he left the army in disgust. The honor of a would-be gentleman demanded nothing less. So he returned to his home, already aptly titled Soldier's Rest.

It was only the return of his friend and neighbor Horatio Gates to command in the South, and a commission as brigadier general by Congress, that drew Morgan out of his Shenandoah retirement. He had not reached the Southern Army before it was destroyed at

Camden in August 1780, and Gates was disgraced for both that loss and his hasty flight from the battlefield. Despite the departure of a man he regarded as a friend, Morgan stayed. The new commander, Nathanael Greene, gave Morgan command of most of the elite formations of the Southern Army and sent him west into the Carolina backcountry to make trouble and yet avoid defeat. That was how Morgan came to be at the Cowpens the night he decided to stop running from Tarleton.

MORGAN's interest to any reader of American history rests on much more than his success in battle. Morgan was an uncommon man of the common people who washed up in the lower Valley of Virginia, by choice without family, and as a consequence penniless, homeless, and placeless. In nearly every respect he seems to have been a prototypically country-style "good old boy" who liked playing cards, brawling, drinking rum, shooting, and women.

But closer inspection reveals him to have been astute and driven. Like the ambition of Abraham Lincoln—another man dismissed as a backcountry hick—Morgan's ambition was "a little engine that knew no rest."[1] His ascent through the ranks of Virginia society amounts to an outline for how to get ahead in colonial America. From laborer to overseer; from hired wagoner to independent wagoner; and from wagoner to wagon owner, farmer, entrepreneur, and captain in the county militia, Morgan fought his way upward through the social hierarchy with as much vigor as he ever fought a country brawl—or more. When he arrived in the valley he was illiterate, and he remained that way until at least the late 1760s. By the beginning of the Revolution he was capable of writing his own letters, and by the 1790s, reading and writing had given him a talent for confident yet still colloquial self-expression.

Daniel Morgan provides us with a rare opportunity in the history of early America to examine the life of someone who came from the often-silent ranks of the colonial poor. When Lincoln was asked to describe his family's history, he said there was not much there that could not be described with the phrase "the short and simple lives of the poor." He was quoting Thomas Gray's "Elegy Written in a Country Churchyard," a poem known to many in Lincoln's and in Morgan's time. Like Lincoln, Morgan was another one of those who came out from the obscurity of poverty.

But Lincoln knew his Gray, and in his double-edged way was undoubtedly also suggesting some of the succeeding lines in the poem. There the poet muses upon those "simple lives" and wonders what greatness lies around him that never had opportunity to display itself to the world, living and dying in this small corner of existence:

> Perhaps in this neglected spot is laid
> Some heart once pregnant with celestial fire;
> Hands that the rod of empire might have swayed,
> Or waked to ecstasy the living lyre.

Lincoln believed he was one of those special people who had rescued himself from poverty and obscurity and was destined for greatness. It is doubtful that Morgan—who, insofar as he was familiar with self-reflection, purposefully avoided it—articulated his own history as Lincoln did. But in his actions, which were his chosen form of expression, Morgan echoed that same self-understanding.

This is why so much of this book is focused on the context of Morgan's early life rather than speeding directly to the Revolution and the "good part." It is also why so much attention is devoted to Morgan's life after the Revolution. We cannot understand Morgan as a military commander and as a prosperous establishment figure without first understanding—insofar as we can, given the limitations of evidence—his early life in the Shenandoah Valley of Virginia. Without piecing together context and understanding what lives like Morgan's were like in the 1750s, we cannot understand how a poor homeless boy became a general, or how a country squire in Virginia became an ardent Federalist and anti-Jeffersonian, or how a military hero might establish his postwar legacy.

Morgan provides us with an opportunity to see what independence meant for a man like him, a rising man of property and growing wealth who fought his way up from the bottom of society. That he supported the cause of American independence was by no means a foregone conclusion. After all, he had fought for Britain as a British subject. Independence, and the fight for it, threatened the security of his property and all that he had worked to achieve. Surely it would have been easier to stay with the tried and proven, rather than take a leap into the darkness. Many other independent property owners chose to do the same, or to carefully avoid the fight.

But like many of those more prominent than he in the Revolutionary era, Morgan "saw in independence a future for himself and for his countrymen that could never be realized in union with England."[2] In Morgan we see what the hopes and fears of independence might have meant to a far-from-average "average" colonial man, to his family and posterity, and to his community.

THERE are other lessons to be learned from Morgan's life that are related to his persona and more generally to all historical biography. The military historian Mark Grimsley has noted that many fascinated by the Civil War are disproportionately interested in the personalities of statesmen and generals. "A team of Clydesdale horses," says Grimsley, "could not make me let go of the notion that what is going on here is a sort of men's studies hidden in plain sight." In confusing times, biography turns out to be a sort of self-help guide.

There are probably worse things that could be done with it. And at its best, this seemingly naive way of understanding personalities of the past understands something essential about the human personality. As Grimsley goes on to observe:

> Behind the general's scowl, the politician's grin, the diplomat's gaze of cool aplomb, are men, mere human beings, wrestling with questions, trying to squeeze them into answers. The questions most important to them rarely concern affairs of state, no matter how momentous. Instead they involve more personal issues, the same puzzles that afflict less famous, less powerful men. Who am I? What is the world around me like? How can I be happy? Which things, in the last analysis, are truly of importance. Each man answers these questions differently, but his answers affect every other decision he makes.[3]

Every human person is a mystery. Some are more mysterious than others, but each one of us has an enigma or riddle inside of us that most of us are unaware of—and in our more enlightened moments we are aware of this ignorance. The great literary answers to this self-ignorance have been the novel and the biography. In both genres we live the lives of others, and in doing so hopefully come to terms with our own. To read the life of Daniel Morgan while considering one's own life is not a misuse of biography but perhaps its most important use.

Therefore, in the following pages there are three intertwining stories. The first is, of course, Dan Morgan's. The second is something of the history of Morgan's place and his era, particularly as it influenced him and others around him. Finally, there is that story that results from the intertwining of the previous two, that of the era of the American Revolution.

In his dictionary of 1755, Samuel Johnson gave as his first definition of *revolution* the "course of any thing which returns to the point at which it began to move," a straightforward borrowing from Latin. It was his fourth definition that approaches the concept of revolution that is perhaps the most common today: "Change in the state of a government or country." Johnson would certainly have been horrified that future generations might see such a change as a good, and dismissive of extending it to cover the vagaries of an individual's life.

Calling Daniel Morgan's life "revolutionary" also has several nuances of definition. On the one hand, as I have already suggested, it was a perfectly ordinary life. Nor was Morgan by the end of his life, and perhaps never, a radical political revolutionary. Yet his was a life that was revolutionary in both senses of Johnson's term. Following his arrival in the Shenandoah Valley, his departures always brought him back to the point from which he first began to move. Morgan was an American Patriot, but he was also a Shenandoah patriot.

Yet Morgan's revolutions were also ones of changes of state. He began his recorded life homeless and ended it with 125,000 acres of land, two or three houses, a congressional gold medal, and a term in Congress. Certainly this was as radical a change of state as could be imagined.

Finally, in Morgan's life we have the context and the outworking of the Revolutionary epoch, drawing together the tumult and creative energy of late colonial America, the sudden alterations of the Revolution itself, and the difficult creation of the early republic. By studying Morgan's life, or that of any of his contemporaries, we make the American Revolution and its entire era personal, its stakes therefore more immediate and intelligible. In it we see that it was not the battles or campaigns that were important, not even for one of the finest soldiers of the Revolution, but the life he sought to build before, during, and after the war; how he built that life; and what it meant to him.

PART ONE

Shenandoah

Chapter One

HOME

S OMETIME late in autumn 1752 or early winter 1753, a
teenage Daniel Morgan walked into the frontier town of
Winchester in the colony of Virginia.[1] He arrived there after
starting his journey in New Jersey or Pennsylvania—we are not sure
exactly where he lived prior to heading south—walking through the
latter colony to Carlisle, Pennsylvania, a small town like Winchester
on the edge of the western frontier.[2] In Carlisle, he had worked for
a few weeks before heading south again on what was already called
the Philadelphia Road or, more romantically, the Great Wagon
Road. A few miles southwest of Carlisle, the road entered into the
Great Valley, the broad expanse bounded in Pennsylvania by South
Mountain to the east and the Appalachians to the west, part of a
geological formation stretching from Lake Champlain in New York
all the way to Alabama. This crease in the earth was an age-old
highway, first for natives traveling north and south and then for settlers heading into the backcountry.

At the Potomac River, Morgan likely crossed at Williams's Ferry,
and kept walking south into Virginia, heading up Opequon Creek,

which flows north to the Potomac. Broken by the merger of the Shenandoah and the Potomac, South Mountain was rechristened by Virginians the Blue Ridge, and they called the valley Shenandoah—or, more simply, "the Valley." When Morgan got to Winchester, he stopped and stayed.

Morgan never really explained why he went to Winchester or why after he got there he didn't keep moving. Certainly thousands of others did. They bought supplies in Winchester and then pushed on south farther into the backcountry. Others took a longer view, bought some land in the Valley, or perhaps more likely squatted on some land, and then ten years later moved on, following the road south through the Shenandoah, over the Blue Ridge, and all the way to the Yadkin River Valley in North Carolina, or farther still, into the backcountry of South Carolina. Others kept making their way down the western side of the Blue Ridge, into the farther reaches of southwestern Virginia.[3]

But Daniel Morgan stopped in the lower Shenandoah Valley and did not travel on; and that determined the shape, if not the direction, of his future. Who knows what Morgan thought as he trudged his way south from the Potomac, but his future life indicates that he thought something like what Civil War chronicler Bruce Catton described: "There may be lovelier country somewhere—in the Island Vale of Avalon, for example—but when the sunlight lies upon it and the wind puts white clouds racing their shadows the Shenandoah Valley is as good as anything America can show."[4]

We know next to nothing about the first decade and a half of Morgan's life; almost the first thing we do know about him is that he chose to stay in the lower Shenandoah. It became his residence, his home, the birthplace of his daughters, and finally his tomb. It was his chosen and particular place. We cannot understand Daniel Morgan without understanding the Shenandoah Valley, and the lower Valley in which he settled.

FOR a surprisingly long time, Virginian explorers persisted in believing that the Blue Ridge was impassable. Given that gaps in the Blue Ridge are not hard to find, the persistence of this belief indicates that no one had gone looking for them. There was no particular reason to do so. The population of Virginia experienced no demographic increase until the 1690s, and the lands of the Tidewater region were more than sufficient to produce the tobacco that made the colony wealthy.

When the first Anglo-Virginians crossed the Blue Ridge, they were in part pushed by the demands of a suddenly increasing population and the resulting economic need for more land, but also by strategic and even cultural imperatives. Not having too good an understanding of longitude, or of the precise placement of the eastern Great Lakes, it was thought necessary by Governor Alexander Spotswood to take steps to block any movement from the French into western Virginia from Lake Erie by establishing a boundary farther to the west. This would also create a route for the Indian trade with western tribes.[5] For this reason it was a matter of considerable importance when, in 1716, Spotswood announced to his council, the upper house of the Virginia legislature, that "some discoverys have lately been made by the Rangers of a Passage over the great mountains to the westward."[6]

Those rangers who first looked down upon the Valley from its surrounding rampart of mountains did not see open plains or meadow. In most places the Valley was still forested with hardwoods, pines in other areas that settlers called barrens. However, in places burned by woodland fires set by lightning or natives, it had been made into a sort of savannah. In other areas, along creeks and rivers, floodplains had been smoothed into meadow.[7]

The middle of the Valley was occupied by yet another mountain ridge, now known as Massanutten Mountain. On either side of it flowed a river, soon known as Shenandoah; the South Fork, on the southeast side of Massanutten, flows north; its twin, the North Fork, rises farther south and flows along the northwestern face of Massanutten before finally joining the South Fork at Masanutten's northern extremity.

This is an ancient landscape; the Blue Ridge hills are geologically the oldest in North America. The valley floor from the height that John Fontaine—a soldier of fortune in Spotswood's company—saw it seems remarkably level. But it actually rolls and undulates, punctuated with occasionally exotic geological features: conical hills, hot springs, chimneys, and a multitude of caves.

Where Morgan stopped his journey, in Frederick County, the Valley changes yet again. Massanutten no longer occupies its center, and the two lines of hills diverge to make the Shenandoah into a basin. This is the lower Valley, so called because it is downhill from the source of the Shenandoah River. The eastern boundary remains the Blue Ridge, but now with the Shenandoah River at its base, running north beneath Ashby's Bent, Mount Weather, and onward until it merges with the Potomac River. Across the basin, as if painted with a five-mile-wide brush, the land is striped with different types of soil. Just to the west of the Shenandoah are limestone lands, then shale, and then limestone, up to the base of the Blue Mountain, the western wall of the lower Valley.

These are not only different soils but different topographies. Limestone lands have terraces and features carved into them from the erosion of thousands of years; water doesn't usually run along the service but instead is absorbed into the porous earth beneath. Shale lands have more flowing surface water, V-shaped valleys, drier soil, and pine woods not found in the limestone areas.

They not only have different topographies but different ecologies. Limestone is—ask any farmer—a highly desirable fertilizer. So limestone lands have fertilizer built in; and they absorb water. Lime makes things base, on the pH scale, so plants that need a more acidic soil don't grow there. Because shale land doesn't absorb water, it's drier, and it's more acidic; pines grow on shale soil in preference to limestone soil.

So shale lands and limestone lands look different from each other. They have different topography; different plants; they even smell different. Moving from east to west across Frederick County was to move from one ecology to another. The limestone lands to the west of the Shenandoah gave way to the shale lands, which in turn give way to yet more limestone lands along Opequon Creek, the geographical center of the lower Valley. From there the limestone lands stretch to the front range of the Appalachians.[8]

Talk of soils and rivers and topographies might seem unrelated to the life of Daniel Morgan, but the divergence of soil conditions in the lower Valley shaped his choices and prospects. Had he settled in western Frederick County, in those limestone lands beneath the Blue Mountain, or in the shale landscape near Winchester, his life would have been shaped by that landscape, that ecology, and those neighbors who settled in that place. But Morgan got a job along the Shenandoah River, and that made all the difference. In large part this was because of the canny actions of Alexander Spotswood's successor as governor of Virginia, William Gooch, and the swift response to Gooch's actions by the wealthiest man in Virginia.[9]

LIKE Spotswood, Gooch was interested in the Shenandoah as a buffer against external pressure from the French to the west and the north. But he was also concerned with the internal pressure of the growing population of enslaved people in Virginia. In 1729, a group of runaway slaves had been tracked to a settlement they established in the mountains near the head of the James River. A series of Anglo-Virginian settlements in the Shenandoah could prevent the establishment of escaped slave communities in the western mountains, like those of the cockpit country in Jamaica.[10]

There was yet another internal threat that Gooch thought settlers in the Shenandoah could resist, and this one was embodied in the domineering, irascible, and generally unscrupulous form of Robert Carter, known to some contemporaries and most of posterity as "King" Carter for the defects rather than the features of his character.[11] He built an enormous fortune not through his career as a tobacco planter but because he was the agent to the Fairfax family's proprietary claim—granted by King Charles II of England—to the "Northern Neck." According to the royal grant the Northern Neck comprised all the land bounded by the Potomac and Rappahannock Rivers and a line drawn between their headwaters.

One of the only things that every Virginia governor could agree on with his legislature was that Charles II's geographical ignorance had led to a deal inimical to the interests of the colony. A long line of governors had always interpreted the Fairfax tract in the most restrictive way possible. While governors and representatives of the Fairfax family agreed that the Rappahannock River rose in the Blue Ridge, no one knew the length of the Potomac. The Virginia government, making ignorance if not a virtue then at least a benefit, insisted that the Potomac only began with the junction of two other rivers, the Shenandoah and the Cohongatarum. Under this interpretation, the Fairfax grant ended at the Blue Ridge. By granting land on his authority to immigrants like Jost Hite of Pennsylvania (the first official grantee in the Shenandoah Valley), Gooch hoped to wall in the Fairfax claims by asserting royal prerogative. Between 1730 and 1732, the government of Virginia distributed three hundred fifty thousand acres in the lower Valley through nine grants, each one requiring settlement by families. With just one exception, none of the settlers were either Virginians or even English, but Germans emigrating down from Pennsylvania. They were precisely the lowly, hardworking, ethical Protestants that Virginia visionaries had long sought to populate Virginia, industrious foreigners who would prove that the colony could be a prosperous and contented place— something generations of British settlement had not hitherto demonstrated.[12]

Those three hundred fifty thousand acres were quickly christened Frederick County and legally incorporated into Virginia, reflecting Gooch's desire to establish an orderly political structure along with a carefully nurtured settlement. It was, even when Morgan arrived in 1753, immense, composed of four present-day Virginia counties—Shenandoah, Clarke, Warren, and Frederick—and five present-day West Virginia counties—Hardy, Hampshire, Berkeley, Jefferson, and (he could not possibly have imagined this in 1753) Morgan.

In response to Gooch's grant, King Carter moved swiftly to protect the Fairfax family's claim, and to benefit himself and his relations—two things he regarded as the inverse and obverse sides of a heavy gold coin. He began a manic distribution of acreage on the eastern side of the lower Valley. He granted fifty thousand to his sons and grandsons one day, and the next day granted ten thousand acres to his son-in-law. By the time of his death in 1732, Carter had given his Tidewater heirs an immense posterity of Valley land.[13]

These heirs had no intention, at first, of settling in the Valley. For the first fifty years or so of their ownership, they and their descendants rented out their land to tenant farmers, or sent their surplus enslaved population to farm it under a white overseer. By the year Morgan first came to the lower Valley and to Frederick County, there were 680 enslaved people, give or take, among a population of eight thousand seven hundred whites. Almost all of these enslaved people were located on the acreage owned by absentee Tide-water landlords.[14]

So Frederick County, from the first land grants, was divided into two parts. On the western side, along Opequon Creek and into the mountains, was a region of four-hundred-acre landholdings, in loose settlements, inhabited by Germans and Scots-Irish. The eastern side, the limestone ground along the Shenandoah, was the preserve of absentee Tidewater aristocrats, all English. On the western side there were few slaves; on the eastern side all the large plantations were worked by enslaved labor.[15] And it was on the eastern side where Morgan got his first job.

WHY Morgan came to the Valley remains a mystery because Daniel Morgan meant it to be one. He never really explained why he left home, what it was that he left behind, or all that much about whom he left behind. His earliest biographers recorded that he only mentioned his early life by happenstance, and then only when conversation was warm and flowing easily. In these moments of ease, or forgetfulness, what he said amounted to this: His parents were Welsh—given the family name this does not count as a revelation—and had come up the Delaware River from Britain in the 1720s. He had been born around 1735 or 1736; he was not exactly sure when. His family had lived in Pennsylvania, or New Jersey, or both. He had quarreled with his father and had then walked away from home in late autumn 1752 or early winter 1753. He had stopped in Carlisle for a few weeks; he had then walked to Winchester and was, when he arrived, without any possessions other than his clothes.[16]

And that was as much as Morgan ever shared about his past. When anyone attempted further questions about his past he withdrew into himself and, if pressed, would "reply in a manner that put a stop to further inquiries of this nature."[17] It does not take much acquaintance with Dan Morgan to realize the elegant understatement of that phrasing.

A few additional scraps of fact can be inferred about his origins. For one, he knew all the skills and talents required for backcountry farming in early America. For another, he was so illiterate that he must have been unschooled—or, rather, unable to write, for in the eighteenth century, writing and reading were two different skills. His inability to write does not indicate that he also possessed an equal inability to read. Yet it is unlikely he ever spent any time in any kind of school.

In the nineteenth century, chroniclers were eager to fill in the large blank spots of Morgan's early life. As his first biographer, William Graham, observed, "generally, there is no part of a great man's career which is regarded with more interest than that with which it commenced."[18] Graham wrote after Parson Weems had done a makeover on George Washington's rather poorly sourced early life, discovering from "neighbors" such stories as the cherry tree, pitching a silver dollar over the Rappahannock, and other tall tales concocted to show just how the boy Washington was the father of the man who became the father of his country. It says much of Graham's seriousness as a scholar that while he expressed his regrets at the paucity of evidence about Morgan's early life, he did not then invent some.

Some of Morgan's biographers were not so scrupulous. At best they made erroneous associations and leaping inferences, but often they just seem to have invented interesting stories. New Jersey historians claimed he was from Hunterdon County; Pennsylvania historians responded that he was actually from Durham County, or perhaps Berks County. He had a long-lost brother whom he visited during the Revolution and provided for from out of his wealth and benevolence, reported one fanciful chronicler. He had a cousin, said others, and that cousin was none other than Daniel Boone. His father was a farm laborer; his father was an employee of the Durham Iron Works; his father was an independent farmer.[19]

Modern readers can be just as bad in this way as any nineteenth-century reader, just as eager to discover the childhoods of the great and good, or the bold and bad. In what seems to be part of the age-old question of nature or nurture, we press to discover the smallest indications of what was to come. It is thrilling to find the future statesman and writer penning a description of a hurricane at age twelve that attracts notice from far and wide (Alexander Hamilton); comforting to believe that the future mathematical genius was a poor student at school (a myth about Albert Einstein). We want to know that adversities have been overcome on the way to greatness—whether they are dyslexia (George Patton), abuse (Bill Clinton), poor education (Lincoln), or poverty (Lincoln again). It interests us that the future war leader played with soldiers (Winston Churchill) and that the future pacifist did too (H.G. Wells). We search childhoods looking for some hint of the future, some sense of the mature person in the action of the adolescent.

Morgan does not allow it. He shows up at seventeen, ready for life, and we have very little idea what, if anything, prepared him for it. There he is, suddenly, in the lower Shenandoah, and we might as well ask where the wind started from as figure out Morgan's early influences. If we want to find out what made Morgan, we have to begin at seventeen. And we have to begin not with the things within him but those things outside him. To interpret him when we lack evidence of his interior life, and even of his actions, we have to understand his context. By understanding the context, we have a better hope of understanding who he was.

Eastern Frederick County was where Dan Morgan got his start, and it was his home for all but the last two years of his life. He got a job with a small farmer named Roberts, clearing land for him, stripping the limestone soil of the trees that covered it—"grubbing stumps," as his lifelong neighbor Benjamin Berry remembered it. Wheat and grains required tilling, as the Valley's settlers saw it, and tilling meant plowing, and plowing meant moving in straight lines across the landscape, and that meant they had to remove the stumps. Thus Morgan worked with ax and mattock and lever to cut free the roots and then pry loose the stump from its long-settled bed. If he was fortunate, he might have had the assistance of a horse or an ox to pry it out.[20]

Morgan apparently did his work well, for as Berry remembered it, Roberts made him the foreman of a sawmill he owned—doubtless the destination of those trees whose stumps it had been Morgan's job to remove. From foreman of a sawmill, Morgan made his next jump to becoming a wagoner. In just a year or a little more after arriving in the Valley, he began to drive a wagon for Samuel Burwell, a scion of one of the great Tidewater families, another beneficiary of King Carter's largesse.[21]

While working for Burwell, he struck up a friendship with Jack Ashby, who turned out to be a good old boy much like himself, or was the model for the good old boy Morgan became. Ashby was from a family that had been on the eastern slopes of the Blue Ridge for long enough that the gap above the Shenandoah was named Ashby's Bent. While the Ashbys were not grandees, they were connected to everyone who was one, in one way or another. They were particularly connected to Lord Fairfax, who lived in a sort of hunting lodge he called Greenway Court, in eastern Frederick. Captain Jack Ashby was known for being a horseman, marksman, brawler, and rum drinker; soon Morgan was known for being all of these things as well.[22]

MORGAN sought, from the very beginning, to get ahead in colonial Virginia. This was a complex social art, and it is worth comparing him to a much better known contemporary who became a noted master of that medium.

By the time Morgan arrived in Frederick County, George Washington had long been a frequent visitor. He had been traveling there since he was sixteen, surveying the Fairfax tract. Washington's advantages over Morgan were considerable, but not as overwhelming as we might now think. He began with these: he was literate and numerate, personable, and from a decent-enough family. Despite having been in Virginia since the 1660s, the Washingtons were not of the foremost rank or anything like it. Furthermore, Washington's father, Augustine, had been a planter, but he had also been employed as an overseer of an ironworks—and being employed meant he was not quite a proper gentleman. George had the further misfortune of being the first child born to his father's second wife. His father's two sons by his first wife inherited the prime property.[23]

At his coming of age, George Washington inherited just a few hundred acres at Ferry Farm, the plantation across from Fredericksburg where his formidable mother lived, and ten slaves. This was wealth that Morgan would spend the entire decade of the 1760s trying to achieve, but it was not enough to make young Washington a true member of the Tidewater aristocracy. Had he been content with just that inheritance, Washington would have spent his years as obscure Virginia yeoman, perhaps rising as high as colonel of a county militia, justice of the peace, perhaps sheriff—and that would be about it.

But he was not content: he was outrageously ambitious, had some valuable learning in trigonometry and a gift for making friends, and was lucky. The connections of family and friendship gave him patronage; numeracy allowed him to take advantage of that patronage and earn a cash income; and luck, if it can be called that, caused him to benefit by the untimely deaths of those he loved.

Through the patronage of his elder half-brother Lawrence, Washington came to the attention of Lord Fairfax. First the Fairfax family sponsored George as a surveyor, both of Culpeper County and their own land. Then, after Lawrence's death, the Fairfaxes were George's patrons when he sought to, in effect, inherit Lawrence's position within the hierarchy of the Virginia militia. Lord Fairfax and his family served as first Lawrence's and then George's access to a higher status than any previous Washington in Virginia had enjoyed. Moreover, with Lawrence's death, the death of Lawrence's daughter and heiress, and the remarriage of his sister-in-law, Washington came into possession of Mount Vernon.

But even before he came to possess Mount Vernon, Washington owned more than two thousand acres of land in Frederick County, including some on Bullskin Run near where Morgan would first settle when he came to the Valley.[24] Trigonometry had made Washington a surveyor, patronage by the Fairfax family gave him the opportunity to engage in that profession, and that combination gave him access to desirable land and then a small income with which to buy some of it.

Daniel Morgan had no one to die for him, no elder brother to win him patronage. And while Washington might have always regarded his education as deficient, it made him a surveyor and got him land; Morgan in his twenties was barely literate.

What Morgan had were two things: a powerful body and a capacity for friendship. Like other men of his status in colonial America—or in any place where the chief means of advancement for you or your family is physical labor—Morgan was in a race against time and bodily deterioration. He had to make his mark or his fortune with the strength and skill of his body before chance or irresistible time took away his greatest advantage. To gain agricultural wealth was to engage in (and, despite all the ingenuities of John Deere, remains) a contest not only against weather, disease, and chance but against the steady deterioration of one's own capacity for labor.

So in addition to his strong body, Daniel Morgan also needed luck—or good fortune, or a beneficial Providence. Call it what you will, he had to live long enough to succeed, to avoid a compound fracture from an oak stump falling on his leg, a foot smashed by an errant horse's hoof, or losing a hand in the sawmill. Getting ahead in colonial America, or any other version of America, required luck.[25]

The other advantage, a capacity for friendship, is as evident throughout Morgan's life as the power of his body. It is indeed one of the most captivating things about him, that reaches out of his creatively spelled and deeply immediate letters to grab the reader, that is the common thread of all the stories told about him by those with reason to know him. Daniel Morgan was as open and free with his emotions as George Washington was stoical and withdrawn. Daniel Morgan hated his enemies and all scoundrels; but Daniel Morgan's love for his friends was stronger than his hatred of his enemies. This capacity for friendship, to men like Jack Ashby and Robert Burwell, would be Morgan's equivalent of Washington's link to the Fairfax family—or the first step toward acquiring such patrons.

BUT that was still in Morgan's future. In 1754 and 1755, Morgan got about the job of wagoner. This was the making of him and his initial fortune, and it was always the occupation through which Morgan saw himself. The night before the battle at the Cowpens, he referred to himself as he went from campfire to campfire as "the old wagoner"; and it helps to see this not as folksy battlefield rhetoric but as something deeper and self-identifying.[26] Being a wagoner was important to Morgan.

By the time Morgan arrived there, Winchester and the lower Valley had only been settled for twenty years, yet both were increasingly a crossroads for trade coming from up the Valley and from even deeper into the colonial American backcountry. Pack trains came up the Great Wagon Road from the Yadkin Valley in North Carolina, or from over the hills in western Maryland, bringing with them skins, furs, and whatever else they had to sell; they bought merchandise in Winchester and then returned to their frontier settlements. From Winchester their goods were taken by wagon either through Carlisle to Lancaster and eventually Philadelphia or across the Blue Ridge to the small ports along the Potomac and Rappahannock Rivers.[27]

It was to these relatively new Virginian ports, and the Scottish merchants who occupied them, that Morgan developed his trade. This was determined by his location in eastern Frederick County and by his developing relationship to the great men who held the land and the tenants who worked it. As Tidewater residents, they had no personal or credit connections to Philadelphia, but they had both with representatives of Glasgow trading firms along the Potomac and Rappahannock, the boundaries of the Northern Neck.

So Morgan's journeys took him east across the Blue Ridge to Fredericksburg and Falmouth on the Rappahannock and to the new towns of Dumfries and Alexandria on the Potomac. He made his way across the fords of the Shenandoah and up the slopes of the Blue Ridge. If going to the Potomac settlements, he took Snickers Gap, named later after his friend Edward Snickers; if going to the Rappahannock River, he went through Ashby's Bent, named after the family of his friend Jack Ashby. Through either gap he came to a Piedmont that was still as wild as the Valley, perhaps even more so in places; there heavily forested, still being cleared by the scions of the Tidewater families, in other places closer to the rivers punctuated with old fields that had once produced tobacco but whose soil was now exhausted and returning to woods.

Morgan and his fellow wagoners drove what were even then known as Conestoga wagons, a term applied to wagons made in southeastern Pennsylvania, western Maryland, and the lower Shenandoah Valley. Like the Pennsylvania rifle, the Conestoga wagon was the product of Pennsylvania German ingenuity, utilitarian and yet with an elegance that transcended utility. The Conestoga's hallmark was a curved body, elegantly raking upward both fore and aft. This curve gave the wagon a taut structural strength, but it also made it beautiful. So too did the canvas cover, bent over hoops. The Conestoga was the prototype for the ubiquitous wagons of the American frontier, the vessels of cultural expansion.[28]

An average Conestoga—and *average* meant something prior to industrial standardization and mass production—was about eighteen feet long, eleven feet high, and four feet wide. Some could carry as many as six tons, but that required a lot of horsepower—or, more probably, ox power: up to six horses or twelve oxen. A cargo of one to two tons seems to have been more typical, with four horses to haul it. Driving a wagon was an athletic endeavor. Anyone who has ridden one difficult saddle horse can only guess at the difficulties encountered in guiding four horses.

Morgan was the eighteenth-century equivalent of a truck driver, if truckers drove everywhere in four-wheel drive vehicles over roads whose appalling condition probably cannot be comprehended by the contemporary mind. Eighteenth-century Virginia roads are best thought of as somewhat parallel ruts that, if well maintained, were kept free of fallen trees.[29] If anything, however, wagoners seem to have had an additional level of panache. During Morgan's time as a wagoner, no one sat atop the wagon on a bench, controlling the reins. Some persisted in the older custom of the wagoner riding the wheel horse, the horse on the left nearest to the wagon, and controlling the rest of the team from that position. When a brake was added to Conestoga wagons, sometime around the middle of the eighteenth century, it was typically mounted on the left front wheel. To have access to it, wagoners began to walk alongside the wagon, close by the brake.[30]

One can imagine Morgan in 1754 traveling down from Ashby's Bent, cajoling, swearing, and coaxing his team by turns, keeping close to the brake—or, if he did not have a brake, then attaching a drag chain to keep the rear wheels from moving, turning it into a barely controllable sled.[31]

He would have traveled through the barely settled woods of the Piedmont of Virginia, passing by the many Ashby farms and kin, heading ever farther south and east toward the Tidewater. Looking at his routes and seeing who lived along them is to find a list of the people he knew the rest of his life. Not only the Ashbys but Edward Snickers settled by his own eponymous gap in the Blue Ridge. Farther down into Fauquier County was the Triplett family; on a January morning at Cowpens nearly thirty years later, Francis Triplett commanded the Virginia Militia gathered on that battlefield.[32] In the port towns were the Scots and Virginia merchants with whom Morgan contracted as a wagoner and to whom he eventually directed his business both as a farmer and an entrepreneur. Perhaps, to show what a hell of a fellow he was, just before he got to Alexandria or Dumfries, Falmouth or Fredericksburg, he left off trudging alongside the team, tidied himself up, maybe put on a fresh shirt, mounted the wheel horse, and rode into town at a brisk clip, the team stepping high, the reins in his hands, a homespun charioteer down from the hills.

This was his school and its curriculum. As a wagoner he had a vital role in a developing frontier economy. Long before many other Americans had articulated it, long before he was publicly concerned about it, he knew the necessity of interstate commerce, of internal improvements, of the need for intelligible commercial relationships. He knew what the prices were throughout Virginia; he knew the gossip, and the news; he was therefore a person to listen to. He was—as Dan Morgan could never fail to be—a local character, a practical athlete displaying his mastery on a regular basis.

Chapter Two

WAR

T HE CONFLICT variously known as the Seven Years' War, the
French and Indian War, and the Great War for Empire also
has a good claim to the title of First World War. Beginning
in Morgan's very own Virginia backcountry, it would, by its end in
1763, have been fought at the walls of Prague and the plains of
Pomerania by the shores of the Baltic; from the borders of Portugal
to the field of Plassey in India; to the walls of Ticonderoga, Louis-
bourg, Quebec, Manila, and Havana. The only continent free from
the conflict was Antarctica—which, to be fair, had not yet been discovered.

But what was tragedy for Morgan as a settler on the Virginia
frontier was potentially an opportunity for Morgan the young man
on the make.

The war began as a dispute between the colony of Virginia and
the government of New France over the destiny of the Ohio River
valley, a region that had been claimed by France since Robert de
LaSalle's expeditions of the 1670s. But as far as the royal government of the colony of Virginia was concerned, the Forks of the
Ohio, the valley that spread west from it, and much else besides was

Virginia and had been since the first charters granted to the Virginia Company. So far as Virginia's elite was concerned, the Ohio valley was the Old Dominion's, not for either French or Quakers.

In 1755, Virginia's leaders began to press that claim. Governor Robert Dinwiddie and elite members of Virginia society knew that the Ohio's bottomland was just the place to expand their ever-growing agrarian slave economy. The result was George Washington's debut on the world stage—as an emissary to a French fort near Lake Erie and then the loser of a series of skirmishes that ended with his surrender of a ramshackle fortification he had dubbed Fort Necessity.

Following young Washington's defeat at Fort Necessity, the first shots of that world war, Governor Dinwiddie split the Virginia Regiment into several companies. Disgusted at losing his regimental command just as soon as he had gained it, Washington resigned. The companies created by this reorganization gathered at Wills Creek on the upper Potomac, and by November they were at work on what was later named Fort Cumberland. Meanwhile in London, the government decided to send a punitive expedition that would land in Virginia, at Alexandria on the Potomac, make its way by Fort Cumberland to the Forks of the Ohio, and seize France's newly constructed Fort Duquesne.

Not even Sir Edmund Braddock, the newly appointed commander of the expedition, thought it would be as simple as that. It wasn't.

WHEN General Braddock arrived at Alexandria on March 26, 1755, with one thousand six hundred troops in two regiments brought from Ireland, the question of how to supply this little army had not been answered. Major Sir John St. Clair, Braddock's experienced, able, and temperamental deputy quartermaster general, had arrived earlier in Virginia. By the time Braddock's army arrived, St. Clair had traveled one thousand miles by horse and canoe through Maryland and Virginia. Much to his chagrin—or more likely disgust—he had discovered that the upper Potomac was unsuitable for transporting the army's needed supplies.[1]

What an eighteenth-century army required for its supply remains astonishing. In 1755, one thousand men required six tons of supplies each day; at one ton per wagon, that was six wagons a day. The horses that pulled those wagons required twenty to twenty-five pounds of good hay each day they were engaged in the brutal labor of hauling a ton of supplies up and down the Appalachian Mountains in the parallel ruts that passed for roads. Braddock was completely dependent upon these wagons and on the cross-grained, cussed wagoners like Dan Morgan, who insisted on being hired at the rate of seventy pounds sterling for a wagon and team of horses (by comparison, in times of peace, the Allasons of Falmouth and Winchester paid Morgan and his compatriots about three pounds per shipment between the two towns).[2]

During his reconnaissance, St. Clair had been, to say the least, dismayed at the condition of Virginia's roads. With the assistance of gold coin he supervised the improvement of roads running through Virginia up to Wills Creek and Fort Cumberland, particularly the Alexandria Road that ran through Winchester. From Alexandria, Braddock dispatched Sir Peter Halkett on this road with the 44th Regiment. They marched up the route Morgan knew so well, across Goose Creek, the crossroads of the Carolina Road, over Catoctin Mountain, down into the Loudon Valley, and then up again over the Blue Ridge to Winchester. With their arrival, Winchester's role as a strategic place, the node of backcountry warfare in Virginia and Maryland, was confirmed.

Colonel Thomas Dunbar led the 48th Regiment and Independent companies from New York and South Carolina on a separate route, across the Potomac at Rock Creek and then north through the countryside to Frederick in Maryland. The difficulties in traversing Maryland were by British standards extreme: dust and heat one day, followed closely by lightning, thunderstorms, and a foot of snow— all this on April 15. So arduous was their journey that when Braddock caught up with the column at Frederick, he saw that his troops had been worn down by the first, and supposedly easiest, phase of their march. Adding injury to insult, they were also without any of the supplies promised them by the governors of Virginia and Maryland, and without wagons in which to haul the nonexistent supplies.[3]

Fortunately for Braddock, one visitor at his dinner table the night he learned of his predicament was Benjamin Franklin. Franklin being Franklin, he naturally volunteered to set things to rights and, being Franklin, he did so with masterpieces of impromptu propaganda, wielding both carrot and stick in two different handbills that he composed on the spot. The stick was the threat that St. Clair would soon lead a "body of soldiers" into Pennsylvania and seize whatever the army needed. The carrot was an appeal for help, with the promise that Pennsylvanians should provide wagons, draft horses, pack horses, and their own service in exchange for generous wages and the promise that they would subjected to the same discipline as British soldiers. That would prove to be, for Dan Morgan, a particularly ironic touch.[4]

Braddock was not quite the simple-minded pompous disciplinarian that American legend has made him out to be. His brief campaign in the colonies showed him to be something of a soldiers' general, concerned first of all for the well-being of his troops. He gave them permission to eat as much as they needed to, rather than set a strict daily ration—certainly wise when they were burning so many calories on a march over difficult terrain. He lightened their carry load by confining it to a small cartridge box, a haversack for rations, a tin canteen, and a small knapsack with additional gear including a blanket. He also directed their officers to be easy in their discipline. Taking it for granted that soldiers would get drunk on their rum ration, he forbade officers to converse with drunken soldiers, lest any soldier say something that he would soon regret. Braddock ordered that the particularly drunken simply be confined and left to sober up, rather than suffering any punishment.[5]

Nevertheless, neither Braddock nor hardly anyone else in British society would have ignored the offense that Dan Morgan soon committed. It is not clear whether it occurred on the march to Fort Cumberland, while the army was camped there, or on the march to the Forks of the Ohio. As Morgan later told the story, a British officer had been abusive and rude to him, and Morgan responded in kind. The officer then struck him with the flat of his sword and Morgan, being Morgan, responded with his fist and knocked the man down, unconscious. Remembering it, Morgan referred to himself as being just a "giddy boy." Giddy boy or not, given the enormity of the crime there was no need in the eighteenth century British army for much of a criminal procedure. Striking an officer was an intolerable breach of military and social norms. Morgan was sentenced to five hundred lashes.[6]

DISCIPLINE in the eighteenth century British army remains legendarily harsh, and this is not an inaccurate view. But it is a limited view. The army was really no different than any aspect of British society in the eighteenth century, on either side of the Atlantic. All legal punishments were harsh, designed not to encourage penitential reform but to enact retribution. Public blasphemy could end with a hole bored through one's tongue; thefts under a certain amount were punished by being branded upon the hand. For many crimes the punishment was death by hanging, which a lenient judge might commute to transportation to the colonies,[7] where punishments would be no more lenient.

So compared to contemporary punishments, the army's were not particularly outrageous. They had been harmonized and simplified as the eighteenth century progressed. In the first quarter of the eighteenth century, punishments included not only flogging but running the gauntlet—being whipped or beaten as you ran down a lane of your fellow soldiers—and "riding the horse": being placed atop a sawhorse with your feet weighted down. These and even more ingenious penalties faded in frequency of application—at least in the regular army—in favor of flogging.[8]

The Royal Army and Navy whipped their miscreants with a cat-o'-nine-tails, a rope handle with nine cords, or "tails," trailing from it. Punishment was administered before the assembled ranks of the condemned's own battalion, drawn up in the center of camp at the end of the day. He would be stripped naked and tied to a tripod of halberds, the pole arms carried by sergeants in part as symbols of their rank. The whipping itself was delivered by the battalion's drummers, supervised by the drum major, each administering twenty-five lashes before switching in order to make certain that their arms did not get tired. Drummers had two qualifications for the job. First, they were the lowest members of any regiment, the bottom of the social hierarchy of that little world. Their arms were also necessarily well exercised. The flogging went on until the sentence of allotted strokes was met, unless the required attending surgeon ended it.[9]

Provincial forces also used flogging as a perennial punishment, particularly the Virginia Regiment. In 1756, when the frontiers were wide open to Indian attack and desertion was destroying the ability of the regiment to protect backcountry Virginians, its commander, George Washington, resorted to doling out fearful rations of flogging to offenders. At one point he ordered one thousand lashes apiece be administered to six deserters; one thousand five hundred to four others; and five hundred to one soldier who had not deserted but was simply believed to have planned to do so. Reporting to Washington the results of one flogging, his second in command and Morgan's future friend Adam Stephen chortled, "We catchd two in the very Act of desertion and have wheal'd them 'till they pissd themselves and the Spectators Shed tears for them—which will I hope answer the End of punishment." Callous brutality was not a monopoly of chinless, red-coated aristocrats.[10]

The particular importance of eighteenth-century punishments was not simply that they were brutal but that they were publicly brutal. Branding, having holes bored in the tongue, running the gauntlet, riding the horse, flogging, even hanging—the goal was not just bodily punishment or death but also social humiliation. A hole bored through the tongue was a humiliation that lasted far longer than the pain. The ceremony of hanging ended not with the death of the individual but with his social exposure: the corpse hung until it rotted, was cut up and its pieces distributed for public viewing, or (in the case of pirates or the particularly notorious criminal), was chained and tarred so that even after the flesh was gone, the bones remained on display. Flogging would not have been flogging if it was done in an empty prison courtyard. It was also essential that it be done not just in public but before miscreants' own public: their neighborhood, their family, or, in the case of the British army, in front of soldiers' own messmates. This made those undergoing punishment in the eighteenth century actors on a stage. How they experienced the punishment, how they endured their social humiliation, was an essential part of the drama. Punishment in the army was sometimes ended before the penalty was complete simply because of the stoicism of the convicted.[11]

So Morgan was tied up to a tripod of three halberds, and his punishers set to work. As he remembered it, only one drummer flogged him. If so there must have been occasional pauses when the boy rested his arm or switched arms. The duration of punishment must have then stretched for more than thirty minutes. Certainly the effects of it remained written on Morgan's back for the rest of his life; whatever his age, the drummer boy was not a puny thirteen-year-old. In the last two years of Morgan's life, when someone always had to be at his bedside to assist him, his pastor, Dr. William Hill, was often with him. Hill later recalled that when helping Morgan turn over in bed during his last illness, he saw that the flesh of his back was scarred and ridged. He asked Morgan how this had happened.

To Hill, as he had many times before to others, Morgan freely recounted the incident. The scars, he said, were the result of punishment that he had gotten from "old King George." As always, he insisted that he had only been flogged 499 times—he had counted along with the drummer, he always said, and marked when the drummer missed count. But he always added—no doubt with a twinkle in his eye—that he had not brought the error to anyone's attention, and "let it go so!" Or, as he laughingly said years later, in 1781, to a British officer captured at Yorktown, "I convinced the drum-major of his mistake, but they wouldn't tie me up again; so I am still their creditor to the amount of one lash."[12]

Morgan's attitude toward his punishment was the response to violence that earned a punished soldier the esteem of not only his fellow soldiers but also possibly his officers. Biographer William Graham reports that the officer Morgan struck actually apologized to him later; and if Morgan took the flogging at the time as well as he later claimed he had, this is somewhat plausible. Stoicism, or better yet cheerfulness, despite the flogging won applause and approbation. It was a sort of external sign of inward redemption. In this sense, Morgan's flogging helped make him somebody. Being flogged gained him his reputation as a man.[13]

Morgan's punishment was soon lost among subsequent events. He and George Washington were just two of the men on Braddock's

expedition who, of course unbeknownst to themselves or their contemporaries, were some of the future notables of the American Revolution. Commanding the 44th Regiment was Lieutenant Colonel
Thomas Gage, later the commander in chief of the British army in
North America and the man who sent troops to seize weapons in
Concord, Massachusetts, and was besieged by George Washington
in Boston. One of Gage's lieutenants was Charles Lee, who, during
that siege of Boston, was Washington's second in command. Farther
back among the provincial forces was Captain Horatio Gates, commissioned in the 45th Regiment, a staff officer in Nova Scotia, now
commanding the 4th New York Independent Company. He would
one day be both Dan Morgan's friend and commander in the Continental army. As if that was not enough, one of Morgan's fellow
teamsters, in the North Carolina detachment bringing up the rear,
was a young frontiersman from the Yadkin River valley named
Daniel Boone.[14]

A few days into Braddock's march from Fort Cumberland to the
Forks of the Ohio, he realized that his army was moving far too
slowly because of the wagons supplying it and because of the siege
artillery brought along to batter Fort Duquesne into splinters. Braddock therefore created a flying column, a lightly equipped, fast-trav-
eling strike force. He left the supply train and artillery under the
command of Colonel Dunbar and moved ahead with the flying column and engineers to build the road. It was probably as part of
Dunbar's column that Morgan drove his way north, following in
his wagon the path created by Braddock's faster-moving engineers.

As part of this column, Morgan also first heard the news of the
Battle of the Monongahela and the defeat of Braddock's advance
column. The wounded Braddock was eventually brought into camp
with other survivors, and when he died, Morgan's wagon and the
rest of the supply train rolled over his grave, the ruts of the wheels
concealing it from the pursuing enemies.

IN the months following the Battle of the Monongahela, Virginia's
backcountry became a center of the developing world war. Open
now to raids mounted from Fort Duquesne as well as locations
deeper in the Ohio Country, the Valley became a strategic place, ful-

filling the purpose that Spotswood and Gooch had intended for it thirty-some years before, a buffer against French attack from the west and a base for counterattacks. This sounds very anodyne and bloodless. The reality was very different. Virginia, for the first time since Bacon's Rebellion in 1676, was at war—suffering all of the particular horrors of American frontier warfare.[15]

The war confronted Virginia's government with military problems for the first time in three-quarters of a century, and the House of Burgesses struggled to develop appropriate military solutions. This was in part because of political cowardice (and a resulting want of foresight), as well as political shrewdness—two qualities often closely aligned in successful politicians, which Virginia had in abundance.

In theory, and thus far in practice, the defense of Virginia relied upon its system of county militias, in which each freeholder was obligated to serve. On paper, then, Virginia possessed an army of thirty-six thousand men. In reality it had nothing of the sort. As Governor Dinwiddie explained to one English correspondent, militia "are Free-holders, who insist upon y're Privileges not to enlist or serve but on imminent danger."[16] This was their political right, and they insisted on it; no one in the House of Burgesses would ever dare to contradict them. But "imminent danger" was often detected when it was far too late, and essential military tasks such as garrisoning a fort or guarding a supply train of wagons did not fall under the rubric of that term. Yet such tasks needed to be done, or Virginia was defenseless.

There were three other problems with employing the Virginia Militia, and two of these were soundly strategic, fitting neatly into the grand strategy of the colony of Virginia—which did not officially exist but was nevertheless present as a default setting. First, if militia were freeholders, they were consequently farmers. One month away from the farm at harvest time could be catastrophic, not only for the individual farmer and his family but, when on a county- or colony-wide scale, for all of Virginia, and possibly even for communities farther away. A missed tobacco harvest could have implications so dreadful they could not be contemplated. Dinwiddie and others were already concerned, in 1755 and 1756, that the drought Virginia was then suffering might lead to famine; such a result would be certain if the militia had a wide callout.[17]

The other necessity for the militia that no Virginia governor could ever ignore was its critical role as an internal security force to suppress the enslaved population. Dinwiddie was particularly concerned that in this time of war the "ungrateful negroes," as he termed them, might take the opportunity to revolt. It was critical then that militia from the eastern Tidewater counties, those most heavily populated by an enslaved population, not be sent to protect the frontier except in times of the most extreme threat—and perhaps not even then.[18]

Finally, there was a social and cultural problem that enraged young Colonel Washington but could not be solved. Whenever the Valley or its outlying regions were threatened by attack and the militia were called out to defend it, many of them (regardless of rank) refused to do so. In such a situation they could not bear to leave their families and neighbors undefended. Washington, of course, tried to reason with them, tried to convince them that by forming up in their militia companies they could take the fight to the enemy and defend their homes. But the chance remained that they would not find the elusive enemy; that an enemy raiding party might bypass the militia, burn their homes and barns, and take their families captive. Much better, in this case, to die defending their homes. Even in peacetime the militia in the Valley were frequently absent from muster, they deserted from service, and they generally placed their concern for their families and very immediate locality over all other claims on their labor and loyalty. With the threat of war, the Valley residents—somewhat less deferential to hierarchical authority than other Virginians—were even more apt to be absent, to desert, and to worry about their families.[19]

Ultimately, Virginia's rulers were forced to rely for the colony's safety on the Virginia Regiment, a professional military unit funded by the colony. Its members were not freeholders or farmers but the poor and landless of Virginia, and even of other colonies or recent English immigrants. They were men without ties to family or community, without any existing responsibilities. It was not a militia, either in duration of enlistment, quality of equipment, amount of pay, or brutality of discipline. Washington aimed to create a regiment that while organized and funded by the colony could be taken into the British line without hesitation. Ultimately it seems he succeeded.[20]

Morgan was never a member of the Virginia Regiment, nor did he develop as a soldier under the benevolent eye of his young commander, as one of his more purple biographers might have put it. He was for a brief time a ranger, an old military specialization in Virginia's history, but which in the crisis of 1755 was being employed in new ways.

The principle problem was geographic. After Braddock's defeat, Washington was charged with defending all four hundred miles of Virginia's western border. This he saw as an impossible assignment, even if he had commanded far more than the one thousand men in the 1st Virginia Regiment. Had Governor Dinwiddie and Washington had their way, they would have organized yet a third attempt to take Fort Duquesne and cauterize the source of Virginia's infection. But the Virginia legislature had no desire to fund such a risky venture.

Instead it voted to establish a chain of forts along the frontier. Eventually there were eighty-one of these, some not much more than a log cabin surrounded by a stockade. So far as Washington was concerned, this was a policy born of complacency resulting in military madness. It was impossible for him to garrison so many forts with the limited number of soldiers in the Virginia Regiment, and it was obviously impossible to call up militia to garrison the forts for any extended length of time.

To be fair, the Virginia legislature's policy was not wrongheaded; it might even have been successful in continuing Washington's fight. That chain of forts provided shelter to the frontier and the Valley settlers and thereby convinced many not to leave their farms for safety east of the Blue Ridge. By remaining on their farms, they could provide Washington's troops with a local source of corn, cattle, horses, and wagons. Washington might vehemently complain about the quality of these supplies, but poor horses were better than no horses; and no horses is what he would have had—or at best an even scarcer supply of horses—had the frontier been completely abandoned.[21]

So in summer and autumn 1755, with the frontier open to attack and the Virginia Regiment just a glimmer in its young commander's eyes, Washington thought the rangers might be the temporary security of the Virginia backcountry. At his urging, the Virginia legislature raised new companies of rangers, one or more companies from each of the western counties to be assigned to garrison and patrol those counties. The company assigned to Hampshire County was commanded by Morgan's friend Jack Ashby. Morgan joined Captain Ashby's company and either from the outset—autumn 1755—or soon thereafter, Morgan was given a commission as an ensign. Within a few months, Morgan had risen from a wagoner receiving five hundred lashes to the rank of an officer, if not yet to the status of a gentleman.[22]

The more immediate attraction that the Virginia rangers provided Morgan and other enlisted men and officers was eight pence a day—one pound every thirty days—minus the money withheld from their salary that paid for their clothing. Although they received the same pay as soldiers of the Virginia Regiment, they were under more relaxed discipline, more like that of the militia (until 1757, when they were brought under the same regulations as the regulars). Yet neither the pay nor the casual attention to detail seemed to attract many more recruits than did the provincial regulars. Though each company of rangers was supposed to muster one hundred men, their actual recorded musters ranged from a lamentable sixty to a downright derisory ten. Ashby's was one of the worst. By October 2, 1755, he reported recruiting just twenty-eight men.[23]

In theory, these companies of rangers were to scout and skulk along the colonial borders, to range the woods looking for Indian war parties and then ambush them long before they reached the settlements of the western valleys, or the Valley itself. But their practice seems to have been a little less than ideal. Adam Stephen complained to Washington that the Indians were discovering the rangers by the tracks of their shoes, since they had no moccasins—which indicates a certain lack of woodcraft on the rangers' part. While reputedly many settlers of the Valley and the western ridges of Virginia did adopt native garb along with a certain understanding of how to live and thrive in the woods, whether the men enlisting in the ranger companies were these backwoodsmen is open to question. Men with actual backwoods skills might not have chosen to join the ranger companies. Certainly Washington was always appealing for them to do so, indicating that they were not, or at least not enough of them were.

Morgan and his fellow rangers seemed to involve themselves in a combination of hard work and goofing off, with the latter in a larger percentage than the former, according to young Washington's acerbic letters. Autumn 1755 found all the ranger companies engaged in building blockhouses in their jurisdictions—thereby creating zones of control (in modern counterinsurgency terminology), part of the elaborate and ineffectual defense plan insisted upon by the Virginia legislature. Rangers also shepherded the supplies that these little "forts" required and guided parties of militia and provincial regulars to garrison some of them. Ashby's company operated along the South Branch of the Potomac, from September 1755 onward, and by December it had constructed a blockhouse on Patterson Creek—fittingly enough the site of present-day Fort Ashby, West Virginia.

The rangers proved to be poorly disciplined when not building, scouting, or guiding, and perhaps even when doing these things. Washington sharply reminded Ashby at the outset that he was for no reason to march his company back to Winchester "on any pretense whatsoever."[24] The temptation to do so must have arisen from the reality of garrison life, which for untrained and undisciplined men with little formal responsibility must have been truly awful. No doubt Morgan's buddy and fellow wagoner Joseph Coombs was regarded as an angel from heaven when he arrived at Fort Ashby in December with a wagonload of rum. Ashby purchased barrels above and beyond the ration allocated to his rangers—whether to sell to them at a profit or to buy their obedience is unclear. Whatever the reason, Ashby's garrison was, as a result, rendered drunk and helpless. When Washington sent the expected snarl of indignation to Ashby, he added that he had heard that Ashby's wife—who, as was not uncommon in the eighteenth century, had accompanied her husband into the field—was a misbehaving nuisance "who I am told sows Sedition among the men."[25]

The rangers did not, then, provide Morgan with the most rigorous military education. But there he nevertheless encountered plenty of opportunities to be killed, wounded, or scalped.

SUCH opportunities were all too apparent to Morgan and his fellows in spring 1756. First, in March, Neally's Fort on Opequon Creek, in the heart of the lower Valley, was attacked. All within it were killed or captured.

But the chief offensive came in April, and it lasted into the summer. Starting around April 10, several war parties moved into the valley of the Cacapon River, which flows north to join the Potomac. Their intention was to sever the supply lines between Winchester and Fort Cumberland, and perhaps to destroy Fort Cumberland itself. To do that they had to destroy Ashby's garrison.[26]

On April 15, Ashby sent a dispatch to Washington at Fort Loudon in Winchester claiming four hundred Indians had demanded the surrender of his post. Moreover, he reported, one thousand five hundred warriors had moved down the valley toward Fort Cumberland, and two thousand were heading farther north toward the Juniata River in Pennsylvania. Washington was dubious about these numbers—he probably wondered if Ashby had been stocking up again on Joe Coombs's rum—and, irritated as usual, ordered Captain Henry Harrison at Fort Edwards (not Jack Ashby) to send out some "good Woodsmen" so they could "get intelligence of the Enemy, and their place of Rendezvous."[27]

When he wrote that order, Washington was unaware that one of the worst defeats ever suffered by his Virginians—either militia, rangers, or Virginia Regiment—had occurred. Captain John Mercer had led a company out of Fort Edwards in pursuit of an Indian war party, which had drawn them into an ambush in which seventeen men were killed. It was not the number of deaths that shocked Washington, but the fact that this had been inflicted by a large force just twenty miles from Winchester. By April 21, he was sending express riders east to commanders of county militias, and to Williamsburg, requesting that the Fairfax and Prince William County Militias turn out and march north in support of his beleaguered garrisons. On April 22, Washington posted yet another broadside, pleading for woodsmen to join the fight.[28]

On the day before Mercer's defeat, Morgan had been caught by one of the roving war bands in the Cacapon Valley. On April 16, he had been at Fort Edwards, to which he and a companion had led some militia—perhaps some of whom were slaughtered the next day. As they returned to Fort Ashby, they came to a narrow place in the trail where seven warriors were waiting. The Indians opened fire. With their first volley they killed Morgan's fellow ranger and gave Morgan a wound that seems impossible he could have survived. The musket ball supposedly pierced Morgan's neck (according to the earliest accounts), passed behind the socket of the jaw, and entered his mouth. There it knocked out all the teeth on the left side before exiting through his upper lip. The entry, however, might well have been in his cheek, just ahead of his jawbone, for it is hard to imagine how a musket ball of .50 caliber or more could have missed both jugular vein and jawbone if it had entered in his neck.[29]

Despite this wound, Morgan stayed in the saddle of his horse, which he understandably remembered fondly as a "fine young filly." She proved herself that in the following moments. Despite the gunfire, she remained motionless while he recovered his senses, holding onto her neck. Soon he nudged her forward, back down the trail toward Fort Edwards (in the course of the attack she had somehow gotten turned around). One member of the war party was approaching Morgan as the mare began to trot away, and he broke into a run; Morgan then put his heels into the horse, and she raced ahead. For a moment, as Morgan later recalled it, his pursuer "ran with open mouth and tomahawk in hand by the side of the horse, expecting every moment to see his victim fall." As the horse surged ahead and the attacker tired, he futilely threw the tomahawk at Morgan with a yell of rage and disappointment. The memory of that yell, like the wound, remained with Morgan the rest of his life.[30]

Mercer, in his last communication to Washington, seemed to refer to Morgan's wounding and his companion's death, yet unfortunately without providing their names. He wrote that "Yesterday Morning one of Captn Ashby's Men, who has been on Forlow some Time, with one Hintch who came down with Us as a Pilot, were in their Return to Ashby's Fort & were fired on by seven Indians, Hintch killed dead on the Spot and the other returned here wounded in the Neck, but no ways dangerous." Mercer's description aligns closely with Graham's description of Morgan's wounding. It is certainly hard to see how the unnamed wounded soldier could not be Daniel Morgan. While it is also hard to see how such a wound could be considered small, Morgan must have been flat on his back at Fort Edwards recuperating when Mercer led his doomed force in pursuit of the war party. It also seems that the wound ended Morgan's service with the rangers. After that attack, his traces fade from the records of the provincial forces.[31]

MORGAN'S experience in the war had certainly been formative, though not in the way anyone would purposefully intend it to be. It left its marks on both his body and his self-conception. His back was now a jagged mess, a monument to the brutality of eighteenth-century punishments. On his face he had an extra philtrum—the scar on his upper lip where the Indian's bullet had exited—that is visible on all of his portraits.

But what Morgan learned from that experience in the war is uncertain. Discipline and attention to detail do not seem to have been part of life in Jack Ashby's company; what Morgan knew of both he could not have learned drinking Joe Coombs's rum. Nor is there evidence that Morgan learned any of the tactics and skills he employed in the skirmishes, battles, and wars to come. Virginia rangers, like those in other colonies, seem to have been much more often ad hoc and ineffective than they were eighteenth-century special operations warriors.

Yet it was nevertheless a tremendously important experience for Morgan, a transition in his self-conception. The first home he established for himself and his future wife he named Soldier's Rest. When at the end of his life he looked back at his origins, he observed that "from my youth I have been a soldier." He had begun the war as a wagoner, but by the end of the war he was—albeit in an uncertain and irregular unit—an officer. Now there was the possibility that Daniel Morgan might someday also be a gentleman.[32]

Chapter Three

BUSTING LOOSE

FTER HIS WOUNDING, Morgan seems to drop out of recorded memory for several years. There is a reference to his carrying dispatches through the western Pennsylvania frontier, from the new Fort Pitt at the Forks of the Ohio up to Fort Venango near Lake Erie.[1] One reference suggests that during this period, Morgan might also have gone on a "long hunt," a winter-long expedition deep into the backcountry to trap and hunt deer and buffalo for skins.[2]

By 1761, Morgan again appears regularly in the account books of Virginia merchants, so it seems that by this time if not before, he had begun once more to drive a wagon. There would be only one more military interlude in his life until Dunmore's War in 1774, and that occurred during the revolt in 1763 against British control by western tribes known as Pontiac's War. After attacks on western Virginia, fearful that the events of 1755 would be repeated, Governor Francis Fauquier called out one thousand militia, five hundred from the northwestern counties, including Frederick. Morgan was appointed lieutenant, and as lowly as that rank was, it probably ensured that years later he would be made a captain in the Virginia

Militia—and had he not been a captain, he would never have become a general. But Morgan's service in Pontiac's War was far from glorious. Though he was given an independent detachment, he was only sent for a few weeks to garrison a settlement near a Quaker meetinghouse just ten miles northwest of Winchester.[3]

That service rendered, Morgan got back to making a life for himself, and it is likely that if anyone had told him in 1763 that he would ever make a name for himself as a soldier, he would have knocked him down out of sheer surprise. He now returned to the battlefield of life, the scrabbling, striving, climbing existence he had embarked on when he walked into Winchester in winter 1753.

FREDERICK COUNTY had changed a great deal because of the French and Indian War. While the war had been at best a wash for Dan Morgan—a slightly higher social rank as an officer in the rangers, set against missing a quarter of his teeth and acquiring 499 scars— it had ultimately benefited the economy of Frederick County.

During the war, Frederick County had been the place from which supply convoys left for the many forts in the Virginia backcountry. Beef and liquor were sent by wagon and mule not only into Virginia but into Maryland and Pennsylvania. The amount of food involved was remarkable. If each soldier required a pound of meat and of flour a day, even Jack Ashby's little company of thirty men consumed one thousand eight hundred pounds of food per month. Multiply that figure by the eighty forts along the Virginia frontier, which, in theory, were to be garrisoned by eighty to one hundred men, and it becomes clear why Winchester had by 1757 six retailers operating stores that sold food to Washington's regiment that came from across the colony and supplies that came from Virginia, from other colonies, and from England.[4]

This wartime economy also brought cash to the Valley. Constructing forts, like Fort Loudon in Winchester, meant builders were needed, and builders had to be paid. Soldiers were paid in cash, which they then no doubt spent quickly in Winchester's burgeoning collection of taverns—or by buying a barrel of rum and cutting out the middleman.[5] Even nursing a sick or wounded soldier was a lucrative business, for which the nurse could collect seven pounds.[6]

So what had been a purely exchange-and-credit economy now had cash added to its complexity. Cash allowed Winchester merchants to trade with strangers, those with whom they had no relationship and therefore no reason to trust or experience upon which to base trust. This meant that the merchants established in Winchester could now do business with places farther away than the local economy in the lower Valley. They established lines of credit with Philadelphia firms, and by the end of the war in 1763, they had transformed the town into a point of transshipment, that place where goods from overseas shipped into Philadelphia made their way by Conestoga wagon before departing for points south and west by pack train.[7]

Winchester had been transformed not only economically but physically. In 1753, it was a village with just sixty houses. Five years later, in 1758, Lord Fairfax himself laid out 365 half-acre lots. Just two years later, Winchester was a town with two hundred houses and one thousand residents.[8] It was now the center of Morgan's legal and commercial life.

As a wagoner, Morgan occupied a position in the midst of a growing intercolonial and international trade. He might have been a rough, tough, independent long hauler, but he was also dependent on trade with and patronage of others. Their patronage was essential not for cash but for a line of credit. The very embodiment of American individualism, Morgan nevertheless needed to keep on his patrons' good side. His ability to do so—perhaps related to his obvious capacity for friendship—was key to his rising in Virginia's hierarchical society.

Some newer merchants and their fancy new stores in Winchester, like those of Bryan Bruin, and the Brush Brothers, did their business with Philadelphia. Wagoners hauled loads of goods up the long wagon road to Carlisle, to Lancaster, and to Philadelphia itself—at least in part the route taken by Morgan as he traveled south. Virginia farmers and planters who did business with these merchants were tied by lines of credit to Philadelphia and became oriented toward the north. That, and the fact that many of them had emigrated south out of Pennsylvania or were the children of those who had, contributed to the lower Valley's Pennsylvania flavor.

Morgan, however, traveled in a different direction. This stemmed not from a psychological aversion to literally retracing his steps but because he resided in the eastern part of Frederick County. The Tidewater planters who owned the tenant farms there and were in occasional residence did their business with Scottish merchants who had established themselves on the upper Potomac at the new towns of Georgetown, Alexandria, and Dumfries, and at the fall line of the Rappahannock in Fredericksburg and Falmouth. As they raised tobacco on their Tidewater plantations, so too did they in eastern Frederick County. Taking tobacco and other goods down to those ports and hauling finished goods back was Morgan's chief employment in the 1760s.

The Allason brothers and their firm were one of the chief sources of his business. They were a family and a firm that stretched across the Atlantic. They were involved in the slave trade, the sugar trade, the tobacco trade—and they owned a store in Winchester.[9]

DAVID ALLASON's ledgers from the Shenandoah Store give a certain narrow view of Daniel Morgan, like looking at a wide and complicated landscape through a paper towel tube. What can be seen is someone who does not quite match up with the rough-hewn woodsman shown in some portraits and engravings. Instead we see a homeless boy who is on the make, a hell-raiser who wanted some of the finer things in life.

Allason's ledgers indicate Morgan was quite the spendthrift. His friend and former commander Captain Jack Ashby, belying his reputation as a drinker and brawler, bought things like nails and a copy of the New Testament; when Ashby splurged it was on turpentine, and osnabrig, a coarse linen cloth used for making clothing for slaves or hunting shirts. Ed Snickers bought thread, ribbons, and varieties of cloth. Morgan, on the other hand, liked socks—worsted socks, or fine English socks. He bought blue broadcloth and Irish linen, the very best kind available; neck lace—literally lace worn around the neck; sleeve buttons in quantity; a horn comb; a worsted cape; and "pinch beck shoe buckles," or fake gold shoe buckles, cheap but flashy. He was a dandy in a frontier town, and it cost him. In one six-month period he ran up a bill of fifty pounds, when others' bills were closer to five or six pounds, and when the Allasons would pay him just three pounds to take a load from Falmouth to Winchester.

Morgan also bought rum, by the pint, the quart, the half gallon, or the gallon—and "1 pint mugs" to drink it in. On some days he accompanied the rum with the purchase of a pack of cards. (Based on the frequency of Morgan's purchases, a pack of playing cards in the eighteenth century lasted about a month; or perhaps he lost them somewhere on the road from Winchester to the Tidewater.)[10]

MORGAN also appears in the circuit court records of Frederick County. Colonial Virginians were not necessarily any more litigious than subsequent generations, but the needs and structure of colonial justice required them to often be in court. For example, a criminal case was not initiated by some functionary of law enforcement but by a citizen or citizens bringing a criminal suit before the justice of the peace. If a colonial Virginian suffered assault and battery, he went to court to bring a criminal suit against the assailant. If someone did not pay a debt, the aggrieved party filed a civil suit against the debtor. It is easy to see, then, why a monthly "court day," when cases were heard by the county court, was something of a public holiday. Not only did it require the involvement of numerous people in the community, it provided a spectacle, and if you attended you could catch up on the news and meet with friends.

Given that Morgan was known as a brawler and entangled with merchants, it is not surprising that he shows up in the court records as often as he does. It is perhaps startling to a modern sensibility that what might now seem like serious misdemeanors were treated more lightly by his cultural contemporaries.

His first appearance in the court records is June 4, 1760, when John Cappon brought suit against Morgan and Thomas Pritchard. On that day, Morgan failed to appear, causing judgment to be granted to the plaintiff. Consequently, Morgan was charged one pound, eighteen shillings, and one pence plus court costs.[11]

This was not an exorbitant cost, compared with the suit brought against him by Thomas Cresap, a frontiersman at the time far more famous and prominent than Morgan. Cresap alleged that Morgan had stolen one of his horses. A jury found Morgan guilty, and he paid Cresap thirteen pounds as well as court costs, which included paying Cresap for the cost he incurred of bringing two of the numerous Ashbys over the Blue Ridge from Fauquier County to testify on his behalf. There may be a story there, between the lines of the court order, of a rift between the Ashbys and Morgan about which we can only speculate.[12]

Of the various suits brought against Morgan, the gravest charge was of being "feloniously burning the tobacco house of Jeremiah Wood." In this instance he seems to have been actually imprisoned in the Winchester jail, penned up behind its heavy oak door while waiting for his case to come to trial. When it did, and he was "brought to the Barr" on December 4, 1762, he pleaded "in now wise thereof guilty." After "several evidences were sworn and examined," the opinion of the justices was that he was not guilty and he was discharged from imprisonment.[13]

THE other criminal suits brought against him were charges of assault and battery, which probably arose out of drunken brawls.[14] It was in these that Morgan gained the local reputation he never shook. Inhabitants of small communities never forget, at least not bad things, and rarely accept the idea of change in character. Reading between the lines of his friend Dr. Hill's eulogy and biographical notes, the local history written in the fifty years after Morgan's death, and Graham's biography, it's clear that subsequent military honors, fortune, political power, and even religious conversion never fully banished the local image of Morgan as a loafer and hell-raiser.[15]

The quantities of rum that appear in his accounts in the store ledgers lend credence to his reputation as someone who would "drink freely at times." Nor was Morgan the kind of man who drank alone. When he was not loafing at the Shenandoah Store in Winchester, drinking rum and playing cards, he and his friends would gather for "gaming drinking quarreling and fighting" at Benjamin Berry's tavern, at the crossroads that are now the center of the town of Berryville but that at the time and for decades after were called "Battletown" by "everybody in that part of the country,"

Graham observes, "excepting the inhabitants of the village themselves."[16]

There on Saturday afternoons, Morgan and his cronies gathered for rum and athletics—meaning foot racing and wrestling, and possibly target shooting. He had a variety of antagonists, including William Darke, a man of about Morgan's age who had also come into the lower Valley at about the same time; forty years later, he would be one of Morgan's subordinates in the Virginia Militia. There also might have been something of a flatland-highland divide in the area: some of Morgan's chief antagonists in his truly serious confrontations were members of the Davis family, who lived up on the slopes of the Blue Ridge, while Morgan's cronies all came from the lowlands of eastern Frederick County. There was at least a year of war between Morgan and the Davises' two gangs, and several encounters between Morgan and Bill Davis, "the strongest and most active" of four brothers "all of whom were men of extraordinary size and strength." Dr. Hill, at Morgan's bedside during his last illness, was helping the old soldier into bed one day when he noticed that one of his toes was bent backward over the foot. Asked what had happened, Morgan responded, "I got that many years ago in a fight I had with Bill Davis, in kicking him at Battletown. I broke that toe, then, and I never could get it to lie in its right place since."[17]

As the anecdote reveals, fighting for Morgan and his Virginia contemporaries did not follow any of the rules subsequently laid down by the Marquess of Queensberry. Those men would be right at home at a cage-fighting mixed martial arts match, though perhaps a bit puzzled by what they would see as overreliance on science and technique. Bare-knuckle prizefighting of the era involved not just the fists but also wrestling throws. To that combination Virginians added not only kicking but eye gouging, biting, clawing, tearing at their opponents genitals, and just about any other means of obtaining advantage and causing an opponent to cry "King's cruse," the words that signaled submission. As a later English observer commented, "An English boxing match though a disgrace to a polished nation, is humanity itself, compared to the Virginia mode of fighting."[18]

Benjamin Berry recalled years later that from the time he first knew Morgan, he was "frequently engaged in affrays and was often beaten, but would nevertheless renew the Combat with those who had just before beaten him."[19] Then, as later, Morgan refused to be beaten or to admit he was beaten. In the standard local legend of his encounters with the Davis family, having first been beaten once or more times, Morgan gathered a sufficient number of compatriots to challenge the Davises on equal terms. The resulting brawl was one of the epic contests in Battletown history.[20]

MORGAN was not exceptional in his penchant for brawling—even an Anglican pastor in the Northern Neck was once discharged from his parish for his love of "drinking and boxing."[21] Every monthly court day—those times when Morgan was arraigned on charges of horse theft, burning barns, or simple assault—was not only a legal and political occasion but a social one that involved brawling as well as cockfighting, dogfighting, and horse racing. Inside the courtroom, more elite members of Virginia society displayed one form of masculine contest and dominance, while outside Morgan and others lower in the colonial hierarchy demonstrated another form of masculinity. Every social occasion in Virginia could be, and usually was, a kind of contest to demonstrate one's manliness. Fox hunting, dancing, card playing, and wrestling were all ways of showing who you really were.[22]

While these amusements were to a certain extent segregated by class—one can't quite imagine Washington wrestling with Morgan, but in the 1750s it was at least a possibility—they in certain ways transcended class and hierarchy. True gentry could show themselves to be patrons of a fast horse or a courageous rooster. But they could also risk life and limb by staying at the very head of a group of riders pursuing a fox and thereby show their courage and masculine prowess. Nor was fox hunting the only way of doing this. Charles Willson Peale, at Mount Vernon to paint his first of sixty-odd portraits of George Washington, was with some other young men throwing an iron bar on the west lawn of the mansion, a popular athletic pursuit in the Chesapeake region (Peale hailed from eastern Maryland). He later remembered that Washington stopped by and, without removing his coat, threw the bar with such force that "it lost the power of gravitation, and whizzed through the air, striking the ground far, very far, beyond our outmost limits . . . [T]he Colonel, on retiring, pleasantly observed, 'When you beat my pitch, young gentlemen, I'll try again."[23]

Morgan, like Peale a poor boy of the southern colonies, would have taken certain lessons from Washington's display. For one thing, Washington had been working while Peale and his friends had been playing at athletics. Nor did he have to even remove his jacket to exert the necessary bit of effort—a first-rate bit of gamesmanship. Such a competition displayed a virility that transcended class. While Morgan would almost undoubtedly have taken up Washington's challenge, it would have been with respect for Washington as a real man.

Why Virginia's culture encouraged such displays—as New England's did not, or at least not to such a degree—remains a continuing subject of debate. But it certainly related to a view of masculinity that resonated with views and practices in the British Isles and throughout the British Atlantic. Morgan as a brawler and good old boy had much in common with the popular interest in pirates, highwaymen, and rakes. He represented a transgressive manliness, a manliness pointed in the wrong direction and corrosive of the social order.[24]

If he had remained pointed in that direction, Morgan might have become no more famous than Bill Davis. But he didn't.

MORGAN was, not surprisingly, also interested in the ladies. In late 1761 and through 1762, Morgan began to buy ribbons, silk cloth, and even a pair of ladies' shoes. Robert Allason noted in his ledger dated June 1763 that Morgan had three different women taking advantage of his credit to purchase sundries. One of them was Abigail Curry. Sometime in the next year they moved in together. By the late 1760s, they had two daughters, Nancy and Betsey.[25]

Abigail was the daughter of a local farmer, a man with a healthy amount of land on the border of Frederick and Berkeley Counties, north of Battletown. He was not a grandee but a yeoman, a man who enjoyed the independence of owning his own property. He was, in other words, just the sort of man Morgan wished to become. Marriage, then as now, was a means for one or both partners to either direct their way further up the societal hierarchy or solidify the position they had.

To be sure, *married* was a relative term by current standards. They were officially married in the Church of England in 1773, but by that time they had been living together since 1763 or 1764. This was not uncommon behavior throughout the English-speaking world for poor or middling sorts, like Abigail and Daniel, who were without much property. Since at least the Middle Ages, marriages for the poor might be a simple verbal contract, made before witnesses or even alone together. They might even do so without permission of their families. All that was required was the couple to join hands and pledge themselves to be wedded to one another. In medieval England, if a parish priest was particularly persuasive, this ceremony of handfasting occurred in front of the church door and was followed by the exchange of rings and a mass. In waiting ten years for the official marriage, Abigail and Daniel, like many other Virginians, were closer to the life of medieval peasants than to the customs of the eighteenth century.[26]

COURT RECORDS also indicate that by the late 1760s, Morgan's behavior was beginning to change. He appears less in cases that originate in brawling—but no fewer than twenty-two times he was accused of indebtedness by impatient creditors.[27] Such lawsuits were perfectly normal in cash-poor Virginia, where there were few means by which to pay off debts and where debts often were credited and credited and credited, and finally collected by probate court after one's death. In any event, indebtedness never seems to have hurt Morgan's reputation.[28] Indeed, it is no exaggeration to say that without indebtedness, he would not have risen to the position he did. Without debt, he could not have acquired 255 acres, just north of a community that Morgan—as much as anyone else— had caused to be named Battletown. Without that acreage, he could not establish himself as a farmer, then as a planter, a slave owner, and an officeholder; a member of the upper levels of the society of the lower Valley. Moreover, indebtedness cemented ties of obligation within Morgan's little society, so long as that debt was to a "diligent gentleman" and not to an "irresponsible rogue"—Virginia gentlemen were not such fools as to throw money down a bottomless pit of drinking and gambling. In a small place where everyone carefully watched everyone else's actions and continually compared them to their words, Morgan needed to demonstrate that he was indeed a diligent gentleman. This, of course, could put men like Morgan into "an infernal economic spiral" since "the planter who wanted to preserve his credit in Virginia, his honor, his claim to personal autonomy, found himself under immense pressure to seem prosperous." To both seem prosperous and to become prosperous were the great tasks of the remainder of Daniel Morgan's life.[29]

Chapter Four

MAKING IT

B UYING that much land placed Morgan at a different level of Virginia's gentry society. He had reached the first rung of that ladder when he purchased sufficient land to be considered by law a freeholder. But now he was becoming a man of prominence in the affairs of Frederick County, placing himself on a level higher than that of the average freeholder.

Virginia society was, and remained for much of its history, hierarchical, shaped like a Mayan pyramid, or a multitiered wedding cake. This is most easily seen by looking at the various political manifestations of its hierarchy, but *politics* is here something of a shorthand, for the political was, in colonial Virginia, not only personal but social, cultural, and economic. Often the entire hierarchical cake is referred to simply as the "gentry." But there were many types of gentry, and none knew this better than the gentry themselves.

At the top of this wedding cake was the Council of State, the upper house of the Virginia legislature. Its members were appointed by the governor—in legal terms, by the monarch—and acted as Virginia's equivalent to the House of Lords, serving, therefore, not only as an upper house but also as a general court. Usually its members were more powerful and potent politically than the governor himself.[1] He was always a British interloper, sent over for a period to superintend the colony's affairs, usually desperate for the income provided by the position. Members of the council were wealthier than the lieutenant governor. They were the most influential members of the Virginia elite, drawn from a minuscule number of families. As members of the council, they not only determined the policy and laws of the colony but were able to direct other family members to lower offices. In a similar manner, any station within the hierarchy of Virginia gentry meant a degree of control and influence on the levels of the hierarchy beneath that status.[2]

Below the governor's council was the House of Burgesses, Virginia's general assembly. Here "Virginia politicians most conspicuously displayed their talents and independence."[3] Its members were necessarily well known in their counties; their participation in the general assembly in Williamsburg made them—along with those men serving on the Governor's Council—members of what might be called colony gentry, the very elite of the elite. Even here, it should quickly be added, wealth and property (and, rarely, learning) established a further level of yet more granular hierarchy.

Below the council and the burgesses were those men inhabiting the political offices in each of Virginia's counties. There justices of the peace and members of the vestry—the system of governance of the Church of England's parishes, both a religious and civil institution—created a tangle of interest. Vestries and justices named their own successors, perpetuating local dynasties. No office was too small not to have a member of the gentry occupying it, even those of great wealth. For example, in England, the office of churchwarden to a parish was occupied by someone of middling status or even lower. But in Virginia, on the verge of the Revolution, one could find Robert Carter III, one of the wealthiest men in the colonies, and a member of the Governor's Council, also fulfilling the duties of churchwarden in his parish.

However, there were other positions to which one could be appointed to achieve county prominence. One could be made a sheriff, a county clerk, a surveyor, a road overseer, or an officer in the militia. Securing such positions meant not only acquiring a small income but perhaps more importantly achieving a greater social status. To advance in Virginia's society, Morgan could not launch a bid for a seat in the House of Burgesses. He needed to achieve the right kind of attention from those men who mattered—and controlled appointment to offices—and gain their favor.

In the late 1760s, Morgan apparently began to wean himself from his brawling and drinking. Not that he ever stopped brawling or drinking—even as late as 1794 he "broke the mouth" of someone who displeased him.[4] By 1770, he and Abigail had their two daughters, Nancy and Betsey, and—as children often do—they seem to have changed the way he comported himself. One old story of the lower Shenandoah, no more reliable than any of Parson Weems's stories of Washington's youth, has Morgan's wife helping him win one last victory at Berry's Tavern before retiring from the field of battle.[5] Whether or not he became "more and more sensible of the impropriety and folly of his conduct," as Graham described it, he certainly began to believe he could do something more than be the hero of Berry's Tavern. He built a house on his 255 acres not far from the tavern, and by the advent of the Revolutionary War at the latest, he had christened it Soldier's Rest, proclaiming his pride in his service and the scars he bore on his face and back.[6]

He began to rise in the ranks of the citizens of Frederick County, putting himself on a plane higher than he must have thought possible as a homeless boy, or a grubber hauling stumps out of Mr. Roberts's field. As early as 1764, he was raising tobacco and selling it via the Allason warehouses in Falmouth. This was unusual in the Valley, because its soil was not suited to tobacco production. Only in eastern Frederick County, where the Tidewater aristocrats demanded its production of their overseers, enslaved people, and tenants, did anyone grow tobacco on a large scale. Morgan's production of tobacco was emblematic of his residence in the eastern valley and the Tidewater planters and Scottish merchants to whom he was beholden.[7] By the late 1760s, he added hemp—a crop prized by the Royal Navy and Admiralty since in effect it was to grow ropes for them—to his crop rotation, securing the bounty offered by the Virginia government to anyone who grudgingly planted something other than tobacco.[8]

Throughout the 1760s, Morgan engaged in hauling, either in person or by hiring someone to do it for him. Since in peacetime wagoners could earn as much as six pounds for hauling a load of tobacco from Frederick County to Falmouth, it would have been hard to give up such an occupation. Almost certainly it was Morgan's ability to continue to haul freight that gave him the wherewithal to buy his land and establish himself as an independent farmer.[9]

There was another way to become respectable: officially marry Abigail. His Anglican minister was Charles Mynn Thruston, formerly a lieutenant in Washington's 1st Virginia Regiment, a resident of Gloucester County who had decided to enter into the Anglican ministry. Now the vicar of Frederick Parish, he announced the impending wedding of Daniel and Abigail and blessed their existing union. Signing the marriage bond as his witness was John Neville, a prosperous resident of Fauquier County, soon to be emigrant and major landowner in the "Virginian" lands along the Allegheny and Monongahela, and father of Morgan's future son-in-law. This marriage—and those who made it possible—was another sign of Morgan's increasing respectability, and Thruston became one of his most important friends and patrons.[10]

Another friend was Isaac Zane, a Quaker from Pennsylvania who had come down to the Valley where he had established an iron forge. He, like Morgan, lived with a woman whom he had not married; unlike Morgan, he did not even intend for her to be a common-law wife or eventually marry her in a Quaker ceremony. Morgan and Zane had a curious relationship over the years that at one point saw Zane sue Morgan for breach of contract. But they nevertheless maintained to the end of their lives a relationship that—on the basis of their letters to each other—can only be called tender.[11]

In 1764, Daniel Morgan made a promise of payment to Alexander Woodrow, the administrator of the late Captain Nimrod Ashby's estate, for the fourteen pounds, four shillings of Virginia currency owed to the estate. Such a note was a common document in the financial and social life of colonial Virginia, as death was the opportunity to collect on the debts owed for the benefit of those remaining. So while the note is not particularly remarkable, its signatures tell a story. Or rather its lack of a signature, for next to the name "Danl Morgan" is a crudely scrawled "X," and beneath that the words "his mark." Daniel Morgan was illiterate.[12]

In 1764, Daniel Morgan could only put his mark on a promissory note; by 1768 (or perhaps a few years later) he was able to write a letter.[13] Not a very fluent one, not very coherently, but he was able to do it. This change is one of the most important revolutions in Morgan's life. How does a man in his thirties set about learning to read and write? Why does he do it?

Probably for the same reason the wagoner became a farmer: ambition. Graham reports that he began in the late 1760s to take "a lively interest in public affairs," an observation that should not be dismissed as mere post facto tidying of the hero's reputation. To be a member of the gentry necessarily meant being part of public life. And to be in public life, to be on display in the community, meant he had to be literate. Because learning was not for oneself, but for the community. A man like Morgan did not learn to read and write so he could keep a journal, write poetry, or read polite literature. Reading, and writing one's thoughts, led to public speaking; and facility in public speaking was a necessary prerequisite to any sort of political power in colonial Virginia.

Indeed, almost all education in colonial America was directed in some way toward a public display or public use, not to mere private improvement. The first colleges in America were really seminaries for training ministers, and the ministry was itself a public office, particularly in colonies that had an established church—which was nearly all of them. As the eighteenth century progressed, the needs of political life in the colonies were a further reason for self-culture and improvement of one's mind, and that meant an unusual attention to reading books on law and legal theory. Edmund Burke, in his speech of March 22, 1775, striving for a final attempt at conciliation with the colonists, observed to his fellow members of Parliament that in the colonies, "all who read, and most do read, endeavour to obtain some smattering in that science [law]. I have been told by an eminent bookseller, that in no branch of his business, after tracts of popular devotion, were so many books as those on the law exported to the plantations. . . . I hear that they have sold nearly as many of Blackstone's *Commentaries* in America as in England." Morgan was almost certainly not attempting to puzzle his way through Blackstone's legal maze. But the impetus for his self-culture, participation in public life, was the same.[14]

Moreover, most education was necessarily self-education or self-culture. There were few schools and fewer colleges. Self-culture and collegiate education were, in fact, regarded as complementary. A "liberally educated person possessed a knowledge of many subjects . . . that rarely formed part of the collegiate curriculum," and therefore the best-educated college graduate still strove to complete his education.[15]

If Morgan learned to read, he never seemed to be comfortable with writing. A friend of his during the Revolutionary War chided him, "I wrote you four letters after you left Camp and never recd. a scrape from you." This was a characteristic pattern in Morgan's life. Washington would many years later observe "it is not denied that he is illiterate." This was not strictly true, but certainly Morgan's letters never obeyed even the uncertain eighteenth-century guidelines for spelling, punctuation, and grammar.[16]

Such education as Morgan acquired came from listening and conversing with others better trained and informed than he. This was, again, a perfectly standard and accepted means of self-culture in the eighteenth century. Indeed, "most forms of gentlemanly self-education involved contact with others." Isaac Watts, an English congregational minister, prolific hymn writer, and author of a book of advice on self-culture, recommended conversation as the best means of learning. Correspondence was simply a conversation conducted on paper over long distances.[17]

So we can imagine Morgan's conversations shifting somewhat over the course of the 1760s. In the early part of the decade they were jokes over rum and cards. As he acquired property, a family life, and a matching sense of self-importance, he began to spend time with other property holders of a higher status than himself. This was one of the natural consequences of the hierarchical nature of Virginia's society. It was also a manifestation of the pressures Virginia placed on each of its property holders to engage in public service.

IN the Roman republic, young patrician men engaged in the *cursus honorum*, which was a trajectory of expected services to the republic before it was a career path or a route to political power. Colonial Virginia lacked such a meticulously designed series of offices in which young men were expected to serve, but it had expectations of all free white male citizens, more of property holders, and even more of any who might be considered gentry, the highest level of property holders.

All free white men, for example, were expected to serve at least in the militia, and greater levels of service were expected of property holders. Those who failed to serve, in whatever capacity, were penalized. There were penalties for not appearing at the monthly militia muster, and they were not small by the standard of Virginia incomes. Officers and enlisted men who missed a training assembly could be fined five pounds, and if they could not pay it they would be imprisoned. Free blacks, Indians, or mixed-race men were not allowed to carry arms, but they were still expected to serve in some capacity. Only Mennonites and Quakers were exempt from service, and they were required to hire a substitute and equip him properly.[18]

Jury duty was another expectation of freeholders—men who had £100 of property. Morgan's first appearance on a Frederick County jury in 1765 indicates he had achieved a higher level of economic, legal, and political status than he had enjoyed in the previous decade.[19]

Other steps up the hierarchy of status and political participation were yet to come. Morgan's next rung on the ladder was to be part of a committee of local men assigned to survey the course of a road that ran from the White Post—a marker set up by Lord Thomas Fairfax to show the direction to his hunting lodge cum manor house—to Cunningham's Chapel, now called Old Chapel, between Berryville and Boyce, Virginia, roughly following the course of modern Virginia Route 340. This was a distance of only a few miles, but it was the sort of service envisioned by Virginia legislators when they directed that when a road was requested, the "court shall appoint three, or more fit and able persons, to view the lands whereon the said roads are proposed to be cleared, or altered, who, upon oath taken before a justice of the peace, faithfully and impartially to perform the said service, shall make report to the next court, of the conveniencies and inconveniencies of the said intended road, or alteration."[20]

The next step was to become the road overseer of that same stretch of road in 1770, and again in 1774. As overseer he was legally obligated to keep this road "well cleared, from woods, bushes, and other obstructions, and all roots well grubb'd up, thirty feet broad at the least," and make certain that no-one cut down any trees and left them lying in the highway. To keep the road cleared, he had coercive powers over the labor of each "tithable free male labouring person" living along the road. Should they fail to "attend with proper tools, when required by such surveyor, or refusing to work when there, or not providing and sending another person to work in his room" then the law specified that they "shall forfeit and pay five shillings."[21]

Overseeing a road was one of the most minor of all public positions. But it was more than Morgan could have expected to attain as a young man when he was grubbing stumps in the same vicinity. His service was further complemented by perhaps his most important commission: captain of the Frederick County Militia. On May 10, 1774, the order book of the Frederick County Circuit Court noted, "Daniel Morgan took the usual oath to his Majesty's Person & Government, took the abjuration oath, repeated & subscribed the Test as Capt. of the Militia of this county." With that commission, Morgan marched west in the last colonial war.[22]

MICHAEL CRESAP was the son of Thomas Cresap, noted troublemaker, Indian trader, and the man who had sued Dan Morgan for stealing one of his horses. Unlike Morgan, young Cresap had the advantages of education and a certain amount of refinement. He had been educated in a Baltimore school but had returned to his family's lands above Fort Pitt on the Monongahela. From there he traveled the Ohio River on the family business of trading and land speculation. It was on one such venture that Michael Cresap initiated a series of events that, as the story is often told, started a war— a small one, quickly forgotten, but no less brutal to those who experienced it.

In response to rumors that an Indian attack was imminent, a group of would-be Kentucky settlers and other woodsmen along the Ohio drafted Cresap to be captain of their impromptu militia company. They intended to attack an Indian village on the northern side of the Ohio, which in their way of thinking would be an act of retaliation—though they would not have been able to explain what they were retaliating against. Indeed, when Cresap took command, he told his company that there was no war and he believed they should take no actions that might start one. Instead they should retreat up the river to the settlements near Wheeling Creek and wait to see if war actually broke out.

At Wheeling Creek, Cresap's party found the same all-pervasive fear of Indian attack as downriver. All were convinced that some sort of war had already begun. Rumors of attacks in the neighborhood were earnestly believed. Some woodsmen set off to take revenge, returning with scalps—taken from whom, no one knew. When the militia sighted a canoe coming downstream, Cresap intercepted it in his own canoe. As it turned out, the three men in the canoe were traders for William Butler of Fort Pitt. Two were Indians—a Delaware and a Shawnee—the third a white man named Stephens. When the traders saw an approaching canoe, they feared that it was paddled by hostile Indians and fled. Gunfire killed both Indians, and Stephens went into the water. There he was picked up by Cresap and his two men—who then scalped Stephens's companions.

This was one in a series of confused accidents of violence and murder during that last week of April 1774. The final act occurred April 30 at Baker's Bottom, thirty miles above Wheeling. Stories told throughout the frontier about what happened were different, yet equally horrific. One story had the head rowdy, Daniel Greathouse, purposefully inviting Indians over the Ohio to kill them. Another story said some of the Indian men were invited to a marksmanship contest and then shot when their guns were empty. Another claimed that Greathouse slashed open the belly of a pregnant woman, scalped the fetus, and hung its body on a tree.

Making matters worse was the fact that one of the victims, the mother of the surviving infant, was the sister of Talgayeeta. Known in Pennsylvania and Virginia as James Logan and usually called by his last name, Logan was one of the most formidable warriors in the Ohio River valley. This murder, bloodshed, and confusion provoked what Virginians called Lord Dunmore's War.[23]

In 1763, following victory in the war with France, the British Parliament decreed a "Proclamation Line," a demarcation between the colonies along the seaboard and the western lands. These were to be preserved for the Indian tribes who, once subjects of the French king, were now subject to Britain's.

Confusingly, from a legal and administrative perspective, at more or less the same moment as the decree of the Proclamation Line, Parliament authorized western land grants to veterans of the Seven Years' War. In one of numerous examples of over two centuries of how ignorant British statesmen could be about the nature of America, Parliament seems to have believed that there was plenty of land available for governmental taking on the eastern side of the line. Since there was not, colonial governors continued to blithely offer grants in the forbidden western lands.

Yet another wrinkle in Parliament's land grant decrees was neatly ironed out by colonial willfulness. Parliament had imagined that these land grants were only for veterans of the regular army and navy, but this was not made clear in the language of the proclamation. Since colonial governors and legislators had no cash, the land grants were the perfect means—really the only means—by which they could indemnify veterans of the provincial forces who had served the colonies.[24]

This stew of legal confusion and political expedience, together with the simple pressure of population growth, meant that by 1774, some fifty thousand settlers resided on the western side of the Proclamation Line. Not only were they distributed along the rivers and creeks of western Virginia and Pennsylvania, they were by then planning to settle sites all along the Ohio River, deep within the territory reserved for the king's Native American subjects.

Morgan might not have served in this, the last of the colony of Virginia's wars. Some did not, most prominently Horatio Gates, his relatively near neighbor and recent immigrant to Virginia. Gates, a career soldier desiring advancement, had gotten tired of the British army; an increasingly radical Whig (or liberal, as that party later titled itself), Gates was consequently tired of British politics. He had immigrated to the newly created Berkeley County, just north of Soldier's Rest. The cash Gates had at hand as a recently retired officer of the British army allowed him to set up a fine establishment, with a new house, over a hundred acres of meadow, and a number of enslaved people—as radical as he might be in politics, Virginia's slave system did not seem to give Gates any qualms.

But going to war in the Ohio valley did. When summoned by Adam Stephen, his direct superior, to join Stephen's regiment, Gates demurred. When commanded to attend by the governor of Virginia, Robert Murray (more usually, Lord Dunmore), Gates refused again. He had a fever, he wrote, and could not serve. In fact, he actually did not serve because he thought the war wrong and unjust, and contrary to his political principles.[25]

Morgan had no such qualms. "As to war, I am and always was a great enemy," he wrote in his last years, "at the same time a warrior the greater part of my life, and were I young again, should still be a warrior while ever this country was invaded." There is every reason to believe that Morgan's military past and military present were essential parts of his identity. Already, by 1774, his home was called Soldier's Rest, surely a significant indication of his self-conception. His commission in the militia was undoubtedly no accident. Such things were recognitions of ability and local reputation, and further increased it. They enabled someone like Morgan to spend the rest of his life referred to by his neighbors as "Captain Morgan," or George Washington to be always referred to as "Colonel Washington." But his militia service was, as Morgan demonstrated, an important avocation.[26]

On June 11, 1774, a month after Morgan received his commission as captain, his superior, Major Angus McDonald, wrote to him with orders. A character seemingly invented by an author of romantic fiction, McDonald had been a soldier of Prince Charles Stuart's at the disaster of Culloden, when a British force under the Duke of Cumberland crushed that last rebellion of the Stuart claimants to the British crown. Fleeing from the Highlands to Virginia, he was a major in the Virginia Militia by 1765, swearing an oath to the grandson of the king against whom he had rebelled. Educated at least partly at the University of Glasgow, he was a merchant, surveyor, and land speculator as well.[27]

Now McDonald wrote to Morgan that eight or so people had been killed on the Ohio and that Morgan should prepare to march. "I think that you ought to get 50 or 60 men in order to set out next week," he instructed, and "therefore get what you can of your own company and send or go to the other companys to get and to make up your number for I expect orders from the Gov. about Monday or Tuesday next and I do not want to draft any but to get Volunteers as the pay will be very good you can get good men and I beg you to take none but such as can be depended on that you may do service to our country and honour to ourselves."[28]

McDonald reveals here a common practice in the Virginia Militia. The local company that one mustered in and trained with was not the same as the one that fought. Rather it was the reserve base from which tactical units were selected and deployed. The numbers mentioned by McDonald, "50 or 60," were typical for a deployed company, while a mustered local company would be about twice the size. Moreover, McDonald hoped that given the pay offered by the Virginia legislature, men would be quick to take arms and march west. Morgan, he hoped, would then be able to choose from the best of the available manpower.[29]

By the time Morgan had received orders from McDonald, George Washington was hearing from the man who represented him in Ohio valley real estate deals, Captain William Crawford, that, "Our hole Country is in Forts, what is Left, but the Majr Part is gon Over the Mountain."[30] Raids from out of Ohio had fallen on settlements along the river, around the Forks of the Ohio, and deeper into western Pennsylvania. Virginia's elites feared that all the area around the Forks would soon be evacuated and that an Indian war would begin that would once more threaten the Shenandoah Valley.

In mid-July, Lord Dunmore—determined to act not only as Virginia's governor but also as the field commander of Virginia's military—arrived in the Valley and established a temporary headquarters at Lord Fairfax's Greenway Court. He designated Winchester as the rendezvous point for the right wing of Virginia's army, assigning it a route to Fort Pitt via Braddock's Road. A left wing, composed of militia from the upper Valley and from farther into southwest Virginia, would meet at a meadow on the Greenbrier River and march down the Kanawha River.[31]

While the two noble lords shared accommodation at Greenway Court, and Dunmore planned his future movements, Morgan marched north with his company to join McDonald. They met at Wheeling, where Morgan and his company were made part of the force McDonald was to lead on a raid into Indian country. Leaving Wheeling on July 26, McDonald's battalion was composed of four hundred men. Its officers included not only Daniel Morgan but Michael Cresap and George Rogers Clark, who in a few years would be as notable a soldier as Morgan. They paddled canoes twenty miles down the Ohio before disembarking with rifles, ammunition, and rations for just seven days. Their target was the Shawnee town of Wakatomica, on the Muskingum River, ninety miles away.

The expedition marched for four days before encountering three Indians on horseback, on Sunday, July 31, 1774. After a night spent in a defensive perimeter, resting on their arms—that is, with rifles loaded and at hand, rather than discharged and stacked near each campfire—McDonald and his expedition assumed they would be ambushed sometime during the day.

When that next day the advance scouts encountered what seems to have been an Indian scouting party, McDonald divided his companies into three parallel columns. In the right column were two companies from Frederick County, that of Captain James Wood of Winchester and Morgan's. When the entire battalion came within range of the ambush, concealed Indians opened fire. McDonald formed a line with the center column, directing the left and right columns to advance and take the enemy from behind. Morgan's and Woods's companies did this, driving the attackers from their ambush. But the Shawnee gave ground slowly, shooting and then scooting from one tree to another for about thirty minutes.

McDonald paused the advance to rally and re-form his companies. That done, he left a detail to guard the wounded and continued the advance toward their objective, reaching the bank of the Muskingum opposite Wakatomica five miles later. Skirmishing began, with sniping back and forth across the river, while McDonald held a council with some local Delaware tribesmen to convince them not to take the side of the Shawnee and Mingo tribesmen in arms against the Virginians.

On the eighth day of the raid, the Virginians finally brushed aside some light resistance, crossed the Muskingum, and entered Wakatomica. The town was deserted. Before burning it and cutting down seventy acres of standing corn in the surrounding fields, the Virginians reprovisioned themselves as best they could from what they found in the town's storehouses. The Delaware villages they left untouched—part of McDonald's diplomatic initiative. Collecting their wounded from the site of the earlier ambush, they returned cross-country to their canoes, consuming just one ear of corn per day plus whatever plants and game they could scare up. One soldier described it later as a journey of "hardships and perils."

They returned to Wheeling and the newly built Fort Fincastle on August 9. According to the letter of their original plans, they had succeeded, for Wakatomica was destroyed. But its destruction resulted in no gains for the Virginians. "Considered strategically," argues Glenn Williams in the most authoritative account of Dunmore's War, "the raid on Wakatomika did little to change the course of the war or hasten its conclusion."

It probably did convince Dunmore that only the overwhelming invasion of the Ohio Country by the northern and southern divisions of the Virginian army would win the conflict. He set about implementing that plan. Moving down the Ohio from Wheeling was the northern division, under the command of Adam Stephen, accompanied by Dunmore. In late September, it reached the mouth of the Hockhocking River, where it built a small fortified supply depot called Fort Gower. The southern division, commanded by Colonel Andrew Lewis, made its way down the Kanawha River to Point Pleasant on the Ohio. There, on October 10, 1774, it was attacked by Shawnee under the leadership of Cornstalk, who sought to defeat one division of Dunmore's army before the two joined together. The battle lasted most of the day before Cornstalk broke off his attack.

Cornstalk had not been defeated, but neither had he achieved his aim; his tactical draw was his strategic defeat. Dunmore won his war because the two divisions joined together. Faced with that overwhelming force, Cornstalk could not see a way of continuing the fight. By the time Lewis's southern division advanced within fifteen miles of the Shawnee towns on the Scioto River, Dunmore had concluded a preliminary peace treaty and ordered the militia to return home and be discharged.

It was Virginia's last colonial war; indeed, it was "the last conflict of America's colonial era." The last royal governor of Virginia had fought a limited war that achieved very eighteenth-century military and diplomatic objectives: "an established border, a promise to cease cross-border incursions, return of captured property, and repatriation of prisoners." The same results might be expected from an equally forgotten war between Savoy and Tuscany over a chunk of the Mediterranean coast, or a naval tussle between Venice and the Ottoman Empire over an Adriatic island.

But there was the slightest indication of things to come. When the northern division gathered at Fort Gower at the mouth of the Hockhocking River, prior to the hard paddle upriver, its officers met together to discuss the ongoing disturbances around Boston. The result was a document they called the "Fort Gower Resolves." Its author is unclear; whoever sent it to the *Virginia Gazette* in Williamsburg described the meeting as beginning with an address by one of the officers to the assembly.[32]

"That we are a respectable body is certain," that officer announced proudly, "when it is considered that we can live weeks without bread or salt; that we can sleep in the open air without any covering but that of the canopy of Heaven; and that our men can march and shoot with any in the known world." With, no doubt, "hear him, hear him" being chanted by his assembled peers—eighteenth-century listeners were much more interactive than their descendants—he pressed on. "Blessed with these talents, let us solemnly engage to one another, and our country in particular, that we will use them to no purpose but for the honour and advantage of America in general, and of Virginia in particular." In other words, their fellow Virginians and other British Americans should not fear that they were an army that could be used for the suppression of English liberty.

The officers then approved the following resolves, possibly written by the original speaker:

> *Resolved,* That we will bear the most faithful allegiance to his Majesty King George the Third, whilst his Majesty delights to reign over a brave and free people; that we will, at the expense of life, and every thing dear and valuable, exert ourselves in support of the honour of his Crown and the dignity of the British Empire. But as the love of Liberty, and attachment to the real interests and just rights of America outweigh every other consideration, we resolve that we will exert every power within us for the defence of American liberty, and for the support of her just rights and privileges; not in any precipitate, riotous, or tumultuous manner, but when regularly called forth by the unanimous voice of our countrymen.
>
> *Resolved,* That we entertain the greatest respect for his Excellency the Right Honourable Lord Dunmore, who commanded the expedition against the Shawanese; and who, we are confident, underwent the great fatigue of this singular campaign from no other motive than the true interest of this country.[33]

Morgan later remembered this event very simply. Last colonial war or no, it merged in his memory with the Revolution that swiftly followed. References to the king and respect for Lord Dunmore were gone. What was left in his memory was this:

> When we had beat the Indians and brought them to order and a treaty of peace confirm'd . . . on our return home at the mouth of the River Hockhocking we were informed of hostilities being offered to our Brethren the people of Boston—we as an army . . . formed ourselves in to a society pledging our word of honour to each other to assist our Brethren in case hostilities should commence. Which it did on the ensuing 19th of April at Lexington.[34]

Morgan connected that meeting on the Ohio with events still to come, making it a prelude to the Revolutionary War. But it is highly unlikely that he did so at the time. The second of the Fort Gower resolves was, after all, praise of Lord Dunmore. Memories, even Dan Morgan's, are not history. They are simultaneously selective and eclectic, not holding onto the past but reconstructing its order and its harmony, enriching it, manipulating it, and adapting it in order to allow us to "enrich and manipulate the present."[35]

Other Virginians also lauded their royal governor. An address of the "Freeholders of Fincastle County" (a newly formed county whose boundaries included all of the modern state of Kentucky) praised Dunmore. "Notwithstanding the unhappy disputes that at present subsist between the Mother Country and the Colonies, in which we have given the publick our sentiments," the address pronounced, "yet justice and gratitude, as well as a sense of our duty, induce us collectively to return your Lordship our unfeigned thanks for the great services you have rendered the frontiers." They particularly praised Dunmore's willingness "to forego your ease, and every domestick felicity, and march at the head of a body of those Troops many hundred miles from the Seat of Government, cheerfully undergoing all the fatigues of the campaign, by exposing your person, and marching on foot with the officers and soldiers."[36] A fellow Scot dryly observed that Dunmore was "as popular as a Scotsman can be amongst weak prejudiced people."[37]

It is good to recall how this praise was intermingled with protest, for it highlights the shock of the news from Massachusetts that swept through the colonies in late April 1775. For Virginians, it helps illuminate the feelings of betrayal and dishonor they felt when the man who had marched along with them into battle with the Shawnee then illegitimately—as they saw it—seized the colony's gunpowder the night of April 20, 1775.[38]

When the Revolution came, it came as a revolution—violently, suddenly, shockingly—even to those who had expected it.

PART TWO

A Call to Arms

Chapter Five

REBELLION

I MAGINE Dan Morgan in early April 1775. He has been back from the Ohio Country for some months, back with Abigail and his girls. It is planting time in the Shenandoah, and he has hired two extra hands.

He is about forty years old. His fine hair was once fully Welsh-red, or red-gold; now it has started to show a few streaks of white. His eyes are blue. The average height in 1775 is about five feet nine inches; at six feet or a little over, Morgan is a tall man.[1]

He remains strong and fast. His muscles are long and ropy, those of someone who has labored all his life. His fast twitch and long twitch muscles vie for supremacy. He can push and carry heavy wooden boats through the wilderness and yet still win a footrace against men half his age.

That strength is casually deployed, like a snowplow against a moderate drift. There is an impulsiveness to his physical actions. He is the first to run to something, first to push something, first to knock someone down, first to jump out of a boat. He does not go around things, he goes through them or over them, and does not much mind the consequences. When he tangles with a briar bush in the process of carrying a boat, it leaves its scratches, and Morgan proceeds onward.

And the voice. All the memoirs mention his voice: loud, yes, but also resonant and carrying and (to some) exhilarating. The voice, like the body, sprawls out.

Body and voice are meticulously clothed. Throughout his life, Morgan showed a careful attention to his appearance. His tailor billed him for altering red and green coats, for making a red jacket, and making a "fine cloth suit." Morgan liked to impress—with size, strength, voice, and sartorial splendor.[2]

The body, the voice, and the personality all make it seem as if Morgan was intended for the American Revolution, as if he was made to command a group of contrary, cross-grained, backcountry hoodlums in battle. But he really wasn't. What he had become, against all odds, was a rising member of the Valley gentry. For a homeless boy who had cut himself off from his family—a fundamental act of rebellion if ever there was one—the place where he found himself in early spring 1775 must have been astonishing.

IN THE CAROLINAS, during the Revolution, the backcountry was a scene of continual civil war between Loyalists and Patriots.[3] Throughout the war there were raids, massacres, turncoats, traitors, and reprisals. Yet this was not the case in Virginia. Though enslaved people sought freedom with the British army and navy whenever they could, and there was considerable disorder and hostility between socioeconomic classes as the war progressed, Virginia did not descend into the same maelstrom of violence as the Carolinas. Not even the ethnic fissures of the Valley led to any conflict. This lack of conflict—the curious incident of the dog that did nothing in the nighttime—requires some brief explanation.[4]

In the lower Valley, this lack of conflict was in part because Robert Carter had given away so much of Lord Fairfax's land, and because farsighted governors had established settlers' claims to whatever was left after Carter was done. Therefore, from the earliest European settlement in the Valley, the Valley had been integrated into the concerns of Virginia's Tidewater aristocracy, whose wealth was based on the cultivation of tobacco by slave labor along the tidal rivers of eastern Virginia. In the Carolinas, the backcountry was a separate world, its inhabitants aliens to those living in the Carolina Lowcountry. In Virginia the inhabitants of the Valley were either yeoman with recognized land titles or tenants of Tidewater aristocrats. So while the inhabitants of western Virginia (that is, anywhere outside of the Tidewater) were in various ways second-class citizens until after the Civil War, they were nevertheless fully integrated into the political order of the colony. Unlike the back-country Carolinians, backcountry Virginians were not as ready to be radicalized for either king or rebellion.[5]

True, there were fewer Anglicans and more Calvinists, Lutherans, Baptists, and even Quakers in the Valley; more Germans, Scots Irish, and whoever else got off the ship at New Castle, Delaware, and Philadelphia and straggled their way down the Valley; and there were also more small independent landowners of the middling sort. But these differences never led to the political or social cleavages found in the Carolinas. As Morgan's case demonstrates, even a yeoman farmer in the Valley could be politically and economically linked to Tidewater aristocracy. The roads Morgan traveled on his wagon, the bridges, ferries, and fords he used to cross the streams of Virginia, all of these tied him and men like him into the interests of the colony of Virginia.

So when the crisis of revolution struck, Frederick County was as ardent in its public support of the embattled Bostonians as any county in the Tidewater. On June 8, 1774, while Morgan was leading his company of militia into the woods of the Ohio valley, Frederick County's prominent citizens issued a declaration against the Boston Port Act of 1774, declaring that any attempts to uphold it would "raise a civil war" and result in disunion.[6] When news of Lexington and Concord reached Winchester, the Patriots of the Valley were ready for action.

The committee directing the Revolutionary efforts in Frederick County had as key members Isaac Zane, Angus McDonald, and Charles Mynn Thruston—all three of their names had been on the resolutions of 1774, and they also signed the resolutions that were issued in May and June 1775. All three had already proved good patrons of Morgan's career, and now they were the gate through which he passed to his future prominence. Thanks to the patronage of the Valley elite, Morgan was soon known as a frontiersman and Revolutionary rifleman.

FREDERICK COUNTY was just one of the many places in the thirteen colonies that, following the news of Lexington and Concord, were seized with *rage militaire,* a moment when it seemed that "every breast had felt military ardor and every lip had spoken words of self-sacrifice."[7] One of the symptoms of that ardor was rifle mania, a fixation on rifles and riflemen that swept through the colonies.

Perhaps it was Richard Henry Lee who started it. The tall, beaky, austerely lipped Virginian was a political radical and ally of similarly radical New Englanders. He was also proud of anything within the Old Dominion's borders and ready to brag about it to anyone, even to his younger brother Arthur, then in London. "The inclosed Address to the Virginia Delegates published a few days since in the Gazette," he wrote Arthur from Philadelphia:

> [W]ill shew you the spirit of the Frontier Men. This one County of Fincastle can furnish 1000 Rifle Men that for their number make most formidable light Infantry in the World. The six frontier Counties can produce 6000 of these Men who from their amazing hardihood, their method of living so long in the woods without carrying provisions with them, the exceeding quickness with which they can march to distant parts, and above all, the dexterity to which they have arrived in the use of the Rifle Gun. Their is not one of these Men who wish a distance less than 200 yards or a larger object than an Orange. Every shot is fatal.[8]

Most of the legend of the American rifleman is present in that paragraph: numbers, hardiness, woodcraft, patriotism, and uncanny marksmanship. None of it was necessarily true.

IN the simplest analysis a rifle is simply a tool, a technological advantage that man uses to exert force upon the surrounding environment. But no other tool has been so mythologized in American history, so appreciated and misunderstood at one and the same time.

One of the men as close to a philosopher of the rifle as the twentieth century produced observed that the rifle "realizes the ancient dream of the Jovian thunderbolt, and as such it is the embodiment of personal power. For this reason it exercises a curious influence over the minds of most men, and in its best examples it constitutes an object of affection unmatched by any other inanimate object."[9] The rifle has become an icon, an object that reveals something more to its beholder than it physically contains. Partly because of this, the misinformation and misunderstanding of eighteenth-century rifles may outstrip any topic other than slavery. So some attention must be paid to first principles.

Imagine that you are inside an eighteenth-century gun barrel the size of a subway tunnel. If you were inside a musket, the smoothbore shoulder arm most commonly used in the eighteenth century, than you would be within as smooth and round a tunnel as the technology of the era could produce.

Now imagine a bullet the size of a subway car. Fortunately for their occupants, subway cars do not fit tightly within a subway tunnel. Nor did round bullets within a musket barrel. They would be rammed in with powder, often with a paper cartridge to keep them fixed down the barrel. But they were not quite as big as the barrel.

Imagine now that you are watching from safely behind some armored glass. A load of powder as big as or bigger than a round bullet the size of a subway car is packed into the bottom of the tunnel. A bullet, swathed in crumpled paper, is jammed down with a ramrod. There is an almighty explosion. The fragments of paper combust along with about 50 percent of the black powder—from your perspective you see that much residue remains in the barrel. As the bullet travels up the battle, it knocks against the sides.

Black powder is a low-yield explosive that does not detonate but burns quickly. The bullets it propels, therefore, travel at low velocity. Thus, on the eighteenth-century battlefields, there could be seemingly miraculous escapes from death—moments when a small New Testament in a breast pocket stopped a bullet, and why numerous belt plates, snuffboxes, watches, coins, and gorgets absorbed the force of a bullet, protected their owners, and became treasured family heirlooms. So commanders did not open fire at long range but waited until fifty yards separated them from their enemy. Observers at the Battle of Quebec in 1760 noted that the French fired the first volley from too great a distance, the result being that while the British suffered six hundred wounded, only forty were killed.[10]

Back to our subway tunnel thought experiment. If you were inside a rifle barrel, you would immediately notice grooves cut into the metal walls around you, spiraling along the direction of the tunnel. This is the rifling that gives the rifle its name. These grooves overcome the problem of bullet fit, and that enables them to do even more. When a bullet is fired it engages with these grooves, and they impart spin to it—in a perennial metaphor, it is the spiral of the thrown football. Spin stabilizes the flight of the bullet, making its trajectory flat and long. Yet bullets, until the middle of the nineteenth century, were not designed to engage the rifling.

To do that, Morgan and his fellow eighteenth-century riflemen followed this procedure. Hanging from their shoulder was a horn— made from that of a cow—and a leather pouch. From the horn they would pour fine gunpowder into an attached measure and drop this powder down the barrel. Then they would remove a lead ball from the pouch, along with a greased patch. The ball was placed atop the patch, and both were forced down the barrel with a ramrod. It was the patch that was the decisive factor, for it was what engaged with the rifling. Should a rifleman put a ball down the barrel without a patch, his rifle was no more accurate than a musket. The final procedure was to prime the lock of the rifle with more powder. If the flints were still able to make spark (and they had to be turned or changed every eight or ten shots), then the rifle was ready to fire.

The long rifle came about as a result of the same cultural fusion that was shaping the British colonies in North America. A conventional telling of the story is that the German rifle, introduced into Pennsylvania, was gradually adapted by a series of gunsmiths to the American environment. The short, heavy rifle used by German hunters became longer and lighter. What additionally made the long rifle unique was that it became ever more ornate. Early rifles looked more like muskets, with blunt, heavy stocks that, despite an antiergonomic appearance, were effective in absorbing the recoil of a heavy powder load. (The lighter the gun, the harsher the recoil to be mastered by the shooter.) Yet in Pennsylvania, gunsmiths quickly began to alter the fundamental designs of German rifles. Pennsylvania craftsmen used curly maple as their wood of choice rather than the equally abundant and traditional walnut. They highlighted the whorls and twists of the maple, and they used its strength to make ever more slender stocks and furnishings. Most notably, the butt of the rifle—the surface that rests against the shoulder of the shooter—began to be fashioned ever more delicately, and a box was carved in it to hold the greased patches in which to enclose the rifle balls. Already by the 1760s, the American rifle was a unique tool that could not be mistaken for a product from any other culture.[11]

A rifle's greatest disadvantage, offsetting its accuracy, was the time required to load it. The Germans had short-barreled rifles into whose muzzles they forced the patched ball with a little hammer—that took time. In America, riflemen dispensed with the hammer, but it still took force to start the ball into the muzzle, and this also took time. American gunsmiths, therefore, made the muzzle of the long rifle longer to make it more convenient for the rifleman to hold in one hand while using the other to start the ball with the ramrod. The time required to load a long rifle was made yet longer by the need to measure the powder before loading. The time required for an expert to load a long rifle could be as long as thirty seconds; for a very expert rifleman, perhaps twenty seconds. A trained musket man, on the other hand, could always be ready in twenty seconds, and an experienced one in as short as twelve or fifteen seconds. For a hunter it made little difference how long it took to load, so long as the first shot went where it should. But for a soldier on the battlefield, that slow loading time was a severe handicap.

RIFLES did not create a fusion of middle European folk culture and colonial English engineering—they were a result of that fusion. Technology does not determine culture; culture determines technology and directs it within certain channels.

Likewise differences between the rifle and the musket made riflemen and musket men representatives of almost different cultures, certainly of different mentalities. Musket men were American and British soldiers. German riflemen—called Jaegers or Chausseurs—were soldiers despite their name. Morgan's riflemen, though, had been hunters before they were soldiers. The key to employing them in battle was to use their skills while simultaneously transforming them into soldiers in such a way that they were not stripped of their skills. At this task, Morgan would prove to be preeminent.

Inasmuch as anything was standardized in an age of handcrafts, it was the British Long Land Pattern musket of 1722, known colloquially or perhaps affectionately as the "Brown Bess," and used with only small variations for over one hundred years. Each was as close to identical as human hands could make them. They were meant to be used by men who also were made to look the same— in uniform, hairstyle, drill, and discipline. The musket was a uniformly constructed weapon designed to be uniformly used. It was a communal instrument whose most effective use was the result of the most effective discipline. While British sergeants of the eighteenth century often taught their trainees to shoot at a target, the musket's effective range of one hundred yards privileged volume of fire over accuracy. There is a natural human tendency to fire high; experienced platoon leaders therefore always directed their musket men to fire low, at the waist level of their enemy. Nevertheless, as the smoke of succeeding volleys collected into a drift that obscured both battlefield and enemy, units in the age of black powder would fire progressively higher. Firsthand accounts from the late seventeenth century to the American Civil War often describe the damage done to trees above a line of infantrymen as their opponents' bullets went over their heads.

From the perspective of musket men, riflemen were all dangerous individualists. They fired separately, not in a volley. The proper use of the rifle relied on an individual's self-discipline, not on group discipline. Moreover, the need to aim meant riflemen could not fight in ranks even if they had been disposed to do so. Black powder creates massive clouds of smoke whose size and thickness are beyond the comprehension of most inexperienced modern imaginations. If a rifleman wanted to aim for a target on a calm day, he had to be clear of his neighbor's smoke as well as the smoke of his last shot. As a consequence, riflemen were forced to usually adopt a loose and broken formation, different from the stiff ranks of the musket men. Doing so was not necessarily an advantage in eighteenth-century warfare. Fighting shoulder to shoulder with friends offered musket men courage and support. Riflemen did not have that, and scattered formations made riflemen psychologically prone to scatter—as Morgan found out on more than one occasion.

The rifle was itself built for this individualism. Its length and other physical characteristics were determined by the height and size of its owner. So, more obviously, was its ornamentation. Each rifle resulted not from the gunsmith's whim but from a consultation between gunsmith and client. In 1775, as many as fifteen gunsmiths were at work in Winchester and Frederick County. The consumer chose the smith he admired the most, and together with him created something that suited him as an individual.[12] Long before de Tocqueville coined the term *individualism*, it was manifest in the longrifle. Each rifle in Morgan's original rifle company was, in some way, as unique as its owner.[13]

FROM the very beginning of the war, before Morgan had even raised his company or set out on the road to Boston, the rifleman became a symbol of American virtue. Part of this was the belief that Americans would not only fight, but they would always win; that they were born with a gun in their hand, and that this gun was a rifle.

Even James Madison, sickly, small, secluded, and profoundly intellectual, was not above claiming a familiarity with the rifle to credulous Yankees. "The most inexpert hands rec[k]on it an indifferent shot to miss the bigness of a man's face at the distance of 100 Yards," he wrote his best friend and fellow Princetonian William Bradford. "I am far from being among the best, & should not often miss it on a fair trial at that distance."[14] So the humble brag about one's own marksmanship, a great American tradition, was first preserved on paper.

To fuel rifle mania and militia prejudice, Madison, Richard Henry Lee, and other Virginians had not only the events of Dunmore's War, and their considerable Virginia pride, but events of April 1775 in Virginia. While the British army in Boston was marching on the powder magazine and arms depot in Concord, at more or less the same moment Lord Dunmore was having a detachment of royal marines spirit away the colony of Virginia's powder supply from its place in the octagonal magazine sitting in the heart of Williamsburg.

The resulting crisis was far more explosive than all those barrels of black powder. Ultimately, thousands of Virginia militia marched on the colonial capital, choosing Virginia's foremost political radical, Patrick Henry, as their leader. They wore hunting shirts and many carried rifles, although those were certainly mixed up with muskets, fowling pieces, and probably antiques of uncertain date of manufacture. Militia from Culpeper County reputedly carried a flag bearing a rattlesnake and the words "Liberty or Death."[15]

As news of this uprising filtered north, its messengers no doubt passing others heading south with news of Lexington and Concord, it became a story of backcountry riflemen driving the royal governor into the sea—or at least into Chesapeake Bay, where Lord Dunmore took refuge on one of His Majesty's ships. New Englanders in attendance at the Second Continental Congress in Philadelphia wrote their friends and family explaining the miraculous power of the rifle and the patriotic fervor of its users. Their comprehension was limited. "It is a sort of musket," explained John to Abigail Adams, revealing that he still did not have much more knowledge of what it was than did his wife after she read his letter.[16]

How precisely Congress raised the regiments remains something of a mystery of American bureaucratic history. The Virginia Convention, the Patriot alternative to the royal government of Virginia, was then meeting to raise regiments to fight Lord Dunmore and to send to the main army in the north. But it did this of its own volition, without responding to any request from Congress. So the rifle regiments were really the first truly American army: "authorized by Congress; . . . paid by Congress; they took their orders from Continental officers."[17]

We do not have many existing records from the Virginia companies of riflemen, but those of Maryland just across the Potomac exist, and it is reasonable to assume that the requirements of Congress were the same for Maryland, Pennsylvania, and Virginia. Congress probably sent an express rider with a request from the Virginia delegation directly to the necessary committees in Berkeley, Frederick, and Augusta Counties—possibly even as far south as Fincastle. Those committees then chose the captains of each company. In Frederick County, the Committee of Safety, the county's Patriot leadership, chose Daniel Morgan.

THE stated and required size of the rifle company was to be sixty-eight privates; a drummer; four corporals; four sergeants; three lieutenants; and the captain. Volunteers swore this oath: "I, A˙ B˙, have, this — day of —, voluntarily enlisted myself as a Soldier in the American Continental army, for one year, unless sooner discharged. I do bind myself to conform, in all instances, to such rules and regulations as are, or shall hereafter be, established for the government of the said Army." They brought their own guns and their own clothes. Each private was offered six and two-thirds dollars a month. Captains were to be paid twenty dollars. The money to pay them did not exist.[18]

The enthusiasm to enlist in Pennsylvania was so great that while Congress had requested eight companies, ten were raised. Two companies were requested of Virginia, and it sent three off to Boston. Morgan, supposed to only have sixty-eight in his company, marched north with a total strength of ninety-six. Captain Hugh Stephenson in neighboring Berkeley County had nineteen men over the quota.[19] After this first flush of *rage militaire*, recruiting was never again so easy.

There are three sets of lists of members of Morgan's company, and collating them gives an idea of who joined him. At the top of them all were three officers: 1st Lieutenant John Humphreys, 2nd Lieutenant William Heth, and Ensign Peter Bruin of Winchester. Billy Heth was the son of an Ulster immigrant to the James River near Richmond and probably served with Morgan on the Ohio during Dunmore's War in 1774. Blind in one eye, Heth was almost insufferably proud of his Virginia roots, a trial to any Yankee within earshot. Bruin, like many others, served with Morgan as often as he could. In addition to these three men there was Charles Porterfield, sometimes listed as a sergeant, other times as a cadet, and who was probably what the British army would have called a gentleman volunteer, a young man serving as a private soldier until an officer's position was available.

Then there were the noncommissioned officers and enlisted men. The first of these were two sergeants, William Fickhis and Benjamin Grubb. Among the privates were several Germans from the Valley, and they formed a little group that was either then or later called the "Dutch Mess." There was also Private George Merchant, described as "large and handsome." This was a particular honor in Morgan's company, as many commented on the height and handsomeness of its members on their march north and their arrival at Boston. They were, said an admiring fellow rifleman from Pennsylvania, "as elegant a body of men as ever came into my view . . . adroit young men, courageous, and thorough-going." Or, as another Pennsylvanian simply said, "they were beautiful boys, who knew how to handle and aim the rifle."[20]

These men were not settlers from the edge of the frontier but were from the lower Valley. Some might have already fought alongside Morgan in Dunmore's War, some might have gone on a long hunt. But the true frontiersmen, the long hunters, men used to living in the woods, were those who followed George Rogers Clark down the Ohio to Kaskaskia and through Illinois to Vincennes. The predominant outdoors experience that men of Morgan's company had had was hunting in the Valley for deer, a different affair than it had been when Morgan first walked into Winchester. A local historian, Samuel Kercheval, a boy when Morgan raised his company, remembered the Valley hunters of his childhood. They hunted the west side of the Shenandoah Valley along the front range of the Appalachians. "As soon as the leaves were pretty well down, and the weather became rainy accompanied with light snows, these men, after acting the part of husbandmen . . . soon began to feel that they were hunters." They became discontented with their normal agrarian routine, would in the mornings sniff the wind, look longingly at woods and their rifle, until that day they loaded their packhorses with necessaries and rode up to their hunting camp. From their shelter they ventured out not for amusement, in a "mere ramble in pursuit of game," but with "Skill and calculation." Indeed, Kercheval observed, "the whole business of the hunter consists of a succession of intrigues" in which he pitted his knowledge of wind, weather, and geography against a deer with "superior sagacity and watchfulness."[21]

It was from this human material that Morgan chose his company. They could shoot, had the intelligence of a hunter, and had the woodcraft that allowed them in a few hours to build a camp that was defended from the weather and that in a day would allow them to be defended against any other humans as well. They came with their rifles, their shot pouches, and their powder horns. They even brought their uniforms to their final muster. Atop everything was a hunting shirt, which quickly became as symbolic as their rifles. This was a linen shirt, coming down to their waists or a little lower, open at the front, and held together by a belt, short ties, or both. A decorative short cape descended from the collar to just over the shoulders, and decorative fringes were placed wherever the owner desired. The hunting shirts could be worn over whatever else they had, ranging from leggings, loincloths, and moccasins, to overalls and hobnailed shoes, giving a pleasing military uniformity to a company of riflemen. In effect, the hunting shirt was in modern military parlance the Battle Dress, Utility, of the eighteenth century.[22] But the standardization of their field uniforms did not make them into soldiers.

Morgan had less experience soldiering than many captains in the British army. Yet he had what many officers in either army lacked: a great, burning ambition combined with a deep empathy that approached and often achieved a kind of curious tenderness. From the very first, he was determined to achieve preeminence, to do more, to be better. He therefore imposed discipline and order on his men that other captains, used to a freewheeling democratic militia system, could not imagine imposing on theirs. Yet that empathy was always close at hand, and Morgan could switch from one emotional state to another with surprising ease and speed.

His first task, Morgan determined, was to get to Boston and the new Continental army before any of the other Virginia or Maryland rifle companies—particularly Hugh Stephenson's from Berkeley County. Without waiting for Stephenson to finish securing men and rifles, Morgan gave him the slip. He put his ninety-six men on the road and marched north.

On Wednesday, July 19, a "Gentleman of Fredericktown, Maryland" wrote, "On Monday last Captain Morgan, from Virginia, with his company of riflemen, (all chosen,) marched through this place, on their way to Boston. Their appearance was truly martial; their spirits amazingly elated, breathing nothing but a desire to join the American Army, and to engage the enemies of American liberty." Morgan marched his men through town without stopping, cheered by the "acclamations of all the inhabitants who attended them." They were escorted via a kind of honor guard composed of companies of Maryland militia, and a sister company of Maryland riflemen. A mile or so outside of town, the accompanying soldiers halted, and Morgan kept on his march.[23]

What happened in Frederick was a kind of pattern for Morgan's march north. These were the first American troops from another region that anyone in the mid-Atlantic or New England colonies had ever seen; for many, they might have been the first people from another colony, certainly the first southerners, they had ever seen. Morgan's company was the first demonstration of a truly united colonial resolve to resist the tyranny of Parliament. It was an indication to all colonists that the Revolution was to be a truly continental effort and fought by a continental army.

Morgan moved quickly; some, probably long after the fact, referred to it as the "Beeline March." He crossed the Potomac on July 15 and went through Fredericktown, Maryland, on the seventeenth. By that time he and his men were just reaching their cruising speed. They marched into Cambridge, Massachusetts, on August 6. Stephenson's company, which had left the day after Morgan's, arrived August 11. Thus, for twenty-one days, give or take, Morgan's company had done twenty-three miles a day, every day, marching 484 miles altogether. The march to Boston was something of which Morgan always remained proud, particularly because "I did not leave a man behind."[24]

In the late nineteenth century, John Esten Cooke (a Virginia writer then living in a house that Morgan had built) imagined the scene when Washington greeted Morgan and his riflemen. Morgan, he said, had saluted the mounted commander in chief, saying, "From the right bank of the Potomac, General!" At this Washington dismounted, and "with tears in his eyes went along the ranks, shaking hands in turn with each of the men."[25]

Cooke's imagination outstripped the facts of his sources. If by some miracle Washington did weep when Morgan and his riflemen arrived in camp, within a month it is certain he was anxious to get rid of them.

Chapter Six

THE MARCH
UPCOUNTRY

JOHN JOSEPH HENRY was an unusual sixteen-year-old. In 1772, at age thirteen or fourteen, his uncle had taken him from Lancaster, Virginia, to Detroit to be his apprentice gunsmith. Finding that business was not as good as he had hoped, he sent him home with a guide. During the journey, the guide died somewhere in the wilderness of Ohio. John Joseph continued alone across Ohio and most of Pennsylvania to Lancaster. Strangely eager for yet more adventure, with the outbreak of the Revolution, Henry enlisted in one of the Pennsylvania rifle companies and marched to Boston in summer 1775.

A few months later he found himself starving in the Maine wilderness. He was part of a scouting party sent ahead of an expedition to attack Quebec led by Colonel Benedict Arnold of Connecticut. Lost in the woods, Henry and his companions soon ran out of food. When they returned, starving, to the main body of the army on October 17, 1775, one of the first men they encountered was Christian Febiger. He was yet another of the curious characters that appeared in the ranks of the Continental army. A veteran of the Danish army who had gone to Boston via the Virgin Islands (where his uncle was governor), Febiger had joined the Massachusetts Militia, fought at Bunker Hill, and then volunteered for Arnold's expedition.

Febiger "with a sudden and involuntary motion and much tenderness . . . handed me his wooden canteen, (which contained the last spirits in the army). . . . The heart of Febiger seemed overjoyed at the relief he had and could afford us," Henry recalled decades later. Then Febiger sat the returning soldiers down by the fire, and they ate from a kettle of pork and dumplings. "This meal to all of us seemed a renewal of life. . . . By and by, Morgan came—large, a commanding aspect, and stentorian voice. He wore leggings and a cloth, in the Indian style. His thighs, which were exposed to view, appeared to have been lacerated by the horns and bushes. He knew our story . . . and greeted us kindly."[1]

This story captures the curious binaries of Arnold's expedition. It was a time of starving and privation and unimaginable suffering, yet it was also a time of friendship and of tenderness such as Febiger expressed. The army that marched through the Maine wilderness was small; by its arrival it had dwindled to roughly six-hundred men. From it emerged notable characters and reputations.

Morgan's was one of those reputations established on the march to Quebec. In that small army he became a character of note. He combined visible fortitude, a disciplinary urge uncommon to other American officers in 1775, and that tenderness that Henry noted in Febiger and would later discern in Morgan. "His manners were of the severest cast," Henry remembered, "but where he became attached he was kind and truly affectionate. This is said from experience of the most sensitive and pleasing nature. Activity, spirit, and courage in a soldier, procured his good will and esteem."[2]

Long before Morgan became a contemporary legend in Revolutionary America, he was a legend in the Continental army. The march to Quebec is when that legend was created.

HAVING gotten to Boston, Morgan's men and the other riflemen who soon joined them quickly made themselves a scourge of British soldiers and George Washington.

The first happened upon arrival in August 1775. Eager for sport, Morgan's men and riflemen of the other companies soon made things difficult for any British soldiers who stuck their heads above their guarding earthworks. James Warren, president of the Massachusetts Provincial Congress, reported to his friend John Adams that the riflemen had killed "four Captains and a subaltern" in the few days between their arrival and the beginning of August. But "the General has been obliged from Principles of frugality to restrain his rifle men. While they were permitted Liberty to fire on the Enemy, a great number of the Army would go and fire away great quantitys of Ammunition to no Purpose." Washington was particularly irritated by this practice—an understatement, really—because he had discovered that gunpowder was in such short supply there was only enough for about ten rounds per man.[3]

Over the month following their arrival, the riflemen became less and less an asset. They were as undisciplined and unmilitary as any of the New England troops. Their officers, with the possible exception of Morgan, not only failed to exert control over them but did not seem to understand why they needed to do so. Fighting other colonial soldiers seemed to give the riflemen as much enjoyment as fighting the British—or more. They were all versions of the earlier model of Daniel Morgan.

By September 11, Warren was writing his friend Adams that "the greatest difficulty seems to be to govern our own Soldiery. I may say the rifle Men only for I hear of no other."[4] He was referring to a riot by thirty-two riflemen, all from the 1st Pennsylvania Regiment, whose attempt to break out of jail some of their comrades had been thwarted by Washington's direct intervention. As one Pennsylvanian remembered it, "Genls. Washington, Lee, and Greene came immediately, and our thirty-two mutineers who had gone about a half a mile toward Cambridge and taken possession of a hill and woods, beginning to be frighted at their proceedings, were not so hardened, but upon the General's ordering them to ground their arms they did it immediately. The General then ordered another of our companies, Capt. [George] Nagel's, to surround them with their loaded guns, which was immediately done, and did the company great honor." But Washington, not taking chances, had the Pennsylvania company surrounded by some of Nathanael

Greene's Rhode Islanders. Jesse Lukens, serving in Thompson's regiment, reported, "You cannot conceive what disgrace we are all in, and how much the General is chagrined that only one regiment should come from the South, and that set so infamous an example."[5] He was not wrong. With some of the snarling, desert-dry wit he shared only with his brothers or intimates, Washington wrote to his brother Samuel—a landowner in Berkeley County in the lower Shenandoah—that, "The Riflemen have had very little oppertunity of shewing their skill, or their ignorance, for some of them, especially from Pensylvania, know no more of a Rifle than my horse, being new Imported Irish many of whom have deserted to the Enemy."[6] Artemas Ward, who had been pushed aside by Washington for command of the army outside Boston, took waspish delight in the fall from grace of another group of southern interlopers into Yankeedom. "They do not boast so much of the Riflemen as heretofore," he wrote. "Genl. Washington has said he wished they had never come. Genl. Lee has damned them and wished them all in Boston. Genl. Gates has said, if any capital movement was about to be made the Riflemen must be moved from this Camp."[7]

THE trepidation with which British Americans had regarded French Canada had been replaced, after its shift to British rule, with a near-perpetual annoyance. First had come the 1763 decree of the Proclamation Line, which seemed a ministerial policy to fence in British Americans within the Appalachians. In 1774 came the Quebec Act, establishing viceregal rather than representative government over Canada. Worst of all, Canadians persisted in remaining both French and Catholic.

This long-standing prejudice shifted with the growth of the insurgent rebellion following the closure of the port of Boston. Committees in the thirteen lower colonies began to reach out to potential cobelligerents in Quebec, imagining that they might join the cause of the English-speaking rebellion to the south. The Quebec Act was seen as an injustice perpetuated against the Quebecois. They, too, were suffering under the legislative tyranny of the British Parliament.

While this was imaginative, it was not necessarily delusional. Like the other colonies throughout British America, Quebec was divided into several political and cultural factions. Its politics were more intelligible to other colonial Americans then they often are to contemporary Americans. Ultimately, the attempt to take Quebec was "no more quixotic than the patriot struggle to control divided New York or government-dependent Georgia, or in fact, the entire concept of the American Revolution."[8]

INTO these dreams of a fourteenth colony marched Benedict Arnold of Connecticut. The fourth generation of American colonists to bear that name, a descendent of a governor of Rhode Island, Arnold had been a teenage deserter from the Connecticut forces fighting (or not fighting, which was why he left) at Fort William Henry in northern New York in 1756. He went on to be an apprentice, a druggist, a ship owner, and a merchant with vessels on the routes from New Haven to Quebec and the Caribbean. His wealth was matched by his rebellious sentiments and commitment to militia service. When news of Lexington and Concord reached New Haven, he broke into the powder magazine on New Haven Green, equipped his company with its contents, and marched to Boston.[9]

One of the many revelations of revolution was that this teenage deserter, former apothecary's apprentice, and old blood turned nouveau riche was also a military genius. The first indication of this gift was his plan to take Fort Ticonderoga and open the waterway of Lake Champlain to the heart of British Canada. Arriving at Ticonderoga to discover that such an attack was already under way by local hero Ethan Allen, Arnold persisted in his vision even after Ticonderoga's capture. He occupied the decayed fort at Crown Point, seized a local sailing vessel, and with it launched a strike against St. John's at the northern end of Lake Champlain. By the time he left Lake Champlain in June, he had established American control over the water route into Canada.

Arnold's strategic insight, along with his attention to logistics, supply, and discipline, caught the attention of George Washington. Sometime before the middle of August 1775, Arnold—until then an officer serving at the pleasure of the provincial Congress of Massachusetts—traveled to Cambridge to meet with the Virginian. Perhaps, one biographer of Arnold suggests, it was at this meeting that

Arnold mentioned a proposal he had made in June to launch an invasion of Canada via an overland route through the Maine woods.

It was not a completely new idea. The French in Canada had, during the course of their seventy-year struggle with the New England colonies, meditated on an attack on Boston using the same routes. An English lieutenant of engineers, John Montresor, now in the British army besieged within Boston, had traveled in 1761 from Quebec city to the Maine coast. And sometime in the early summer, an officer from Massachusetts, Colonel Jonathan Brewer, had proposed an expedition of five hundred men along that route.[10]

Washington told Arnold he needed a few days to review the proposal. On August 20, he sent an express courier to Major General Philip Schuyler, commanding the Continental army in New York, proposing a joint attack on Canada. "The Design of this Express," Washington wrote, "is to communicate to you a Plan of an Expedition, which has engrossed my Thoughts for several Days: It is to penetrate into Canada, by Way of Kennebeck River, and so to Quebec, by a Rout 90 Miles below Montreal—I can very well spare a Detachment of 1000 or 1200 Men." In an unusually careless and foolhardy phrase he added "the Land Carriage by the Rout proposed is too inconsiderable to make an Objection." He would, in a few months, regret those words.[11]

The commander in chief did not necessarily believe the plan would inevitably succeed. For him it was enough simply to attempt it. The chief attack called for in the plan was against Montreal by way of Lake Champlain. Any attack through the Maine woods would simply be a diversion that might possibly gain something more. Washington suggested to General Schuyler that Guy Carleton, governor of Canada, "must either break up and follow this party to Quebec, by which he will leave you a free passage or suffer that important Place to fall into our Hands: an Event which would have a decisive Effect and Influence on the public Interests." Washington intended to gore Carleton with the horns of a dilemma. By the time Schuyler responded, Washington had already decided to entrust Arnold with command of the expedition.[12]

His orders to Arnold—and thereby to Arnold's army—were passionate and meticulous. Arnold and his men were to consider themselves as liberators entering an enslaved land:

I [charge] you therefore and the Officers & Soldiers [under] your Command, as you value your own Safety and Honour, & the Favour and Esteem of your Country that you consider yourselves as marching not through an Enemies Country, but that of our Friends and Brethren, for such the Inhabitants of Canada & the Indian Nations have approved themselves in this unhappy Contest between Great Brittain & America.

Most particularly did Washington order Arnold to discipline his men so they avoided giving any religious offense to the Catholic Canadians:

I also give it in Charge to you to avoid all Disrespect or Contempt of the Religion of the Country and its Cere-monies—Prudence, Policy and a true Christian Spirit will lead us to look with Compassion upon their Errors without insult-ing them—While we are Contending for our own Liberty, we should be very cautious of violating the Rights of Conscience in others; ever considering that God alone is the Judge of the Hearts of Men and to him only in this Case they are answer-able.[13]

The expedition was assembled with incredible speed. Orders from Washington's headquarters in Massachusetts were sent to Fort Western in Maine for the construction of two hundred bateaux, the flat-bottomed, shallow-drafted, double-pointed rowboats used to navigate the lower Kennebec River. The plan was for Arnold's army to use these boats to convoy one thousand men and approximately sixty-five tons of supplies up the Kennebec River to a twelve-mile portage known somewhat unimaginatively as the Great Carrying Place. This portage would lead them to the Dead River, a tributary of the Kennebec. They would travel up the Dead River to yet an-other portage that crossed the Height of Land, the aptly named little continental divide from which streams and rivers flow north to the St. Lawrence and south to the Gulf of Maine. Portaging the Height of Land would lead them to Lake Megantic, headwaters of the Chaudiere River. Navigating the Chaudiere would take them straight down to the banks of the St. Lawrence, very near to Quebec city itself. Using Montresor's map, Arnold estimated that the entire journey was about 180 miles and would take twenty to thirty days.

In truth, it was a distance of 350 miles. Had Washington and Arnold known the actual length of the route, the time it would require, or the cost at which it would be undertaken, they might never have launched the expedition.[14]

But they did not know, and so they launched it. On September 5, 1775, the general orders to the Continental army directed that as part of

> A Detachment . . . to go upon Command with Col. Arnold of Connecticut . . . one Company of Virginia Riflemen and two Companies from Col. Thompson's Pennsylvania Regiment of Rifle-men, to parade at the same time and place, to join the above Detachment: Tents and Necessaries proper and convenient for the whole, will be supplied by the Quarter Master Genl immediately upon the Detachment being collected—As it is imagined the Officers and Men sent from the Regiments both here, and at Roxbury, will be such Volunteers, as are active Woodsmen, and well acquainted with batteaus; so it is recommended, that none but such will offer themselves for this service.[15]

The little army was about 1,050 men strong. It marched to the Massachusetts town of Newburyport, where some of Arnold's officers took pieces of cloth and perhaps even bones from the corpse of the evangelist George Whitfield, which rested in the crypt of the Congregational Church. These holy relics were perhaps, in Arnold's mind, the reason a favorable wind blew them north on September 19 to the mouth of the Kennebec and three days later saw them dropping anchor off Fort Western, site of present-day Augusta, Maine.[16]

The officers of Arnold's little army were a collection of the Continental army's most interesting soldiers. In addition to Arnold and Daniel Morgan there was Rhode Island Quaker captain Christopher Greene, second cousin of General Nathanael Greene's, and—as he demonstrated at the Battle of Red Bank in 1777—as courageous a battlefield commander as either Morgan or Arnold. From Connecticut came the unforgettably named Return Jonathan Meigs, who also became one of the great combat leaders of the Continental army. A number of volunteers also accompanied the expedition—

young men who were either officers detached from their regiments or young gentlemen hoping for a battlefield commission; among them were a young man from New Jersey, Aaron Burr, and his stepbrother Matt Ogden.

There were other, less-promising officers. One of the two Pennsylvania rifle companies was commanded by the less-memorably-named Matthew Smith. He was from Paxtang, a community now close to modern Harrisburg, and a handsome, indolent drunk, according at least to the memories of rifleman John Joseph Henry, who served in his company. Smith's previous brush with fame had been as a leader of the so-called Paxton Boys, who had murdered a number of peaceful Indians and then marched on Philadelphia to chastise the provincial government for failing to protect them. Morgan would find Smith to be a continual problem.

Arnold divided his command into several divisions. He had intended to place Christopher Greene in command of the first division and compose it of five companies: two of musket men, as well as the three rifle companies. But, Arnold explained to his commander in chief in a letter of September 25, when he appointed Greene to that command, "This was objected to by the captains of the rifle companies, who insist on being commanded by no other person than captain Morgan and myself." This the three rifle captains claimed to have been Washington's intention, since they had been raised by Congress itself rather than any state and were therefore outside the normal command structure of the army. Rather than immediately engage in a dispute over command, Arnold sensibly sent the three rifle companies ahead with Morgan in command of that first division.[17] Greene followed with the second division, then Return Jonathan Meigs with the third, and finally Colonel Roger Enos of New Hampshire commanding the rear guard.[18]

THE first recorded correspondence between Washington and Morgan resulted from circumstances the latter would have certainly preferred to alter. Washington responded to Morgan's dispute with Arnold over command of the rifle companies by sending Morgan one of those stiffly written letters of his that were sharp enough to etch the recipient's name on glass. By that time he had had quite enough of enlisted riflemen and was now short of tolerance for their officers as well. "My Intention is and ever was that every Officer should Command according to his Rank," he informed Morgan. "To do otherwise would Subvert all military Order & Authority which I am Sure you could not wish or expect." Having stated matters clearly, Washington then twisted Morgan's arm behind his back. "Remember," he wrote, "that by the Same Rule that You claim an independant Command & break in upon military Authority others will do the same by you: And of Consequence the Expedition must terminate in Shame & Disgrace to yourselves and the Reproach and Detriment of your Country—To a Man of true Spirit & military Character farther Argument is unnecessary."[19]

To Morgan's credit, further reproofs were never needed again, which could not be said for many officers in the Continental army. In addition to reprimand, Washington's letter also offered Morgan a certain kind of status. In accepting Washington's censure, he demonstrated himself to be "a Man of true Spirit & military Character." The former wagoner, the yeoman farmer with 499 scars on his back, was now recognized as a gentleman of honor, a man of such spirit and character.

MORGAN set off with the first division up the Kennebec on the morning of Monday, September 25, 1775. His orders were to scout and clear the route the rest of the army would take, a task for which Arnold believed the riflemen were ideal. Not that Arnold thought they or the army would encounter many difficulties. When John Montresor, now besieged with the rest of the British army in Boston, traveled from Quebec city to the Kennebec River and then down to the coast of Maine, he had navigated the Chaudiere River in eight days and then traveled from the headwaters of the Chaudiere to Fort Halifax on the Kennebec in twelve.

But by the time Morgan and his men made it to Skowhegan Falls on the Kennebec, just thirty-five or forty miles north of Fort Western, their badly made bateaux were already beginning to break apart under the strain. On October 2, they reached Norridgewalk Falls, a ninety-foot drop over a mile in length, the demarcation line for Maine frontier settlements. Catching up with Morgan's ad-

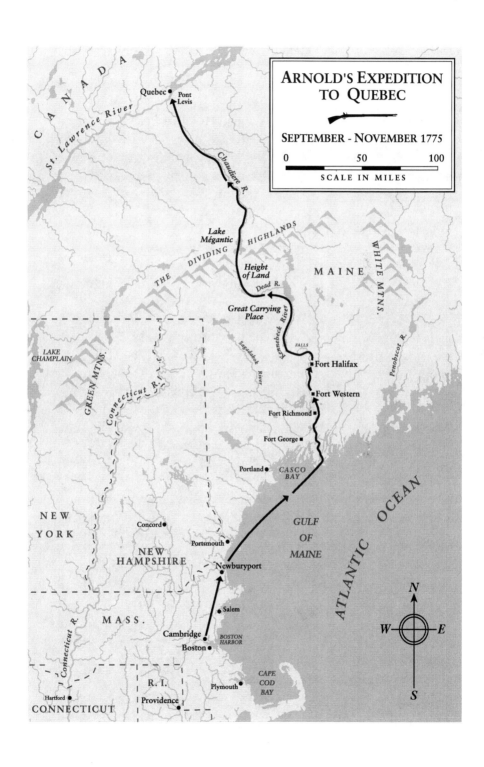

ARNOLD'S EXPEDITION
TO QUEBEC

SEPTEMBER - NOVEMBER 1775

0   50   100

SCALE IN MILES

vanced division, Arnold encouraged the riflemen by assuring them they had already traveled a third of the way to Quebec.[20]

On October 3, Arnold sent Morgan and his division forward to locate and clear a path across the Great Carrying Place, the portage from the Kennebec to the ironically named Dead River—ironic because the portage would allow the army to bypass a series of rapids. Reaching the first of three ponds that stretched along the portage, the riflemen with Morgan dined on salmon, trout, and a moose unfortunate enough to wander into the range of the largest collection of rifles on any continent.

However, nature refused to cooperate with Arnold's plan. On October 8, it began to rain, and that rain persisted for days. The Great Carrying Place portage became a stream of muck and bog and roots. The ponds overflowed, submerging the landmarks that indicated the trail as well as the trail itself. The rain was followed by winds that blew down trees whose roots had been loosened, and nights with temperatures below freezing. All this would have been bad enough if they had been traveling with packs alone, but Arnold's little army was also carrying unwieldy, ever-collapsing bateaux. They became walking cases of exposure, hypothermia, dysentery, and all the other illnesses to be expected when malnourished men cluster together in unsanitary camps.[21]

Morgan's advance division reached the Dead River on October 13; the rear guard, under Colonel Enos, arrived seven days later. And on October 13, despite the adversities of the previous five days and their ever-compounding consequences, Arnold wrote to General Schuyler that he and his army would arrive at Quebec city in two weeks.

THEY did not. On October 19, rain returned in full force, raising the height of the Dead River "upwards of 3 feet," Arnold recorded. On October 21, what seems to have been a late-season hurricane struck the Maine coast and rolled inland to further torment the beleaguered expedition. "It rained very fast all Night," Captain Henry Dearborn laconically wrote in his journal. "The river rose very fast." It did; in fact, the Dead River rose another eight feet, and the army's campsites, baggage, and supplies were inundated. The route forward along the riverbank was flooded, so that the men were wading as they moved forward. Then it began to snow.[22]

By this time, Captain Greene's division had passed Morgan's as his riflemen worked to clear brush from the portage trails. When even Enos's rear guard pushed up behind him, Morgan ordered his men to now remove only the worst obstructions from the trail; he could not bear the prospect of falling so far behind the lead. When the rains of October 19 and 21 struck the expedition, Morgan's men were intermingled among the other divisions.[23]

Through all this, Morgan maintained a discipline that was offensive to some of the riflemen, especially the company from Pennsylvania led by Captain Matthew Smith, who was not the kind of man who took command responsibility very seriously. Morgan's two "principal rules," remembered rifleman Henry "were, that there should be no straggling from camp; and no firing without authoritative permission." Morgan particularly detested the unnecessary firing of weapons, either for target practice or as a lazy way of removing a round at the end of the day. (The more disciplined method involved using a screw rod to tease out the bullets, and then carefully shaking out the powder, returning it to the powder horn. Perhaps unsurprisingly, many riflemen lacked sufficient patience for this practice.) As far as Morgan was concerned, firing betrayed the position of the shooter, wasted irreplaceable powder, and indicated all-around slovenliness. Imposing this discipline on the riflemen "was left to the energy of Morgan's mind," wrote Henry, "and he conquered."[24]

When on October 19 a Pennsylvanian fired off his rifle, it happened that Morgan was nearby. Running to the scene, he accused the rifleman of violating his order, a charge the rifleman denied. In Morgan's casual, Battletown-formed way of exerting authority, he seized a stick of firewood and proclaimed that unless the rifleman confessed, Morgan would strike him to the ground. This was unusual even by eighteenth-century standards of military justice, and Captain Smith took exception to it. Rifleman Henry remembered this incident as the only time Smith showed much passion or backbone about anything.

Rather than having it out with Smith then and there—as a not-much-younger Morgan certainly would have—Morgan let the infraction, and Smith's challenge, pass. Since it is nearly impossible to believe that Smith intimidated Morgan, it seems likely Morgan concluded that pounding a junior officer into a pulp would be prejudicial to discipline and unit cohesion.[25]

The riflemen trudged and paddled through the late autumn deluge along the banks of the Dead River; only experienced boatmen could now handle the bateaux against the powerful current and navigate upstream through its rapids.[26] They regularly lost equipment and supplies, either washed away by capsized bateaux or ruined by prolonged exposure to the rain. At times boatmen dragged themselves forward against the current by catching hold of trees and bushes along the banks.[27]

ON October 28, thirty-three days after setting out from Fort Western, Morgan's division reached the Height of Land. All memoirs concur that the four-and-a-half mile track across this little continental divide was the worst leg of the terrible journey. This was especially true for Morgan's company. While each of the Pennsylvania rifle companies portaged just one bateau each, Morgan insisted on taking all seven of his across what one private remembered as "The Terrible Carrying Place." The path was slicked by a few inches of snow and ice, enough to obscure its rocks, roots, and fallen trees. That was agony enough, but they were also carrying bateaux.[28] Other division commanders, including those of the rifle companies, had by this time cast aside the hated boats, but Morgan refused to do so. He would not be beaten, even by the Maine woods. Rifleman Henry recalled, "It would have made your heart ache to view the intolerable labors of his fine fellows. . . . By this time an antipathy had arisen against Morgan, as too strict a disciplinarian."[29]

Finally, by November 1, Morgan and his men reached Lake Megantic, the headwaters of the Chaudiere, which flowed down to the St. Lawrence near Quebec itself. The Virginians loaded and launched their seven remaining bateaux, Morgan boarding the first one. Within a few miles of setting off on the Chaudiere, they discovered why the French had named the river cauldron, or boiling pot. Morgan's bateau, followed by the other six, ran into rapids, hit rock, broke up, and sank. It was probably as close to death as

Morgan came at any time during the war. But they had also lost all the food, all the equipment except what they were carrying on their backs—and some of that as well—and the medicine chest for the entire army.[30] "Their condition was truly deplorable," wrote Private Abner Stocking of the riflemen, "they had not when we came up with them a mouthful of provisions of any kind, and we were not able to relieve them, as hunger stared us in the face. Some of us were now entirely destitute and others had but a morsel of bread, and we now supposed ourselves 70 miles from the nearest inhabitants."[31] Miraculously, only one of Morgan's men died; everyone else made it safely to shore, and they saved what hard money the expedition had with it.[32]

By this time Arnold's little expeditionary army was a straggling line of ragged, starving, suffering soldiers, stumbling forward along the banks of the river. Anything leather was considered a possible source of one last meal; Private Stocking assures his readers that they cannot imagine the gourmet treat of a boiled shot pouch—though presumably one must be malnourished and close to starvation in order to properly enjoy it. Morgan, staggering on his feet from the effects of malnutrition, made his way up and down the line of his division, joking, cajoling, and giving what hope he could.[33]

On November 2, relief finally arrived, traveling up the Chaudiere to encounter the starving army. The lead elements of the remaining 650 soldiers saw cattle being herded toward them; some at first thought they were hallucinating. Canoes arrived loaded with provisions. Men built fires and devoured scorched, mostly raw beef, a few dying of the shock. Abner Stocking "got a little piece of flesh, which I eat raw with a little oat meal wet with cold water, and thought I feasted sumptuously."[34] Others, strength almost immediately returning, went back up along the river to look for the missing. As they pressed on deeper into Canada, Arnold kept moving ahead of the column, purchasing supplies and sending them back to his recuperating and advancing army.[35]

On November 6, Arnold, Morgan, and the surviving army began the last leg of their journey across the plain of Quebec to Pont Levis, on the banks of the St. Lawrence across from Quebec city. Rain and snow transformed the roads into a semiliquid slurry, which Doctor

Isaac Senter, the expedition's surgeon, described as "Mud and mire to the horses belly."[36] If that observation was accurate, Morgan and his men were slogging through muck that could have been waist deep. On Thursday, November 9, moving through "gusts of swirling snow," the army reached the banks of the St. Lawrence and glimpsed, across the broad river, their goal of the last two months. "Few of us had any shoes, but moggasons made of raw skins— many of us without hats," wrote Stocking, "and beards long and visages thin and meagre. I thought we much resembled the animals which inhabit New Spain, called the Ourang-Outang."[37] Now all that Arnold's army had to do was take the city.

THE number of journals and memoirs left by the soldiers who suffered through Arnold's march is truly striking. Kenneth Roberts, searching for research material for his novel *Arundel*, collected twelve journals. To this number more can now be added, and there are probably a few more as yet undiscovered. Some were more or less plagiarized from other accounts, with a few personal details salted into the narrative. Yet the fact that veterans of the march did that indicates something important. Those who survived the Maine woods realized they had achieved an astonishing feat. They seemed to also understand that because Arnold's army did not acquire the fourteenth colony, their bitter march and remarkable survival would be forgotten, so they established memorials to their suffering. Many American victories are less well documented than this heroic failure.

Through their words, these veterans expressed a comradeship that seemingly every one of them felt, the forging of a suffering brotherhood. This recognition became all the more poignant as the Revolution unfolded; the passion of *rage militaire* faded, and costs personal, familial, and financial mounted. By Revolution's end, the public image of American enlisted soldiers was that of the dregs of society, mercenaries taking the place of others for dubious profit; men, in short, who, if they had not been soldiers, would have been migrant laborers. The revolutionary ideology in vogue by the end of the war meant that the citizens of the new republic viewed those serving in the army with at best ambivalence.

But, as the veterans' memoirs—particularly those that record the experience of Arnold's expedition—suggest, survivors looked back and saw a different picture. They remembered themselves as citizen-soldiers who suffered and overcame for the cause of liberty and for their new country. These memoirs, and the applications for governmental pensions for veterans of the Revolution that began in 1818, became a source for national repentance at their former ingratitude.[38]

Of course, for many this was far too late, and in any event it was somewhat irrelevant. They already knew what they had done, and with whom they had done it. Certainly there was no nonsense about the greatest generation from them, nor some sentimental attachment to all those who had suffered with them—they might continue to regard some of their fellow sufferers as thieves, rogues, and liars, and treat them as such.

But some of them had forged friendships, had become a group of suffering comrades who, despite differences of rank or background, could show themselves to be "kind and truly affectionate," as Febiger was to Henry and his fellow scouts. That mutual sympathy was linked in their minds and the minds of other soldiers to the love they had for their cause. It was also a virtue that sustained them in the worst moments of the war—which, they soon learned, could exceed the worst that had happened in the Maine wilderness.[39]

Chapter Seven

QUEBEC

I N MANY WAYS, Arnold's attempt to take Quebec was proof of Marx's dictum that history repeats itself, the second time as farce. Perhaps a term stronger than *farce* is required when comparing Arnold's 1775 arrival at Quebec with Brigadier General James Wolfe's of 1759. Wolfe led eight thousand five hundred men; Arnold about six hundred. The Marquis de Montcalm had defended the city against Wolfe with twelve thousand five hundred. When Arnold arrived at the St. Lawrence, one hundred or fewer armed men guarded it. Wolfe had arrived in a grand fleet of forty-nine sail, and many more smaller craft; Arnold slunk quietly into camp at Point Levis, and he scoured the area to find a few canoes with which to cross the river.[1]

Arnold had discovered on November 5 that one of his messengers into Quebec had been captured and that his army's presence on the south bank of the St. Lawrence was now known to loyal defenders of the city. But he also knew that Guy Carlton, the governor of Quebec, and what regular troops he had available remained inside Montreal, besieged by Brigadier General Richard Montgomery.

For five days the Americans collected boats, eventually assembling about forty canoes, and built scaling ladders with which to ascend the walls of Quebec. They planned to undertake a task that Wolfe had thought impossible: storm the walls of the city in the dark of night.

While thanks to the capture of the messenger the presence of Arnold's army was known, it remained undetected until a roving longboat from a British frigate poked its way to the south bank of the St. Lawrence near a mill where Morgan and some of his men had taken shelter. As the boat grounded on the shore, Morgan's men opened fire. The sailors pushed off, leaving behind the young midshipman commanding them to his fate; he had jumped out and now was stranded knee deep in the water. He dove into the St. Lawrence, but with the boat continuing to pull away, he turned back to shore. Riflemen and Indians raced toward him, hoping to claim their first scalp of the campaign. But Morgan also broke into a run, reached the boy first, and interposed himself between the abandoned sailor and his would-be killers.[2]

In the meantime, the garrison of Quebec was being strengthened. Colonel Allan MacLean, a veteran of the French and Indian War who had raised a regiment of 170 Scottish emigrants, arrived in the city on Sunday, November 12, discovering to his shock that Arnold was camped on the south bank of the St. Lawrence. MacLean was soon joined by 150 men from Newfoundland, many of them carpenters who built hasty barricades to wall off the streets of the Lower Town, with platforms behind them for cannon that could shoot over the barricades and sweep with shot any approach to the barricades. To these numbers were added sailors from ships in the harbor and, slowly and reluctantly, six hundred French Canadian habitants from the city and the surrounding countryside. By November 13, there were 1,126 defenders of Quebec city versus Arnold's six hundred effectives (that is, soldiers able to fight).[3]

On the night of November 12, Arnold convened a council of war attended by Morgan and his other captains. A local mill owner, John Halstead, presented them with intelligence of events in the city. After Halstead spoke, Arnold asked for his captains' opinions on what he saw as the central problem: should the Americans attempt a surprise strike against the city as soon as they arrived on the other side of the river? Given the unprepared state of Quebec's defenses, Arnold wanted an aggressive, lightning quick strike against the city.

Naturally Morgan agreed, as did Christopher Greene. But the majority of officers feared a trap and worried about the terrible odds they and their march-weary men faced.

At 3 AM on November 13, Arnold was ready to cross the river. The winds that impeded a crossing during the previous four days had subsided, and there promised to be a cloud cover over the moon. The destination was the very same cove on the northern riverbank that James Wolfe used in 1759.

Morgan was in the first canoe, leading the initial wave of boats across more than a mile of water, paddling between the British warships anchored in the middle of the stream. As the canoes returned across the river for the next load, Morgan led his men to the top of the narrow path from the river up to the Plains of Abraham. Morgan then sent Lieutenant Heth forward with a squad to scout toward the walls of the city while he posted pickets on the plain and along the shoreline of the St. Lawrence.

The boats returned for a second time, bringing Arnold, Greene, and 160 men. Half of Arnold's force was now on the north side of the St. Lawrence. There remained approximately three hundred men and, almost as important, the scaling ladders left to ferry across the river.[4]

SOMETIME after Arnold arrived but before the canoes landed a third time, Heth returned with extraordinary news. Everything between Wolfe's Cove and the city was quiet; the city was quiet too. There was no indication that anyone had an inkling that the Americans had crossed the river. Calling a council, Arnold consulted with his captains. Only Morgan endorsed an immediate assault, using just the men already there and those just being ferried across. There was no need for more men or scaling ladders, he thought. Attack now and achieve surprise.

Arnold would, in time, be as aggressive as Morgan ever was. But now was not that time. He had imagined simply establishing a perimeter around the city to invest it (that is, surround it and prevent anyone from moving in or out) until Montgomery arrived from Montreal. Attacking Quebec was not a consideration.

Any opportunity or interest Morgan might have had to convince Arnold otherwise was interrupted by gunfire. A British patrol boat, either out in the river or approaching the shore, had discovered the American crossing. After the boat withdrew into the night, the decision was made: alarm had been raised, the advantage of surprise had been lost. Attack would be suicidal. They would proceed with surrounding the town.[5]

Morgan led his riflemen toward the city walls. At the home of Colonel Henry Caldwell, he encountered a forward guard post, which fired on him. His immediate, and characteristic, response was to attack the ambush. He ran at the door of the mansion with a squad of his men, broke it down, and captured the guards without suffering any losses. Rifleman Henry recalled Caldwell's residence as "a great pile of wooden buildings, with numerous outhouses, which testified the agricultural spirit and taste of the owner. . . . [E]verything within and without the house, became a prey. . . . [W]rapped in my blanket, fearless of events, casting my person to the floor of an elegant parlor, I slept until two in the afternoon." His taste in residence was approved by Arnold, who made the mansion his headquarters.[6]

Also sleeping, in a thicket near the St. John's Gate of Quebec city, was George Merchant, one of Morgan's company from Virginia, "an excellent marksman and one of Morgan's favorites." A group of defenders led by a sergeant "who, from the manner of the thing, must have been clever" burst out of the city gates, seized Merchant, and dashed back inside the city before the riflemen could do anything about it. (Merchant was taken to London on the last ship to leave before the freezing of the winter ice; there he was displayed as an exemplar of the American hunting shirt man.)[7]

Caldwell was the seigneur of Point-Levis—the feudal lord in the system that remained in place in Quebec—and it was at dethroning these local tyrants that American propaganda had been directed. Over the six days, Arnold's force made several demonstrations before the walls, encouraging disloyalty among the French Canadians, the *habitants*. Arnold distributed copies of Washington's address to the citizens of Quebec, and some *habitants* visited the camp to see the Bostonnais (Bostonians, as they called all Americans), and voice their approval—an attitude that Arnold cultivated by purchasing from them supplies for his force.

When Col. MacLean sent out scouts, he could not have been pleased to discover that those who had dealt with the Americans thought them "a good set of men who take nothing by force." He must have been even less pleased when he discovered that the countrymen who came to market in Quebec city brought with them copies of Washington's address.[8] Yet Arnold had just 650 troops, and he discovered that among those whose weapons had not been lost during the march, his men had an average of five rounds of ammunition each.

On November 17, Arnold learned that Montgomery had taken Montreal. He decided it would be the better part of valor to withdraw up the river in the direction of Montreal, to Point aux Trembles twenty miles up the St. Lawrence.

On Sunday, November 19, Arnold and his men began to march. They did so, as rifleman Henry remembered, "in a slovenly style, accompanied, probably, by the validations of the clergy and nobility, but attended by the regrets [of] the host of well-wishers among the peasantry." As they trudged through snow flurries they saw a merchant ship sailing down the St. Lawrence. Unknown to them, it carried Governor Sir Guy Carleton, fleeing the capture of Montreal and bound for Quebec city. When Arnold's force arrived at Point aux Trembles, they "enjoyed as much comfort as tight houses, warm fires, and our scantiness of clothing would admit."[9]

But just a few days later, on November 29, Morgan returned to the suburbs of Quebec with a detachment to prevent sorties from departing the city. Arnold, anticipating Montgomery's momentary arrival and returning to his "action this day" mentality, asked Morgan to investigate conditions in Quebec. Morgan scouted around the city, billeting his man with agreeable habitant families and in captured Loyalist mansions. From buildings close to the city walls, riflemen began to snipe at any who showed themselves, outraging British officers and persuading their soldiers to stay behind cover.[10]

After a week so engaged, Morgan's detachment was joined not only by Arnold and his men but also by four hundred more soldiers and Brigadier General Montgomery, Arnold's superior. An Anglo-Irish professional soldier who had immigrated to New York and then married into the powerful Livingston family, he seems to have been a character from a Jane Austen novel. "He was well-limbed, tall, and handsome," Henry remembered, "though his face was much pock-marked. His air and manner designated the real soldier"; "straight-limbed and tall," remembered John Pierce.[11] Multiple witnesses described Montgomery as "genteel appearing . . . of an agreeable temper," and "born to command," having an "easy and affable condescension to both officers and men." He may have been dilatory and uncertain so far in the campaign, but Montgomery had presence and charisma.[12]

The problem that now confronted Montgomery was fairly simple. First, Carleton and the garrison of Quebec city had sufficient provisions to last until help arrived from Britain in spring. Second, the enlistments of the majority, if not all, of Arnold's force were slated to end January 1, 1776. Third, even with Arnold and Montgomery's combined force, the Americans lacked the numbers, equipment, and provisions capable of mounting a sophisticated siege on the fortifications of Quebec, during a Canadian winter. They had to take the city by assault.

Sometime in mid-December, Montgomery held a meeting of all officers and explained his assault plan. On the first dark and stormy night (no, really), Arnold would lead his column from the north along the bank of the St. Charles River. Near the head of his column would be a sled carrying a six-pounder cannon to batter the way open for the troops that followed. Montgomery would simultaneously attack with his New Yorkers from the other direction, moving from Cape Diamond along the banks of the St. Lawrence toward Quebec's lower city, clustered around the base of the cliffs on which the upper city and its citadel were seated. As Arnold and Montgomery attacked, diversionary assaults would occur against the gates of St. John and St. Louis, announced by what artillery they had and with much firing of muskets and rockets. Uniting in the Lower Town, Montgomery and Arnold would then attack up the Rue de la Montagne, Mountain Street, the one street that led to the Upper Town.[13]

Unfortunately for the Americans, Governor Carleton understood just as well as they did the logic that necessitated an assault. He also understood that the only possible time for such an undersized force to launch an effective assault was during the confusion of a blizzard. The only thing either side could do was wait for that night.

THE dark and stormy night came in suitably cinematic fashion, on December 30, 1775, the night before enlistments expired. A north-easter hit that afternoon, with strong winds and flurries that, at sun-set, swirled and raged against the walls and cliffs of the city. As Morgan remembered, he was, in the hours prior to the battle, full of fear and doubt. He knew it would be a desperate assault. If there are atheists in foxholes, there are probably far fewer leading assaults on fortified positions: Morgan was driven to prayer. He found a "secluded spot," probably to escape the storm and the incredulous eyes of his riflemen. On his knees, he begged God to preserve his life, the lives of his soldiers, and "for a triumph of his country." One of those requests was answered.[14]

He gathered his command. Arnold, characteristically, chose to lead his column with a group of about thirty men, preceding the sled-mounted cannon. Behind the sled marched Morgan and his three companies of riflemen, and then the rest of the column. Be-cause of the perennial impossibility of attaching bayonets to their rifles, the riflemen were issued half pikes— either simple short spears or spontoons, spears with blades attached. These were, in eigh-teenth-century warfare, typically signs of rank for either noncom-missioned or junior commissioned officers. That night they proved to be not anachronistic relics but eminently practical.

The advance began at 4 AM. Rockets fired by Montgomery's col-umn at Cape Diamond illuminated the swirling dome of snow over the city. The feint on the St. John and St. Louis Gates then began, as Arnold started forward with his detachment, and officers and sergeants shouted "Turn out! Turn out!" through the streets of Que-bec. Americans in both attacks moved forward, picking their way through floes of ice thrown up along the river bank. Arnold's men encountered an additional barrier—the ice-encrusted ropes mooring ships to the bank.

The snow and wind were punctuated by sounds of attack and battle. City bells clanged through the storm, alarm guns sounded, and other cannons fired at soldiers both real and phantom. Then Arnold's advance guard came to the first barrier on the main street of the Lower Town of Quebec, called the Sault Au Matelot. As they spread out and waited for their one artillery piece to arrive, a blindly delivered but highly consequential volley was delivered from the barricade. One musket ball hit Arnold in the left leg. He leaned against a wall, watching his men pass by. Morgan appeared from out of the snow, shouting to Arnold that Captain John Lamb's sled-mounted six-pounder was caught in a drift; they would have to assault the barrier without it. Seeing Arnold was wounded, Morgan called over a rifleman and a chaplain and ordered them to take their colonel back to the hospital. As they carried him away, riflemen fired through the embrasures at the defenders behind them, and Morgan ordered up the ladders to scale the more-than-ten-foot-high walls.[15]

Volleys of gunfire from behind the barricade did not prevent soldiers from propping ladders against it, nor did they prevent Morgan from being the first to climb and the first to crest the barrier. As he did, witnesses reported, a blaze of gunfire blew him backward off the ladder. He landed in the snow, flat on his back, motionless, the wind knocked out of him. There were bullet holes in his cap or clothing or both, and a bloody crease on his cheek to join his collection of scars. He had been so close to the mouths of the firing muskets that he had powder burns on his face. But he was alive.[16]

Not only was he still alive, he was still all-Morgan, which he proved by immediately rescaling the ladder, calling on his Virginians to follow him. Charles Porterfield followed, then probably Billy Heth, then others. Morgan went over the top like a falling pine. There was no gunfire this time. He landed atop a cannon, falling so that his back absorbed the full force of the impact. It "hurt me exceedingly," he laconically recalled—and it almost certainly cracked a vertebra, ruptured a disc, or both.[17] Fortunately for him he then rolled off the cannon and sheltered beneath it, making it difficult for the soldiers on the platform where he landed to skewer him with their bayonets. Then Porterfield and a mob of howling Virginians came over the wall, scattering the enemy before them.[18]

Limping and staggering from the hurt, Morgan pressed the next assault. The defenders had taken refuge in ranks of stone houses lined up side by side along the next block. The Virginians charged in the low doors to clear them out, using not their rifles but their half-pikes, stabbing and heaving opposing militia like forkfuls of hay in the Shenandoah Valley meadows. While the riflemen went in the front of one house, Morgan ran alone around to its back door. Militia driven out by the attack met him there—over six feet, bleeding, face blackened with his enemy's gunpowder, the snow swirling around him. When he demanded their surrender, they very naturally offered it at once. Within minutes, over a hundred Quebecois militiamen up and down Sault au Matelot were surrendering to the American attackers, screaming *"Vive la liberté!"*[19]

Morgan, meanwhile, gimped his way down the street to the next barricade, accompanied only by a Quebecois interpreter. Not a sound or a shot emerged from it. There was a door in its face, and to his amazement he found it unlocked; to his further amazement, he found that when he opened it—no doubt with a certain amount of caution—no one was behind it or the barricade. He and the interpreter went down Sault au Matelot Street a little farther, encountering nothing and no one. It is difficult to know exactly how far they traveled, but it was probably to the foot of the Cote de Montagne, Mountain Street, the one way into the Upper Town. On a summer day it does not seem like a very far distance; in the cold and dark, amidst the storm, with the threat of sudden attack, adrenaline flooding the veins, it must have seemed like a mile.[20]

When he returned to the rest of the detachment, ready to lead them forward into the quiet streets of the Lower Town, he encountered chaos within the minds of his fellow officers. There was no second in command; neither Arnold nor anyone else had foreseen the need. Just three hundred yards away, Canada lay open and vulnerable to one final attack, the dreams of a fourteenth colony on the verge of reality. But at the other end of the long street, where the Americans had clustered, officers saw only barriers, not opportunity. Not enough troops had arrived; there were too many prisoners to leave behind; there were too many prisoners and too few guards; and most clinching of all, Montgomery had not yet arrived at the second barrier, and they must wait for him. Morgan later wrote in his very brief autobiographical notes that his fellow officers "were sure of conquest if we acted in caution—to these arguments I sacrificed my own opinion and lost the town."[21]

So they waited for Montgomery. And yet, with first light, there was still no sign of him. However, there was evidence that the

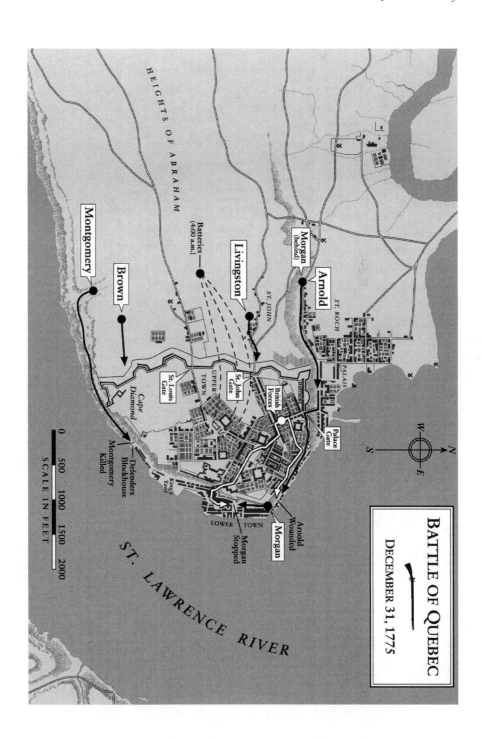

HEIGHTS OF ABRAHAM

Montgomery

Brown

Batteries
(4:00 a.m.)

Livingston

Morgan
(behind)

Arnold

ST. JOHN

ST. ROCH

PALAIS

St. Louis
Gate

UPPER
TOWN

St. John
Gate

British
Forces

Cape
Diamond

Montgomery
Killed

Defenders
Blockhouse

King's
Yard

LOWER TOWN

Morgan
Stopped

Morgan

Arnold
Wounded

Palace
Gate

0
500
1000
1500
2000

SCALE IN FEET

W
N
S
E

ST. LAWRENCE RIVER

BATTLE OF QUEBEC

DECEMBER 31, 1775

British had reoccupied the second barricade through which Morgan had earlier passed and returned. No one had thought to place sentries or guards atop it. Morgan ordered up the scaling ladders and began to prepare men to storm a position that the enemy had been allowed to reoccupy.

Then the door of the barricade opened and an officer stepped out. Morgan could not know it, but it was a former British naval officer, a Captain Anderson. Accompanied by several sailors who fanned out behind him, Anderson shouted for the Americans to lay down their arms and surrender. Morgan raised his rifle and shot Anderson through the head. Message received, message returned.[22]

Morgan's men then charged the barrier, scaling ladders in hand. Volleys of musket fire met them as they placed their ladders against the wooden wall, and canister from cannon exploded over the barriers' top and ricocheted down the street. Morgan again clambered up a ladder, joined this time on others by Lieutenants John Humphreys and William Heath of his own company and Archibald Steele of the Pennsylvania riflemen. As they stuck their heads over the top, more gunfire came at them from the second stories of houses on either side of the street; they also saw ranks of enemy with fixed bayonets prepare to receive the assault. The volume of gunfire drove Morgan and his fellow officers back; others joined them. A second attempt was made. Then a third. Then a fourth. None could cross.[23]

To contest the enemy's fire, Morgan sent riflemen into the houses on the American side of the barrier. They discovered that the cannon were on a platform a little farther down the street, sited so they could fire over the barrier. Riflemen soon cleared the platform and made it impossible for anyone to work the cannon. They also returned fire to the soldiers who were shooting from the upper rooms of houses across the way.[24]

But those enemies were joined by reinforcements. Some fired from the ramparts of the Upper Town directly into the street where the majority of Americans were still clustered—shooting fish in a barrel might be just a little harder. Worse, Captain Henry Dearborn's company, situated to protect the rear of the American force, was overrun at about 8 AM, and a party of Quebec's defenders seized the first barricade. The Americans were now trapped in a crossfire, running low on ammunition. Lieutenant Humphreys was dead in the street, almost six months to the day since he had marched out of Winchester; Lieutenant William Hendricks of Pennsylvania had been killed in one of the houses by return fire; Archibald Steele had lost three fingers to another bullet; Captain Lamb of the New York artillery had been terribly wounded, "nearly one half of his face carried away by grape or canister shot."[25]

Morgan, "brave to temerity, stormed and raged."[26] Private Morison recalled his voice "betwixt every peal" sounding through the gunfire, rallying men to him, directing their fire, appealing to them to fight on. His "gigantic stature and terrible appearance carrie[d] dismay among the foe wherever he [came]."[27]

At some point during this final period of the battle, Morgan held a brief council of war with the remaining officers. He proposed that they collect the remaining soldiers and break out back along the line of their original assault. But again he was overruled by their hope that Montgomery would eventually appear. If they successfully retreated, Morgan's fellow officers argued, they would expose Montgomery to destruction.

But Montgomery did not come. The trap had closed, and what remained of Arnold's force was surrounded by nearly the entire Quebec garrison, at the barriers in front of and behind them, and on the walls above. Sometime about 9 AM, Americans began to surrender. Morgan wept.

Graham reports that British soldiers demanded Morgan surrender his sword and he refused, backing up against a wall, daring them to come and take it from him. The enemy threatened to shoot him, and still he refused. His captured riflemen urged him to give up, but he would not listen to them. Finally he saw a priest in the crowd gathering around him. "Morgan delivered his sword to the clergyman, observing, 'Then I give my sword to you; but not a scoundrel of those cowards shall take it out of my hands.'"[28]

Years later, at the moment of his greatest military triumph, Morgan reputedly shouted with equal rage, "Old Morgan was never beaten!" But of course he was, once. Unless he did not count surrendering his sword to a priest as a defeat, or unless—like a great athlete—he forgot failure and thought only of the next contest. Or if he had never, in spirit, been conquered.

From any perspective, Arnold's expedition and the trouncing at Quebec was not just a defeat but a calamity. Consequences were felt not only in Canada but in the lower Shenandoah: in Battletown and Winchester, along Opequon Creek and the Shenandoah River. Morgan and his men were prisoners. When Morgan's company marched out of Winchester in July 1775, they were ninety-eight-men strong. When they arrived on the south bank of the St. Lawrence in November 1775, their number had been reduced to about eighty. As they surrendered in Quebec, their dead lay about them. Many, many more would die in captivity. Of the ninety-eight who'd left the Valley, only twenty-five returned.[29]

Chapter Eight

MORGAN'S RIFLEMEN

I T IS HARD to come up with a person, or a personality, less likely than Daniel Morgan to succeed in the capacity of prisoner. Exile and imprisonment have been fertile creative grounds for certain figures, those of a mathematical or philosophical bent able in the enforced solitude to nourish their rich interior intellect (Boethius, John Bunyan, and Dietrich Bonhoeffer spring to mind). Daniel Morgan was not among them. No *Consolation of Philosophy, Pilgrim's Progress*, memorized poetry, or "Letters and Papers from Prison" were nourished in his cell. For a man of action, a laborer, one who had passed most of his days outdoors and who was accustomed to going to sleep exhausted by hard work, confinement must have aligned closely with his personal conception of hell.

After their surrender, the American prisoners were herded up the steep streets of the city to the Jesuit seminary in the Upper Town of Quebec. It was then that Governor Carleton proved himself to be one of the few people who understood what the war was about and how to fight it. According to rifleman Henry, Carleton suggested that if the colonists would not agree to be brothers, then at least they could agree to be cousins. Carleton's actions demonstrated that this was his philosophy of practice. The rations and conditions given the officers and enlisted soldiers were, by far, the best that American prisoners experienced during the entire Revolution. (Other prisoner experiences included the infamous HMS *Jersey,* or the "Sugar House" of lower Manhattan, so the bar of comparison is admittedly low.) Given the shortage of food and other supplies necessary for Quebec to survive until British relief in the spring, Carleton's generosity to the prisoners is even more amazing. In addition to these material comforts, he also offered them honor and respect by treating General Montgomery's corpse with reverence.

The fate that befell Montgomery and the men in his assault column is quickly told. The path he took on his assault along the banks of the St. Lawrence brought him to two barricades. Each of these he opened, according to others, with his own hands. Beyond the barricades was a blockhouse made of logs, with loopholes for musket men on the ground floor and two or three cannons mounted on the second floor; behind the blockhouse were no other defenses, only the open streets of Quebec leading to the juncture of Sault au Matelot and Mountain Street. Supposedly, in a story that appears in several of the survivors' diaries, the entire garrison of the blockhouse fled, and only one member returned briefly to fire the cannon whose shots cut down Montgomery and those around him—leaving only his recently appointed aide, Aaron Burr of New York. Montgomery's second in command, Lieutenant Colonel Donald Campbell, took counsel of his fears and withdrew. Morgan and his fellow officers had waited for a relief that could never have come.[1]

Carleton gave Montgomery a proper and honorable military funeral; like so many men in the war, they had been friends once upon a time. He also gave the officers a supply of wine and visited them and the enlisted men, listening to whatever complaints they had with a serious and kindly air.[2]

Morgan was visited by numerous British officers who respected him because of his performance in the battle. One of them was the older brother of a midshipman named McKenzie, the boy whom Morgan had rescued from scalping at Pont Levis. Perhaps it was the elder McKenzie who was the "Naval officer" of Graham's account who, after several meetings, finally spoke at length to Morgan of the Revolution and the impossibility of a successful outcome for the rebellious colonists. This naval officer said that since Morgan was a brave and noble man, he deserved a braver and nobler employment then was afforded him by an impossible cause. Morgan could, the officer assured him, have a colonelcy in a royal regiment. Graham reports that Morgan "rejected the proposal with disdain," saying finally, "I hope, sir, you will never again insult me in my present distressed and unfortunate situation, by making me offers which plainly imply that you think me a scoundrel!"[3] Or words to that effect: Morgan's actual vocabulary was surely more direct.

The officer's proposal was not as ridiculous as it might seem. After all, Robert Rogers had reacquired a position with His Majesty's forces to once again lead his rangers in the field against the rebellion. In slightly more obscure circumstances, the elder brother of New Hampshire hero John Stark (a New England analogue of Morgan) had also been recruited to the royal cause. Many men in the Carolinas began as Patriots or Whigs and ended the war as Loyalist exiles in the Bahamas or farther afield. There is no reason to believe that Morgan was not so tempted, or that the offer was insincere.[4]

Throughout the winter months the wounded Arnold and his much-reduced force, having avoided capture, maintained their watch on the city. While it was no siege in the formal sense, they did prevent anyone from selling potatoes or any other kind of winter food to the garrison; Quebec was completely reliant upon its stores. As firewood began to run out, Carleton sent armed groups out to the near suburbs to cut what they needed. Barely able to even counter them let alone attack the city, Arnold ordered buildings near the city and ships in the river to be set afire to deprive them of fuel and possible provision. In the meantime, smallpox was devouring the uninoculated (nearly all of them) in Arnold's force.[5]

Arnold, his aggressive instincts unfettered by humiliation, had begun to plan a second assault while in his first week in his hospital bed recovering from the wound to his leg. He directed the placement of artillery batteries, planned a post-thaw attack by fireships on the waterfront to serve as a diversion for a "massed escalade against the western wall," and ordered the construction of scaling ladders.[6]

Then an opportunity for a second assault dropped into his lap. The American enlisted prisoners had been moved from the Jesuit seminary to the old jail, located near St. John's Gate. Discovering in a room there iron intended for barrel hoops, the ingenious craftsmen among them began to fashion spears and swords. They elected a council of officers from among their number and planned an assault on the guardhouse near the prison to be rapidly followed by seizure of St. John's Gate. Having seized the gate, they would turn the artillery sited there to fire upon the city and hold their position until Arnold arrived with his army to enter Quebec. One prisoner escaped from the city and informed Arnold of the plan, also arranging signals between the rebel prisoners and Arnold. But another American prisoner, a deserter from the British army, informed on the plot to secure his freedom. In the end, the American enlisted men were placed in chains from which they were not removed until their final release in July 1776. Carleton attempted to lure Arnold into a trap using the informant's intelligence, but Arnold proved to be too wary a fox and did not enter it.[7]

His wound for the most part healed, Arnold left Quebec city in early April. On May 5, facing a shortage of supplies, Major General John Thomas, the American commander in Canada who replaced Montgomery, decided to withdraw. As fate would have it, on the next day the frigate HMS *Surprise* was sighted sailing up the St. Lawrence, preceding two transports carrying supplies and British regulars, the first three ships of a relief fleet from Britain. No sooner had they appeared than a kind of panic overtook the American army, and it fell back along the St. Lawrence. It was the final whimpering end of Arnold's expedition through the Maine wilderness.[8]

It was undoubtedly no consolation whatsoever for Morgan that after British relief arrived in Quebec, he now had more British visitors, eager to see the imprisoned leader of the "hunting shirt men." Nor was the arrival of Canadian spring likely to improve his mood. It must have been irreparably soured as he learned of the string of American disasters that led to the complete expulsion of the Continental army from Canada by mid-June 1776.

Other American prisoners became the object of some of Morgan's frustrations, particularly Captain William Goodrich of Massachusetts. He, along with Captain Oliver Hanchet of Connecticut, had been the constant, semimutinous antagonists of Arnold during the march upcountry and through all the preparations for an assault on Quebec. Morgan and other officers—certainly his Virginians—regarded these two and their particular crony, one Lieutenant Andrews, as venal, lying, and altogether despicable. Billy Heth and Charles Porterfield in their diaries describe a few encounters between Morgan and these three. Once, Morgan gave Andrews "a blow or two in his jaws" for lying.

Then there was the incident of the watch, one of those small episodes that, during close confinement, becomes very important. During the assault on Quebec, Goodrich carried a watch belonging to a Canadian citizen. (Perhaps he borrowed it in order to know the time of the assault.) Given the opportunity to return it on June 23, 1776, Goodrich refused, saying he did not trust the messenger who had requested him to return it to its owner. Morgan, according to Charles Porterfield, grew "pretty warm"—one can only imagine the emotional range concealed by those laconic words, given that his next action was to seize Goodrich by the throat and throttle him until he gave up the watch.[9]

Goodrich might have learned his lesson from this encounter, but apparently he was stupid as well as venal. On July 3, Morgan was talking with Major Timothy Bigelow when he saw Goodrich eavesdropping—a practice of his, Porterfield claimed, aimed at not being left out of any news yet "knowing that he is detested by all . . . for his rascally conduct." Morgan told him to push along. When Goodrich was slow to leave, Morgan seized him and "shook him severely." Andrews and some others came to Goodrich's rescue. Some grabbed Morgan and held him up while Andrews hit him. Then Morgan rallied with a "severe kick" to Andrews's stomach, a move that his old sparring partner Bill Davis could have warned Andrews about if he had been on hand to offer advice. Goodrich's rescuers, making a swift tactical decision, retreated from the field bearing their fallen with them. So great was the indignation of Goodrich, Hanchet, and Andrews that they brought a complaint against Morgan to Carleton. "Think of what a despicable opinion these gentlemen must entertain of us," lamented Porterfield, "or of any set of men in our situation, that would call their enemies to be arbiters in such contests—much below the conduct of any gentleman, much less an officer in the army."[10]

Perhaps Carleton decided he did not want to be blamed for damage done to imprisoned American officers when, really, the culprit was one of their own. Or perhaps he was moved by the appeal Captain Christopher Greene drafted on behalf of the imprisoned American officers in June 1776, requesting their release on parole.[11] More likely it was because with the American presence swept away from Canadian soil, and the dream of the fourteenth colony rendered a smallpox-infested nightmare, Carleton no longer had need of the prisoners. His attention was focused on building a Lake Champlain fleet that would sweep down into the colony of New York from the north as Sir William Howe sailed into New York harbor from the south.

On August 11, Morgan and his fellow prisoners were released on parole. They were sent to New York City in several transports, arriving there on September 10 to discover that Howe had defeated Washington at Brooklyn Heights and that the Continental army had withdrawn to Harlem Heights on the north end of Manhattan Island. As their ship lay in New York harbor, they witnessed the burning of New York. "The flames were fanned by the briskness of the breeze, and drove the destructive effects of the elements on all sides," Henry remembered. "When the fire reached the spire of a large steeple . . . the effect upon the eye was astonishingly grand... The deck of our ship, for many hours, was lighted as at noon day."

Finally, on September 24, just over a year since they had started out to march from Cambridge to Quebec, the former prisoners were loaded onto a group of small boats and sent around Staten Island to the American-held port of Elizabethtown, New Jersey. "Adverse winds retarded us. It was ten or eleven at night, before we landed; the moon shone beautifully. Morgan stood in the bow of the boat; making a spring not easily surpassed, and falling on the earth as it were to grasp it, crying 'Oh, my country.'"[12]

Though it is tempting to declare this anecdote the product of Henry's classics-saturated imagination (an analogue of Caesar falling on the coast and grabbing soil in his hand to prove that it was not an ill omen), no one could ever accuse Morgan of suppressing his emotions or of passing up the chance of a gesture, or a phrase. It probably happened as Henry described it.

It is more interesting to speculate on what country, precisely, Morgan was referring to. He had been born in New Jersey (or Pennsylvania), and lived in New Jersey (or Pennsylvania) until that fateful day he left home in anger. So perhaps this Virginian by choice was embracing the country of his childhood, his lost former home.

But it is more likely Morgan was embracing America. He had long ago rejected New Jersey's soil. He returned to it having marched through Maine and assaulted the strongest fortifications in North America with a group of Pennsylvanians and true down east Yankees. Some were worth only grabbing by the neck and shaking until their teeth rattled, but others were as good men as you could find anywhere. The march through the north woods and the attack on Quebec had made him into an American. A British prison located in a Jesuit monastery in French Canada made him into an American nationalist. His country was now not Virginia, not New Jersey, but the United States of America—a conversion neatly coinciding with the Declaration of Independence. Daniel Morgan was an American from the very beginning of the republic.

It is not clear if Morgan visited Washington at his headquarters, located in Harlem Heights. Regardless, Washington was aware that Morgan and the other prisoners had returned from Canada. Moreover, Washington knew what he wanted Morgan to do. Hugh Stephenson had recently died while back in the Valley, recruiting a new rifle regiment, and Washington wanted Morgan as his replacement. Accordingly he wrote to Congress, saying:

> I would beg leave to recommend to the particular notice of Congress, Capt. Daniel Morgan just returned the prisoners from Canada as a fit and proper person to Succeed to the vacancy occasion by his death. Because he ranked above them and as a captain when he first entered the service. His conduct as an officer of the expedition with Gen. Arnold last fall; his intrepid behavior in the assault upon Quebec . . . all in my opinion entitle him to the favor of Congress and lead me to believe that in his promotion, the states will gain a good and valuable officer for the sort of troops he is particularly recommended to command.[13]

For the moment, though, Morgan was on parole, a genteel custom of the military enlightenment that allowed a former prisoner to return home so long he had nothing to do whatsoever with the war effort. Therefore, Washington warned Congress that Morgan's appointment must be kept "Close" and not revealed, otherwise "his acceptance of the commission under his present circumstances might be construed a violation of his engagement." European nations had, over the course of centuries, developed cartels and treaties that governed the treatment of prisoners and parolees during wartime. Britain had no such conventions with its rebelling colonies, and the colonies were apt to be just as intransigent with the home country. Washington's promotion of Morgan, and his plans for his new regimental command, were an example of such intransigence and underhandedness.[14]

OF course, much changed following Morgan's 1776 return to the new United Sates. First, Washington's army was brushed away from the environs of New York City. Then it was pursued across New Jersey to the other side of the Delaware River. And then Washington reversed his course and America's fortunes with the raid on Trenton, followed by the maneuverings of the Second Battle of Trenton and the Battle of Princeton. As a result, the British army suddenly found itself confined, more or less, to a triangle of land in northern New Jersey, its forward position the village of New Brunswick.

The Continental army spent the remainder of winter 1777 in a wide arc centered on the village of Morristown, tucked away then and now behind Watchung Mountain, a semicircular hill like a bent horseshoe that rises steeply from the coastal plain. It is not much of a precipice anywhere other than at the pancake-flat New Jersey coastal plain, but there it was a natural fortress. Beneath the Watchung to the south is the Raritan River, flowing slightly southeast to its bay beneath Staten Island. The middle section of the Raritan valley was occupied by the British army, its chief encampment at New Brunswick, on the Raritan's west bank and extending into the villages up and down the river. The lower Raritan was also occupied by the British, particularly the port of Amboy at its mouth, and additional British detachments occupied Bergen and other villages with direct access to the North River or to New York harbor.

During the months that followed the Continental army's encampment at Morristown, Washington played one of the most dangerous games of the eight years of the war. The 1776 enlistments expired, and nearly all of his army departed, leaving him with just a mere remnant of his previous force. Even by March 15, when new enlistments began to arrive from the states, there were just 2,543 Continental army soldiers fit for duty and under Washington's immediate command in New Jersey, and there were only 976 New Jersey militia in the field to shore up the Continental army. Those who were unfit and unable to fight were often so because Washington had insisted that his army be inoculated with smallpox to prevent a virulent epidemic. Now Washington's army was not only miserably small at best, but most of it was literally pox-ridden.

To conceal this weakness, Washington deployed his paucity of troops in a wide arc in towns and hamlets along the slopes of Watchung Mountain and out into the coastal plain to watch key bridges and fords. In this way they kept a perimeter around the British forces in the Raritan valley and on the coast. Washington and his commanders then sought to convince the British commanders that this loose arc was a cordon restricting their movements rather than the thin layers of a large onion that was empty at its core. At Morristown itself there were only forty-six men from some Pennsylvania regiments, as well as Washington, his Life Guards, and headquarters staff (also dangerously understaffed); at Chatham, also behind Watchung, were just 260 soldiers. The remainder of the army was scattered in places like Princeton, Bound Brook, Westfield, Spank Town, and Quibbletown. These were the screen that concealed the empty center, often just two or three men garrisoned in a house. As part of this exercise in deception, and to keep life as uncomfortable as possible for the British garrison forces left in New Jersey while protecting his own sources of forage, Washington began a campaign of continual partisan warfare that lasted through the winter and spring.

PARTISAN became a favorite word of officers in the American Revolution, and Morgan became one of the Revolution's preeminent partisan commanders. Subsequently overlaid with other military concepts, such as guerrilla, the term *partisan* must have some of the dust of age and disuse scraped off of it in order to understand what Morgan and his contemporaries meant by it.

For those studying military tactics and strategy in the 1760s, *partisan* was a military term referring to a concept that is greatly admired but untested or untried by most who admire it: *blitzkrieg, aerial envelopment, air-land battle, air-sea battle, low-intensity conflict, revolution in military affairs*—the historical list of such terms is nearly endless. Partisan had become fashionable through stories of battles by the Austrian Empire against the Turks, using the light Hungarian cavalry, Hussars. These stories were soon put in the shade by the success of Hussar detachments in the Seven Years' War, most notably against the epitome of Enlightenment generalship, Frederick the Great of Prussia. In 1757, the Austrian general Andras Hadik, with just five thousand hussars, circled around Frederick's army, seized Berlin, and held it for ransom. This victory, the hussars' colorful uniforms, and the success of Frederick's own hussar regiments in his endless wars, prompted imitation of hussars and ideas of partisan warfare throughout Europe by soldiers interested in tactical innovation, fancy dress, or both.

But partisan warfare involved more than light cavalry and fancy dress. Some armies assigned hussars to the same tasks as their light cavalry: reconnaissance and securing flanks during battle. Such an employment was not particularly different from the practices of the last fifty years. Educated soldiers instead found the key to partisan warfare in the title of a treatise by M. De Jeney, *The Partisan, or the Art of Making War in Detachment*. Partisan warfare was not simply light cavalry but the art of employing small, detached units that performed on their own under the command of junior field officers. It was what the French called *petit guerre* before the Spanish term *guerrilla* took hold of the popular imagination. These were instinctive tactics of ambush and surprise, based on local knowledge and aimed at the opponent's weakest points.[15]

Partisan warfare therefore required not hussars, or even cavalry, but intelligent field officers capable of understanding the situation in front of them, making clear decisions, and executing them. If well-trained, intelligent field officers were unavailable, the practice of partisan warfare was an excellent way to identify and train intelligent officers.

Indeed, the practice of partisan warfare was the only officer training school the Continental army could afford. "We have now a fine nursery of officers," exulted Nathanael Greene in January 1777, and while he was probably talking about the Trenton-Princeton campaign, as well as the ongoing reorganization of the army's regiments, the partisan war conducted over the next five to six months in central New Jersey was a vital part of that nursery's activities. It was a lengthy live-fire exercise, with perilous consequences for the Continental army if mishandled. After all, the perennial problem with partisan war was and remains that it depends on the good sense of the junior officers who lead the small detachments, and this is always a commodity in short supply. A captain or lieutenant might take it upon himself to lead twenty or forty men into British territory to lay an ambush and succeed only in getting his entire command killed, wounded, or captured.[16]

Nearly every day of winter and spring 1777 saw a skirmish or report of one between the Americans—whether of the Continental army or the New Jersey Militia—and the British in New Brunswick and Perth Amboy. But this was also part of an ongoing political and internal warfare. After Princeton, and the army's encampment behind the Watchung, Greene gloated to his wife that the "Tories are melting away in this country." To Governor Nicholas Cooke of Rhode Island, Greene observed that due to their mistreatment by the British and Hessians, Jersey "High Tories" had by late January 1777 become "warm Whigs." Having been ravaged by British troops, these former supporters of the royal government now desired revenge against those whom, just a month before, they had welcomed.[17]

Partisan war blurred the lines between politics and warfare, logistics and looting, revenge and retaliation in a way none of the manuals and texts on warfare ever had. Daniel Morgan was both a student and schoolmaster in this partisan war. Not only did he learn how to conduct skirmishing, ambushing, foraging, and all the other military skills necessary for a partisan war, he also learned how to appeal to—and threaten, if not actually terrorize—a civilian population. And then he trained a nursery of his own officers in all that he had learned.

What Morgan and other Continental army officers began to practice in winter 1777 was not an adaptation of Native American tactics and strategy to European warfare. Native warfare had a different rhythm. Consider as an example the raid in which Morgan was wounded in the face, during his service as a Virginia ranger. As best as can be reconstructed, the Indians moved in a distributed body of several small groups, ranging roughly parallel across the Pennsylvania, Maryland, and Virginia backcountry, all moving toward an agreed-on point and possibly via agreed-on routes. Because these parties moved quickly, maintained high security and watchfulness, and had no supply train or supply line connecting them to either their base or to each other, they could not be defeated in detail. Their independent actions spread confusion, rumor, and contradictory reports as Washington, Adam Stephen, and others in Maryland and Pennsylvania attempted to discern which was the "real" war party and what was the objective. Their raid completed, their objective attained or unattained, the Native American parties immediately and quickly withdrew with whatever captives and portable plunder they could carry—and both would be discarded if they hampered the raiding party's speed.

Morgan's partisan warfare was distinct from Native American raiding. It required not speed so much as persistence. It operated along the battle lines of armies, at night and during the day. Patrols moved out to determine the placement of enemy outposts, intercept British patrols, capture prisoners, and bring them in for interrogation. As they operated, patrols kept an eye on the houses of those they believed to be traitors to America and watched the roads and paths for any communication between suspected Loyalists and the British. This was not the kind of warfare that Native Americans necessarily enjoyed—as the British discovered at Saratoga.

MORGAN did not join the partisan war until late April 1777 at the earliest. Until then, he was trying to recruit his new regiment in the lower Valley.

Washington had succeeded in communicating his apprehensions at the size of his army, and the continual press of the partisan war, to some of the governors—at least to Governor Patrick Henry of Virginia, who soon began to communicate his displeasure to the newly minted Colonel Morgan at the slow pace of recruiting. Raising troops, said Henry to Morgan in a letter of March 15, 1777 (not the first he had sent to Frederick County), was a "pushing necessity." Morgan must not lose a moment to get his regiment on the road. "Surmount every obstacle and lose not a moment," Henry exhorted, "lest America receive a wound that may prove mortal."[18]

Morgan had already begun to recruit, but he had encountered formidable obstacles. Simply enough, it was much more difficult to find recruits—both officers and men—then it had been in summer 1775, almost two years before. Morgan's mentor, Anglican-minister-turned-major Charles Mynn Thruston, had been offered a colonelcy and command of a new Virginia regiment. Now also seeking to raise troops in the lower Valley, he referred to Virginia as being "cull'd."[19] Little wonder, given that in addition to Morgan and Thruston, John Peter Gabriel Muhlenberg was also in Winchester attempting to reconstitute his 8th Virginia Regiment after a disease-plagued tour defending Charleston, South Carolina. Muhlenberg claimed he had twelve or fourteen vacancies among the officers of his regiment alone.[20] Angus McDonald, whom Thruston desired to be his lieutenant colonel—the regimental second in command—declined the appointment. When impeccably qualified men like McDonald refused to serve, with what materials could a new officer corps be constructed?

Officers were important because they served as recruiters. But recruiting men also took money. Thruston requested £200 of enlisting money to go with his adjutant and recruiting officer on a foray into the relatively untapped districts of southwestern Virginia. Recruits expected an initial bounty when joining their country's cause. As Thruston lamented, "I fear there will be but too great Need for every assistance to be had, in order to filling up the Regiment."[21]

Morgan encountered similar problems, but he did slightly better in the officer department. He had a cadre of young men who had served with him on the march to Quebec. Nor did it matter to him if they hailed from Virginia. John Joseph Henry of Lancaster, Pennsylvania, had been promised a lieutenancy and a platoon before he took ill over winter 1777. Lt. Col. Christian Febiger had joined the army from Massachusetts, but Morgan was delighted to have "Old Denmark" as his Danish-Massachusettsian second in command. While Morgan remained in Winchester and continued recruiting,

Febiger marched north with the first company of the 11th Virginia Regiment, arriving in Philadelphia and having his men inoculated and placed in quarantine. When Febiger wrote Washington on March 6, 1777, he informed the commander in chief that two more companies under Captain Peter Bruin—another of Morgan's Quebec veterans—and Captain Gallihue of Prince William County were on the road and daily expected in Philadelphia. Three more companies would follow, Morgan arriving with the last. This brought the total number of companies in the 11th Virginia to five, around two hundred men or a little more, not enough to amount to a full line regiment.[22]

Shorthanded or not, Washington needed what soldiers there were. By the middle of April 1777, Morgan and what there was of the 11th Virginia arrived in the vicinity of Morristown, New Jersey. They were almost at once in the field while continuing to reorganize. It was a complex human-resources Rubik's Cube, solved while soldiering.

As Morgan, Febiger, and the rest of the commissioned and non-commissioned officers shook the 11th Virginia into shape in early June 1777, Washington simultaneously created a new unit. This he christened the Provisional Rifle Corps, and he made Morgan its commander. The Provisional Rifle Corps is often called "Morgan's Riflemen" or "Morgan's Rifles" and is sometimes confused with the 11th Virginia. In fact, for the next two years, Morgan commanded both the 11th Virginia and the Provisional Rifle Corps. In his absences, Febiger commanded the 11th Virginia.

Washington established the Provisional Rifle Corps because many regimental commanders had come to dislike rifles. Muhlenberg's 8th Virginia had been, interestingly enough, equipped solely with rifles, and he had not found them worth the trouble. "The Campaign we made to the Southward last Summer fully convinces me," he wrote Washington, "that on a march where Soldiers are without Tents, & their Arms continually exposd to the Weather; Rifles are of little use." This was not necessarily a result of technological conservatism but of trial. Washington, responding via an aide to Muhlenberg's request to transition from rifles to muskets, said, "[I am] satisfied of the Justice of your Observations about Rifles, [and] determined to have as few used as possible." From now on, he directed, Muhlenberg was to put "Musketts into the hands of all that Battalion that is not very well acquainted with Rifles."[23]

The converse was also true. Washington would have rifles into the hands of all those who were very well acquainted with them. No longer would riflemen be ignorant fellows who knew no more of rifles than Washington's horse. In general orders of June 1, 1777, Washington directed, "The commanding officer of every Corps is to make a report early to morrow morning, to his Brigadier, of the number of rifle-men under his command—In doing which, he is to include none but such as are known to be perfectly skilled in the use of these guns, and who are known to be active and orderly in their behaviour—Each Brigadier to make a collective return to the Adjutant General of these men."[24]

As late as June 13, 1777, when the Provisional Rifle Corps had already engaged in combat, Washington was still directing that "Such rifles as belong to the States, in the different brigades . . . be immediately exchanged with Col. Morgan for musquets—Officers commanding brigades are desired to pay attention to this matter, as the nature of the service requires the utmost dispatch. If a sufficient number of rifles (public property) can not be procured, the Brigadiers are requested to assist Col. Morgan, either by exchanging, or purchasing those that are private property."[25]

So Morgan took into his provisional corps those men from Pennsylvania, Virginia, Maryland, and New Jersey regiments who knew how to use a rifle. Nine rifle companies had been raised from Pennsylvania and then distributed among the line regiments of that state during their reorganization in the spring. Two companies had been raised in Virginia (Morgan's and Hugh Stephenson's), and two in Maryland. The Maryland companies had been in the Maryland and Virginia Rifle Regiment captured at Fort Washington, on Manhattan Island on November 16, 1776. But as Muhlenberg's regiment shows, there were rifles and riflemen in regiments not officially organized as rifle companies in 1775—in Virginia, Pennsylvania, and other states as well. Major Joseph Morris of the Provisional Rifle Corps was a Jerseyman serving in the New Jersey Brigade who had gained his experience with the rifle in the Wyoming Valley of northwestern Pennsylvania.[26] Thus Morgan's Rifles was a culturally and professionally hodgepodge unit, provisional in name and nature.

There could be no greater test of a commander than making such a disparate group of men work together as one.

"PRAY, what can these Gentry be about?" wrote Major General Nathanael Greene on June 9, 1777. "I never was more perplext to unravel and adjust the contradictory intelligence."[27] Morgan, now scouting the British lines daily with his new regiment, must have been equally mystified.

On June 12, Washington called a council of general officers at which Morgan was not present. The memo of the proceedings indicates Washington began the discussion with the intelligence that "General Howe had collected nearly the whole of his Force at Brunswic [New Brunswick]." Washington and his subordinates considered at length what Howe's aim might be. The consensus of the meeting was that Howe would fix the Continental army in place, then move for the Delaware River, which he would cross to capture Philadelphia. It was also agreed that additional troops should be brought down to New Jersey from positions on the Hudson to reinforce the main army against Howe's expected move.

The very next day, the proceedings of the council were rendered moot when two British columns, which together added up to a little under seventeen thousand men, marched up the Raritan River toward the American position at Middlebrook. This powerful force moved to within four or five miles of Washington's camp at Middlebrook. British officers and enlisted men alike expected that this was the beginning of the campaign that would finish what had been started the previous winter, the destruction of the Continental army and the capture of Philadelphia. A pontoon bridge had been prepared in New York City and was either with, or was soon to follow, the army. The British now knew—with considerable accuracy, considering the failure of their intelligence in the late winter—that Washington had between "7 or 8,000 men" at Middlebrook. (Indeed, he had precisely 7,763 soldiers ready for battle.) Howe's own German aide, Friedrich von Münchausen, believed that "General Howe has planned a forced march at dawn in order to cut off and to throw back General [John] Sullivan, who is at Princeton with 2,000 men."[28] June 14, then, was the beginning of the Continental army's defeat in detail. Washington had amateurishly dispersed his forces. Howe would separate them by intervening his powerful force in the geographical space between them, then set about separately destroying each.

When Howe issued forth from the camps around New Brunswick, Washington did not choose to respond with immediate action. Instead he sent forward Morgan and his riflemen, Maxwell's Jersey Brigade, and the increasingly battle-hardened and effective New Jersey militia to skirmish with the British troops. Howe then marched a grand total of five miles and dug in.

Once again, Greene and his fellow generals were bemused. "It was unaccountable that the people who the day before gave out in very gasconading terms that they would be in Philadelphia in six days should stop short when they had gone only nine miles," said Henry Knox, too generous by four miles. Knox and his American colleagues were joined in their bemusement by British officers, who themselves now began to wonder just what their commander could be up to. Sullivan, in the meantime, had retreated over the Delaware River into Pennsylvania and looped about to the north to recross the river and join the main army; Washington, it turned out, was not quite so amateurish as all that.

And then—nothing happened. Washington, perplexed, gave orders that Morgan keep scouts out and in contact with the enemy while having his corps ready to move "without confusion, and free from danger."[29] These scouts and Captain von Ewald's German Jaegers engaged in desultory skirmishing—desultory, at least, for all those who were not killed and wounded. Captain Montresor continued to direct the building of the redoubts. Redcoats and Hessians began to loot the nearby inhabitants, provoking the same cycle of Loyalist defections that had occurred the previous autumn and winter. And yet more New Jersey militia arrived in Washington's encampment, now eager for the fight they had not offered before. "We are under no more Apprehensions here than if the British Army was in Crimea," wrote John Adams to his wife from Philadelphia.[30]

Nor should he have been. After five days of camping out beneath Watchung Mountain, Howe decamped on June 19, 1777, and marched back to New Brunswick, burning about fifty farms and houses on the march. After some initial hesitation on Washington's part, he ordered Greene to follow Howe with three brigades; but they started their march too late to do any damage to Howe's rear guard. The grand movement toward the Delaware and Philadelphia, and the accompanying destruction of Washington's army, had turned into nothing more than an elaborate spring excursion.[31]

The day after returning to New Brunswick, Howe made preparations once again to leave it. On June 20, hundreds of boats, small ships, and six ships of the line began to arrive at Perth Amboy. On June 22, Howe marched out of New Brunswick. The British crossed the bridge over the Raritan River and marched down the road to Perth Amboy. The rear guard, resting on the heights above Raritan Landing, watched the arrival of, at most, three thousand Continentals and militia led by William Alexander, Lord Stirling, marching to intercept them from Bound Brook. These were some of the best American troops, all of them seasoned by months of partisan war. Two brigades of Continentals—the Jersey Brigade led by Brigadier General William Maxwell and the Pennsylvania Brigade led by Brigadier General Thomas Conway, known for its unusually high level of drill when compared with the rest of Washington's army. Temporarily under Stirling's orders were Morgan's riflemen and a small corps of German American riflemen under the titular command of a mysterious German mercenary, Nicholas Baron von Ottendorf, but commanded now by Charles Armand, an enthusiastic French volunteer who had renounced his title of Marquis de la Rouiëre to serve in this republican army.[32]

Morgan's riflemen began skirmishing on the east side of the river, driving in the British flankers, then being driven back. These American attacks on the rear guard, commanded by Howe himself, continued as the British marched toward Amboy, burning houses behind them as they went. New Brunswick was hardly in better shape. American soldiers found that the houses in the town had been deliberately vandalized, probably as the British departed. According to one report, though, the British had also buried the dead in the cellars of houses throughout New Brunswick, perhaps to keep the number of deaths secret. The artist and sometime-soldier Charles Willson Peale wrote that while there were hundreds of houses in the town, at the moment of the British evacuation only thirty families remained in all New Brunswick. Along the line of their march to Amboy, green wheat had been reaped, orchards cut down, some houses burned, others torn apart.[33]

Washington, meanwhile, had marched out of the protection of the Watchung with the vanguard of his army and paused at Quibbletown. Stirling's force, Morgan in advance, pursued Howe to the outskirts of Perth Amboy, attacking the rear guard as he was able. Stirling then fell back to camp in the Short Hills area between Westfield and Perth Amboy. Howe began to ferry troops and baggage to Staten Island. More troops were sent forward to Stirling's position as Washington meditated an attack on a divided British army.[34]

In the process, Washington had divided his own Continental army, and that division was exactly what Howe had been hoping for since the campaign began. The disembarkation of troops to Staten Island had been Howe's bait to draw Washington from cover; he ferried them back to the mainland after nightfall. After midnight on the morning of June 26, two British columns marched out of Amboy. One, led by Major General Charles Lord Cornwallis, made for Woodbridge; the other, led by Major General John Vaughan and accompanied by Howe, set out on a roughly parallel course to Bonhamtown. Howe's column attacked and defeated Stirling; Cornwallis flanked Washington and prevented him from retreating behind the Watchung. It was the Battle of Long Island all over again, and it was a taste of things to come.

Cornwallis's force encountered Stirling's pickets first. These, mostly of Armand's independent company, were terribly mauled and driven back, with thirty-two of eighty men killed or captured. Stirling had arranged some six hundred troops and three cannon (captured from the Hessians at Trenton) atop the crest of a hill blocking Cornwallis's path, their flanks protected. The battle soon focused on the cannon, British and Hessian troops racing forward at the run, bayonets extended, vying for the honor of capturing Stirling's cannon. At one point in the swirl of combat, a young British nobleman drove off the gunners and matrosses from the cannon, and then, seeing Stirling, called, "Come here, you damned rebel, and I will do for you." Whereupon Lord Stirling showed that while he might be concerned enough with his honor to appeal for his Scottish title to the House of Lords, he was no romantic on the battlefield. He ordered four riflemen near him—possibly Morgan's men—to shoot Captain John Finch. They did, and Finch went down, a casualty along with about half of his light company of the Guards. In the end, Stirling lost his cannon anyway. But the action, combined with the oppressive heat (summer 1777 was, by all accounts, a remarkably hot one, as was summer 1778) stalled the British pursuit.[35]

Washington had been completely let down by his scouts and spies. According to the recollections of the acidulous Colonel Timothy Pickering of Massachusetts, Washington's adjutant general, the commander in chief was unaware of the British attack until the redcoats were about two-and-a-half miles from Washington's headquarters in Quibbletown. The army was alerted, put to arms, and marched up the slope of the Watchung. Howe arrived, surveyed Washington's lines, slept in Westfield that night, and then marched back to Perth Amboy.[36]

Westfield was no battle, in any strict understanding of the word, but the majority of those killed in action during the Revolution died in just such skirmishes and almost-battles.

AFTER Westfield, Howe turned his army around and ferried it over to Staten Island. Then it boarded the transports anchored in New York harbor. Day after day, Morgan and his scouts watched for any sign of movement. The transports and all accompanying warships continued at anchor for so long that it seemed they might soon run aground on the garbage they threw overboard. "Pray, what can these gentlemen be about?" seemed to be a phrase in perennial use that summer.

But common sense told Washington that Howe would now join Lieutenant General Sir John Burgoyne, who by that time had reached Fort Ticonderoga on Lake Champlain; that the transports were a means to use the superior naval forces of Britain to beat the Continental army up the Hudson; and that the delay was just a way of wrong-footing him. So he ordered Morgan to keep a particularly close watch on the fleet from the Jersey shore of New York harbor.

On July 19, Morgan sent a messenger to Washington's headquarters bearing news of the long-expected movement. "This morning about seven oClock," he reported, "the enemies fleet ware all in

Motion, thay fired several guns which I looked upon to be signals, thay saild about for the span of two hours, and Come to at the watering place, except a few that fell down towards the hook and seemd to go round statan island toward Princes bay." Later that night or early the next morning, he received a reply indicating that there was every reason now to believe that the British fleet would be heading up the Hudson. "It is therefore his Excellency's Orders," wrote Colonel John Fitzgerald, one of Washington's aides-de-camp, "that upon receipt of this you March your Corps to the Bridge at the great Falls, from thence to Paramus, thence to Kakegate & thence to Haverstraw, then to observe the motions of the Enemy, & if they land on the west side of the river below the Highland you are to take possession of the Road to the forrest of Dean Furnace, & oppose their penetrating that way—but if the Enemy push up the River you are to get over the Mountains to fort Montgomery & there wait for further Orders."[37]

Then, against all expectations, the British fleet raised anchor, moved into the outer harbor, out around Sandy Hook, and to sea. Morgan had by this time recruited an informant, "a man whome I believe to be a Great Vilion, but it appears to me through him some inteligence may be had, as he has free excess in New york, Mr [ ] says he has made use of him that way." Having captured this man, Morgan then "let him make his escape, he is to go [to] New York this evening, and tell thare he has been taken, and made his escape, and is afrad to be seen at home in the day, and is to Colect what News he Can in the day, and deliver it to Mr — at Night." Then perhaps Morgan—and Washington—might be able to find out what Howe was up to.[38]

But Morgan's messenger must have passed another coming from Washington. He brought orders from the commander in chief to "Immediately on receipt of this . . . march with the Corps under your Command to the City of Philadelphia & there receive Orders from the Commanding Officer—You will proceed as expeditiously, as you can by the shortest Routs—You will take no Heavy Baggage with you, but leave it to follow with an Officer and a proper Guard."[39]

So around Morgan and his rifle corps turned, and south they marched. When they reached Trenton, they received further orders to wait there. For the next few weeks, in response to other orders, Morgan (and most of Washington's army) were in a sort of continual pas de deux, moving to and fro across northern New Jersey—a complex game of Simon Says involving thousands of soldiers.

Finally, by August 16, Washington knew what was going on. Amazing as it was, Howe had not intended a feint. He had sailed around into Chesapeake Bay and showed every intention of landing his army at its northern reaches, where the Susquehanna River flowed into it. The entire army was therefore put under marching orders for Philadelphia and the road south to Delaware—the entire army, that is, except for Morgan's Provisional Rifle Corps. Burgoyne's advance toward Albany, wrote Washington, "has made a further reinforcement necessary, and I know of no Corps so likely to check their progress in proportion to its Number as that under your command. I have great dependance on you—Your Officers & Men, and I am persuaded, you will do honour to yourselves, & Essential services to your Country."[40]

The most important portrait of Daniel Morgan was painted by Charles Willson Peale, perhaps in 1794, probably before. It served as a model for John Trumbull when he sketched it as a study for his portrait of Morgan in his 1821 painting of Burgoyne's surrender at Saratoga. Morgan here is not in a hunting shirt, but in his Brigadier General's uniform. Just visible on his upper lip is the scar of the exit wound from the bullet that struck him in April 1756. The entry wound is probably the seam on his left cheek, just above the jaw-line. A later revision of this portrait, either by Peale himself or by his son Rembrandt, was owned by Morgan descendants into the late twentieth century; it is now in the permanent collection of the Virginia Historical Society. (*National Park Service*)

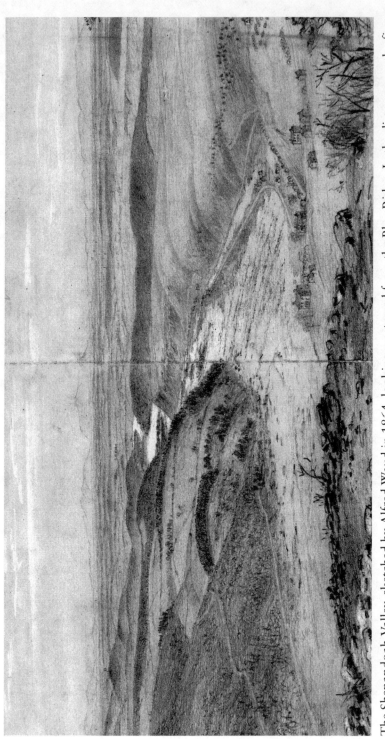

The Shenandoah Valley, sketched by Alfred Waud in 1864, looking westward from the Blue Ridge. In the distance are the first ridges of the Appalachian Range. Between is the lower Valley, where Daniel Morgan lived his entire adult life. This was his fortress, his refuge, and his home (*Library of Congress*)

This Conestoga wagon is a later version of those that Morgan drove. The wagoner is on the left wheel horse, as Morgan would have been. The lazy board, in between the wheels where the woman is sitting, was a later innovation. But the curved lines of the wagon's "box" are just as Morgan would have known them. These provided both strength and beauty to the wagon.. (*Library of Congess*)

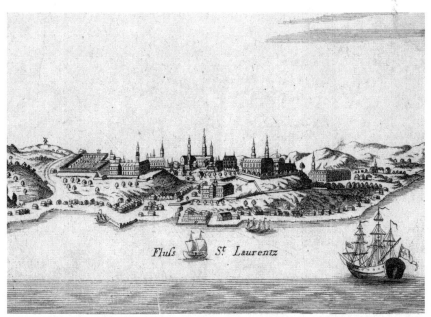

Flufs   St. Laurentz

"View of Quebec," 1775. The city of Quebec, perhaps the most formidable fortress in North America, sat atop a great rock promontory above the St. Lawrence River. Benedict Arnold's force attacked from the right of drawing, moving along the banks of the frozen river. Morgan seems to have made his way with a local guide to the foot of street leading from the Lower Town to the Upper Town, seen here in the center of the drawing. The battle took place roughly in the area of the town between the rightmost ship, and the two ships closest to the wharf. All of the action was confined to two or three rows of houses, in a space not much longer than two modern city blocks. (*Library of Congress*)

Generals Horatio Gates, left, and Benedict Arnold, right.
(*Library of Congress/New York Public Library*)

The Battle of Bemis Heights from the American lines. This nineteenth-century engraving does give the viewer a sense of the distances involved in the two battles we now collectively call "Saratoga." Both the Battle of Freeman's Farm and the Battle of Bemis Heights were fought two miles away from the American lines. Burgoyne never was able to even examine the American fortifications that Gates's army had built to block his route down the Hudson. (*New York Public Library*)

Opposite: John Trumbull's 1821 painting of British general John Burgoyne's surrender at Saratoga. Burgoyne hands his sword to Gates; Morgan leans casually on his own sheathed sword, dressed in a white linen hunting shirt. It is unlikely that Morgan would have chosen to be so depicted. While he wore leggings and a loincloth in the field, like his men, he was also a man who enjoyed fancy clothes—as bills to his tailor reveal. Here, Trumbull was cleverly making Morgan part of the developing myth of the American backwoodsman, showing him in his utilitarian field dress rather than in his uniform. Future artists would then show Morgan in the same dress, but in a posture similar to that of Daniel Boone, who by the mid nineteenth century was his more famous contemporary. (*Architect of the Capitol*)

Americaner Soldat.

An American soldier wearing a rifleman's fringed hunting shirt and mitre hat, published in 1778. The original caption read, "An accurate representation of an American soldier, by a Bavarian officer presently in the English service in America, drawn and sent from there. Their clothing is of ticking, they have long guns with bayonets, and are very rugged and healthy." (*Staatliche Museen Preussischer Kulturbesitz, Kunstbibliothek, Berlin*)

A post-Revolution example of the long rifles which Morgan and his men were employed from Boston to Cowpens. While this long rifle was made in Kentucky, they were made by artisans up and down the Great Wagon Road that stretched from Pennsylvania to the Carolinas. A rifle maker needed to be a master of numerous skills: blacksmithing and foundry work, to create the barrel; "whitesmithing," to cast the brass or silver ornamentation; woodworking, to carve the stock. Gunsmiths had their own approach to building a rifle, based on their years of apprenticeship, yet each rifle was a response to the needs of the customer and the location in which its made. Its caliber, length, weight, balance, and decoration were all done to his request. The result was a uniquely individual weapon, found only in Pennsylvania and the colonies to its south, unknown in New England or Britain. (Worman, *Firearms in American History*)

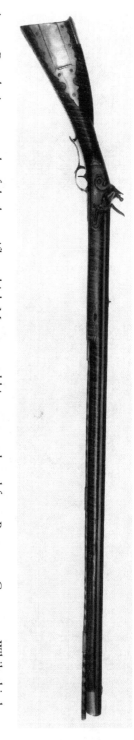

A reproduction hunting shirt, crafted of original materials. Contrary to common belief, hunting shirts were not made of deer skin, but of coarse linen fabric, or a linen-wool blend. This made for a utilitarian garment, which could be left its natural color, or dyed into a variety of colors—some Virginia regiments wore hunting shirts dyed purple. The fringe was purely for decorative purposes. Open at the front, it was closed by strapping a belt over it, or by some attached laces. The hunting shirt was, like the rifle, a product of the Great Wagon Road. In British eyes, this utilitarian garment was an exotic symbol of the American frontier, just as much as the rifle that its wearers carried. (*Colonial Williamsburg Foundation*)

Generals Nathanael Greene, left, and Henry "Light Horse Harry" Lee, right. (*National Park Service*)

Colonels William Washington, left, and Otho Williams, right. (*National Park Service*)

Opposite: The Battle of Cowpens by Frederick Kemmelmeyer, c. 1809. Kemmelmeyer (?–1819) was in all likelihood a former Hessian soldier who remained in South Carolina after the British evacuation. He ended his life as an intinerant artist in the lower Shenandoah, not far from Winchester. Perhaps during his time in South Carolina he became familiar with the stories of Cowpens. Here he shows the final moments of the battle, as William Washington and his cavalry drive off their British counterparts. At the center of the painting we can see the ensign-bearer aiming his pistol at a British trooper about to strike an American. The British trooper is probably supposed to be Tarleton himself, and William Washington the unheeding American. (*Yale University Art Gallery*)

General Andrew Pickens, left, and Col. John Eager Howard, right. (*New York Public Library/National Park Service*)

Soldier's Rest, just on the edge of today's Berryville, Virginia. Morgan's first home was either on this property, or is now part of the fabric of this house. When Morgan first lived here, he was convenient to Benjamin Berry's tavern, where he and his cronies would drink, run races, shoot, and fight one another. This was one of the three houses that Morgan built in the lower Shenandoah Valley. (*National Park Service*)

Chapter Nine

SARATOGA

WHEN Morgan began marching his Provisional Rifle Corps to the assistance of the Northern Army, it had been just one year and one week since he had been released from prison and placed on a transport in the St. Lawrence River. Since that time, the Northern Army had been shattered, first by the British attacks of May and June 1776, and then from the near-simultaneous attacks of the smallpox bacillus. It had first retreated when the British fleet appeared in the river below Quebec city and then been driven south from Montreal. Over a ten-day period while the Northern Army paused during its retreat on an island in the Richelieu River north of Lake Champlain, nine hundred men had died of smallpox. What was left of the army made its way down Lake Champlain to the fortress of Ticonderoga, where the upper part of Champlain is connected to Lake George and to the almost-separate lake that constitutes Champlain's southern extremity.

There the army had been rebuilt over summer 1776 by Major General Philip Schuyler, commander of the Northern Department, with much time, labor, and expense.[1] To contest British control of Lake Champlain, a small and pitifully equipped navy had been built under the leadership of Morgan's old commander Benedict Arnold. Its creation led to further building by the British, and then more building by the Americans, until suddenly it was autumn, there was snow on some of the higher Adirondacks, and the British had twenty-five ships and the Americans an undergunned fleet of seventeen (two British vessels alone had a greater firepower than all of Arnold's ships combined).[2] On October 11, 1776, the two miniature navies finally met and fought at Valcour Island. The American force, badly hurt, fled that night and was systematically snapped up and destroyed over the next two days by the British fleet.

It was not the battle given by the sacrificial American fleet that halted the progress of Carleton's army, but the shipbuilding race of the summer. Given that it was late in the year when Carleton's lake-borne army finally arrived at Ticonderoga, he decided it would be impossible to successfully besiege the fort during the early winter, and he returned to the north.[3]

These dramatic events happened as Morgan returned to the new United States from Quebec and made his way south to his family in the Valley. By the time he was marching to New Jersey with his pitifully small collection of 11th Virginia Regiment recruits in early April 1777, the Northern Army's winter quarters were thawing and a new leader was sailing to the British army in Canada. Carleton had been replaced by one of the more gifted and flexibly minded British commanders, Sir John Burgoyne. He commanded an army of four thousand four hundred British soldiers and four thousand seven hundred Germans. Also among his number were Canadian irregulars, some Loyalists from New York—Burgoyne expected the latter to increase—and an uncertain number of natives from the Six Nations and from nations along the Great Lakes. Superintended by five hundred artillerymen were 138 pieces of artillery, of which thirty-seven were heavy guns firing a twelve-pound or heavier ball. Their purpose was to demolish Fort Ticonderoga. There was also a German regiment of dragoons, without horses. This imperial power was carried down Lake Champlain in the fleet built in 1776, preceded by bateaux and countless canoes. It was not a fast-moving army, but it seemed an inexorable one.[4]

The British army leveled its power at Fort Ticonderoga. Although scenically situated, Ticonderoga had proven, during its short life, to be in a terrible tactical location, given that no fewer than three positions within cannon shot look down on it. Two had been carefully fortified since Ethan Allen and Benedict Arnold captured it in 1775. But the third, the smooth, steep slopes of Sugar Loaf Hill, which dominated the approaches to Ticonderoga if not the fort itself, seemed impossible to exploit. William Phillips, the experienced commander of Burgoyne's artillery, took a different view. "Where a goat can go," he supposedly said, "a man can go; and where a man can go he can drag a gun." Whether he said these words or not, his actions demonstrated that he believed them.[5]

On the morning of July 5, 1777, American defenders in and around Ticonderoga observed the remarkable sight of a British battery atop Mount Defiance, commanding the two waterways to southern Lake Champlain and to Lake George, able to toss cannon balls into any attempt to retreat from Ticonderoga as casually as throwing bread crusts off a footbridge to ducks.[6]

Major General Arthur St. Clair, commanding Ticonderoga, decided to abandon the fort and retreat south to the Hudson River. Burgoyne moved in quick pursuit. In a delaying action at Hubbardton, the Americans fended off the British and gained some distance. On July 12, the various units of the Northern Army joined together at the ruins of Fort Edward, on the banks of the Hudson. Only fifty miles separated them from Albany, and another 150 miles lay between Albany and New York City. The Northern Army was now a very uncertain screen of Continentals and militia guarding against Burgoyne and whatever British detachment chose to force its way up the Hudson. It was a thin, brittle crust defending the colonies against disaster.[7]

This continuing litany of disaster from the north was, by July 1777, too much for the Continental Congress. It replaced Philip Schuyler with Major General Horatio Gates.

Gates had the assistance of the supply lines that Schuyler had established from 1775 to 1777, as well as the engineering expertise of Colonel Tadeusz Kosciuszko. Together Gates and the Polish engineer determined that the right place to make a stand against Burgoyne's approaching army was Bemis Heights, a plateau a few miles north of Stillwater, New York, that rose three hundred feet above the Hudson River. Its bluffs above the river, combined with marshy low ground along the bank, would hinder an approach along the river while enabling the Americans to place it under intense fire from the heights. The terrain on the east bank, and the growing American strength east of the Hudson in New England, made Bemis Heights an unavoidable obstacle for Burgoyne.

Gates posted one division on the east side of the plateau, under his immediate command, to defend the river road. The left wing of the army he placed under now-Major General Benedict Arnold. Just south of the fortifications on the heights, Kosciuszko's engineers built a pontoon bridge across the Hudson, enabling retreat or offense as necessary. Breastworks were built for half a mile along the crest of the bluff overlooking the Hudson, and another line was added along the crest of the plateau looking north. Batteries of cannon were placed on either end, and one was placed in the middle. Yet another set of breastworks ran across the river flats from Bemis Heights to the banks of the Hudson. As reinforcements arrived, both militia and Continental, Gates put them to work building additional fortifications, strengthening the complexity and sophistication of those already developed.[8] He was determined to remain on the strategic and tactical defensive; he knew that Burgoyne must come to him, and given his green troops—both regular and militia—that suited Gates perfectly.

On August 31, Morgan and his riflemen reached Albany, arriving on the same day Arnold returned from a successful expedition up the Mohawk Valley, where he deterred a British force that intended to join Burgoyne at Albany by taking the Northern Army from behind.

Gates placed Morgan and his riflemen in Arnold's division. They joined two brigades already under Arnold's command, one led by Brigadier General Enoch Poor composed of New Hampshire and New York regiments of the Continental army as well as some regiments of Connecticut militia, and the other commanded by Brigadier General Ebenezer Learned and composed of three Massachusetts regiments and a battery of New York artillery. These were Gates's best combat troops, and he gave them to his best and most aggressive commander.

From Morgan's point of view, the most decisive of Gates's organizational moves was to detach a battalion of New Hampshire musketmen from Poor's brigade and assign it to Morgan. The battalion was commanded by Major Henry Dearborn, who was Morgan's friend, a veteran of the march to Quebec, and a fellow prisoner at the Jesuit seminary. Dearborn's battalion was assigned to Morgan to serve as a light infantry auxiliary to his riflemen. With it he had a screen of bayonets to guard his vulnerable, slow-loading rifles, in effect a primitive combined arms force, able to undertake multiple tasks simultaneously, staffed by men he knew and trusted.[9]

BY September 12, the entire Northern Army had moved into the new fortifications atop the plateau. Gates had established his headquarters in Woodworth Farm, at the center of the plateau, lodged in a log cabin so small he shared it only with one aide, Major James Wilkinson, a nineteen-year-old sprig of a Maryland plantation family.[10] One-third of a mile north was the Nielsen Farm, where Arnold and Morgan shared quarters. Just north of the Nielsen home was the family barn, which Morgan's riflemen transformed into a fort with a double tier of logs and entrenchments that covered an area of about half an acre. It was located at the center of the north-facing fortifications on the plateau and was the expected focus of any British attack. Gates unquestionably envisioned a Bunker Hill scenario, but this time with British and German soldiers falling to rifle bullets at two hundred yards out. Morgan had 451 riflemen fit for duty, and they camped in the area north of the barn.

But Morgan did not intend his riflemen to spend their time in their new fortifications waiting for an attack or in building defenses alongside the other Continentals and the militia. As in New Jersey, he assigned them to scout and to engage in partisan warfare. These nightly scouts, and the raids that developed from their intelligence regarding the terrain and the movements of Burgoyne's army, were Morgan's most important contribution to the eventual victory of Saratoga.

ON September 18, Burgoyne established camp about five miles north of Bemis Heights. His contingent of Native Americans, originally about five hundred, had dwindled to fifty warriors who did not seem very eager to scout the American lines.[11] Despite this lack of intelligence regarding the American army's position, on September 19, Burgoyne ordered an attack. He did know that it was impossible to proceed farther down the river road, and he did not want to cross the river; that would put him on the opposite side of the Hudson from Albany. So he decided to flank the American position to its left, to the west. His intelligence and knowledge of that area were so limited he had to rely on the actual assault to gain that information. His German division proceeded down the river road, acting as a diversion and a means of engineering new bridges and causeways. The light corps, under the command of Brigadier General Simon Fraser, led the advance to the west, followed by the British division. Gates might be lured into devoting his troops to attack the German division, thereby leaving himself vulnerable on the west; or he might do the opposite. Either way, Burgoyne intended to take advantage of his inattention.

Gates, learning of Burgoyne's movement to the west from Morgan's scouts, sent the rifle corps out in force to learn more. They deployed in crescent formation, the horns pointed toward the enemy, with Morgan at the apex, in the rear. To communicate with his men, Morgan carried into battle a turkey call, the device used to lure the most cautious of woodland creatures within range of rifle shot. Though Morgan must have employed the turkey call during New Jersey skirmishes, his use of it as a communication tool appears only in accounts of Saratoga. Like British light infantry officers, Morgan probably had no fixed system of signals but used the call primarily to rally his men. He may also have used it to get the attention of his officers so he could then signal with his hands or hat—many British light infantry officers would flourish their hats in a kind of simple semaphore or wigwag code.[12]

After a march of four miles, Morgan and his rifle corps reached the fields belonging to John Freeman, upon which stood a house, a log barn, and a few other structures. Freeman was a Loyalist who had already sold his livestock, or most of it, to the British army. He was a tenant of none other than Major General Philip Schuyler, and like other lower-status tenants of the great Hudson valley landholders, Freeman's loyalty to the king was also an act of rebellion against his landlord.[13]

Within range of some skirmishers and pickets of the British 9th Regiment, the riflemen opened fire. The lead companies, commanded by Major Morris, Morgan's third in command, pursued the retreating pickets, and they swiftly encountered the main British force. Major Gordon Forbes of the 9th Regiment responded with the perfect tactic when confronting American riflemen at short range: he fixed bayonets and charged, scattering the riflemen and capturing, among others, Captain Van Swearingen, who had recently joined Morgan with a company of riflemen from the 8th Pennsylvania Regiment. Other British units, arriving and falling into line, began to volley fire at the scattered riflemen.[14]

The effects were dramatic. Morgan's riflemen fled into the woods, ahead of an assault they had no ability to withstand. Morris's company scattered to the four winds, and others quickly followed. Dearborn attempted to withstand the British assault with about forty or so of his New Hampshire musket men. Gates's aide James Wilkinson, arriving on the field with a dispatch from Gates, rode toward the sounds of firing and found Major Morris retreating from his attack on the British. A little later, he discovered Lieutenant Colonel Richard Butler of Pennsylvania, Morgan's second in command, perched in a tree with three other men, where they had taken refuge from British bayonets. Finally finished with his perambulations around the battlefield and ready to return to camp, Wilkinson heard "an uncommon noise." Making his way toward it, he found Morgan blowing his turkey call, accompanied by just two men. Seeing Wilkinson, Morgan burst into tears of rage and vexation. "I am ruined, by God!" he wept. "Major Morris ran on so rapidly with the front, that they were beaten before I can get up with the rear, and my men scattered God knows where." But even as Wilkinson attempted to console Morgan, riflemen began to return to their commander, rallied by his signal to a position about 275 yards south of Freeman's house and barns.[15]

Dearborn's light infantry was now separated from Morgan's slowly regrouping riflemen, off to the left of the rest of Morgan's command. As Gates swiftly sent reinforcements, each new unit tended to interpose itself into a gap between the riflemen and Dearborn's musket men. By the end of the day, every other American unit on the battlefield separated Dearborn's battalion from the rest of Morgan's corps. So the little experiment in combined arms, and the advantage it provided Morgan's riflemen, had failed. Morgan set some of his men to building barricades and obstacles, cutting down saplings, the tips of their limbs facing toward the enemy and quickly sharpened, creating an improvised barrier against bayonet attack—a field-expedient version of the half-pikes he had requested in New Jersey and used in Quebec. Baron von Riedesel, commander of Burgoyne's German troops, described the American right in front of Morgan's position as protected by a deep natural ditch or gully, the other side of which had been "rendered inaccessible by stones, underbrush and barricades."[16]

Both the day and the battle were far from over. The reinforcements, Poor's New Hampshire brigade, formed with Morgan's riflemen into a crescent adhering to the tree line around Freeman's farm. They were evenly matched with the opposing British force; and Dearborn and those New Hampshire troops near him attacked, driving the British back and taking one of their cannons. But the Americans were just as swiftly driven back at bayonet point by a counterattack. As each British attack ended, the Americans had enough time to re-form and launch another attack of their own.

This litany of attack and counterattack continued through midafternoon, at which point all of Arnold's division was committed. That meant there were now about two thousand two hundred Americans on the battlefield, outnumbering the British. Opposite Morgan's corps, the British 62nd Regiment had been devastated, suffering 50 percent casualties. As the 62nd retreated from the field, a gun battery was forced to retreat along with it, and it was only saved by a sacrificial charge by the 20th Regiment of Foot at about five o'clock in the afternoon.

By that time the Americans' superior numbers, surprising courage and ability with the bayonet, and marksmanship were grinding down British resistance. Of this last Burgoyne reported that many of Morgan's men were "in the high trees in the rear of their own line . . . any part of our lines without officers being taken off by a single shot." The ubiquitous Sergeant Roger Lamb of the 9th Regiment of Foot agreed: "Several of the Americans placed themselves in high trees, and as often as they could distinguish a British officers uniform, Took him off by deliberately aiming at his person."

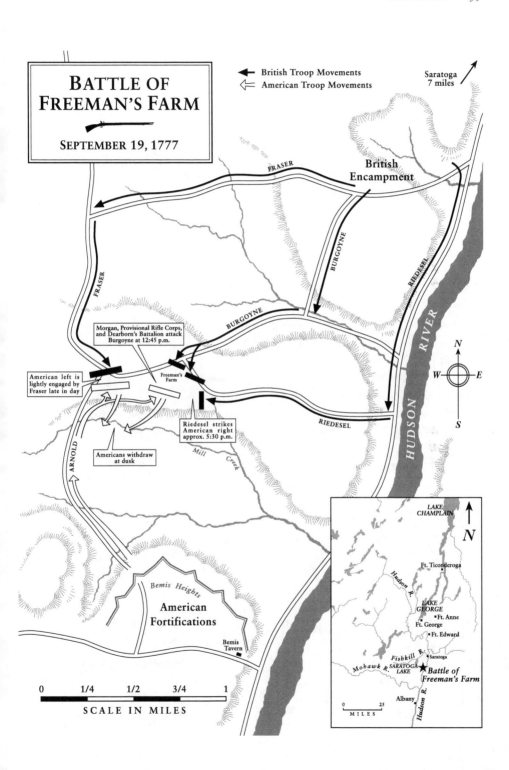

BATTLE OF
FREEMAN'S FARM

SEPTEMBER 19, 1777

◀━ British Troop Movements
⇐ American Troop Movements

Saratoga
7 miles

FRASER

British
Encampment

BURGOYNE

RIEDESEL

FRASER

BURGOYNE

Morgan, Provisional Rifle Corps,
and Dearborn's Battalion attack
Burgoyne at 12:45 p.m.

HUDSON   RIVER

American left is
lightly engaged by
Fraser late in day

Freeman's
Farm

N
W   E
S

ARNOLD

Riedesel strikes
American right
approx. 5:30 p.m.

RIEDESEL

HUDSON

Americans withdraw
at dusk

Mill   Creek

Bemis Heights

American
Fortifications

Bemis
Tavern

0   1/4   1/2   3/4   1

SCALE IN MILES

LAKE
CHAMPLAIN

N

Ft. Ticonderoga

Hudson R.

LAKE
GEORGE
        • Ft. Anne
Ft. George
        • Ft. Edward

Fishkill R.   • Saratoga
SARATOGA
LAKE
Mohawk R.   ★ Battle of
                Freeman's Farm

0   25
MILES

Albany   Hudson R.

Perhaps the only thing that dissuaded Morgan was counterfire delivered by German Jaegers, who were shooting rifles that were the ancestors of those his men carried.

These Jaegers were the lead elements of a counterattack by the German forces, led by Baron von Riedesel. He had been marching in his feint along the river road, when late in the day Burgoyne summoned him to come to his assistance. Taking half of his men, following a rough road up to Freeman's farm from the Hudson, he made his way toward the sound of the guns. This took time. Determined that his men would arrive fresh upon the battlefield, he gave them several stops to rest. Sometime between five and six o'clock, the German rescue arrived. Von Riedesel's men caught Morgan's by surprise and drove them back, reversing the right horn of his crescent formation and beginning to roll up the 3rd and 1st New Hampshire Regiments along with the riflemen.[17]

This should have been the moment that Arnold's division broke and the moment the Northern Army suffered yet another ignominious defeat. But the Americans refused to be destroyed. They continued to hold their right flank and resist Burgoyne's advance, which allowed time for the rest of the left division to grudgingly and stubbornly fall back. They fought their entire retreat back to the Middle Fork, where they rallied and then returned into the lines atop Bemis Heights.[18]

Under the rules of eighteenth-century warfare, the British were victorious since they retained the field at the conclusion of the battle. But Morgan, his riflemen, and the rest of Arnold's division had demonstrated that the rules of eighteenth-century warfare did not always apply. After all, by nightfall, Burgoyne was no closer to New York City then he had been in the morning. Nor had he managed to damage Gates's army. Only half of the Northern Army had been committed to the battle; the other half remained fresh and undeployed. More importantly, Burgoyne had used up resources that he could not replace. Morgan and his corps had targeted officers and artilleryman, and they and the other regiments of Arnold's division had rendered at least two regiments incapable of further fighting. No reinforcements were coming to replace Burgoyne's losses. But militia and other reinforcements were daily joining Gates's Northern Army.

Burgoyne had not lost. The British army, officers and enlisted men, were accustomed to fighting battles that lasted longer than one day and campaigns that were decided over the course of several engagements. The Americans were not. The greater experience of the British and German forces meant that after the day's struggle over John Freeman's fields, the contest was still evenly balanced.

HISTORIANS often describe the two weeks in late September and early October 1777, following the battle at Freeman's farm as a kind of interlude between the two principal engagements that compose the Battle of Saratoga. But those two weeks were the deciding factor of the battle, the balance on which its result pivoted, and they were dominated by the actions of Morgan and his Provisional Rifle Corps. For Morgan, every previous experience of combat contributed to his performance. For his riflemen, the partisan warfare in New Jersey during spring and summer 1777—not their innate woodcraft or their backcountry hunting experience—had served as a lengthy training exercise preparing them for the task at hand.

Those two weeks were characterized by partisan warfare, *petit guerre,* war by small detachments. Each night Morgan directed groups of men in scouting forays and skirmishes around the British positions, now extended forward to new fortifications being built on Freeman's farm. The British still did not know where precisely Gates's camp was located or how it was defended, and by ambushing, and killing or capturing their scouts, Morgan prevented them from closing this gap in intelligence. In addition to thwarting their efforts at intelligence gathering, he wore down Burgoyne's men by keeping their pickets on continual alert. The battleground for this partisan warfare was the no-man's-land between the armies, the gullies, woods, and thickets along the Middle Ravine and Mill Creek. A chronicle of this *petit guerre* might read something like this:

> September 21—A group of several hundred Germans clearing roads toward the American position were attacked by an American force. They beat the Americans off, but only after calling the entire British army to arms.[19]

> September 22—British pickets drove off scouts and skirmishers. Oneida Indians captured two British sentries, killed

and scalped another. A group of drunken militiamen intimidated and captured thirty British sentries. An American scouting party intercepted an Indian messenger between Fort Ticonderoga and Burgoyne.[20]

September 23—Outposts on the left wing were attacked by what British commanders believed to be a large force; so too were detachments in other areas.[21]

September 24—Rangers and light infantry detachments were supposed to scout, but they stayed in camp. German pickets sounded the alarm several times about the approach of American skirmishers.

September 25—"At dawn, the enemy again tried something against the Hesse-Hanau pickets . . . to compel one noncommissioned officer with ten men to retreat" The Oneidas brought in twenty-seven British and German prisoners and two Loyalists.

September 26—Eighteen prisoners were taken by American patrols from foraging parties near Saratoga. British pickets were under attack all day. Oneidas brought in eleven British regulars and two scalps.

September 27—Americans in bateaux attacked German positions along the river.

September 28—Colonel John Glover of Massachusetts and one hundred men of his brigade attacked a strong German outpost, which was quickly abandoned. The soldiers fled back to their main lines, many abandoning their guns. The Germans lost three dead, more wounded. Glover lost no one.[22]

So it went, night by night. British scouts went out, and returned reporting they had seen nothing. And yet on those same nights when nothing was seen, pickets were attacked, and British, Germans, and Loyalist were killed, wounded, and captured. The "prudent and necessary" precautions taken by Burgoyne to defend the camp resulted—after three weeks— in an exhausted British army that still knew little about either the terrain or the disposition of Gates's army. When Burgoyne eventually once more went on the offensive, he drew his troops from those garrisons who had been least under attack—indicating either apprehension at further attacks, that those soldiers had been worn down from partisan war, or both.[23]

This skirmishing against the British occurred at the same time that American officers were skirmishing among themselves, battle lines drawn in a now-lethal conflict between Horatio Gates and Benedict Arnold. In the past year, Gates had defended and protected Arnold, particularly in attempts to railroad him with a court-martial on highly questionable claims of malfeasance while commanding in Montreal. But Gates's defense of his focused and aggressive commander was forgotten, and the two were in a state of raging conflict.

The immediate cause of their rupture was over who commanded Morgan and his Provisional Rifle Corps. Morgan occupied a curious place in the command structure of the Northern Army since he had been detached to the army by Washington and was a colonel in independent command of a formation larger than many Continental army brigades. (Given the riflemen's temporary detachment and the size of the corps, Gates had not incorporated them into any of his existing formations but left them intact, albeit within Arnold's division.)

However, in his general orders of September 22, Gates announced that all reports and requests by Morgan be directed not to Arnold but to his own headquarters. Arnold soon arrived at Gates's cabin and demanded to know why. Major Wilkinson reported that Arnold was "in great warmth" during this conversation and that Gates, in response, ridiculed him. "High words and gross language ensued." Gates removed Arnold from command, taking personal charge of the left division. Arnold, left with nothing to do, requested permission to leave camp. Gates granted permission, but Burgoyne intervened in the execution of Arnold's plan.[24]

Hemmed in by skirmishers, his supply lines to the north under attack, Burgoyne was sustained by hope that Sir Henry Clinton would soon advance from the south and the two British forces would crack Gates like a walnut. Burgoyne, a once-decisive cavalry commander, a brilliant leader of dashing raids and sudden assaults in Portugal, was now paralyzed with waiting. Morgan and other Americans practicing partisan war had rendered him blind. Lacking essential intelligence, Burgoyne was unable to orient himself. Unable to orient himself, he was unable to decide; unable to decide, he was unable to act.[25]

Burgoyne needed provisions and information, and he also wanted to turn Gates's left flank. On October 7, he decided to kill at least two birds with one stone. Stretching south from Freeman's farm were wheat fields now ready for harvest. A foraging party would harvest that wheat, well defended by a force capable of withstanding any skirmishers. It would, simultaneously, scout the American lines as his Indians and Loyalists had proven unable to do. It might be possible to secure some advantage, but it would certainly be possible to secure wheat from which to grind flour.

MORGAN'S SCOUTS—who that day included, or were exclusively, Stockbridge Indians detached to serve in his corps—reported the British movement as soon as the redcoats stepped foot out of their camp, sometime just before one o'clock in the afternoon. Morgan had been out the night of the sixth and seventh on a "scout" with eight hundred men. They took seven prisoners, and, caught in heavy rain, "we got Bewildered in the woods," Henry Dearborn recalled, "and Stayd all night." Returning after sunrise, Morgan's corps slept through the rest of the morning.[26]

This intelligence was quickly relayed to Gates, who was having dinner with his generals in his cabin. At Arnold's pleading, Gates allowed him to scout the advance, but he sent Major General Benjamin Lincoln with him. He also sent Wilkinson to have a look. That worthy, moving to the west and within sight of the September 19 battlefield, watched three enemy columns advance into a wheat field south of Freeman's farm and there stop for a rest while foragers moved out to cut grain and officers climbed a cabin roof and with their telescopes attempted to survey what they could see of the American left.[27]

Riding back to Gates, Wilkinson offered the opinion that the advancing British force meant "to offer you battle." Gates, somewhat amazingly, was unaware of the terrain over which the two armies had struggled for the last month, asking, "What is the nature of the ground, and what is your opinion?" Having heard what Wilkinson had to say, Gates replied tersely, "Well, then, order on Morgan to begin the game."[28]

Wilkinson found Morgan and his corps at the center of camp, near Fort Nielsen, already deployed in their crescent formation. Morgan was pulling at the proverbial leash, anticipating the order from Gates that would make him the first unit onto the battlefield. However, when Wilkinson gave that order—apparently with some more terrain considerations and tactical directions than Gates provided—Morgan paused to consider and evaluate it. Unlike Gates, Morgan knew the ground well, and he saw how to use it to his advantage. Questioning Wilkinson closely on the disposition of the British troops and their location on the battlefield of September 19, Morgan advised some modifications. He would circle his rifle corps around the British right, moving to the northwest, then appear on some wooded heights just to their right rear. In the meantime, he advised, Poor should take the New Hampshire Brigade and some New York militia and make a direct assault on the British front and left flank. They would coordinate their attacks. As soon as Poor had attacked and caught the attention of the British, Morgan would strike.[29]

Miraculously enough for a battle plan, it unfolded just as Morgan had imagined it. As Poor attacked the grenadier detachments on the British left, the light infantry stationed to the right and to the front of the British protective line began to maneuver to support the grenadiers, opening a gap in their lines into which Morgan inserted his corps like a pry bar. Morgan "poured down like a torrent from the hill," and this time Dearborn's New Hampshire light infantry were close to his riflemen. They formed a screen for the riflemen, moving in advance of Morgan's crescent formation, and also acted as a bayonet-equipped shock force for the bladeless rifles. Like the left hand of a right-handed boxer, they were able to guard and keep distance for the devastating right, yet still able to jab.[30]

Meanwhile, Gates stood in the doorway of his cabin, waiting for word from the battlefield. Northern Army generals began to congregate, heads cocked as they listened to growing, surging, diminishing, then growing again volleys of musketry, punctuated by the irregular staccato of rifles. Benjamin Lincoln and Benedict Arnold returned to the group after examining the ground near the river, where American forces were skirmishing with German troops. Lincoln suggested to Gates that any movement near the river was merely a feint and that Burgoyne's real attack would be on the American left. Gates replied that he had sent Morgan and Dearborn to prevent that from happening. Arnold then burst out: "That is nothing. You must send a strong force." Gates responded, "General Arnold, I've nothing for you to do. You have no business here." Lincoln intervened, advising Gates that he "must send a strong force to support Morgan and Dearborn, at least three regiments."[31]

It is uncertain whether Lincoln, Arnold, or even Gates knew that Poor's brigade was now also engaged. But it must have impressed Gates that the defensive-minded Lincoln was advocating an attack. Gates ordered Brigadier General Learned to send out two of his regiments and requested Brigadier General John Nixon of Massachusetts to send another forward. These came into line on Enoch Poor's left, extending his line and attacking the British center. The entire left of Burgoyne's reconnaissance was now seized by a strong claw while Morgan slashed and raked at its right.

This he did, as he had done three weeks before, by targeting officers, artillery, and Loyalists. Morgan's men had attacked at about 2:30 PM. By three o'clock or a little after, the British line began to collapse, gradually bending back into a *U* shape. Learned's detachment then punched back the center. Gates added a brigade of some three thousand New York militiamen to the assaults. What they lacked in experience they made up for in sheer numbers and aggression. By now there were some eight thousand Americans either on or moving to the battlefield.[32]

Brigadier General Simon Fraser, mounted on a big gray gelding, attempted to re-form the British right. He was laying out a second line behind the collapsing *U*, and bringing disintegrating units back into cohesion. Just after three o'clock, Morgan pointed out Fraser to his best marksmen. "He is a brave man," he said, "but he must be killed." Years later, a British officer dining with Morgan asked him about Fraser. Morgan turned to their host and asked "if he remembered a certain person, a most remarkable rifle shot. . . . He then told him that having been ordered to seize a height contiguous to the British posts at Saratoga, . . . he saw an officer on a grey horse advancing, . . . he therefore sent this man, who was such an excel-

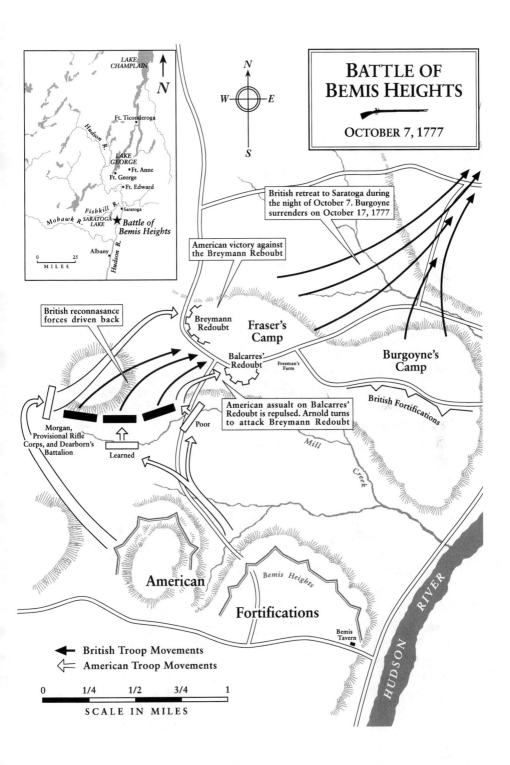

BATTLE OF
BEMIS HEIGHTS

OCTOBER 7, 1777

LAKE
CHAMPLAIN

N

Ft. Ticonderoga

LAKE
GEORGE
• Ft. Anne
Ft. George
• Ft. Edward

Fishkill R.
Saratoga
Mohawk R. SARATOGA
LAKE ★ Battle of
Bemis Heights

Albany

0   25
MILES

N
W ⊕ E
S

British retreat to Saratoga during
the night of October 7. Burgoyne
surrenders on October 17, 1777

American victory against
the Breymann Reboubt

British reconnasance
forces driven back

Breymann
Redoubt

Fraser's
Camp

Balcarres'
Redoubt   Freeman's
Farm

Burgoyne's
Camp

American assault on Balcarres'
Redoubt is repulsed. Arnold turns
to attack Breymann Redoubt

British Fortifications

Morgan,
Provisional Rifle
Corps, and Dearborn's
Battalion

Poor

Learned

Mill

Creek

American

Bemis Heights

Fortifications

Bemis
Tavern

HUDSON RIVER

◀━ British Troop Movements
⇐ American Troop Movements

0   1/4   1/2   3/4   1

SCALE IN MILES

lent shot, into a tree, with orders to take aim at that officer." Fraser was the target of more than one sharpshooter that day. His horse was hit by two or three shots, his staff and their horses hit by at least another three, and all this before Fraser himself was shot through the stomach from one side to the other.[33]

By 3:30 PM or a little after, Burgoyne knew that he had lost the fight. His flanks were bending inward, his center collapsing, Fraser was down, and by that time about four hundred men had been killed, wounded, or captured. Burgoyne sent orders to Phillips and Riedesel to withdraw. A bullet clipped his waistcoat, and another nearly took off his hat. The artillery battery accompanying the reconnaissance force had slowly lost its officers, its surrounding infantry support had fled, and all its horses were killed in their traces.[34]

Then the Americans—the 1st New Hampshire—swept forward and took the guns. The soldiers halted, shouted, tossed up their hats, and exulted. They had made British regulars run. And what was better, they had made them flee their guns. Colonel Joseph Cilley, their commander, arrived, vaulted onto a cannon, and from his iron mount rejoiced along with his men. Then, as the British artillerymen fled without removing the ammunition, the 1st New Hampshire turned the guns around and fired at the fleeing enemy.[35]

Morgan continued to press his advantage—then, and later, one of his favorite phrases. He moved his men forward as quickly as the British retreated, killing them as they fled, spurring them to still greater speed and increasing their disintegration. As Morgan's men approached the second line that Fraser had been forming when he fell, they flanked it and began to gut it from one end; their loose crescent formation was perpendicular to the British line and left all the British soldiers exposed to American gunfire. The line broke, and Learned's and Poor's brigades surged forward again. This time, mounted on a chestnut stallion named after his good friend Joseph Warren, Benedict Arnold rode forward with them, shouting, waving his hat, and flourishing his sword. He had left the camp and joined the battle. Later his enemies would allege that he was drunk or mad. In either event, he had no official status on the battlefield, leading only by the power of his charisma.[36]

It was about 5:30 when Burgoyne's troops fell back to their camp, a series of redoubts and breastworks built along a ridge above Freeman's farm.[37] With the British leaving the field, the battle was—according to convention—over and the Americans were the victors. It was Arnold's decision to make this victory a great one by attacking Burgoyne's camp and forcing him to either fight or retreat.[38]

In the two weeks since the battle of September 19, the ridge and buildings of Freeman's farm had been turned into fortifications. A great breastwork, the Balcarres redoubt (named after its commander, Alexander Lindsay, 6th Earl of Balcarres), had been built around the buildings of John Freeman's farm in the weeks since the September 19 engagement. To its right along the ridge, opposite the American left, was what later was called Breymann's redoubt (also named after its commander, in this case Lieutenant Colonel Heinrich von Breymann of Brunswick) occupied by German soldiers. Between them were some cabins occupied by Canadian militia.

Arnold first led assault after unsuccessful assault on the Balcarres redoubt. Each was repulsed by the size of the fortification and the gunfire defending it. Abandoning this attempt, Arnold now galloped between the blazing ranks of Americans and the British in their redoubt, came upon some of Learned's men, and led them in an assault on the cabins, putting the Canadians to flight. Now there was only empty air between the two redoubts; it was possible to circle around them.

In the meantime, Morgan had edged his men to the right flank of Breymann's—he always moved to the flank, to the flank—and the left horn of his crescent formation was beginning to overlap the open rear of the redoubt. It was not a sophisticated fort, but a U-shaped field fortification, meant to give simple cover on the battlefield; and by then it only held approximately two hundred men. Arnold, leading the men of Learned's brigade, appeared around the other side of the redoubt, driving forward from the redoubt's left. Dearborn's light infantry—on the left end of Morgan's crescent—fell in behind him, as did Major Joseph Morris with twelve riflemen, Richard Butler with some of his Pennsylvanians, and possibly Morgan himself. Some Germans fled before them after a brief resistance; others standing and firing out from the ramparts turned and opened fire at the attackers in their rear.[39]

A German—maybe wounded, maybe fleeing—fired and hit Arnold in the same leg in which he had been so badly wounded at

Quebec. The first wound had hit only muscle; this one broke his femur in several places before wounding his horse and dropping it atop Arnold, pinning his unwounded leg. Riflemen were now flooding into the redoubt, Morgan with them, his voice rising above the roar of battle just as it had the last time Arnold was wounded. The Germans were fleeing, somehow, leaving everything behind them, their retreating backs making excellent target practice for the riflemen. Dearborn leaned over Arnold after the horse had been dragged off of him. "Are you badly wounded?" he asked. Arnold looked up at his old companion of the attack on Quebec and said, "In the same leg." He paused before continuing, "I wish it had been my heart."[40]

The Northern Army had won the greatest and one of the most consequential American victories of the entire Revolution. But that was not yet clear. At the moment Morgan wanted something simpler and more substantial than victory. When he returned to camp, Gates embraced him and said, "Morgan, you have done wonders this day! You have immortalized yourself and your country; if you are not promoted immediately, I will not serve another day!"

"For God's sake, general, forbear this stuff," Morgan said, "and give me something to eat and drink, for I am ready to die with hunger, fatigue, and exhaustion."[41]

In taking Breymann's redoubt, the Northern Army had outflanked the entire British position. The Americans had done to Burgoyne what he had dreamed of doing to them. There was now nothing Burgoyne could do other than retreat to his original position of September 21. Any hope of Clinton's arrival was now gone.

Before Burgoyne retreated, there was a hasty funeral, and Simon Fraser was buried within the "Great Redoubt," the center of the British position. American cannon, now within range, continued firing throughout the ceremony, much to the indignation of all those assembled. At 8 PM, the British began to retreat: the baggage went first, while the bridge of boats across the Hudson was broken up; then came the Germans under Riedesel, then the artillery moved out; and by 11 PM, the entire army was on the move, the dependable William Phillips commanding Fraser's "Advanced corps," which, despite the name, now protected the rear of Burgoyne's army.

By six o'clock on October 9, the Americans knew that the British were in retreat. A roving detachment of Nixon's brigade simply walked in and took possession of the earth works and hospital. When Gates heard of this he sent Dearborn forward with his light infantry and some riflemen. In the hospital they found 340 British and German wounded. Patrols Dearborn sent out to find Burgoyne discovered him only a few miles away, moving slowly north up the Hudson; Dearborn doubled the guard and waited for the rest of the army to march through the October rain to join him, and begin the pursuit of the British.[42]

On October 10, the American army caught up with Burgoyne at Saratoga on Fishkill Creek, where he had taken possession of former Northern Army commander Philip Schuyler's extensive estate on the north side of the creek's gorge. Morgan placed his corps at the center front of the line, a mile in advance of the rest of the army. From there he began to mercilessly harass the British pickets. Wilkinson recalled crossing the creek on a raft, surrounded by a deep fog, and when moving forward to investigate some gunfire, finding Morgan on the spot. "He was of the opinion, the main body of the enemy had not moved, but could not ascertain the fact," Wilkinson remembered. "[H]e knew the creek was in his rear, disliked his situation, and was desirous to change it, but was a stranger to the ground." Wilkinson, unlike Morgan, had been across the ground during the American retreat south from Fort Edward two months before and could describe the terrain to him. So Morgan, as he almost always did, sought his enemy's flank, moving around to Burgoyne's far right side. Other American brigades soon crossed the creek and fell in on Morgan's own right, and the final encirclement of Burgoyne was under way. American artillery arrived, was sited, and began an incessant bombardment of Burgoyne's position. Throughout the bombardment, "the outposts were continually engaged with those of the enemy."[43] Morgan was once again wearing down Burgoyne with a war of outposts.

Three days later, Burgoyne knew that surrender was his only option. His army was exhausted, under cannonade, under rifle fire, and had been under arms for six nights. Supplies were dwindling, and the last of his Indians and Loyalists were leaving rather than face capture. Morgan had his riflemen and light infantry engaged in nearly continual skirmishing with the opposing forces. At about 10 AM on October 14, Burgoyne sent a messenger to General Gates. After the typically polite eighteenth-century negotiation, by the evening of October 16, the two generals had agreed on articles of surrender. At ten o'clock on the morning of October 17, the defeated army marched out of its works to surrender.

Wilkinson escorted Burgoyne to Gates's tent, pitched a half mile south of Fishkill Creek. The sides of the marquee had been rolled up and a long table set for dinner. Burgoyne dismounted and was introduced by Wilkinson to his captor. Introduction was, in this case, a mere formality: in 1745, fifteen-year-old Horatio Gates had been the fifteenth man listed on the rolls of the Duke of Bolton's regiment; sixteenth on the rolls was Lieutenant John Burgoyne, five years Gates's elder. (No one looking at them would have guessed that Gates was the younger.) Major General William Phillips was another old acquaintance of Gates's; the British army was a small world. Gates in turn introduced Burgoyne to his brigade commanders and to Colonel Daniel Morgan.[44]

Whether Morgan attended the dinner Gates offered his prisoners is to be doubted. Biographer William Graham, citing the authority of not only Dr. Hill's notes but also the memories of Morgan's son-in-law Presley Neville, says he did not. This he attributes to Gates's growing hostility toward Morgan, of which "the cause was buried in the bosoms of the parties themselves." According to Graham's account, Morgan did at one point enter the dinner to conduct some necessary business with Gates. When the British officers learned who he was, they rose and took him by the hand.[45]

Whether Gates and Morgan were indeed in conflict, whether Morgan was at the table or only came in briefly to discuss business, Morgan's usefulness to Gates and the Northern Army was at an end. On the next day, October 18, he and the Provisional Rifle Corps began their march south from Saratoga to rejoin Washington and his army near Philadelphia, where they were greatly needed.[46]

⟨～ð⟩

BIOGRAPHERS are often tempted to magnify the importance of their subjects out of proportion with the historical record. Equally dangerous is the temptation to minimize a subject's contemporaries in order to amplify the subject's historical position. Such biographers seem to believe in the perennial scarcity of reputation. Because of this scarcity, every contemporary, every other actor, becomes a competitor for a limited piece of historical legacy. If Adams is to rise, Washington and Franklin must also fall. Jefferson cannot triumph without Hamilton losing, and Hamilton cannot be hip without Jefferson being out of it.

In accounts of Saratoga, biographers have crowned either Gates or Arnold as the true victor and denounced the other. This has been the generally accepted pattern of tit for tat since Benedict Arnold defected to the British army. Nor can this cycle be broken by insisting that neither Gates nor Arnold won the Battle of Saratoga, but that Daniel Morgan did.

Yet it is difficult to see how, without Morgan's contribution, the battle would have unfolded as it did. Gates meticulously prepared for a battle that did not happen as he intended. All entrenchments and fortifications, the very site he chose to defend, indicate he envisioned a second battle of Bunker Hill. He imagined that Burgoyne's army would break upon the rock of Bemis Heights, that he would win a great defensive battle. He behaved with great strategic insight, maintaining a strategic defensive, situating himself in the perfect geographic position to block Burgoyne and receive reinforcements from other Continental units and from the militias of New England.

Gates's limitation, if it was such, was to imagine he would be able to maintain a strategic and a tactical defense. He could not. Burgoyne acted differently than Gates planned, and Morgan's partisan warfare tactics, combined with his advantage-pressing personality, were more aggressive than Gates had expected.

In his way, Morgan anticipated the teachings of Air Force Colonel John Boyd, who, beginning in the 1960s, began to teach an unwilling Air Force (and a more interested United States Marine Corps) a principle he termed OODA loops: Observation-Orientation-Decision-Action. As Boyd contemplated dogfights of the Korean War, he realized that it was not always the best aircraft that won but the one with a pilot who was best able to see what was going on around him. This was observation—seeing the actual circumstances. Observation led to orientation—understanding the circumstances. Orientation led to decision and action—the capacity to make an informed decision and lead its execution.

Boyd suggested that the ideal means of action was to infiltrate and disrupt an opponent's OODA loop. To do this, one must continually confuse, startle, and baffle the enemy, such that one's actions ultimately seem confusing and unpredictable. Simultaneously, one shuts down the information being received by the enemy, leading to further disorientation.

If the enemy is expecting an attack and the attack never comes or occurs somewhere else, the commander has successfully interrupted his cycle. Through flexibility, a leader must be able to temper tactical patience with initiative to create an unrecognizable tactical tempo to the enemy and constantly operate within his OODA loop. It is hard to think of a better description of what Burgoyne experienced between the first and second battles of Saratoga.[47]

Not all of the engagements that made up the Battle of Saratoga were at Morgan's initiative. But when even drunken militiamen attack British outposts, it suggests that some of Morgan's advantage-pressing mentality had filtered into the American army. Whatever Horatio Gates's gifts as a general and leader—and it is foolish to diminish or underrate them—aggressiveness was not one of them. Arnold, of course, was aggressiveness personified, as can be seen from the attacks that led to the taking of Breymann's redoubt. While some of this activity might have been informally encouraged and even sketched out at Arnold's dinner table, it was Morgan who had day-to-day tactical contact with the British lines and who, as Wilkinson's memoir attests, was intimately familiar with the terrain and with Burgoyne's dispositions. It was Morgan—together with Henry Dearborn, John Glover, unnamed Oneida and Stockbridge leaders, and other small unit commanders, and all the men who followed them—who infiltrated and disrupted the British OODA loop.

The results of that disruption can be seen not only in the memoirs of generals but in those of a noncommissioned officer, Sergeant

Roger Lamb, then of the British 9th Regiment. Even in 1811, the defeat at Saratoga still confused and angered him. It did not seem to him, in the final analysis, that Burgoyne's army was truly beaten. Everything other than the American army, Lamb believed, had defeated Burgoyne. It was "the tide of unprosperous affairs (increased with an unforeseen torrent of events) [that] had overtaken" Burgoyne. It was "delays, disappointments in various ways, and unfortunate failures of co-operation"; that Burgoyne was in a "wilderness," and only when his army was "unprovided with means of subsistence" was he forced to surrender. The Americans' success was ultimately "providential," and their victory could only be explained by divine power working to use the weak to overthrow the strong.[48]

An unsympathetic American reader might point out to Sergeant Lamb that means of subsistence and intelligence had been purposefully interrupted, that delays and "unfortunate failures of co-operation" had been inflicted by American action, and that the "torrent of events" might well describe both battles of Saratoga and the intervening weeks of *petit guerre*. If Boyd was right in judging that creating confusion and disorder in the enemy's mind is the first condition for victory, Lamb demonstrates that confusion can persist for decades in the minds of the defeated.

Chapter Ten

THE
WASHINGTONIAN

O N THE MORNING of November 1, 1777, a mile outside New
Windsor, New York—then, as now, a sleepy town north of
West Point on the Hudson River—Morgan and his Provi-
sional Rifle Corps encountered Alexander Hamilton, who was sur-
prised to meet them. Though Hamilton was only six months in
Washington's employ, the commander in chief had dispatched him
on a politically delicate mission: inveigling reinforcements from
Gates to aid in the campaign against General Howe in Philadelphia.

After Gates's Northern Army triumphed at Saratoga in October,
Washington presumed Gates would immediately send troops south
to assist Washington's army outside Philadelphia. So far as Washington knew, reinforcements from New York were delayed. Hamilton was heading north to "lay before [Gates] the State of this Army;
and the Situation of the Enemy and to point out to him the many
happy Consequences that will accrue from an immediate reinforcement being sent from the Northern Army."[1] Since Gates had not
sent Washington any communications following the battle, Wash-

ington did not know he had dispatched Morgan to return south the day after the convention was signed with Burgoyne. Nor had Gates let the commander in chief know he was already sending three brigades to reinforce the scattering of troops around the post at West Point.[2]

"I told him," wrote Hamilton to Washington of his conversation with Morgan, "the necessity of making all the dispatch he could so as not to fatigue his men too much, which he has promised to do." Then Hamilton rode north to find what Continental troops he could to send to Philadelphia in "endeavoring to crush Mr. Howe."[3]

THE potential to "crush Mr. Howe" was tied to Howe's dependence on coordinating actions with the Royal Navy and his inability to access it while occupying Philadelphia. The power of that synergy had been on full display during summer 1777, when Howe used the fleet first to confuse Washington and then to do an end run around the barrier of New Jersey.

But living by the fleet also meant dying without it. The occupation of Philadelphia had become a potential trap for Howe's army, as it was cut off from contact and, more importantly, resupply.

Barring the might of the Royal Navy were two pitifully small forts—Fort Mifflin on the Pennsylvania shore of the Delaware River and Fort Mercer on the New Jersey side—occupied by a few hundred men of the Rhode Island Brigade and covered by a collection of glorified rowboats optimistically titled the "Pennsylvania navy." Yet this seemingly insignificant force had withstood a Hessian assault on Fort Mercer and numerous Royal Navy attempts to force its way through the river's main channel, which was blocked by underwater obstacles as well as by the few heavy guns of the Pennsylvania navy. These two forts were Washington's thumbs, placed firmly on Sir William Howe's carotid arteries. If Washington could maintain his grip, then crushing Mr. Howe was not an idle fantasy.

WHILE Gates had been defeating Burgoyne in New York, Washington had been losing to Howe in Philadelphia. After sending Morgan to Albany, Washington had marched his army south toward the northern head of Chesapeake Bay, where Howe had finally arrived with his army. A series of maneuvers culminated in a confrontation at Brandywine Creek on September 11, 1777. There, in the largest land battle of the War of Independence, Washington's army was very nearly destroyed. As he had done on Long Island, Howe distracted Washington's attention with a move to his front while taking the majority of his army in a long march around Washington's right flank, suddenly appearing about three miles behind and to his right. Only the exhaustion of the British army after a seventeen-mile march in full kit during summer heat, ferocious fighting by the outlying divisions commanded by Major Generals John Sullivan and Lord Stirling, and a quick march by Major General Nathanael Greene's division saved Washington's army from being neatly sewed up in a tactical bag.[4]

What Washington particularly wanted, at Brandywine and in the weeks that followed, were well-organized and well-led light infantry. As he marched south from Philadelphia, he established an ad hoc formation composed of select marksmen from each regiment, placed under Brigadier General William Maxwell, commander of the New Jersey Brigade. According to one of Morgan's trusted proteges, Maxwell's performance was to blame for the Brandywine defeat. William Heth, who along with Charles Porterfield had fought in Maxwell's light infantry corps, wrote to Morgan that Maxwell "has some how or another acquired a character which by no means fits him."[5] This allegation of Heth's was entirely unfair, given Maxwell's leadership during the partisan warfare in New Jersey in spring 1777.[6] The problems with the light infantry at Brandywine lay not with Maxwell but with the temporary nature of the light infantry organization in that campaign. Soldiers did not know each other, and officers did not know their soldiers or each other. And while the marksmen might have been selected, the same attention had not necessarily been given to the choice of officers.

Morgan, on the other hand, commanded a now-cohesive corps of veterans, led by officers he had chosen, who had risen along with him and were competent, intelligent, and loyal.

Washington wanted them badly. In many ways, he used Morgan's corps to make up for his deficit of cavalry, performing the duties of screening and hiding the main body of the army while scouting enemy forces. At Brandywine he had almost been destroyed for lack of knowledge of the terrain around him. At Paoli, on September 20, Anthony Wayne's Pennsylvanian regulars were almost destroyed because of poor security against attack. Going into the attack at Germantown on October 18, Washington could have benefited from the knowledge of terrain that Morgan's corps would have provided him, as well as their ability to make war on pickets and outposts.

Morgan and his corps arrived at camp in Whitemarsh, sixteen miles outside Philadelphia, on November 19. No sooner had they arrived than Washington immediately sent them back across the Delaware River. On November 16, the commander of the forces at Forts Mifflin and Mercer, Brigadier General James Varnum of Rhode Island, had decided that Fort Mifflin could not be maintained against an imminent British assault and withdrawn its garrison. A slight possibility remained that even without Fort Mifflin, the Americans could, by holding Fort Mercer, continue to block the Royal Navy and its transports from resupplying Howe's army. The successful American blockade of the Delaware meant that only small British boats traveling at night were able to make the journey, and the supplies they could transport were insufficient to meet the requirements of the British forces.[7]

Every piece of intelligence indicated that Howe's army was low on provisions of all sorts and that just another week of stopping up the Delaware might result in the destruction of Howe's army. Not only were Philadelphia beef prices rising dramatically, but when the British Guards occupied the recently abandoned Fort Mifflin, these best equipped and groomed of soldiers dug up the graves of American dead to take their shoes. British soldiers set up lotteries to see who could correctly predict the date their general would order the evacuation of Philadelphia. Desperate to press his advantage and put down any further attempt to take Fort Mercer, Washington sent Major General Nathanael Greene, his most trusted subordinate, to save the situation.[8]

NATHANAEL GREENE, like Daniel Morgan, was always lucky when it came to selecting subordinates. Not only did Morgan join him in New Jersey that autumn, but he had a pantheon of the best combat commanders in the Continental army of 1777: Muhlenberg and Brigadier General George Weedon's Virginia brigades were already in Greene's division, but Gates was sending south some of its best brigades, fresh from the victory at Saratoga. Across the Delaware, moreover, was the Rhode Island Brigade, Greene's first wartime command.[9] These elite infantry formations were supplemented by a small troop of light cavalry led by the young Virginian Harry Lee and the Marquis de Lafayette, recently recovered from his Brandywine wound and along as an observer.

With such a remarkable collection of men and officers it seemed possible to do anything. "I am to march tomorrow morning with my Brigade to Cut off the Enemys Supplies of provisions from the Shiping," wrote Brigadier General Charles Scott of Virginia to his wife. "Colo. Morgan with his lite Coar and Genl. Woodfords Brigd. marches at the same time. I make no doubt of Success and indeed of doing something very Cleaver."[10]

Yet despite this talent, and the safe crossing of his men, Greene had less cause for delight than Scott. While his men were across the Delaware at noon, a shortage of boats prevented his supply train from crossing as swiftly as his men had. At 5 PM, when he wrote to Washington, it looked as if the entire night would be "employd in getting over the greater part of the baggage and artillery." Of more concern than the supply train delay was the news that reached him in Burlington. On the night of November 20, Commodore John Hazelwood, the commander of the mosquito-sized boats of the Pennsylvania navy, had burned most of his fleet just below Philadelphia rather than allow it to fall into the hands of the British.

Then worse news arrived, removing, it seemed, the entire reason for Greene's expedition. On November 19, Varnum had evacuated Fort Mercer as well, knowing he could not maintain it against a joint bombardment by the Royal Navy and an assault by a division led by Major General Charles Lord Cornwallis, which had crossed the Delaware south of Fort Mercer and marched swiftly to the attack. Varnum burned the fort behind him and retreated with his men as far north as Mount Holly, ten miles southeast of Greene's position in Burlington. Greene's plan, in the face of these adversities, was now simply to join with Varnum and see what could be done. "I cannot promise any thing," he wrote somewhat plaintively to his commander in chief, "until I learn more of the designs of the enemy their strength and the position they are in."[11]

While Greene grappled with these strategic setbacks, Morgan was encountering the increasingly difficult problems of supply that had plagued Washington's army during summer and fall 1777. Many of his men were without shoes, and they were not hardy enough to march without them. With only 170 of his corps therefore fit for duty, Morgan nonetheless marched them toward Greene, crossing the Delaware at Bristol, Pennsylvania, while his subordinates scrambled to make deals for more shoes. Major Joseph Morris purchased some with his own funds to enable the march to proceed.[12]

Morgan joined Greene and Varnum in Mount Holly. Greene was painfully reluctant to fight Cornwallis. With Fort Mercer now gone and the Royal Navy resupplying Howe in Philadelphia, confronting Cornwallis seemed to entail a great deal of risk for very little reward. With the benefit of his old Rhode Island friend Varnum's newfound acquaintance with the lower counties of New Jersey, Greene decided he must be certain that Cornwallis did not stay on the east side of the Delaware. What was to be most feared, Greene thought, was Howe maintaining a strong presence in southern New Jersey across from Philadelphia, perhaps a permanent post at Haddonfield on the King's Highway that descended down into the lower counties of New Jersey. If he did, Haddonfield would become a market town, and from that position cover "those Counties . . . some of the most fertile in the State, from whence great Quantities of Provisions can be drawn." He determined that this must not happen and sent Morgan to reconnoiter and screen the area north of Haddonfield.[13]

Eventually Greene overcame his hesitations sufficiently enough to advance from Mount Holly to Haddonfield. When he did so he discovered that Cornwallis's force was crossing over from Gloucester City to Philadelphia, its movements protected by the guns of General Howe's fleet, its flanks protected by southern New Jersey's many tidal creeks. Lafayette scampered forward with the South Jersey Militia, a battalion of Morgan's riflemen led by Lieutenant Colonel Richard Butler and Major Joseph Morris (who when last seen had pushed on too far ahead of support at Freeman's farm), ten cavalry men, and the scrum of French volunteers the marquis always attracted. Butler was pleased with himself, having pushed back his opposite numbers in the Jaegers "and beat them on board under the fire of three ships of war."[14] Lafayette wrote to Washington that "I never saw men so merry, so spirited, so desirous to go on to the ennemy what ever forces they could have as that little party was in this little fight. I found the riflemen above even theyr reputation and the militia above all expectations I could have." But it was an inconsequential skirmish, as he himself acknowledged. Cornwallis returned almost unscathed to Philadelphia after his tour through South Jersey and the Gloucester County countryside.[15]

For Washington, Cornwallis's return to Philadelphia meant Howe could now attack a divided Continental army. Washington based this intuition not on intelligence—not yet—but on his insight and his worst-case imaginings. As soon as he had the news, he summoned Greene to return with all possible speed to the Whitemarsh encampment.

WASHINGTON'S worst-case suspicions were correct: At 11 PM on December 4, the British army marched out of Philadelphia, headed for what Howe hoped would be the final confrontation with the Continental army. Now that his men had hardtack and salt beef in their bellies, and hopefully new shoes on their feet, Howe was determined to once more go on the attack. He saw opportunity to defeat Washington using speed and secrecy: a swift march from the city that arrived suddenly at Whitemarsh and swept over the Continental army in a wave of scarlet uniforms. He would redeem Burgoyne's defeat at Saratoga and decisively conclude the Philadelphia Campaign.[16]

But Washington's network of stay-behind agents in Philadelphia had already penetrated Howe's secrecy: One or more agents reported British preparations to the temporary spymaster, Major John Clark.[17]

As the British reached Chestnut Hill at four the next morning, they heard the Continental army's alarm guns. Morning light brought the British into view of the American encampment, four miles of entrenchments along the ridge extending east from Whitemarsh church. The British set up camp on the western edge of Chestnut Hill, facing the Americans across the valley, spreading themselves out on a three-mile-long front, and Howe tried to draw Washington out.

Not surprisingly, other than sending Brigadier General James Irvine and six hundred Pennsylvania militia out for some ill-fated skirmishing (Irvine was captured, the militia easily thrown back), Washington declined Howe's offer. He was confident in his position and ready to make Howe suffer a second Bunker Hill, this time in the Pennsylvania countryside.

Careful observation persuaded Howe to try another way to skin the proverbial cat. Moving once again at night and circling around to the American left near Jenkintown, Howe hoped that Washington could once again be outflanked, as he had been twice before. Perhaps in yet another attempt to coax Washington out of his position, or as a means of securing his route against Morgan's riflemen, as they had when evacuating New Jersey in the previous June, the British burned the houses and villages they passed.

At Jenkintown, Howe detached Major General Charles Grey with a newly formed Loyalist brigade, the Queen's Rangers; the light infantry of the Guards regiments; and Hessian Jaegers. Grey was to move forward, seeking a way to shift Washington. Washington, in response, sent forward a number of soldiers to oppose Grey, including Morgan and his corps.

Unlike at Saratoga, Morgan had no Dearborn for support. Strangely enough, while Dearborn was present, he was not assigned to Morgan's command, and that would seem to indicate that Morgan did not request him. Nor did Washington provide him with support from a regular formation, instead detaching Colonel Mordecai Gist and a contingent of Maryland militia to Morgan's assistance. They had served creditably at Germantown, and they were beginning to show promise after their autumn seasoning in the field. But inexplicably and inexcusably, they had no bayonets. Morgan could not use them as he had Dearborn, to screen his vulnerable, slow-loading marksmen from a sudden charge by determined infantry. They might be good troops, but they could not be used in the tactical system Morgan had developed at Saratoga.

Morgan deployed his men in the thick woods in front of Washington's position, and they moved toward Grey's right and attacked from cover. The riflemen and militia stopped and pushed back the first companies. One British lieutenant found the firing to be more hot and destructive than any he had encountered in the war. Major John André, serving as an aide to Grey, put the British loss to about "thirty or forty men, killed or wounded." But the British light infantry and their officers knew what to do when faced with riflemen. They fixed bayonets and charged. Without properly equipped light infantry reinforcement of his own, Morgan fell back. He lost twenty-seven killed and wounded, among them Major Joseph Morris, Morgan's New Jersey rifleman, who was wounded in the head. Brought home to his wife, he lingered for a month before dying.[18]

With his skirmishers thrown back, Washington might have expected to now receive Howe's assault. But instead Howe encamped for the night. Early the next morning, much to the astonishment of everyone in either army except possibly himself, Howe ordered his troops to break camp and commence a return march to Philadelphia.

Washington had had a narrow escape, though Howe did not seem to realize it. As formidable as the front of his position was, its flanks rested on air—that is, the American line simply stopped; there was nothing to protect its ends. Had Howe attempted it, he could easily have outflanked Washington or simply marched around him and attacked from behind.

The other great weakness of the Whitemarsh encampment was its nearness to Philadelphia. Washington's spies had succeeded in penetrating Howe's security this time. But future efforts to do so might not succeed. It would be better for the army, its commander decided, to move farther from Philadelphia—but not so far that British foraging parties could range the countryside without concern of opposition. In other words, Washington needed a more defensible position no more than a day's march from Philadelphia. On December 11, he ordered the army to break camp and headed west through the valley of the Schuylkill River to find such a place.

CAMPED at Gulph Mills for a week, Washington's army celebrated the memorable Thanksgiving Day prescribed by Congress and memorialized by the meal Joseph Plumb Martin recalled as "half a gill of rice, and a table spoon full of vinegar"—an indication, if nothing else, of the total breakdown of the Commissary and Quartermaster's Departments.[19] Gulph Mills was a notch in the hills west of Philadelphia. It was, therefore, a windy, steep, miserable camp, not a place to spend the winter. The army resumed its march and, a few miles northwest, stopped in a wide, basin-like valley of woods and fields between the Schuylkill River to the north; a long, high ridge to the south; and a creek within a steep gully on the west that powered and watered a forge. That creek, and the forge, gave the area its name: Valley Forge.

The army set about erasing the valley's forests as it built log huts according to Washington's specifics. Fortunate soldiers, like Martin, were sent inland to other Pennsylvania towns on guard duty or other supporting tasks. There they did remarkably well, in both food and other supplies, for it was a relatively mild winter and had been a productive agricultural season.

Twenty-first century perceptions of Valley Forge are exaggerated or mistaken. The winter of 1777–1778 was not unusually harsh; in fact, it was one of the milder ones of the war. Nor did the hunger of the army mean there were no supplies or food to be had; there were. The reason the army went hungry so often over December and January was mismanagement by a Quartermaster's Department whose main task was organizing transport in order to bring supplies to the army.[20]

But these concerns of supply were not Morgan's. Washington still wanted to restrain British activities around Philadelphia, and he tasked Morgan with waging partisan warfare against Howe and his outposts. No sooner had Morgan arrived at Valley Forge than he and his men were sent back to Gulph and then down to Radnor. Near the Quaker meetinghouse in that village, Brigadier General James Potter of the Pennsylvania Militia was encamped with three hundred soldiers, and together Morgan and Potter were responsible for patrolling the roads of eastern Chester County.

Morgan soon moved again, this time farther south and east, to the Springfield meetinghouse. From that spot a few days earlier, Washington's spymaster, John Clark, had written his commander, "If Morgans Corps was stationed here or near this, I'd venture to keep them usefully employed."[21] Now Morgan had arrived, eager

for that employment, but uncertain of the soldiers he had been assigned. On December 23, he inspected the "selected men" attached
to him by Washington and was unimpressed. "Thay are by no
means fit for scouts," he grumbled to Washington, "being taken
promiscuously from the regts, when thay ought to have been pick'd
men, and thay all Came out without provisions which renders them
almost useless." Add to all that the fact that "thay stragle at such a
rate that if the enemy was any wais interprising thay might get two
from us, whare we would take one of them." But he was nevertheless optimistic. When some of these improvised detachments did not
immediately return, he hoped that "parhaps they have done something clever."[22]

Whatever the shortcomings of his temporary attachments, his
own men did well. They scouted and skirmished successfully around
the British lines, and Lieutenant Colonel Butler attacked a troop of
British cavalry, taking ten men and twelve horses.[23] Morgan scouted
and harassed a British foraging expedition, which had coincidentally emerged from Philadelphia at the same time he had taken command in eastern Chester County. "The enemy," he reported to
Washington, "is incampt from schuylkill to within two miles of the
white horse on chester road—I think thair prencesible view in Coming out, was to get in the hay from the islands, thay have had Nigh
a hundred waggons halling hay every day since thay have been
out—we keep Close round them." He concluded with disappointment that "thay dont offer to Come far out side of thair pequets so
that we have little Chance to take any of them."[24]

IN the meantime, as the huts were built at Valley Forge and the various camp diseases began to afflict the soldiers, officers began to
fight another battle, this one in defense of Washington's reputation.

The greatest indictment against Washington was his record of
1777. Critics of Washington in Congress and elsewhere had an interpretation of events that was something like this:

The British had come out of New Brunswick, and he had done
nothing. They had feigned a retreat to Amboy and Elizabethtown,
he had fallen for the ruse and almost lost a division of his army.
Howe had then surprised him by his movement into the Chesa-

peake, brushed past his army in Delaware, and then nearly annihilated him at Brandywine. Wayne had been surprised at Paoli; Howe had once again feinted and outfoxed Washington at the fords of the Schuylkill and taken Philadelphia. An overly elaborate plan had failed at Germantown, and the army had then failed to hold the Delaware forts. All the while, the support systems of the army—medical, commissary, quartermaster, supply of all kinds—were failing or had already failed.

In contrast, while Washington muddled along between accident and disaster, Horatio Gates and the Northern Army had been brilliantly successful, with militia first destroying the large Hessian detachment at Bennington and then a brilliantly organized force of regulars and militia capturing an entire British army. Such a comparison could lead to only one conclusion: George Washington was a military failure who ought to be replaced.

An increasing number of congressmen, if they did not already hold this view, were at least willing to consider it. John Adams had for a long time been a critic of the Continental army's generals and its other officers. Following Adams's departure to France to join the American diplomatic mission, his friends Benjamin Rush and James Lovell became strong critics of Washington and his misadventures. Within Washington's own army, some generals believed his choice of Valley Forge was yet another example of his rank amateurism: from a military point of view it made no sense to be in a place so destitute of forage, so far from sources of supply in Reading and Lancaster, and yet still so vulnerable to a sudden attack from Howe in Philadelphia. These complaints and increasing congressional mistrust of Washington's ability to lead America to victory provoked the series of incidents now known as the Conway Cabal.

The story of the Conway Cabal has often been told like this. Beginning in autumn 1777, after the failure at Germantown and news of Gates's victory at Saratoga, a group of army officers and congressmen began to plot Washington's replacement by Horatio Gates. Benjamin Rush, Samuel Adams, Thomas Mifflin, and Richard Henry Lee were the leading congressional instigators of the plot. Gates was their willing co-conspirator. To wrest control from Washington, this "cabal" first made Brigadier General Thomas Conway, an experienced Irish officer in the French army, both a major general and inspector general of the army, with authority for the training of the army as well as for its disciplinary and organizational supervision—examining regiments to see how many men were actually fit for duty, and so on. Both appointments overrode Washington's own desires. Additionally, Congress created a Board of War with the remit of supervising the actions and directions of Washington and his army. On November 27, it appointed Gates president of the Board of War. Throughout the winter, other attempts were made to usurp Washington's authority and potentially remove him from power, including a proposed invasion of Canada that would be titularly led by the Marquis de Lafayette but whose deputy commander would be Thomas Conway. Eventually, through patient resistance, Washington succeeded in outwaiting and outwitting the plotters.

Any actual conspiracy is difficult to demonstrate, almost as much as an imaginary one, and the Conway Cabal is an example of that. It was certainly not the carefully laid plot that Washington's supporters reported it to be, though it was perhaps not quite as imaginary as historians have thought it to have been over the last sixty years.[25] What is important for our purposes is that Washington's supporters thought the conspiracy was real, that Daniel Morgan thought it was real, and that he took Washington's side.

That he did has indicated to some, including his earliest biographer, James Graham, that some rift had occurred between him and Horatio Gates during the battles at Saratoga. This would seem by the evidence to be an ex post facto logical fallacy, with the following reasoning: if Morgan defended Washington, he was defending him against Gates; and if he defended him against Gates, then he must no longer have been friends with Gates; and that loss of friendship could logically only have occurred during Morgan's detachment to Saratoga. Therefore, Morgan and Gates fell out during the Saratoga Campaign, and this led Morgan to support Washington against the Conway Cabal.

These are stories that seem suspiciously as if they are crafted after the fact—possibly by members of Morgan's family, memory and desire playing their usual tricks upon family lore and legend—to explain that Morgan was on the side of the father of his country. But there are better reasons for why Morgan made the choice he did.

One is simple admiration. Late in the war, Morgan lamented to Washington that it was "my peculier fate that during the whole course of the present war I have never on any important event had the honor of serving particularly under your excellency. It is a misfortune I have ever sincearly lamented."[26] This was certainly how he felt in 1778. Morgan had come to hold Washington in an increasingly holy awe, as had so many officers. For the rest of his life, he would find any reason he could to do Washington service, either militarily or personally.

But more important were their political, social, and geographic connections as Virginians. Washington was Morgan's social superior, a possible political and economic patron—a man to whom he owed deference in the Virginia hierarchy.[27] Moreover, he was near neighbor to Washington's younger brothers, who had established themselves in the Valley, as Washington himself would have had to do had Lawrence lived. As congenial a companion as Morgan might find Gates—and he certainly did—the self-exiled Englishman lacked George Washington's prominence. Angus McDonald, Charles Mynn Thruston, and Isaac Zane Jr. had once been Morgan's patrons; now his own fortune and reputation was firmly tied to Washington's. Like Nathanael Greene, Henry Knox, and Alexander Hamilton— among many others—Morgan was now a Washingtonian. Their rise and fall was intertwined with, and dependent upon, Washington's. Before he could be the father of his country, Washington had to first be the chosen leader of its army.

BORED at Valley Forge, the skirmishing not intense enough to occupy him fully, Morgan was probably an unpleasant commander to have around. Febiger, Butler, and his other officers would have been delighted when Morgan took a furlough to return home to the Valley in middle or late January. Away until early May, Morgan witnessed neither the new training regimen instituted by Friedrich Baron von Steuben—the Prussian émigré who wrote a new manual of discipline to be followed by every regiment of the Continental army— nor the celebrations of the French alliance.

His journey home took him along precisely the same route he traveled as a youth running away from his family. But now he was the center of attention in Frederick County. He was, in the words of his old sometime-friend Isaac Zane, "a man that has so often left all that is dear to him . . . to serve his country." Morgan the vagabond, wagoner, and brawler was now Colonel Daniel Morgan, hero and Patriot. Zane, sick and unable to come into town or to Soldier's Rest, begged Morgan to come see him. They had been at times friends, occasionally at legal odds, and Zane wished to settle any misunderstanding. "Probably after thy now going," he wrote, "we may not meet again. I should like that no room for dispute should be left behind."[28]

In Winchester on furlough, Morgan met a group of men who turned out to be unlikely friends, Quakers who had refused to take the oath to the Commonwealth of Pennsylvania and who urged their fellow brethren to maintain pacifist principles. One of them, James Rutherford, was Isaac Zane's brother-in-law, and it is likely Morgan grew to know the Quakers through that connection. Their preaching of pacifism had been compounded by a strong dose of Patriot paranoia, which led to rumors that Quaker leaders were in alliance with British emissaries. Accordingly, the Quakers had been exiled to Winchester and the surrounding area as prisoners of conscience.[29]

Some of them remembered Morgan decades later, and he them. He believed they had been wrongfully imprisoned since they had no hearing or trial prior to their exile. "I recollect about 20 years since that a number of Quaker friends were sent to Winchester by Government," he wrote one of them in 1798, "for some cause which I never understood so well, not being in the Legislature, but in a Department, the employment of which afforded little time to enquire into the propriety or impropriety of your Banishment—but I well recolect you among others of the unfortunate—am sorry to observe that such misfortunes generally take place on revolutions, and often very unjustly." He might now be a Revolutionary leader and a public figure, but Morgan had a simple and forthright sense of plain dealing. Just as he did not like a rascal, a scoundrel, or a coward, so too could he not explain to himself why obviously good men should be considered traitors, rascals, or scoundrels.[30]

Certainly he was also aware, as were nearly all officers of the Continental army, of the financial and bodily sacrifice he was making in order to serve. Being home for however short a time gave him a chance to look at his fields and livestock, review his accounts payable and receivable, and make plans for the short term.

According to Graham, Morgan may have requested furlough because of chronic poor health. "The fatigues and sufferings experienced by him in the Canadian campaign, had seriously impaired a constitution, naturally very robust."[31] What Daniel Morgan needed was rest and recuperation. But after a few short months, he returned to Valley Forge and the beginning of the 1778 campaign.

Chapter Eleven

MONMOUTH

MAY at Valley Forge brought blossoming trees, chirping birds, a French alliance, a newly trained army, and a consequent surge of Washington's aggressive instincts. He was, by his taciturn standards, almost frantic to get fuller and better information about circumstances in Philadelphia. Daily he expected an attack, a last attempt by General Howe to bring some further polish to his tarnishing reputation prior to his return to England.

Consequently Morgan, like others occupying forward observational positions, received a blizzard of notes from the commander in chief and his staff and subordinates. As a further means of gaining intelligence, and to prevent the British from foraging after their winter nap, Washington sent Lafayette forward with two thousand one hundred troops to augment Morgan and the other partisan commanders keeping a close eye on the city. On May 18, 1778, Lafayette crossed the Schuylkill and encamped in and around the church crossroads on Barren Hill, about five miles west of Germantown. His chief American aide-de-camp, John Neville's son, Presley, sent missives to Morgan requesting him to report to Lafayette for consultations, to detach one of his companies of riflemen under Captain James Parr of Pennsylvania, and then to support Lafayette's movement.[1] Washington attached recently arrived Oneida Indian allies to Parr's detachment, perhaps thinking they might be an improvement on the manners of the hunting shirt men but more likely because he thought one group of savages deserved another.[2]

Lafayette's reconnaissance was a large target, too close to the British army not to tempt Howe. He might be on the verge of departing America for the last time, but Lafayette's two thousand one hundred troops were sufficient bait to reawaken the fighter who had slumbered over the winter. Planning one of his characteristically elegant flanking maneuvers, on the night of May 19, Howe pushed directly and obviously at Lafayette's position while sending a larger attachment around Lafayette's left to block him from retreating across the river.

Howe's attempt failed; Lafayette received sufficient intelligence of the British movements and melted back across the Schuylkill River, Morgan moving to assist him by blocking any attempt of Howe's to pursue Lafayette's retreat. That brief excitement ended, Morgan and his corps continued routine scouting, interrogated those moving in and out of the city, and watched and waited for British movement.

By May 30, it was clear that Sir Henry Clinton, Howe's replacement as British commander in chief in North America, would be leaving Philadelphia for good. Some forces would sail for the Caribbean to defend British islands against French attack, but the majority of the British forces would march across New Jersey. On June 18, Washington sent word to Morgan that Clinton was leaving the city and that he should send a party to scout and be ready to join up with Washington's army "at first orders."[3] First orders came later the same day: Morgan was to march to meet the main army, guarding its rear as it marched toward Coryell's Ferry on the Delaware, on an interception course with the British army.

WASHINGTON's army moved fast by any account, not only when measured against Clinton's slow and cumbersome progress. It crossed the Delaware at Coryell's Ferry—today, New Hope, Pennsylvania, and Lambertville, New Jersey—on June 22. Clinton was now thirty miles to the south, and Washington wanted to deter his progress with more than just the New Jersey Militia and the New Jersey Brigade. Early on June 23, he sent Morgan and the Provisional Rifle Corps south to link up with the New Jersey Militia commanded by Major General Philemon Dickinson. Either Morgan or Washington or both understood the lessons of Saratoga and Whitemarsh: to be effective in the field against British troops, riflemen must be supported by musket men. Dearborn's New Hampshire men were available, but Washington instead gave Morgan almost all of his Life Guards, "the two light infantry companies in the North Carolina Brigade," and "picked men," the twenty-five best marksmen of each infantry brigade led by "an active spirited officer."[4] This slapping together of soldiers from different regiments into temporary units was one of the Continental army's greatest weaknesses during the Monmouth Campaign, as it had been for Maxwell's light infantry corps during the maneuvers before Brandywine the previous autumn. Though von Steuben had drilled them to a new level of discipline that channeled and directed their experience, the unit cohesion gained by that drill and experience was now frittered away as detail after detail of "picked men" were separated from their home regiments, battalions, and companies to serve with details and under officers quite unknown to them. In the British army this was handled by detaching the flank companies of light infantry and grenadiers and combining them to form their own units, or to support other units.[5] But there were hardly any grenadier companies in the Continental army. Washington's Life Guards, chosen for their size, neatness of appearance, and fighting ability, were about the closest to the grenadier ideal. The Continental force had in June 1778 just a few purposefully created light infantry formations—like those Morgan took from the North Carolina Brigade.

Morgan's orders were easy to understand. He was, said Washington, "to take the most effectual means for gaining the enemys right flank, and giving them as much annoyance as possible in that quarter."[6] Such simple instructions, and yet so difficult to fulfill, for ever-present was that immaterial force that a future German theorist called friction. "Everything in war is very simple," Karl von Clausewitz would observe, "but the simplest thing is difficult. These difficulties accumulate and end by producing a kind of friction that is inconceivable unless one has experienced war."[7] During the Monmouth Campaign, Washington and his men provided enough proof of friction to fill several books.

Morgan attached his new additions to his corps, set the order of march, distributed his orders, and set out in pursuit of Clinton. First he headed south, leaving the main army's camp in Hopewell, New Jersey, at 3:00 AM on June 24 to begin the march in the cool of the early morning. He headed toward Trenton and the bridge leading across the Assunpink Creek to Bordentown beyond. By Morgan's standards, his progress was slow. He and his men made only twelve miles in about nine hours and by early afternoon had not reached Trenton. At first Morgan's intention was to camp that night in Trenton, but since some British troops were on the south bank of Crosswicks Creek at Bordentown, he pressed on—prodding, goading, teasing, encouraging his men, just as he had in the Maine wilderness, this time on the sandy roads of South Jersey. That night he camped along the north side of the creek above Bordentown, the British just over the water. After a brief morning rest, Morgan marched his command along the north side of the creek, paralleling the British line. Picking up speed, he was in Allentown, New Jersey, the morning of June 25, and there he made contact with the British rear guard.

After a few shots, the British moved on, and Morgan rested his men. Then, following Washington's orders, he moved around to Clinton's right flank.[8] With the three small militia battalions attached to him, he commanded about eight hundred men. He reported to Washington:

> I fell in with the enemies rear—we exchangd a few shot—no harm done—thay drew up on one side of the Creek and we on the other—I sent some parties to scarmish with them when the[y] emmediatly made off. . . . I moved my whole party after them about A mile, and then filed of[f] to thair right, I intend to gain thair right this evening if possible I am afraid I shant be able to do them much damage, thay encamp in a body so compact that it is empossible to get any advantage of them— except we ware able to beat thair rear gard which is pretty strong.[9]

Clinton, the son of an admiral, ran his army like a tight ship: "the British army was now akin to a Royal Navy ship-of-the-line, deadly and unstoppable wherever it was for a given moment, but plowing through an increasingly hostile sea."[10] More aptly, Clinton handled it not like a single ship of the line but a fleet of warships in convoy with vulnerable transports, all keeping perfect station on each other. Morgan, like the commander of a powerful and efficient frigate, was unable to attack any single ship of the line on his own or participate in the line of battle. But he could shadow a convoy, take advantage of its mistakes, and perhaps provoke others. And he could provide his own ships of the line with intelligence that could help them win a great battle. So he hovered about Clinton's flanks, doing what he could to give them "as much annoyance as possible," delay their progress, and look for an advantage.

Skirmishing was also under way in Washington's headquarters, as of June 24 still located at Hopewell. There the commander in chief held a council of war in the front room of the house where he was lodging. Eleven generals attended, and Washington began with an appreciation of the situation confronting the army. He named the numbers of the enemy, the current American forces that were in its vicinity, and Dickinson's suspicion that Clinton was moving so slowly because he wished to predicate a battle with Washington. Finally, Washington posed a question to his assembled subordinates: "What precise line of conduct will it be best for us to pursue?"

They arrived at no consensus. On one side was General Charles Lee, whom Lafayette remembered saying he would "erect a bridge of gold for the enemy" to assist them to get into New York rather than risk the Continental army in battle. Lee's position seems to have swayed the council, who agreed that the British should not be attacked—a position that, Alexander Hamilton sneered, "would have done honor to the most honorable society of midwives, and them only."[11]

More creative generals quickly reasserted themselves, first among them Nathanael Greene. He wanted to hit the enemy hard because he did not want the American army to impotently allow the British to pass through New Jersey. "People expect something from us and our strength demands it," he wrote. "I am by no means for rash measures but we must preserve our reputation."[12] Greene was one of the few generals in either army "who understood that wars are not won by battles alone; popular morale and political support are critical as well." Fortunately, Washington himself shared this insight, though he was one of the few who did.

The complete story of Monmouth is too complex to be told here, but soon preparations for a major attack by part of the army on the rear guard of the British were under way. It was commanded by Charles Lee, by seniority second only to Washington. Composed of four thousand five hundred men, "it was large enough to hurt an isolated or careless component of Clinton's army or to fight its way out of trouble if the British came after it in force." But it was also a compromised force, commanded by a man who opposed the attack, directed by unclear orders and poor staff work, fought by a collection of ad hoc formations in which men and officers were often unknown to each other. These factors, combined with the oppressive heat that killed men and horses as they walked, placed immense friction on the Continental army, all without reckoning up any of the capabilities of their skilled and ready opponents.[13]

MORGAN'S greatest contribution to the Battle of Monmouth came not on June 28 but on June 27, "an especially active day" for skirmishing as Lee's force and the rest of the army closed in on the rear of Clinton's army.[14] The British had been continually harassed since Allentown—not too coincidentally, from the moment Morgan and his corps had joined the fight. Skirmishing on June 26 and 27 was intense. The British camped in and around Monmouth Courthouse, and Morgan kept them under constant observation. Militia continued to press the western edges of the British encampment; one German officer reported that nearly all the pickets came under fire some time that day, though his patrol could find none of the attackers. Foraging parties were disrupted and sent back empty-handed. Morgan was calling plays from the book he had prepared at Saratoga.

The one recorded engagement that day was when some of Morgan's men—riflemen, militia, and Life Guards—snapped up a cluster of British grenadiers washing laundry in a brook south of the courthouse. When the prisoners were brought before Morgan, he was convulsed with laughter, not at the prisoners caught with their guard down but at Life Guards whose lovely uniforms were covered with the mud and slime of a Jersey creek. Morgan liked order, discipline, fancy clothes, and neatness better than most officers in the Continental army, but it seems to have pleased him to see the "toy soldiers" of Washington's guard doing some real soldiering.[15]

Dr. Hill recorded Morgan's account of another curious event that occurred on June 26. That night, a Loyalist spy calling himself Smith—perhaps not the most original of pseudonyms—entered Morgan's camp and attempted to persuade him that some of the British baggage train was weakly protected and could easily be captured. As Morgan told it to Hill, he thought for a moment and then said, "Look at me sir!" As he did, he "saw the man's eye fall and his countenance change." Convinced now that this was a spy, he then carefully concealed his suspicion, slapped him on the shoulder, and said, "Well, my good friend, I am 1,000 times obliged to you for your valuable information. I have to request, however, that you will be my guide to the enemy's baggage." Morgan set their rendezvous time as four o'clock the morning of June 27. Smith returned to the British and told them that Morgan would be attacking sometime after 4 AM. As soldiers waited in ambush for him, Morgan used the opportunity to attack a British party at a mill about a mile from where the ambush waited. "He soon silenced the troops at the mill, took them all prisoners, and marched them off without loss or difficulty." Believing that Smith had been a Patriot double agent the entire time, the British hung him from the nearest tree.[16]

In addition to prisoners and spies, civilians fleeing the British army also came into Morgan's camp. Fearing the return of those troops who had ravaged and raped New Jersey in winter 1776 and 1777, they had fled into the thick woods in summer 1778 and, in one way or another, made their way to Morgan. It is unclear how many civilians he protected, how he fed them, or the extent to which they slowed execution of his orders. For a few days before and after the battle, he seems to have moved with less than his usual speed. This was due in part to the oppressive heat—all of those days saw temperatures above one hundred degrees Fahrenheit—as well as the need to maintain contact with British pickets. But it is interesting to speculate that some of his slowness and hesitation might also have occurred because he had a mobile refugee village following him around the countryside.

On the evening of June 27, the presence of that insidious, and lethal, friction that made simple things difficult for the Continentals became more obvious. Morgan's troops were now at Richmond Mills, south and east of the British encampment at Monmouth Courthouse. General Charles Lee required their support for his attack on the morning of June 28.

He sent a series of messengers to bring Morgan into the fight, but they had to find him first. Numerous indications in the messages and dispatches flying along the sandy roads in the two days prior to the battle suggest that no one quite knew where Morgan was at any given hour. Alexander Hamilton, writing to Brigadier General Charles Scott, whose orders mirrored Morgan's, requested that should Scott stumble upon Morgan in the course of his own harassment of Clinton's army, "let him be desired again to keep close to the enemy and attack when we attack." He added, "You will endeavour to keep up a communication of intelligence."[17] Morgan was, as it happens, exactly where Washington's orders directed him to be; but he was not easy to locate. Nor was he keeping up that communication of intelligence, the principal benefit he could provide to his commander in chief.

Two couriers arrived from Washington, one directly in response to a message from Morgan and one indirectly via Lee. While the message does not survive, a dragoon sent by Morgan sometime after midnight on June 28 suggested that Morgan and his forces make a daylight attack. Washington thought this risky and responded with a note by the same rider. "Your Corps is out of supporting distance," he admonished Morgan, and "I would have you confine yourself to observing the motions of the enemy . . . and by no means to come to engagement with your whole body unless you're tempted by some very evident advantage."[18] Washington then dictated another order to Lee, instructing him to send out a "party of observation," and then another dispatch to Morgan, ordering him to hinder the enemy from escaping in the middle of the night or early in the morning. Washington sent the dispatches forward to Lee, instructing that Morgan's orders be forwarded to him, wherever he should be.

At about two o'clock on the steamy-hot morning of June 28, Lee sent a courier out to find Morgan, which he did at Richmond Mills about an hour later. This letter quickly became, and remains, the source of much controversy and confusion. It seems to have confused Morgan when he received it. The letter no longer exists, but in a dispatch that Morgan drafted on June 29, he referred to a message he had received from Lee "Yesterday" that was written at one o'clock in the "evening." So either Morgan did not read the dispatch properly, or Lee's staff committed a kind of clerical error. Certainly Morgan knew he was to attack, but he seems to have thought he was to attack on the morning of June 29.

As the battle began the morning of June 28, Morgan heard the increasing noise of the volleys of musketry and the crescendo of cannons, and he began to wonder what exactly he should be doing about it. Before noon he sent a dragoon with a dispatch to Lee. Coming onto the developing battlefield, the dragoon looked for Lee and found General Anthony Wayne, who was at that moment directing the withdrawal of his brigade in the face of an aggressive British counterattack. Asked for orders, Wayne said the rider could see for himself how well things were going. That, of course, was not information Morgan could use, nor was it a positive order. Worse still, Wayne did not direct the dragoon on to Lee.

As a result, Morgan and his corps were completely sidelined in the Battle of Monmouth, with one exception: Captain Josiah Huddy, an artillery captain of the Monmouth County Militia, perhaps impatient at Morgan's inactivity, took fifteen men and attacked the baggage train of the British army six miles east of Monmouth Courthouse. Baggage train guards ably resisted this small force, repelling its seemingly suicidal bayonet charge with volleys that ultimately killed two of Huddy's men. But by the time Huddy retreated, he had some horses and had overturned two or three wagons. More importantly, he created confusion and panic up and down the British baggage train.[19]

WHEN Morgan learned what had happened around Monmouth Courthouse the day before—that the Continental army had, after an unsuccessful attack, successfully repulsed several British counterattacks—he sent his congratulations to Washington. "They have, from every account, had a severe flogging," he wrote, which was a provocative metaphor, considering his personal history. He continued, "if I had had notice of their situation, to have fallen upon them, we could have taken most of them, I think. We are all very unhappy that we did not share in the glory."

It is hard in retrospect not to blame Morgan for this failure to have attacked the British army, even if Washington did not do so. (And he was certainly never afraid to reprimand subordinates who displeased him, either in the army or on the farm.) Morgan's absence during the battle seems to be the Revolutionary version of General Jeb Stuart's infamous ride around the Union army prior to Gettysburg: trusted subordinate and able partisan warrior, depended on for constant intelligence and intelligent independent action, suddenly disappears without a trace. When most needed he is unavailable. It raises questions of just how useful Morgan would have been at Brandywine and Germantown had he been with Washington rather than Gates at Saratoga.

It is also hard to understand why, and how, an advantage-pressing fighter would hesitate to involve himself in battle. In the week leading up to Monmouth, Morgan had been in near-constant contact with the British army. Surely he must have seen what was under way on that scorching day? Could he not have deployed his hard-won partisan skills and intervened in some way, in some aspect of the battle? His failure seems all the more visible given the brief and unlimited success of Captain Huddy's New Jersey militia against the baggage train. (Militia! What must Washington have said when he heard that.) If with fifteen or sixteen men Huddy had been able to do so much, and more importantly create so much confusion, what might Morgan have done with six hundred?

His inaction at Monmouth might suggest that Morgan lacked the confidence to operate independently. The lack of specific orders and the absence of fallback contingency plans might have been a problem of divided command or of poor staff work. But despite the manifest shortcomings of both, something else seems to have been going on. After Monmouth, Morgan pursued Clinton's rear guard, hemmed them in with small parties, and engaged in a sharp skirmish on July 1. But by that date, the vanguard of the British army was already marching up Sandy Hook, the long sandy peninsula that frames the outer bay of New York harbor. From there the British boarded transports for the twelve-mile trip to Manhattan. The fox had returned safely to its den. Washington and the main army felt they had gained something of a victory. Morgan did not.[20]

PART THREE

Victory

Chapter Twelve

HONOR

I N textbooks and many history books, Clinton's retreat into New York after Monmouth began a period of boredom and inactivity that lasted until the swift march south to the siege of Yorktown in September 1781, an eighteenth-century phony war. Yet this was not how it seemed to those American soldiers who for three years maintained a loose cordon around New York City. For them it was like war usually is for those who experience it from within—long periods of boredom punctuated by days of terror.

Considering this period an interlude of unrelieved tedium during the War of Independence would seem impossible to Washington and indeed to Morgan, for it was impossible that an enemy with so many advantages would continually fail to use them in offensives directed at the Continental army. But while the British took many nips, nibbles, and even bite-size pieces of the Americans over the next three years, they never delivered the mauling that Americans continually anticipated.

The first episode of terror—or at least extraordinary anticipation of it—began mere days after Clinton took refuge in New York City. A French fleet arrived off the coast of New York on July 11, just after Royal Navy transports carried the British army to safety in New York's inner harbor. After a tense face-off, with an inferior British fleet blocking passage through the bar that shielded New York's outer harbor, the French fleet departed north for easier prey.

The French fleet's arrival in July inspired Washington. He quickly began preparations for a land-sea assault on New York City that he intended to make after the British fleet had been destroyed. As part of the preparation for the attack, most of the Continental army moved across the Hudson River to White Plains in Westchester County, and in the process Morgan was separated from his riflemen. Instead of leading his corps, Washington appointed him to take temporary charge of Brigadier William Woodford's Virginia brigade after Woodford took sick. Morgan led his new brigade to White Plains, leaving the Provisional Rifle Corps on the New Jersey side of the Hudson. Though separated from them, he retained command not only of the corps but also of the 11th Virginia Regiment. (If visualizing these command machinations is confusing, imagine what the paperwork must have been like.) In late September, when Sir Henry Clinton probed out from New York along either side of the Hudson, Morgan and his brigade, under the command of Lord Stirling's division, returned to New Jersey as part of a force designed to oppose a force led by Lord Cornwallis. After Cornwallis withdrew to New York City, Morgan's brigade was stationed in Newark.

Both before and after the September incursions, the British were in a state of continual preparation, apparently for some larger campaign. Washington assumed this would be directed against the forts in the Hudson Highlands, focused on the developing fortress at West Point. As part of the preparations for resisting any British attack, Morgan's brigade, together with many others, was put to work building or improving roads and fortifications, and Morgan was further tasked with securing intelligence and engaging in reconnaissance of the British advance posts.

By November 1, it seemed clear to Washington and all his subordinate commanders that the British were about to attack—from movements of the British army and reports coming from within the city. As part of Washington's defensive preparations, Morgan moved from Newark to defend the Clove through the Hudson Highlands.

But this expectation was, ultimately, disappointed. In December, once that previous set of fears had subsided and Morgan had marched his brigade back into New Jersey, it seemed Clinton would finally attack. On December 3, 1778, just as Burgoyne's captured army was being ferried from across the Hudson toward prisoner of war camps in the Virginia Piedmont, Clinton headed north out of New York City along the Hudson in considerable strength, aiming for the convoy of British and German prisoners. The entire army, including Morgan's brigade, marched toward the Hudson Highlands, anticipating a climactic confrontation with the British army. But long before they arrived, Clinton had contented himself with burning three log cabins and several barrels of spoiled herring at King's Ferry—Stony Point on the Hudson's western bank and Verplanck's Point on its eastern bank—and then returning to New York City.

Given Clinton's relative inaction, Morgan's most rigorous conflicts in late 1778 involved navigating overwhelming administrative detail—a daunting challenge for a man who, fourteen years before, signed a contract with his mark but was suddenly tasked with managing a medium-sized business, which is what a brigade of eight hundred to one thousand two hundred men was. But Morgan was up to the challenge. His papers and those of his commanders are full of his reports regarding food, equipment, the passing on of general orders, and musters.

In this he was no doubt helped by a small but competent staff. It is an overlooked fact of his life as an army commander that he was able to attract to him literate and clever staff officers who compensated for his lack of formal education. To be sure, some must have been more of a burden than a support. These were European officers who, wanting to see the hunting-shirt men for themselves and to observe firsthand the curious methods of *les sauvages de l'Amerique*, attached themselves to Morgan's rifle corps or to himself. At Saratoga he had been accompanied by Denis-Jean-Florimond Langlois de Mautheville, chevalier Du Bouchet, who not only had a name longer than the Marquis de Lafayette's but was the brother-in-law of the troublesome Brigadier General Thomas Conway. He was also accompanied by Gilles de Kermorvan, most recently a lieutenant colonel in the Turkish army who departed the

American army when he was refused the rank of brigadier general. (Du Bouchet was a better investment than Kermorvan, returning to America after a spell in a British prison ship as one of the Comte du Rochambeau's aides, helping to manage the French army that arrived in 1780.) And at Cowpens, Morgan had the dubious services of the Baron Glaubeck, whom he mentioned favorably in his dispatches to Greene, Washington, and Congress, and who returned the favor by running up bills of $1,000 against Nathanael Greene's credit. (Congress pondered repaying Greene's estate for the fraud until 1795.)[1]

But others offered real assistance. Christian Febiger, for example, was administratively competent in Danish, French, and English. His last recorded service as an officer involved sorting out supply problems in Virginia for Greene's Southern Army following the surrender at Yorktown. During his tour in the Carolinas, Morgan benefited from the assistance of two veteran officers of the Maryland line, Major Edward Giles and Captain Benjamin Brookes. Giles and Brookes were members of what he, like Washington, Greene, and other general officers, referred to as family. Brigadier generals had two aides: an aide-de-camp and a brigade major (in effect, a chief of staff). As Woodford's substitute leading the Virginia brigade, Morgan had access to administrative help that polished his spelling and grammar, making it easier for him to bring his instinctive leadership to bear on the brigade.[2]

For Morgan, the problem of enlistments trumped even the challenge of his new administrative responsibilities. By winter 1778–1779, large numbers of Virginia troops had reached the end of their service terms and, despite offers of land, had no intention of remaining. Though he had a special rapport with enlisted men, Morgan was unable to persuade them to remain with the army.[3] The end result was that Virginia's complement of regiments, as well as those of other states, had to be shrunk from their theoretical high point in spring 1777. The 11th Virginia was struck from the books, and Morgan was made commander of a reorganized successor, the 7th Virginia.

By this time—late autumn 1778—the life of the Provisional Rifle Corps had come to a final end. Following Monmouth, Washington began to dispatch companies from Morgan's corps to the frontiers of Pennsylvania, northern New Jersey, and New York, all open to raids from the Six Nations of the Iroquois Confederacy. Eventually there were no more companies of riflemen left to constitute Morgan's corps. By the end of August 1778, the fine instrument that Morgan had used so effectively in New Jersey, Saratoga, and Pennsylvania was no more.[4]

It is a common modern conceit that the rifle won American independence; or that the rifle could have done so quicker if only employed more often. This has more to do with twenty-first-century views of technology and cleverness than it does with the reality of the American Revolution. Because we now use rifles, contemporaries of Morgan's like George Washington, Anthony Wayne, or John Burgoyne who valued muskets and bayonets are seen as hidebound reactionaries who did not understand the revolutionary promise of technology. It is a curiosity of our time that we believe technology to be one of the most important ingredients for success—or that the failure to rapidly adopt new technology shows an almost moral failing.[5]

Technologies are not devices but systems. The rifled barrel was just one part of a system that took decades to finally come of age and arguably did not do so in full until the invention of highly energetic propellants that increased rifle bullet velocity and made their firing "smokeless." Without that innovation—and without breech loading—the rifle had considerable drawbacks. Oftentimes those who declined to adopt technology experienced and understood drawbacks that we now do not.

Moreover, no technological system is useful without a culture that understands it and knows how to best use it. On the narrow point of military culture, this is what military professionals mean by *doctrine*.[6] For example, inventing an amphibious tank or a landing craft did not mean that the skill to use it automatically existed once it was procured by the US Marines. It had to be tested, trained with, and used again and again, until its limitations and benefits were understood and internalized. The result of this was amphibious warfare doctrine. Likewise the first attempts to use tanks, in the Battle of the Somme in 1916, trusted solely in the technological prowess of the new armored vehicles. It was not until 1917 and 1918, after further testing and employment, that armored doctrine began to emerge, and it took decades to refine and improve.

Morgan lacked the formal concepts of doctrine and training as part of his mental equipment. But through a synthesis of instinct and experience he in effect developed one. His genius as a commander of riflemen was to understand the limitations and the benefits of the flintlock rifle and work with them. He had used spontoons successfully in the attack on Quebec city, and it is not surprising that he requested them again during the spring and summer 1777 campaign in New Jersey. The breakthrough came when he joined a relatively small number of musket men with a mass of riflemen at Saratoga. This made a decisive tactical difference, as can be seen in the very different results he achieved first at Freeman's farm and then three weeks later in the fight to push the British away from their reconnaissance in force and in taking Breymann's redoubt. Without support of the rapid-firing, bayonet-wielding muskets, rifles were almost always of limited use on the eighteenth-century battlefield when employed in isolation. Morgan would demonstrate at Cowpens that he had not forgotten that lesson: rifles and muskets in an integrated and mutually supporting formation could prevail against a conventionally armed one.

When the Provisional Rifle Corps was dissolved, the Continental army lost not the use of the rifle but the cultural institution of Morgan's rangers—the doctrine, however informal, of massed rifles on the battlefield, working as sharpshooters as needed—supported by muskets and bayonets that could defend them, or even act as an assault force depending on tactical necessity. It was the unit using the technology that made the difference, not the technology in the hand of one or two or even fifty trained individuals. Morgan's brilliance as a tactical commander was his ability to fuse a disparate group of riflemen and musket men from different units and then use them as one weapon. The American army deployed no unit quite like it on the battlefield until the twentieth century.[7]

By June 1779, Morgan had fixed his determined and ambitious eyes on another command possibility, one that also promised advancement in rank and authority.

Washington had decided to create an effective light infantry arm of the Continental army. As part of the reorganization of the army, each regiment had created a light infantry company as part of its formation. Washington determined—in line with British practice during the War of Independence—to detach the light infantry companies from their parent formations during the summer (or any campaign period) and group them into a corps of light infantry. This new unit would succeed the Provisional Rifle Corps and would be composed of young men, healthy, strong, trained in the bayonet, and with at least two years of service. They were precisely the kind of unit Morgan was best suited to lead, by virtue of inclination and experience.[8]

But there were other factors to be considered rather than accomplishments and capabilities. Brigadier General Anthony Wayne of Pennsylvania had just been involuntarily replaced as commander of the Pennsylvania line by his fellow Pennsylvanian, Major General Arthur St. Clair, his superior in rank and inferior in combat. Each cordially despised the other, but since St. Clair outranked Wayne, the command was his for the asking. Smarting from what he regarded as a personal humiliation, Wayne sought command of the Corps of Light Infantry as a balm to his wounds and let it be known that he would resign if he did not attain it.

So far as Morgan was concerned, Wayne was very welcome to resign, and the faster the better. Wayne was pugnacious, but his pugnacity was rarely combined with good judgment. He had judged, for example, that harassing the British army during the Philadelphia Campaign meant camping just two miles away from it. As a result his brigade was savaged by a bayonet attack so severe that it was called the Paoli massacre and Wayne was court-martialed for dereliction of duty. (He was acquitted, probably wrongly, but that shame lingered as well.) Wayne might have gained back some respect for his behavior at Monmouth Courthouse, but how could his record possibly compare to Morgan's? The now-famous march to Boston, the even more epochal march through the Maine woods, the assault on Quebec city, and all his service of 1777 and 1778, particularly at Saratoga. Daniel Morgan would not have been caught sleeping at Paoli.[9]

But while Morgan possessed experience, he lacked rank. The new command would be equivalent to a brigade in size, requiring the command of a brigadier general. Morgan was a colonel, but there was no chance he could be promoted into the position. Washington was loathe to give any indication of favoritism toward officers from his native state (though favoritism was suspected no matter his actions). So promotion was based strictly on seniority, by state. Promotion was further complicated by the rise and fall of enlistments, a matter that dogged Morgan in his role as interim commander of Woodford's Virginia brigade. If the number of regiments in, say, Virginia's complement of regiments shrunk, not only was there less need for colonels commanding the regiments but there was less need for other lower-ranking officers as well. Those officers allowed to remain serving in the regiments or in command were those who had seniority—not necessarily those with skill, intelligence, charisma, or simple common sense. Moreover, even if by some miracle Morgan was promoted, Wayne's commission predated his. So whatever Morgan might want, the Light Infantry Corps command was Wayne's for the asking.

The inability to get the command that seemed rightfully his deeply outraged Morgan. But it is significant, for those seeking to understand his personality, that he kept his anger to himself. He wrote his friend Dolphin Drew in Winchester that he was determined to resign if he was not given command of the corps. But, he said, he would not share his resolution with fellow officers because he did not choose to fuel their growing discontents—an act of a man who had truly become a Washingtonian.

On June 30, 1779, Morgan learned that Wayne had been promoted to what he believed was his natural place. It was, perhaps, even more galling because Richard Butler, his protege, his subordinate in New Jersey and at Saratoga, one of the preeminent members of his nursery of officers, was appointed Wayne's second in command. That very day, Morgan requested from Washington, apparently in person, a pass to travel to Philadelphia and tender to Congress his resignation from the Continental army. Washington gave him the following letter:

To the President of Congress:

Sir: Col. Morgan, of the Virginia line, who waits on Congress with his resignation, will have the honor of delivering you this. I cannot, in justice, avoid mentioning him as a very valuable officer, who has rendered a series of important services, and distinguished himself on several occasions. I have the honor to be With the greatest respect & esteem Yr Excellency's Most Obedt ser.[10]

That was all Washington had to say publicly. It seems outrageous that he would so coldly dismiss one of his leading combat soldiers. Washington was indeed furious with Morgan. A year later, when Congressman Joseph Jones inquired about the possibility of promoting Morgan to brigadier general, the commander in chief made it fairly clear that he did not approve of Morgan's being promoted. Morgan, Washington wrote, was "a brave Officer, and a well meaning man, but his withdrawing from Service at the time he did last year, could not be justified on any ground—there was not, to my knowledge, the smallest cause for dissatisfaction—and the season and circumstances were totally opposed to the measure, even if cause had existed, till matters assumed a different aspect than they were at the time of his preffered resignation."[11] What Washington meant, of course, was that Morgan should not have been dissatisfied with a superior officer getting a command to which he was entitled.

Richard Meade, who took Washington's dictation for the letter and included a personal note from himself to Morgan in the same envelope, told Morgan that their commander's letter was "concise, but in justice to your merit makes handsome mention of your services." But it is hard for anyone—not least an ardently devoted Washingtonian and a trusted aide—to see the carefully equivocated sentence as a "handsome mention." Meade was doing what he could to play the peacemaker and cajole Morgan to remain, concluding his note wistfully: "It were much to be wished that you could have reconciled a longer continuance in the service."[12]

But Morgan would not. He was done, and he left camp and rode to Philadelphia. He had to wait a bit, until his letter of resignation was read along with Washington's on Monday, July 19. Morgan's was dated July 18, but writing it could not have been quick work for him, given the difficulty that writing remained.

In it he first describes his service in the Maine woods and at Quebec, proudly saying that "I cheerfully obayed every order I recd—I with pleasure underwent every hardship, not doubting but my faithfulness would recommend me to my country, and my merits meet with thare just reward." (How many of those who began that expedition could not say that?) At Saratoga, he says of his rifle corps and its performance that "during the time I commanded that corps I often attact the enemy with success I at all time lay close round them, I never was surprised or lost any troops through negligence or inattention" (a pointed reference to Wayne's negligence at Paoli).

"As it is generally known that I commanded the light troops of our army and that this command is now taken from me, it will Naturally be judged that this chang of officers has taken place either on account of some misconduct in me, or on account of my want of capacity—I cannot therefore but feel deeply effected with this injury done my reputation, by reduceing me from a respectable station in the army, which I believe None will say I did Not fill with propriety."[13] Not being appointed to command the Corps of Light Infantry was, given Morgan's long public record of exemplary service, an imputation of some hidden fault on his part. Since no fault existed so far as Morgan was concerned, his being overlooked for the position was an injury to his honor. Therefore, that same honor required him to resign from the army.

HONOR SOCIETIES are shame societies. Whether the world of Homer's *Iliad*, an open-air drug market on a street corner, or a typical suburban high school, a shame-based society does not value the interior lives of its members. If you are a member of such a society, then whether you might know yourself not to be a coward is of no interest to anyone else; what matters is whether you are perceived as a coward. What and who you are is external and performed, not interior and concealed. A medieval knight's coat of arms was not simply an indication of his lineage, it was a statement of his personality.

Honor societies are also hierarchical societies. Admiral Horatio Nelson is often quoted as saying, "Aft the most honor, forward the better man!" Less frequently quoted is the rest of the sentence, which makes clear that Nelson quoted a common sailor's phrase in order to dismiss it as an "erroneous principle." This offends egalitarian sensibilities, but it would be more surprising if Nelson had not thought this. From his perspective, the lower one's position in a hierarchical society, the less honor one could have, and the more inferior a human one was. Thersites, the ugly, clamoring foot soldier—the only common soldier to appear in the *Iliad*—is a vulgar member of the herd who says what he thinks without thinking about it and who cries when beaten by Odysseus for his impudence. He is quite literally shameless; and because he has no shame, he can possess no honor.

In ways that are difficult for us to understand, the American Revolutionary world was in certain ways closer to Homer's world than to our own. Jacksonian democracy leveled the political distinctions that had formed some of the lower tiers of the hierarchical pyramid in the eighteenth century. Simultaneously, evangelical Christianity popularized the interiority of identity and replaced shame with guilt more effectively than any previous religious or intellectual movement. In a roundabout way, the self-identification of American southerners as members of an honor culture did further damage to the concepts of honor and shame. A New Englander in 1750 could have subscribed to the concept of honor, at least as a hypothetical. His descendants in 1850 saw honor and dueling, and all the other apparatuses for the distinction and preservation of honor, as the pretensions to nobility of a corrupt southern slaveocracy or of an equally decadent European aristocracy. Hence Nathaniel Hawthorne set his story of shame and honor, "My Kinsman, Major Molineux," in the eighteenth century, an excavation into a dark New England past that haunted the transcendental present.[14]

Hawthorne's story was not Morgan's past but his insistent present. For a man so recently and laboriously self-fashioned as Daniel Morgan—or Nathanael Greene, or Henry Knox, or John Sullivan, or even George Washington—the system of honor was what preserved their new positions in the hierarchical pyramid. Having reached their eminence, they were bound to maintain themselves atop it by meeting with all the resources and powers at their command any attempt to shame or deprive them of position—even if that required resisting a beloved commander in chief or the Congress of the United States.

In hopes that officers of the Continental army would put aside their political honor for the greater good, let alone his fantasy of Congress yearly electing generals, John Adams was—at least at that moment—as unrealistic and naive about human nature as his friend Thomas Jefferson.[15] Since Congress could not bestow money on its generals, having none to give, all Congress could reward them with was the status of rank and a guarantee of future property. Having honored a general with the status, revoking it was akin to demanding that an executive return a year's worth of wages since business had not gone as well over that year as projected. The most that Morgan had as a general was the status of rank, a symbol of the approval of the nation. In such a small society, built around status, it was natural that "anxiety over rank and other kinds of public recognition [would be] severe.[16]

But Morgan was also—perhaps more than any of his colleagues—just as sensitive to his financial position as he was to the status and honor of his rank. Nathanael Greene could return to the family business in Rhode Island. Henry Knox had married an heiress, and perhaps their fortune would be intact at the end of the Revolution. Washington, whatever damage might befall Mount Vernon in his absence, had thousands and thousands of acres of equity behind him. Others had some prewar political or social position to fall back on. Morgan alone among them had begun the war as a yeoman farmer, a small slaveholder, dependent on the yearly production of his land. He had nothing to fall back on, no family, not too much property, no great local position, and now he did not even have his body—those days of grubbing stumps from fields were now long gone, the Maine woods and the hardship in Quebec had seen to that. What pay he received was inadequate to support his family and maintain himself the way a gentleman should in the capacity of a commander of a regiment or brigade.

Many officers in the Continental army felt similarly, and as undemocratic as it might seem to us now, they considered themselves to have a much harder time of it than enlisted men or noncommissioned officers. Many of the enlisted man of 1779 had been landless laborers, penniless immigrants, or homeless boys, much as Morgan had been when he arrived in Winchester twenty-five years before. Having the occasional meal in a smoky hut might be considered something of an improvement on their previous circumstances. But gentlemen like Morgan not only suffered personal privations, they did so at the further expense of their family's well being. Eventually many had to choose between the needs of their most personal community and those of the national community.

After all, before the founding fathers founded anything they were fathers. Their greatest status and economic power came from how they developed and superintended their families. That category included not just wife, children, and house but servants, enslaved people, animals, land, and all that was under their stewardship. In the honor culture of the eighteenth-century Virginia gentry, one could not be a successful and honored founder if one was a failed father. Revolutionary leaders were, therefore, often absent from their public duties, to a degree that is sometimes surprising to those who hold them up as models of tireless public servants. They, however, did not think they could be public servants if they did not first engage in service to their families.[17]

So Morgan rode home, again along the route he had probably walked, west from Philadelphia to Lancaster, Carlisle, and then down the Great Valley, across the Potomac, and into the Shenandoah. He was beset not only by the haunting concerns of honor, wealth, and status but by great bodily pain. It is worth considering, in a systematic way, what Morgan's body had endured in just over forty years of life.

He had aches and pains all over. He had scars across his back and on his face, and who knows where else. His back hurt nearly all the time. Occasionally he also complained about pains in his chest. At least one of his digits had been poorly set after breaking, and one can only suspect that others were as well. For thirty years he had been damaging his musculoskeletal structure up to and beyond the point of failure. Now his body could no longer recover as it once had. By frontier standards and the state of medical care, his body was old.

Despite his injuries and chronic pain, his life and the lives of all who depended on him required his farm to be improved. This he began to do in fall 1779. His financial circumstances, though pressing, may not have been dire, since it is likely during this interlude that he began initial work on the farmhouse-mansion he eventually christened Saratoga.

During winter or spring 1780, Morgan began to visit Horatio Gates at his home in Berkeley County. As Don Higginbotham observes, "if he had believed him hostile to Washington in the winter of 1777–1778, Morgan harbored no ill will toward him now."[18] They visited together, swapped stories, and no doubt drank a fair amount of rum. It was probably not because of the influence of the rum that Morgan advocated that Gates take command in the south if it was offered to him.

THE American Revolution in the American South—that is, in Maryland and Virginia, down through the Carolinas and Georgia, and into what was then East and West Florida—had been going on for just as long as the Revolution in the North, dating from Lord Dunmore's seizure of gunpowder from the armory in Williamsburg, a more successful attempt to seize military stores than occurred at Concord, Massachusetts. There were lulls and periods of inactivity in the south, but the same could be said of New England or any of the other states with the exception of New Jersey and New York.

What gave the war a slightly different character in the South, from its origins, was the open armed conflict between districts, neighborhoods, neighbors, and families. The North was not free of such troubles, though local and national histories often ignore the unsightly factional cracks that existed even in places seemingly so revolutionary as Pennsylvania, Delaware, Maryland, and New Jersey. Nevertheless, the fighting that characterized all eight years of the southern War of Independence was particularly bloody and personal. All visitors saw it; most residents felt it themselves, even though they rarely had any standard of comparison.

The campaigns in South Carolina and North Carolina during the early years of the war were rebellions against rebel governments, as Loyalist militia attempted to resist or overthrow the new Patriot governments. These attempts were successfully suppressed, some-times—and here is a particular southern wrinkle to the American Revolution—by men who would, in five years, have changed from Patriots to Loyalists, from Loyalists to Patriots, or from neutrals to either.

From the beginning of the war, British strategists attempted to secure some advantage or foothold in the American South, starting in 1776 with seaborne attempts at landing in the Cape Fear region or Charleston Harbor. In the last days of 1778, a large force from New York City seized Savannah, Georgia, and set about making Georgia a royal colony. Forces operating out of Savannah made a surprise attack that almost captured Charleston in June 1779, and they held Savannah against a siege by French and American troops that summer.

Success in Georgia increased the enthusiasm of British generals and statesmen for what has been termed the southern strategy. In 1779, this was in part a sensible desire to reinforce success. But it was also the result of an excellent lobbying effort on the part of Loyalists in London and in New York, who convinced Sir Henry Clinton, commander in chief of the British army in North America, and Lord George Germain, the secretary of state for America, that there was a large and enthusiastic Loyalist population in the Carolinas waiting for its liberation. Once control was established in the loyal, less-rebellious southern colonies, the rest would be more ready to negotiate—or at least more easily conquered by a combined force of regular and trained provincial forces.

There were a great many Loyalists in Georgia and the Carolinas, but the problem with the southern strategy was that it was also seen as a way of doing counter-rebellion on the cheap now that France's entry in the war necessitated sending troops to the Caribbean.

Cultivating and protecting the loyal southern population required vast resources, as evidenced by the experience of Loyalists responding to British recruiting efforts shortly after the seizure of Georgia, when a British force occupied the frontier settlement of Augusta and used it as a base for remarkably successful recruiting attempts (raising, for example, one thousand one hundred men into twenty militia companies). Loyalist lieutenant colonel John Boyd, responding to the summons, recruited some six hundred men in the

South Carolina backcountry. But as he marched his recruits to Augusta, they were ambushed at Kettle Creek by Patriots under the command of Colonel Andrew Pickens and Elijah Clark. In an irony that Boyd would not have appreciated, at the very moment he was ambushed, his British supporters were already withdrawing from Augusta.

Militias like Boyd's could not exist without the active support of garrisons of trained regular troops serving in the threefold role of trainers, protectors of the local loyal population, and mobile strike force. Yet establishing those garrisons required resources and manpower that the British army in America did not have and that London was not willing to commit.

Following the successful defense of Savannah in autumn 1779, Sir Henry Clinton doubled down on the southern strategy by capturing Charleston. In March 1780, the Royal Navy blockaded the harbor and landed Clinton's army of ten thousand southeast of the city. The city was defended by an army of about two thousand seven hundred Continental regulars and about the same number of militia, the regulars essentially making up the total strength of the brigades of South Carolina, North Carolina, and Virginia. Following some brilliant maneuvering, Clinton bottled them up on the peninsula between the Ashley and Cooper Rivers. Following the cutting of the supply line to Charleston, the outcome of the siege was only a question of time. It began April 1, and on May 12, Major General Benjamin Lincoln formally surrendered the city. When news of the surrender reached the American outposts of Fort Ninety Six, South Carolina, and Camden, they also capitulated. There was no longer an American army in the South and no longer a ruling American government in South Carolina or Georgia. If there was a moment at which the southern strategy seemed to be truly brilliant, this was it.[19]

What then followed was an unforced error by Clinton. At first he craftily asked surrendering militia officers and soldiers to sign only an oath of neutrality, in which they promised not to involve themselves in further conflict. But just before he departed for New York on June 5, he altered the terms of the oath, now requiring a declaration of loyalty to the king. This was a calamitous choice. It drove many former Patriot leaders from a disarmed neutrality to a renewal of their opposition to the Crown. Nothing served to renew a conviction to oppose tyrannical and arbitrary government like a tyrannical and arbitrary decision.

Other factors beyond Clinton's control also undermined his victory. Some men, among them Thomas Sumter and Francis Marion, never submitted and gathered resisters around them. Perhaps even more importantly, the Loyalists who were now free of Patriot domination had their opportunity to take their revenge on their Patriot neighbors, and they took it. Andrew Pickens, the Patriot victor at the Battle of Kettle Creek, had taken the oath of neutrality. When Tories destroyed some of his property and threatened his family, he renounced his oath. Such defections as his in time made both British and Loyalists regret Clinton's decision and their own inability to imagine a future beyond immediate revenge.[20]

On Wednesday, June 21, 1780, Gates wrote to Morgan letting him know that the Board of War had appointed Gates to command the Southern Department. "I am also informed," he added, "that Congress had it in contemplation to call General Weedon and yourself into service, and to employ you immediately to the southward. I shall set out on Monday morning. . . . I am too much employed to return your visit; but if you can come to me before I leave home, I shall be glad to inform you of all particulars."[21]

Morgan was over the moon. "Would to God you'd a had it six months ago," he wrote back. "Our affairs would have a more pleasing aspect at this day than they do."[22] He wanted to meet Gates, but he was again feeling his sciatica—which was either the result of that flogging or, more likely, the result of falling atop the cannon in Quebec—and did not think he could ride even as far as Gates's home, Traveller's Rest, just twenty miles away. In the end they met on the morning of June 28, 1780, at Benjamin Berry's tavern, the site of Morgan's famous brawls and within eyesight of Soldier's Rest. Gates then offered command to Morgan of a unit similar to the one he had led at Saratoga. If possible, Morgan was even more delighted. His only request was that Congress finally grant him the rank of brigadier general so he would not be forced to take orders from state militia officers who outranked him. That was a tall ask: George Washington was no more willing to intervene on behalf of Virginians than he had been before, but Gates agreed to try.[23]

In the meantime, Morgan began to busy himself with the business of supporting Gates and the Southern Department. He circulated a muster order in western Virginia and prosecuted deserters in Frederick County Court. Despite his enthusiasm, his body stubbornly refused to cooperate, and he suffered chronic pain that sometimes left him unable to rise from his bed.

WHILE Morgan struggled to do his duty as best as his injuries permitted, the victor of Saratoga was encountering Lord Charles Cornwallis on a sandy, pine-studded savannah about five miles north of the South Carolina village of Camden.

From his arrival in North Carolina, Horatio Gates had behaved quite uncharacteristically. Hitherto a master of logistics, training, and planning, he began his command by ignoring all three. On July 25, he took command of the remainder of the Southern Army—the regulars of the Maryland and Delaware Division, commanded by Major General Johann de Kalb—at Buffalo Ford on the Deep River in North Carolina. Two days later, he began to march his one thousand four hundred men down the long road into the heart of South Carolina. Despite the advice of those who knew the land in front of them, he took a route through a relatively unpopulated territory that had been, during the previous six months, stripped of forage. Joined by militia, their numbers served only to increase their own and others' hunger. By the time they reached a point just north of Camden, the goal of their march, the entire army was immensely hungry and suffering from diarrhea—a condition that Gates's adjutant, Lieutenant Colonel Otho Williams of Maryland, attributed to "a hasty meal of quick baked bread and fresh beef, with a desert of molasses, mixed with mush, or dumplings."[24]

While his soldiers suffered from gastrointestinal distress, Gates suffered from a lack of information: he had no idea of the force that lay in front of him. From the beginning, he set upon acting with a strategic offense and tactical defense. Driving deep into South Carolina to a position just north of Camden, he would then dig in on some defensible position. This might have been intended to be on the ridge just north of Camden, or perhaps behind Saunders Creek, just a little farther north. This proximity to the British garrison would force the British to attack, and he would be able to inflict on them the southern Bunker Hill, or another repeat of Bemis Heights.[25]

So much for Gates's imaginings. The maxims "no battle plan survives contact with the enemy" and "plans are dispensable but planning is indispensable" were not yet formulated. Gates would learn the truth of both of them.

At about 2:30 on the morning of August 16, the advance guard of the American army encountered a British force at Saunders Creek, the very location Gates had considered as the place to dig in. In the fight that followed, Gates took a few prisoners and learned while interrogating them that he was facing none other than Cornwallis—the British commander in the Carolinas—and a force of three thousand men that the noble lord was leading north in search of Gates. Calling a first council of war, Gates asked "gentlemen, what is to be done?" The only option offered was to fight; no one demurred, and Gates and his army prepared for battle.[26]

On August 16, at first light, the two armies found themselves separated by a little less than three hundred yards. Both divided themselves into long lines of regiments with some reserves behind. As it happened, Gates placed his Virginia and North Carolina militia on his left. Quite by chance, Cornwallis placed his most experienced and highly trained regulars on his right, facing these inexperienced troops. Gates's right, composed of the 2nd Maryland Brigade—possibly the finest combat force in the Continental army other than the 1st Maryland Brigade, which waited as a reserve force—faced Loyalist militia from the Carolinas and the Volunteers of Ireland, a unit composed mainly of deserters from the Continental army or prisoners from the fall of Charleston who sought to avoid imprisonment on the rotting ships moored in the harbor.

In the first moves of the battle, the British facing the American left began to deploy from column into line, a moment of extreme vulnerability in eighteenth-century warfare. When a request was made of Gates to send forth the Virginia Militia to interrupt this movement, Gates said simply, "Sir, that's right—let it be done"— an order as casual in its panache as his Saratoga order committing Morgan to the fight, "let Morgan begin the game."[27]

The result was not the same. The Virginians fled before a bayonet charge; some may have fired before fleeing, but many did not. On their right, the North Carolina Militia do not seem to have even bothered to shoot; they simply ran. Only the Continental regulars remained, with some of the best British troops in North America or anywhere else turning their left flank, catching them in a vise from which they could not escape.

Otho Williams attempted to come to the rescue of the front line with the reserve of the 1st Maryland Brigade, but the fleeing militia disrupted his maneuver—much like trying to enter an emptying arena after a football game. After two hours of combat, or a little bit more, it was over. Those who were not killed or wounded, among them Williams and John Eager Howard, fled into the swamps, or north in a loose fugitive mass. Gates was ahead of them. By the evening of the battle, he reached Charlotte, North Carolina, sixty miles away; by August 19 he had reached Hillsborough, North Carolina, 180 miles away from the bloody field near Camden. "Was there ever an instance of a General running away as Gates has done from his whole army?" Alexander Hamilton snickered, "and was there ever so precipitous a flight? One hundred and eighty miles in three days and a half. It does admirable credit to the activity of a man at his time of life."[28]

Left behind on the field were the dead and the wounded. Among the latter was Baron Johann von Kalb, once the son of a Bavarian blacksmith, later an officer in the French army, husband of a wealthy heiress, spy, and most recently a major general in the Continental army. He had been shot three times and bayoneted repeatedly before finally being taken prisoner. With him in both wounding and captivity was Charles Porterfield. Once a cadet in Morgan's first company, the second man over the first barricade at Quebec, Porterfield had served, in time, as captain in the 7th Virginia Regiment (commanding its rifle company) and had fired the first shot at the Battle of Brandywine. He had accepted an appointment as lieutenant colonel of the Virginia State Garrison Regiment—state troops, somewhere between militia and Continental regulars—and led his men to Gates's aid. Now he was wounded and once again imprisoned. De Kalb died of his wounds in three days; Porterfield, his shin shattered by a bullet, lingered for three months.[29]

For the second time in just three months, an American army had been utterly destroyed in the south. There was now no regular army south of Philadelphia. North Carolina was open to the invader, and so too was Virginia, the largest, most populated, and richest of the colonies. There never was a darker moment in the American Revolution.

On receiving this terrible news, Daniel Morgan did the only thing he was probably capable of doing. He rode south.

Chapter Thirteen

SOUTH

ORGAN once more took leave of Abigail and his girls and rode out of the Valley, but for the first time he pointed south. He might have wished he were leading armed and experienced men. But he was lucky to bring even one proven man along with him whose quality he knew and trusted. Peter Bruin had been an ensign in Morgan's original company, then a captain in the 11th Virginia Regiment, then one of Major General John Sullivan's aides during the Battle of Rhode Island and later in the 1779 expedition against the Six Nations. In 1780, Bruin found himself on furlough in Frederick County serving as a supernumerary officer. When Morgan went south, Bruin remembered, "the General (without much difficulty) prevailed on me to accompany him." He hoped that he might get some position in the wrecked Southern Army.[1]

Morgan's financial and physical health had declined since 1775, when he and Bruin had marched together the first time. To look after his continuing want of cash, Morgan left with an extra horse, which he sold in Richmond to pay for his travel expenses. His physical problems could not be solved, only mitigated by traveling slowly and stopping often. Though he was somewhat recovered, his body was not quite ready to do what his spirit was determined upon.[2]

Given his slow travel, Morgan did not arrive at the Continental army's camp in Hillsborough, North Carolina, until late September 1780. Otho Williams, later remembering early autumn 1780, wrote, "About this time, Colonel Morgan of Virginia . . . arrived at camp, without command, and with only two or three young gentlemen attending him."[3] The remnants of the Maryland and Delaware Division had collected there, about six hundred to seven hundred men, living not in tents or huts but in brush shelters—"wigwams" they called them—made of fence rails and cornstalks and whatever else a soldier's ingenuity could scrounge and use. When Morgan arrived, it might have seemed to him that those wigwams held the only hope for the Revolution in the South. But all was not as it seemed.

THE humiliating defeat delivered to Gates at Camden had been a terrible, crippling blow to the Southern Army. Sumter's rout by Banastre Tarleton and his British Legion at Fishing Creek two days later—in which Tarleton killed approximately 150 men and took 300 prisoner—seemed, if possible, even more devastating to the militia of central South Carolina. Yet, as the always-perceptive Otho Williams later noted, "Victory is not always attended, perhaps never, with all the superiority it seems to bestow." Not only did Cornwallis hesitate to take full advantage of the victory that his opponents expected him to exploit, but the rebellion that had begun in the Carolinas in June 1780 (galvanized by Clinton's shortsighted alteration of the loyalty oath) gained strength, until it became a series of events that opened threats and opportunities unsought, unexpected, and unanticipated, not only by the British but also by American leaders.

Cornwallis, after Camden, gathered supplies and wagons in the Waxhaws region spanning the border of South and North Carolina and then drove north toward Charlotte Court House. The sole opposition facing him across the border of the Carolinas was a twenty-four-year-old Princeton graduate, Colonel William Richardson Davie, who led a group of roughly four hundred mounted riflemen—among them fourteen-year-old courier Andrew Jackson. At

Wahab's Plantation, on September 21, Davie attacked Tarleton's British Legion, killed fifteen, wounded forty, and lost only one of his own—shot by a fellow soldier. Five days later at Charlotte Court House, Tarleton's legion was ambushed and humiliated before the entire army, including Cornwallis. The only consolation in that defeat was that Tarleton was, at the time, deathly ill with a violent fever. For his part, Cornwallis encountered so much resistance foraging in the countryside that he termed all of Mecklenburg County "the hornet's nest."[4]

As Cornwallis's army foraged in the hornet's nest, the Loyalist cause in the Carolinas experienced tremendous disaster—perhaps even its defining defeat. Major Patrick Ferguson, a clever son of an Edinburgh intellectual family, had been appointed inspector of militia, in which capacity he was raising, equipping, and training Loyalist militia in the South Carolina backcountry. His effort was a classic example of successful counterinsurgency, outguerillaing the Patriot guerilla. Throughout summer 1780, Ferguson led a force of New York and New Jersey Loyalist infantry. His men were as trained and experienced as any British regular. To this number he added an ever-growing group of Carolina Loyalist militia. Together they suppressed Patriot forces from Fort Ninety Six, South Carolina, to the North Carolina border.

Patriot leaders from Georgia all the way to southwest Virginia and far northeast Tennessee saw Ferguson as their greatest immediate threat. Organizing at Sycamore Shoals in far east Tennessee, near modern Kingsport, eight hundred men marched for two weeks to confront Ferguson along the border between North and South Carolina. These "Overmountain Men" augmented a larger group of Georgia and Carolina militia. Turning on their tormenter, on October 7, 1780, they caught up with him at Kings Mountain, a frying-pan-shaped ridge whose summit Ferguson and his Loyalist army occupied. (It is noteworthy that the only Briton on either side in the following battle was Ferguson; all other participants were American Patriots or American Loyalists.) In the end, after surrounding the mountain and engaging in a long firefight, the Patriots took the hill. Ferguson was shot down, hit by multiple bullets. Many surrendering Loyalists and wounded were shot or stabbed to death; others of the wounded were left to die. Nine of the prisoners were hung without trial a few days later. Without Ferguson's mobile, fast-moving detachment to shield them, the garrison at Fort Ninety Six and others in the backcountry were left isolated and defenseless.[5]

In addition to Davie and the other partisans of the Carolina backcountry, the Patriot cause was served by Thomas Sumter and the hundreds of South Carolina militia he commanded. Sumter was cross-grained, acquisitive, narrow-minded, experienced, and an utterly focused fighting man. Sumter "would wade through blood to achieve his objects," wrote Lieutenant Colonel Harry Lee (Princeton graduate, partisan leader, and father-to-be of Robert E. Lee) in his memoirs years later. Incapable of cooperating or playing well with others, Sumter was also incapable of remaining defeated. Certainly he inflicted more defeats than he suffered, and he was yet another of the partisan leaders who kept Cornwallis—who christened Sumter "the gamecock"—in a perpetual and increasing condition of strategic uncertainty.[6]

But the paragon of Carolina's partisan leaders haunted the swamps and fields of the low country. Francis Marion was a South Carolina infantry officer, a disciplinarian who won no friends among his enlisted soldiers—one of whom once referred to him as "a damned hook-nosed son of a bitch." In April 1780, he left Charleston with a broken ankle—broken while trying to leave a drinking party early by jumping out of a window, which gives an idea of his temperament—shortly before Clinton surrounded it. Since Charleston's fall, he had raised a small and motley collection of "miserably equipped" boys and men, both white and black. When he led this collection into Gates's camp to volunteer for the Camden Campaign "their appearance was in fact so burlesque that it was with much difficulty the diversion of the regular soldiery was restrained by the officers."[7] Gates sent him away, back to the swamps of the lower Pee Dee River. That was probably for the best, since it meant that the man who would be christened the "Swamp Fox" was not caught up in Gates's subsequent disaster at Camden. Marion set about demonstrating that no supply line from Charleston to wherever Cornwallis happened to camp could ever be considered safe. In less than a year, his ranks, now swollen with victory, would stand in the battle line and contend with British regulars, proving to be as hardy and accomplished in formal eighteenth-century linear combat as they were at partisan war.

SOME of these events were still to come when Morgan arrived at Hillsborough; but Cornwallis's initial push into North Carolina, with the ultimate goal of establishing a royal government and a supply depot before invading Virginia, was concurrent with Morgan's arrival in the Southern Army. Anticipating Cornwallis's invasion, the North Carolina Board of War wrote to Gates asking him to send those Continental soldiers who still had shoes toward Charlotte so they could assist the militia. It further requested that Brigadier General William Smallwood of Maryland lead the force and that he be accompanied by Morgan. "General Morgan's Character as a Soldier is well known in America," the letter read, which was to be handed to Morgan. "I [the writer on behalf of the North Carolina board] am persuaded that your presence would give Spirits to my Countrymen."[8]

Gates agreed and did even better than that. He gave Morgan command of what light infantry he had and created a sort of combined-arms fighting unit. It was small but beautifully balanced: three companies of Maryland and Delaware infantry, sixty Virginia riflemen, other Virginia state troops and militia, and seventy cavalrymen. These last were the remnants of the 1st and 3rd Continental Light Dragoons who had escaped encirclement at Charleston in April. Though the size of their formations had been reduced due to death, capture, and attrition, they were veterans of hard fighting, well seasoned, and courageous, though unused to victory. They might be nearly naked, or sometimes literally so in their camp in Hillsborough (at least reduced to loincloths), but they knew how to soldier. New recruits were surrounded by a cadre of capable veterans who did not hesitate to instruct them in proper behavior while modeling a certain sense of honor.

But perhaps the best thing about Morgan's new command was the quality of his officers. Like Nathanael Greene, Morgan had always been lucky in his selection of officers as well as skilled in developing them, and this time was no exception. He had the benefits of a long war in his favor. Without systematic training or education, honing and sharpening the skill of officers, noncommissioned officers, and soldiers took years. Now, though, the young men who had begun the war as privates, cadet-volunteers, ensigns, or lieutenants were commanding battalions and regiments. They were supported by noncommissioned officers with experience and authority. By 1780, the true leaders and innovators were finally reaching positions of authority in the Continental army.

Morgan's senior infantryman, John Eager Howard of Maryland, was one of the finest combat officers it ever produced, one whose actions gave Maryland its now puzzling nickname "the Old Line State." Howard was the son of a slaveholding aristocrat, and soldiers like him earned the initial Maryland regiments their sneering nickname, "the Silk Stocking Regiments." Silk stockings or not, Howard quickly proved he could fight. Outside of combat he was known for being placid and reserved—his portraits show a long-nosed, long-chinned fellow gazing almost meekly at the spectator—but in battle he was always at the point of contact. He was now a lieutenant colonel commanding the Continental light infantry in Morgan's detachment.

William Washington was Howard's equal on horseback. He was the second or third cousin of the commander in chief and one of the numerous progeny of his great-grandfather John Washington of Virginia's Northern Neck. When the war began, Washington had been intending to pursue ordination in the Church of England, but like Charles Thruston and Peter Muhlenberg, he had discovered another vocation. Beginning in the militia, one of the two officers wounded at the Battle of Trenton (the other was fellow Virginian and fifth president James Monroe), William Washington served in the 3rd Continental Dragoons after its formation with no record of particular distinction. But just as Howard used every combat engagement as a training opportunity, so too did Washington. By the time this amiable, round-headed, pie-faced Virginian became a lieutenant colonel and Morgan's subordinate in 1780, he had, unbeknownst to anyone else and perhaps even to himself, developed into one of the finest cavalry commanders on the continent, as he would shortly demonstrate.[9]

Morgan also had the privilege of serving with a man he had known since nearly his first wagon journeys across Virginia, Major Francis Triplett. When Morgan had traveled to Fredericksburg, he had guided his team past the Triplett tavern in Fauquier County en route to Tidewater ports. He too had been on Braddock's march and fought in the 1st Virginia Regiment under Washington during the French and Indian War. Now forty-eight and an old man by the standards of Morgan's other officers—both Howard and Washington were twenty-eight—Frank Triplett was fighting once more with Morgan.

In addition to trusted officers, Morgan had two competent aides, Captain Edward Giles and Captain Benjamin Brookes, both of the Maryland line. Giles was his aide-de-camp, his military secretary and amanuensis. The owner of a one-thousand-four-hundred-acre plantation in Harford County north of Baltimore, Giles had been a captain in the 2nd Canadian Regiment—a remnant of the attempt to seize the fourteenth colony, now with very few Canadians remaining in its ranks—before transferring to the Maryland line.[10] Brookes, the son of a Prince George's County merchant and plantation owner, had served in the Maryland line since January 1776. Brookes and Morgan had one thing in common: both had been shot through the mouth, although Brookes's wound at Germantown "split his Tongue & went out at the back of his Jaw-Bone." He served as Morgan's brigade-major, the eighteenth-century equivalent of a brigade's chief of staff.[11]

This combination of musket men, riflemen, and cavalry meant Morgan had under him an ad hoc partisan legion, an innovation that emerged in the last years of the war. Experience had shown both British and Americans that wars of detachments were best fought by adaptable and mobile forces, hence the inclination to assemble legions—combined arms detachments of infantry and cavalry, perhaps also with riflemen and one or two pieces of light artillery. The most famous of these was the 2nd Partisan Corps, led by Harry Lee of Virginia, soon to arrive in North Carolina. But every cavalry regiment in the Southern Campaign soon had some of its troopers dismounted and given muskets, or were augmented by a company of infantry and some riflemen. This gave them an unparalleled ability to be mobile on attack and defense, to function as a miniature army.

On October 7, together with these promising men and their soldiers, all freshly clothed and shod, Morgan marched southwest on the Great Wagon Road toward Salisbury on the Yadkin—the same road that ran through Winchester. It was an assignment without any particular direction, but Morgan used it to get to know the geography of North Carolina: its roads, its fords, the provisions available along the roads, its people, and the number of men in the area who owned rifles.[12] It was a mark of both his newly acquired gentility and position, as well as his natural sociability, that after mourning the inability to acquire food for his men, he fretted that he would be unable to host a dinner for his subordinate officers. "I assure you," he wrote Gates from Salisbury on October 20, "an officer looks very blank when he han't it in his power to ask his officers to eat with him at times." He also had heard there was linen coming in for the officers and requested that his friend the Polish engineer Colonel Tadeusz Kosciusko bring his share along in his baggage when he moved down the road to join Morgan.[13]

Shortly after learning of Cornwallis's retreat south from Charlotte in response to Ferguson's defeat, Morgan advanced toward that important crossroads in Mecklenburg County. By October 20, the slow-moving Smallwood had finally caught up with Morgan, and they camped twelve miles south of Charlotte in New Providence. By that time, Cornwallis had withdrawn to camp at Winnsborough, chosen because it was halfway between Camden and Ninety Six, and the British screen now stretched out to defend South Carolina. Gates arrived suddenly from Hillsborough with the remainder of the Southern Army before withdrawing again with the whole army back to Charlotte when he found no forage along the Carolina border.

Morgan kept position on the border, occupying himself with defending foraging parties and begging his superiors for further opportunities. "Morgan," Smallwood wrote Gates, "is a-fever to go below"—meaning to scout and raid into South Carolina. He was finally allowed to take some wagons and his new corps to seek grain and hay in the Waxhaws territory along the Carolina border whose residents paid no particular attention to either the geographical boundary or the law.[14]

Morgan found neither forage nor cattle, both having been picked clean by Cornwallis. But he did undertake a successful engagement, which amused him greatly and demonstrated the abilities of William Washington. Just ten miles north of Camden was the plantation of a Loyalist colonel, Henry Rugeley, who was recruiting and training a militia. To this end, Rugeley had fortified his barn and built a stockade or an abatis around it. Given that "Rugeley's Fort" was so close to the British garrison at Camden, Morgan did not wish to risk his infantry on a forced march. But neither did he wish to allow Rugeley to continue in his activities, for suppressing the Loyalist militia and its recruitment was the foremost goal of the American forces. Morgan ordered Washington and his cavalry on a raid to capture Rugeley's Fort and its garrison. Surveying the defenses, Washington decided that cavalry alone was unlikely to take the fort, however improvised it might be. So he had his men take a pine log, mount it on some wheels, or on four sticks (sources refer to both), and reveal it to the holed-up Loyalists from a careful distance. To Rugeley's eyes it was no pine log but a cannon. Then Lieutenant Colonel Washington sent a corporal under a white flag to give Rugeley "solemn summons" to surrender. This Rugeley speedily did, delivering over himself, a major, and 107 or so men. Rugeley's words and emotions on discovering that he had been defeated by a log are not recorded. But as Morgan observed later in a letter endorsing Rugeley's request for parole, "I believe he may be depended on, but when they get him there I fear they won't be anxious to exchange him, as they won't, after this, look upon him as a great military character."[15]

In early November 1780, news reached Morgan that Congress was planning to recall Gates on account of the defeat at Camden. Rumor had it that a group of officers in the Southern Department were working to push Gates out and that their leader was William Smallwood. Another rumor had it that Smallwood would be Gates's successor, while others hinted at the appointment of Benjamin Lincoln, exchanged after his capture at Charleston.

By late 1780, Morgan's health seems to have been miraculously restored. It may have been helped along when he discovered that Congress had finally promoted him to brigadier general on October 13, after receiving letters in support of Morgan from Governors Thomas Jefferson of Virginia and John Rutledge of South Carolina. Congress's promotion came even though Virginia lacked the soldiers to justify appointing yet another general. In effect, while the resolution of Congress did not mention Morgan's previous record as a soldier, it was both a response to the requests of southern governors and an endorsement of the Board of War's statement that Morgan "early embarked in the present war, and uniformly distinguished himself as an active, brave, and useful soldier."[16] It was as much of an apology as Morgan could expect.

MORGAN, based on everything written by him or others, would have loved to continue serving under his old commander. But all things considered, the man coming to replace Gates would know how to use Morgan better than any superior ever had. Daniel Morgan's brief service with Nathanael Greene ranks as one of the great military partnerships in the history of the United States, one of the most formidable combinations that any American enemy could face.

It is hard to imagine a more interesting interplay of personalities than between those of Greene and Morgan. Greene was a businessman, an ironworker, raised Quaker in Rhode Island. Unlike Morgan, he had always craved book learning and worked hard from an early age to attain it. Unlike Morgan, he was deeply connected to the place of his birth, surrounded by numerous brothers and sisters, as well as a proliferation of first, second, and third cousins thickly scattered along the western shore of Narragansett Bay. Greene had become a general because he read a great deal, remembered what he read, and experimented with those lessons.

But Morgan and Greene had a few things in common. First, they were both used to working with their hands, which was not only a physical attribute but a mental and emotional one—they both grabbed hold of things. Second, both were gregarious and sociable and reveled in the brotherhood created by the ranks of the Continental army. Third, they were new men, men on the make, gentlemen created by the Revolutionary moment. Finally, they both had a natural talent for wrecking enemy armies—each did this in a different way, and these ways were perfectly complementary.

Greene arrived at Charlotte on December 2, and it was apparently the first that anyone there knew the identity of Gates's replacement.[17] "A manly resignation marked the conduct of General Gates on the arrival of his successor," remembered Otho Williams, "whom he received at head quarters with that liberal and gentlemanly air which was habitual to him." For his part, "General Greene observed a plain, candid, respectful manner, neither betraying compassion nor the want of it—nothing like the pride of official consequence even seemed. In short, the officers who were present, had an elegant lesson of propriety exhibited on a most delicate and interesting occasion."[18] With that, Gates's command was at an end and Greene took charge.

On his ride south from West Point, Greene had already begun to dispose talented subordinates into those positions to which they were best suited—it cannot be said too often: no one in American military history has been so consistently fortunate in the quality of his subordinates, except perhaps Morgan. Until Richmond, he had been accompanied by none other than Baron Friedrich von Steuben; he left him in Virginia to organize recruitment and training. Edward Carrington, an able Virginia officer of artillery, he made deputy quartermaster general. Seeing in William Richardson Davie not only a partisan leader but a brilliant manager, much to that young gentleman's displeasure Greene made him commissary general with responsibility to solve the provisioning problems of the Southern Army. He had, on his ride south, carefully examined the geography of North Carolina, seeing that it was overlaid with a series of rivers and creeks, noting the fords over each. Now he sent out Tadeusz Kosciuszko with specific instructions, among them to chart the locations of every ford and gristmill. Realizing Otho Williams's quality, he kept him as adjutant general but established him even more as chief of staff in camp and on the battlefield.

Most importantly from Morgan's perspective, he decided to make Morgan's detachment into what was known in the eighteenth century as a Flying Army: a division of light infantry and cavalry that moved across the theater as needed—and to which the backcountry militia could flock.

GREENE possessed a profound strategic understanding—probably no general of either side in the War of Independence had a deeper strategic understanding. Like so many American generals, Greene had previously served in the colonial legislature. Whatever military sensibility he developed during the war, or idea of himself as an officer and a gentleman, he was always conscientiously subordinate to civil authority. Moreover, like Washington but unlike nearly all of his peers on either side, he understood that warfare always had political goals. Greene was not interested simply in defeating the enemy or occupying territory seized by the British army. He wanted to shield and protect what civil society there remained in the Carolinas and allow the re-creation of its polities.

This unique strategic understanding is best captured in a response to one of the circulars that Washington issued to his generals from time to time requesting memos from them in response to a query of his. Responding to a question regarding an attack on New York City, Greene observed that he found the British strategy inexplicable. "The great object of the Enemies attention is and ever ought to have been our Army," he wrote the commander in chief. "Destroy that, and the Country is conquerd; or at least this is the most ready way to affect the reduction of the United States. They have seen that taking Cities and marching through Governments answered no other purpose that that of giving them an opportunity to plunder the Inhabitants with more security than by little parties."

"It is like a Ship plowing the Ocean," he continued. "[T]hey have no sooner past than the scene closes and the people rise anew to oppose them. This will ever be the case while the grand Army is considerd as capable of giving support to the peoples endeavors. But destroy this Army and the confidence of the people will sink and nothing but that can overcome us. For the degree of opposition will ever be in proportion to the peoples confidence in their own strength and security. I think therefore this Army may be considerd the Stamina of American liberty; and our position and measures should be taken upon this principle."[19]

In effect, this was a memo describing what Greene would do in his southern campaigns. It would always be Greene's first and highest object to preserve his army, even at—especially at—the moment when total victory seemed possible on the battlefield. If there was no army in the South then there would be no southern governments, no South Carolina, no North Carolina. It was imperative that Greene not be defeated, and therefore every battle was fraught with the possibility of immense loss—something Gates had disregarded before Camden.

It also meant that the opposite was true. Defeating, containing, or constraining the British army—not even allowing it to continue to pass back and forth across the American landscape—meant there could be no support for the Loyalist population, no creation of Loyalist militias to unify and defend that population, no suppression of the American militia whose chief end was to suppress the Loyalists. Outposts like Rugeley's Fort, however small and militarily inconsequential they might seem, were the seeds of royal power. They must be eliminated, not for the sake of tidiness but because where they were could also be militia, and where there were militia there was also the beginning of the reassertion of royal authority.

It also meant that if Greene could destroy or break Cornwallis's army, then he would destroy all the dreams of the southern strategy. Moreover—and here was Greene's particular genius—there were other ways to break an army than by defeating it on the battlefield.

With this strategic appraisal always foremost in his mind, Greene made the most momentous of his decisions. The whole area around Charlotte had been stripped of food and supplies, and no part of the army could continue to subsist in that place. He decided to send Morgan and the Flying Army into the backcountry of South Carolina, toward the British post at Ninety Six, on the trail from Charleston to Cherokee country. Simultaneously, Greene would move the main body of the army to Cheraw, a hilly section of eastern South Carolina along the upper Pee Dee River. Neither of these areas had yet been crossed by the opposing armies, and they would therefore be open to foraging. Most importantly, the presence of the two parts of the army in those areas would encourage the local Patriot population and suppress the Loyalists.[20]

Greene was well aware that this movement violated every principle of classical strategy; one was not supposed to divide an army, for that could allow an enemy to defeat each part of the army separately—what the books called defeat in detail. But the higher needs of logistics and supply demanded this action. Moreover, by splitting the army, he could possibly cause Cornwallis to split his own army. Morgan's Flying Army would threaten Fort Ninety Six; Greene's army in Cheraw would threaten Georgetown and Charleston. If Cornwallis moved his entire force against Greene, then Morgan would be free to attack Ninety Six; if Cornwallis moved his entire army against Morgan, then Greene could join with Francis Marion and attack Georgetown, or even raid Charleston. If Cornwallis split his army to confront both Morgan and Greene, then things were even. Morgan was to cross to the west side of the Catawba River and there join with the South Carolina militia under Thomas Sumter and the North Carolina militia under William Lee Davidson. With their support he would place his army between the Broad and Pacolet Rivers. Green gave him no specific instructions, telling him to act defensively or offensively as "prudence and discretion" led him to, taking only special care to avoid being surprised. "The object of this detachment," wrote Greene, "is to give protection to that part of the country and spirit up the people, to annoy the enemy in that quarter, [and] collect the provisions and forage out of the way of the enemy." He concluded, "confiding in your abilities and activity, I entrust you with this command, being persuaded you will do everything in your power to distress the enemy, and afford protection to the country."[21] Ultimately the object of Morgan's movement into the backcountry was to influence the opinions of the southern people, both Patriots and Loyalists.[22]

They were precisely the kind of orders that showed Morgan the respect he believed his record had earned him. Whatever favor Gates might have showed him, it was, in the end, the bookish former Quaker from Rhode Island who gave Morgan the latitude to show what he was capable of doing.

ON December 21, Morgan headed west. By Christmas Day, the Flying Army was encamped at Grindal's Shoals on the Pacolet River, divided into detachments stretching over several miles in order to facilitate grazing for the many horses that the militia arriving to support Morgan brought with them. "The scarcity of forage," Morgan wrote Greene later, "makes it impossible for us to be always in a compact body; and were this not the case, it is beyond the art of man to keep militia from straggling."[23]

The central camp, where Morgan's headquarters were located, was on the plantation of the Loyalist Alexander Chesney, and his houses and barns were comprehensively plundered. Other detachments were located at nearby mills, invariably sites of conflict during the war in the South because it was there that the warring armies could process raw grain into flour—armies of the eighteenth century marched on the power of complex carbohydrates. Washington's dragoons were at Wofford's ironworks, using the facilities to shoe their horses and repair equipment—possibly also crafting swords for the militia with which Morgan hoped to augment Washington's numbers.

The hope had been that Thomas Sumter and other militia forces would join Morgan once he established himself in the backcountry. Militia did start to arrive at camp, but not Sumter or any of the troops under his command. Sumter was still suffering from a severe wound inflicted during his repulse of Tarleton at Blackstock's Plantation on November 20—and from a no-less-grave fit of pique at what he saw as Morgan and Greene's high-handed regular army behavior. As far as he was concerned, he and no other man should be in command west of the Catawba, and he would allow none of his subordinates to respond to any of Morgan's requests. While Greene continued to alternate cajoling and flattery to motivate Sumter, Morgan had developed an antipathy for the Gamecock.[24]

As his army replenished and prepared itself, Morgan learned that a group of Georgia Loyalists were in the neighborhood around Little Creek robbing and plundering the local Patriot inhabitants; a detachment of South Carolina Loyalists were based nearby in Williams's Fort, formerly a Patriot stronghold. Pursuant to his orders from Greene, Morgan sent William Washington's cavalry detachment along with militia that had recently arrived in Morgan's camp. His orders were to crush the Loyalist raiders and sweep the area between Morgan and Ninety Six free of them.

About noon on December 30, Washington caught up with the Loyalists. They were on a hill on the other side of the valley of the Little River, about a mile away, centered on a location known as Hammond's Store. Washington formed his dragoons in the center of a long line, flanked by the mounted militia. Thomas Young, a teenager serving in the militia, remembered that "Col. Washington and his dragoons gave a shout, drew swords, and charged down the hill like mad men." The Loyalists ran for their horses, but it was too late for them. Before they could mount and flee, Washington and the dragoons were in among them, stabbing, slashing, and hacking. Washington reported 150 killed and wounded and forty taken prisoner, against no losses of his own—numbers suspiciously like a massacre, killed and wounded ratios usually being in reverse of this. In the aftermath of this rout, Washington sent a detachment to attack Fort Williams, but its defenders trickled away before the arrival of the American dragoons. Finding the nest empty, the dragoons burned it.[25]

This was a highly consequential skirmish, though the numbers of Loyalist dead and captured make it almost a small battle. It persuaded Cornwallis that Morgan was on the march toward Ninety Six. The entire resulting campaign, over the next three months, stems from Washington's raid on Hammond's Store.

On his way back to Morgan's camp, Washington fell in with a group of militia from the Long Cane district of South Carolina, an area away toward the Savannah River, the border between South Carolina and Georgia. They were led by a tall, sober, bald, lantern-jawed Presbyterian elder whom the Cherokee called Wizard Owl and of whom one contemporary said that before speaking he "would first take the words out of his mouth between his fingers, and examine them before he uttered them." This was Colonel Andrew Pickens. A successful Patriot militia officer since the beginning of the war, he had sworn the neutrality oath after the capture of Charleston and collapse of the South Carolina government. He had been jailed, but after his release observed his parole until—when he was one day away from home—some Loyalists plundered his plantation. Pickens was not a man to do things halfway when his conscience was at issue. He first rode to Ninety Six, where he informed the Loyalist commandant of the outrage committed against his family and renounced his oath; having done that, he rode away and became one of the most effective partisan commanders in the Carolinas, the equal of Sumter and Marion. While his personality could hardly be more different than Morgan's, it was always one of Morgan's innate abilities to recognize talent however it presented itself. "Col Pickens," he said, "is a valuable, discreet, and attentive officer, and has the full confidence of the militia."[26] He recognized Pickens as the commander of all the South Carolina militia that were then flocking to Morgan's camp. It would prove to be one of the best decisions Morgan ever made.

By the time Washington returned to camp with Pickens and his followers, Morgan had decided his time at Grindal's Shoals was at an end. Because of his dispersed camps, he could not easily defend against surprise. "Situated as we are," he wrote Greene, "every possible precaution may not be sufficient to secure us." He requested that he be recalled and that Pickens and Davidson be left behind in the backcountry as "they will not be so much the object of the enemy's attention, and will be capable of being a check on the disaffected."[27]

Alternatively, he could instead be let off the leash and go deeper into enemy territory. He wanted to hit something, raise a ruckus, start a fight. Perhaps, he suggested to Greene, the Flying Army could attack into Georgia. "To me it appears an Adviseable Scheme. But should be happy to receive your Directions on this point."[28]

By January 1, Cornwallis had had enough of intelligence and rumors of Morgan's activity in the backcountry. He sent Tarleton to deal with Morgan by intercepting his presumed movement against Ninety Six. Just as Greene had anticipated, he split his army in order to deal with Greene's divided army.[29]

It would be impossible for novelists to come up with more appropriate antagonists than Morgan and Tarleton, and if they did they would be accused of taking things too far. Tarleton was about twenty years younger than Morgan, just twenty-six in 1780. He was the third son of a Liverpool family grown wealthy from shipping, slavery, and sugar plantations in the West Indies. Intended for studying law at University College, Oxford, he instead devoted his time to drinking and attending horse races and boxing matches. When he went to London for further legal education, he added whoring and gambling to his repertoire.[30]

Eventually Tarleton threw over a career as a lawyer and purchased a commission in the 1st Dragoon Guards, a suitably fashionable regiment. With the war in America beckoning adrenaline-deprived adventurers like himself, he took leave of his regiment to volunteer with the 16th Light Dragoons. There, under the guidance of its lieutenant colonel, William Harcourt, he developed into a talent. During the occupation of Philadelphia, he began to fight alongside Loyalists. After the return of the British army to New York following its retreat across New Jersey in 1778, a variety of company-sized units of Loyalists formed during the army's occupation of Philadelphia were reorganized into several units. One of these was christened the British Legion and made into a combined-arms unit of cavalry and infantry. Tarleton was made its commander by Sir Henry Clinton, and in time it became synonymous with its leader, so that it was simply called "Tarleton's Legion."

That was perhaps a better name for it, since like Ferguson and his partisans, Tarleton was one of the only Britons in its ranks— everyone else was an American Loyalist or a deserter from the American army. Many American deserters from Camden and from the capture of Charleston chose service in the legion rather than imprisonment in rotting ships in Charleston Harbor. Yet with this "motley group," Tarleton was able to engage in "rapid marches, hard driving attacks," destroy opposition of all kinds, and obtain intelligence for an information-starved Cornwallis.[31] His memoirs are filled with strong verbs and energetic adjectives: he, "instantly forming his troops, ordered them to charge"; his troops engage in "vigorous effort" to pursue the enemy; he generally makes "arrangement for the attack with all possible expedition"; advances are made with "great rapidity."[32] The examples are found with every attack, every pursuit, making it clear that the lesson Tarleton had learned from his six months in the Carolinas is that speed kills the enemy. Speed meant surprise, and surprise was victory. "Speed, shock, and daring" might have been a "crude formula," but Tarleton had sufficient victories to justify his reliance on that arithmetic. Other British campaigns since the beginning of the war had been characterized by lethargy and an inability to take advantage of their American adversaries' numerous mistakes. Tarleton seems to have resolved that he would never be guilty of that. The result was that he was highly effective in Cornwallis's service, hated by Patriots throughout the Carolinas but more importantly, feared.[33]

DESPITE his predilection for high-speed pursuit, Tarleton was forced at first to advance deliberately and even slowly. Like Morgan, he was under logistical pressure as well as busy gathering intelligence from backcountry Loyalists. Behind Tarleton as he marched out to find Morgan were not only the soldiers of the British Legion, about 450 infantry and cavalry, but some of the best troops of Cornwallis's army. There were light infantry detachments from two regiments; the battered and much reduced 7th Royal Fusiliers; and 334 men of the 71st Regiment, "Fraser's Highlanders," a Scottish regiment whose men had probably long ago discarded their tartan trousers but not their hardened and aggressive professionalism. Tarleton had in addition to his legion's cavalry a supporting detachment of the 17th Light Dragoons and two light three-pounder cannon. It was the perfect force with which to hunt and destroy Morgan.

On January 2, 1781, as Tarleton was on the march, a messenger from Cornwallis arrived with further orders. There was one report that Morgan had cannon, Cornwallis wrote, which he disbelieved; "it is, however, possible and Ninety-six is of so much consequence, that no time is to be lost." Therefore, "if Morgan is still at Williams's, or any where within your reach, I should wish you to push him to the utmost."[34]

These were orders Tarleton understood: "push him to the utmost." This is what he had done to the 1st and 3rd Continental Dragoons at Lenud's Ferry when he destroyed them; Buford's Virginia Regiment at Waxhaws, which he had also destroyed; and Thomas Sumter's brigade at Fishing Creek, which he had literally caught napping and destroyed as well. Cornwallis's favorite dog had been released, and the hunt was on.

Chapter Fourteen

COWPENS

ON January 7, probably still considering a descent into Georgia, Morgan wrote an address to the Georgia refugees, those members of the Georgia militia who had fled the British occupation. To be sure, Morgan did not write the final draft; Edward Giles must have rewritten it, or taken dictation, for it is far too polished a composition to have come directly from Morgan's own hand. Yet it is all Morgan: in its spirit, its emphasis on discipline, its disdain for unprofessional behavior, and its insistence on honor and achievement. It is not hard to imagine him pacing back and forth at the camp on the Pacolet while Giles took dictation and then cleaned up the word choice.

> Having heard of your sufferings, your attachment to the cause of freedom, and your gallantry of address in action, I had formed a pleasing idea of receiving in you as a great and valuable acquisition to my force. Judge then, of my disappointment when I find you scattered about in parties, subjected to no orders, nor joining in any general plan to promote the public service. The recollection of your past achievements, and the hope of gaining future laurels, should prevent your acting

in such a manner, for a moment. You have gained a character, and why will you risk the loss of it, for the most trifling gratifications. You must know that in your present situation you can neither provide for your safety, nor assist me in annoying the enemy. Let me then entreat you, but the regard you have for your fame, by the love for your country, repair to my camp, and subject yourselves to order and discipline. I will ask you to encounter no dangers or difficulties but what I will participate. Should it be thought desirable to form detachments, you may rely in being employed in that business if it be more agreeable to your wishes; but it is absolutely necessary that your situation and movements be known to me, so that I may be enabled to direct them in such a manner that they may tend to the advantage of the whole.[1]

It is a curious fact that possibly no one in the American Revolution, on either side, employed militia better than did Daniel Morgan, and yet he seems to have had no love, and indeed much disdain, for militia in general. Charles Lee and Horatio Gates burned with an ideological enthusiasm for militia, and yet both were sadly disappointed by them when they most depended on them. Morgan shared no such enthusiasm with the two English generals, perhaps because he had been a militiaman himself. There was very little that, as a body, he thought they could do correctly. He found their loyalty suspect, such that with a reverse of any kind, those "who have already joined will desert us, and it is not improvable, but a Regard to their own safety will induce them to Join the Enemy."[2] Militia insisted on being mounted on horses, and that meant they exhausted an entire countryside of forage (by lawless plunder); and those horses meant they straggled, so they could never be kept together in the event of a surprise.[3] And then, to add insult to these injuries, militia like the Georgia refugees to whom he made that tart address would not even condescend to come into camp, let alone inform him of where they were or what they intended to do. Moreover, he was suspicious of the unguided militia and their capacity to take advantage of the "law of retaliation," which was no law, only retaliation freed of restraint.[4] Like Greene, Morgan did not believe that the war could be won by lawlessness.

So Morgan did not like or trust militia. He was a professional soldier, and proud of it, and they were not. In this he was in the good company of his much-admired commander in chief. Yet, unlike George Washington, Morgan knew how to use them in the way that best suited them. This apparent paradox is at the heart of his greatest military achievement.

AT Brooke's Rush River Plantation, twenty miles and two days from his starting point, Tarleton paused to receive reinforcements and provisions, and for his baggage to catch up.[5] By January 11, he had both. More dragoons had arrived, along with two hundred infantry who had been intended to reinforce Ninety Six. At the moment his march began from Brooke's, Tarleton had one thousand two hundred men and a baggage train. By the twelfth or thirteenth, he was joined by Alexander Chesney, the man whose plantation Morgan was occupying at Grindal's Shoals. Chesney and fifty other Loyalist militia were Tarleton's guides.[6]

The British crossed the Enoree River at a point thirty miles from Morgan's main camp. As Tarleton turned northwest, he entered an area along Fair Forest Creek that both armies, and numerous militia bands, had been picking over for the last three months; Andrew Pickens had been occupying it the previous week. Tarleton was entering a logistical trap, moving into an area picked clean of food for men and even forage for horses. Since he was traveling fast, he could not delay to allow his troops to forage away from his line of movement. Tarleton was completely dependent on the supplies he brought with him.

On the fourteenth, Morgan received news of Tarleton's advance. He drew in his units and began to march north. His soldiers understood that he wanted to draw Tarleton farther and farther away from any support Cornwallis might give. Morgan sent parties ahead of the army to scout as well as forage for what was necessary. All the while, more groups of Carolina militia were finding him and joining the Flying Army, falling into its northward march.

On the morning of the sixteenth, Tarleton left his campfires burning to deceive American scouts (it worked) and stole a march on Morgan. During breakfast in the American camp, a scout raced in with word that Tarleton was only six miles away. Morgan had the Continentals up and marching without finishing their breakfasts; North Carolina militia followed behind, riding out at noon as Tarleton's scouts arrived. The British force was soon enjoying the Americans' cooked meals and warm fires. Those meals might have been a very welcome sight: after a four-days march, it is possible Tarleton had nearly used up his supplies. An interrogation of a captured militia colonel convinced Tarleton that if he held onto Morgan like a bulldog biting an ox's leg, he could prevent him from crossing the Broad River and wait for Cornwallis to arrive to ensure Morgan's destruction. That night, as his men got some sleep, Tarleton stayed up listening to the reports from scouts on Morgan's new location, a place called the Cowpens.[7]

Morgan had arrived there in the afternoon with his aides and the dragoons detailed to be his bodyguards. Alerted to the presence of local resident Captain Dennis Trammell in the ranks of the South Carolina Militia, Morgan had him escort him around the landscape, the savannah of trees and grass where Carolina protocowboys rested their cattle on the drive down to Charleston. When he began his ride with Trammel, Morgan knew that a fight was coming but not where or when. By the time he was finished with his survey, he was determined that this was the place where he would fight and that it would happen either that night or the following morning. "Captain," Trammell recalled Morgan saying, "here is Morgan's grave or victory."[8]

EVEN shortly after the battle, Morgan seems to have already been tired of being asked why he had decided to fight at the Cowpens. In a letter he wrote ten days later to his friend William Snickers, he said, "I did not intend to fight that day, but intended to cross the Broad River early that morning to a strong piece of ground, and there decide the matter, but as matters worse circumstanced, no time was to be lost, I prepared for battle."[9]

Daniel Morgan seems to have been one of the only people to ever find the Cowpens an ideal place to mount a defensive battle. Tarleton in his memoirs described what he termed "the vulnerable situation of the enemy." Writing in the third person, he said, "The ground which General Morgan had chosen for the engagement . . . was disadvantageous for the Americans, and convenient for the British: An open wood was certainly as proper a place for action as Lieutenant-colonel Tarleton could desire; America does not produce many more suitable to the nature of the troops under his command." Charles Stedman, a Loyalist officer engaged in that campaign who walked the ground not long after, and who despised Tarleton, in this one instance agreed with him—as well as with generations of subsequent visitors to the battlefield. Stedman observed that Morgan's flanks were open, the savannah of fields with scattered trees was perfectly suited to cavalry, and the location of the Broad River a mile or so behind the American position meant that if defeated, there was no way for Morgan to retreat.[10]

Years later, Morgan claimed he had chosen the position precisely because of its disadvantages. If they had been closer to the Broad and there had been a swamp nearby, then the militia would run for its cover at the first opportunity. "As to covering my wings, I knew my adversary, I was perfectly sure I should have nothing but downright fighting. As to retreat, it was the very thing I wished to cut off all hope of. I would have thanked Tarleton had he surrounded me with his cavalry. It would have been better than placing my own men in the rear to shoot down those who broke ranks. When men are forced to fight, they will sell their lives dearly . . . and had I crossed the river, one half of the militia would immediately have abandoned me."[11]

This sounds like a load of special pleading. But there is something there that coheres with Morgan's pre- and post-Cowpens experiences and with his personality. At the battles of Saratoga, he had directed his men of the Provisional Rifle Corps from slightly to the rear of their line, in part to watch the battle as it developed but also to shame those who might consider running. A few weeks later, he specifically advised Greene that a suitable battle plan would involve stationing chosen men behind the line of militia with instructions to shoot the first to flee. Morgan clearly believed that psychological and physical threats were perfectly in order to make reluctant citizen-soldiers do their duty. That he combined this with a common touch, a certain degree of empathy, and clear directions made him a truly formidable battlefield commander.

All these abilities, and many more, now came into play. First was Morgan's ability to see the ground. The Cowpens was not quite as it seemed to either Tarleton on the morning of the battle or Stedman a few days later. What seems flat at first glance is actually rolling, shallow swales crossing the landscape. These swales do not seem like much. But each of them is large enough so that when arriving at the south end of the Cowpens, the very place from which Tarleton surveyed the landscape, troops sheltered in them were hardly visible.

Having assessed this ground, Morgan began to organize and distribute his troops according to everything he had learned in five years of Revolutionary warfare. He had five varieties of troops, based on their organization and armament: Continental cavalry, armed with swords; Continental infantry, with muskets and bayonet; mounted militia, armed with swords; militia with rifles; militia with muskets. There were, moreover, differing levels of experience in each of these units. The capacity and numbers of each meant none could succeed without the other, and all their qualities had to be taken into account. Morgan first began to do this by creating a plan for a defense in depth. By nightfall, or some time a little later when it became clear to him from scouting reports that Tarleton would not arrive until first light, he had altered the original plan into the mode by which he fought the battle.

British reports of the battle referred to two lines of defense. There were actually five parts of Morgan's defense, all working toward the end of breaking Tarleton's army. First were the scouts and skirmishers pushed forward to throw off Tarleton's speed. On the battlefield itself there were four components. First was a line of skirmishers, riflemen from Georgia and the Carolinas, placed 150 yards out, screening the entire Flying Army, carefully coached to fire once or twice before falling back to the second line. This was another line of militia, all from North Carolina, South Carolina, and Georgia, armed predominately with rifles.

The third line was actually more like three dashes spaced apart to create two gaps so that the second line of the militia might retreat through them. It was composed of those units that had been under Morgan's orders since Gates had given him command of the light troops after his arrival at Hillsborough. At its center were John

Eager Howard's Continentals, light infantry from Virginia, Maryland, and Delaware. On the flanks were Frank Triplett's Virginians and some North Carolina militia. Notably, both wings of the third line were anchored by riflemen from Rockbridge and Augusta Counties in the upper Shenandoah, here fighting in linear formation, their rifles sweeping the center of the battlefield.

Supporting these three lines of defense were William Washington's horsemen. As late as that night, Morgan was adding to Washington's strength; sixteen-year-old Thomas Young was given a saber after nightfall and told he would ride the next morning with Washington's 3rd Light Dragoons. With the addition of the mounted militia, Washington had at minimum 120 troopers at Cowpens. Like the other militia at Cowpens, these militia were mounted infantry, riding to the site of battle but then fighting on foot. They were not practiced in fighting with the sword on horseback, an art that took years to master. Morgan and Washington believed that the mass these mounted militia added to the Continental dragoons would make up for their inexperience as dragoons. They were proved right. Never in the previous five years had cavalry proved decisive on a Revolutionary battlefield. Morgan now proposed that they would act both as light dragoons, scouting and screening Tarleton's advance, and then become heavy cavalry, able to charge the British infantry at the decisive moment.[12]

Then, with darkness, Morgan made his way from campfire to campfire. Thomas Young, who had just been issued that saber, remembered him helping the newly drafted militia dragoons with their swords—possibly correcting their overenthusiastic sharpening, or binding some rawhide around the grips—as he "joked with them about their sweethearts . . . telling them that the 'Old Wagoner' would crack his whip over Ben Tarleton in the morning as sure as he lived." He gave the militia in the front two lines repeated simple instructions. "'Just hold up your heads, boys,' he would say, 'three fires, and you are free! And then, when you return to your homes, how the old folks will bless you, and the girls kiss you, for your gallant conduct.'"

There is enough in those two sentences for a small essay on the psychology of exhortation: the diminution, not demonization, of Tarleton as "Ben"; "hold up your head," both an admonition to keep their eyes on the target as well as to be men of honor; precise instructions of what he wanted them to do; an appeal to freedom; an appeal to imagine themselves as heroes with all the benefits. It amounts to a rhetorical and instructional masterpiece in miniature; if a soldier only remembered one thing out of it, then Morgan had done good work. And this speech was not delivered once, but again and again and again, until Morgan was satisfied that every one of his soldiers knew what he wanted them to do. Young reflected years later, "I don't think he slept a wink that night."[13]

THE courier who came into camp at 5:30 AM reported that Tarleton's force had advanced to within three miles of the camp at Cowpens. They had begun their march at 3:00 AM, following in the path of Morgan's army. In the freezing darkness of morning, they had waded across two creeks, each at least knee high, and trudged through the semifrozen mud churned up by the feet, hooves, and wagon wheels of the American army. By the time they reached the first mounted pickets of Morgan's army they were cold, wet, exhausted, and hungry.

As Morgan's infantrymen took their arranged positions, some dragoons from Washington's troop were encountering Tarleton's outriders. Led by Sergeant Lawrence Everheart—few names could be more appropriate to the man or his service—they rode out from the forward post, three miles down the Green River road from the Cowpens. Just a mile away, they found Tarleton, closing as fast as his men could march. The Americans wheeled their horses and fled, ten of them managing to escape and bring final word of the British approach. Tarleton's advance riders were mounted on the best racehorses he could find in the Carolinas (he and his constant American opponents, William Washington and Harry Lee, were all horse proud and none too scrupulous about obtaining the best), and some of them managed to catch up with the rear of the fleeing American troopers. In the melee, Everheart's mount was killed, and he alone was captured.

Marched back on foot to the main body of Tarleton's little army, Everheart was confronted by a young, clean-faced, almost cherubic officer in the green uniform and bearskin-topped helmet of the

British Legion. He dismounted and began to interrogate Everheart, asking him if he expected that Morgan and Washington would fight.

"Yes," said Everheart, "if they can keep together only two hundred men."

"Then," said the officer, "it will be another Gates' defeat"— the name in use in the Carolinas for the Battle of Camden.

"I hope to God it will be another Tarleton's defeat," responded Everheart.

"I am Colonel Tarleton, sir," responded his interrogator.

"And I am Sergeant Everheart."[14]

Tarleton moved on, trying to pick up the pace. Skirmishers began to fire at his forces from ambush, delaying them as best they could, but they were encountering men who knew what to do in such a situation. The cavalry of the British Legion and the 17th Light Dragoons were deployed along both sides of the line of march, the open woods allowing them to sweep it free of skirmishers.

It was not yet sunrise when the first cavalry arrived at the Cowpens, Tarleton with them. Chesney and his other guides had told him all they could about the ground in front of him, describing Cowpens and the country toward the Broad River "with great perspicuity," as Tarleton recalled. Even after the defeat, Tarleton admitted that "an open wood was certainly as proper a place for action as Lieutenant-colonel Tarleton could desire; Americans does not produce many more suitable to the nature of the troops under his command." But at that moment, in the dim light, he could not see what his guides were describing, and it was simply not in Tarleton's nature to wait for brighter light. He could see clumps of what appeared to be militia scattered across the field in cover behind trees, Morgan's line of militia; but he could not see the line of militia skirmishers that had been deployed between his position and that line. Nor does Tarleton seem to have seen either the location of the Continentals or the cavalry. Therefore, Tarleton sent forward the cavalry of the British Legion "to drive in the militia parties who covered the front, that General Morgan's disposition might be conveniently and distinctly inspected." The riflemen from Georgia and South Carolina chosen to oppose them were ready. Morgan had given them specific instructions to hide behind the large trees on the field in groups of three. Only one soldier was to fire at a time, the other two keeping their shots in reserve until such a moment as the cavalry attempted a charge. There was a continual crackle of rifle fire, and Tarleton's cavalry balked, then retreated. He still did not know how Morgan was deployed, and the strength of the rifle fire forced him to deploy at his location.[15]

Meanwhile, Tarleton's infantrymen were arriving at the field, dropping all equipment other than their muskets and cartridge boxes and deploying into a single formation spread out along both sides of the Green River Road. As each formation arrived, Tarleton fed them into the line. The 7th Regiment of Foot (the Fusiliers) and the two light cannon were placed on the west side of the road, and the British Legion's infantry and the other light infantry formations on the right side. They were flanked by Tarleton's cavalry—the horses of the British Legion on the left flank and right, supported by the detachment of the 17th Light Dragoons on the right. The 71st Highlanders, led by the veteran Major Archibald McArthur, were kept in reserve. According to Stedman, Tarleton began to lead the line forward "before it was fully formed," while officers were still stationing themselves in the appropriate positions and before the reserve had reached its designated position. Tarleton himself remembered that "the animation of the officers and the alacrity of the soldiers afforded the most promising assurances of success." As always, speed was Tarleton's measure of imminent victory.[16]

Morgan was now mounted and ranging along the second line of the militia. He repeated many of the things he had said to them earlier that night. Once more he told them to fire just two rounds and then retreat behind the Continentals and re-form. Then he rode back to the third line of the Continentals and Virginia riflemen, where Lieutenant Colonel Howard was also mounted, ranging up and down behind the line. All witnesses agree that Morgan's speech was shorter to them and went something like this: "My friends in arms, my dear boys, I request you to remember Saratoga, Monmouth, Paoli, Brandywine, on this day you must play your parts for your honor and liberties cause." As historian Don Higginbotham aptly observed, "battlefield oratory was not uncommon in the eighteenth century, but it was seldom more effectively employed."[17] But it was more than simply effective. There, in one long sentence, stood everything Daniel Morgan thought was important. First of all, friendship—a friendship that transcended class and origin, that bound him and a Baltimore silk stocking like John Eager Howard together, that bound Howard and himself to a recent Irish immigrant now standing in the ranks before him. Because they were friends in arms, they had suffered together, fought together, and that meant they were "dear boys," and who can doubt the man who cried so easily, laughed so easily, raged so easily, meant something particular by that emotional identification.

And they all had honor. If the Revolution meant anything to Daniel Morgan, it was that he now had honor, and that all of his soldiers now had honor. That meant that he and they now had the moral responsibility to defend that honor as well as liberty itself. And he knew that he and they had the ability to do so.

His attack barely shaken into line, Tarleton ordered his soldiers forward against the militia he could now see in the growing light. Morgan rode to the center of the militia line, taking a post just behind it, encouraging his men to wait until they could see the whites of the enemy's eyes. As the British came forward, they gave their typical deep-throated bellow. "They give us the British hallo, boys," said Morgan to the second line. "Give them the Indian hallo, by God."[18]

Not until the British had reached about forty yards in front of them did Pickens give the word to fire. Some had already begun firing, so that Thomas Young, back with the cavalry, recalled first hearing a "pop, pop, pop, pop" before then hearing the volleys of companies firing together in unison. These blasts of firing by company worked their way down the line of militia. Every one of them fired at least one shot, many two or three or even more. The firing went on for about three minutes until the British infantry dressed their lines, lowered their bayonets, and charged forward.

Militia fell back, in varying degrees of excitement. They passed through the ranks of the third line, after which they were directed to re-form. But some of them kept going, heading for their horses tied in a pine grove about three hundred or four hundred yards behind the Continentals in the third line. As they ran, Tarleton ordered a charge by the Legion and 17th Dragoons on his right flank. They charged forward, sweeping around the third line of regulars and militia toward the unprotected militia now running across open ground to reach the safety of their mounts. "I thought," remembered James Collins, a teenage South Carolina militiaman, "'my hide is now in the loft.'" Just as the British dragoons began to lay about with their swords, William Washington and his cavalry came riding to the rescue, preserving Collins and most of his comrades from a skinning. "There was no time to rally," Collins remembered admiringly; the British cavalry "appeared to be as hard to stop as a drove of wild Choctaw steers, going to a Pennsylvania market. In a few moments the clashing of swords was out of hearing." Then Morgan was there in front of them, waving his sword, bellowing "form, form, my brave fellows. Old Morgan was never beaten." Pickens and he managed to head off the stampede toward the horses and bring the militia into some kind of order, ready to head once more into the battle. They began to march toward the third line, the right end where at that moment the battle seemed in doubt.[19]

The flight of the militia was, in retrospect, the critical moment in the battle. Subsequent accounts by British participants or contemporaries never considered any other possibility than that they, at that moment, had victory in their hand and that the militia were broken and running. Long experience, after all, had taught them that once militia ran, they would not return. At that moment, Tarleton was certain of his victory. He dressed the lines of his infantry, taking no more than two or three minutes to do so, and then they continued their advance.

They then met the seemingly immovable object of the third line. "The fire on both sides was well supported," wrote Tarleton, "and produced much slaughter"—but rather more of British than Americans.[20] For the mixture of both Virginia riflemen and Continental musketry in Howard's third line was even more effective than the mixing of Morgan's riflemen and Dearborn's musket men had been at Saratoga. The rifle fire from the Rockbridge and Fauquier County militias meant that as soon as Tarleton's infantry came within view, before they came within musket range, they were vulnerable. But when they came closer, they could not simply sprint forward with extended bayonets. When they tried, they were

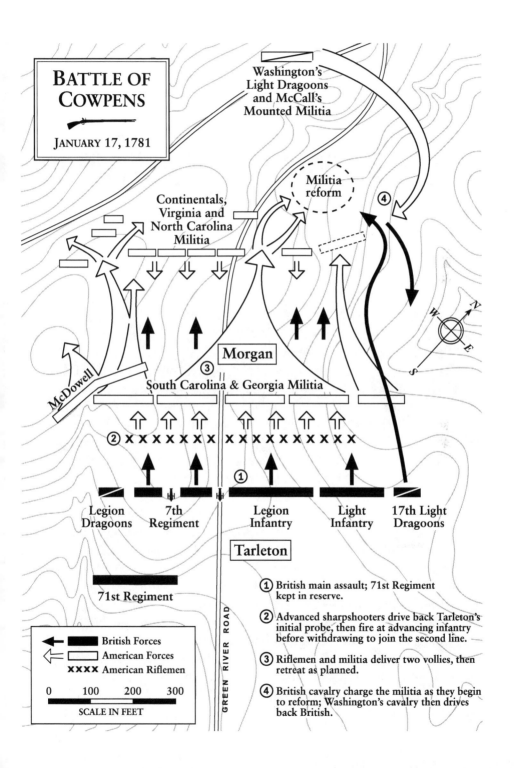

BATTLE OF
COWPENS

JANUARY 17, 1781

Washington's
Light Dragoons
and McCall's
Mounted Militia

Militia
reform

④

Continentals,
Virginia and
North Carolina
Militia

Morgan

③

McDowell

South Carolina & Georgia Militia

② X X X X X X X   X X X X X X X X X X

①

Legion
Dragoons

7th
Regiment

Legion
Infantry

Light
Infantry

17th Light
Dragoons

Tarleton

71st Regiment

① British main assault; 71st Regiment
kept in reserve.

② Advanced sharpshooters drive back Tarleton's
initial probe, then fire at advancing infantry
before withdrawing to join the second line.

③ Riflemen and militia deliver two vollies, then
retreat as planned.

④ British cavalry charge the militia as they begin
to reform; Washington's cavalry then drives
back British.

GREEN RIVER ROAD

◀ ■■ British Forces
⇐ ▢ American Forces
XXXX American Riflemen

0   100   200   300
SCALE IN FEET

stunned by the rapid volleys delivered by the Maryland and Delaware Continentals massed at the center of the line, the Virginia riflemen continuing to pick away at the British officers and sergeants as best they could see them through the smoke.

The fire was "well-directed and incessant," Morgan wrote in his report to Greene. Indeed it was. One Virginia rifleman remembered having used seventeen rounds from his shot pouch. At three shots a minute—excellent practice—this meant the third line was locked in battle with Tarleton's advance for over five minutes. The musket men of the Maryland and Delaware would have, in the course of things, fired that much more, at least twenty rounds, and probably more like thirty would have been expended in such a sharp, toe-to-toe firefight.[21]

Realizing that the moment of decision was at hand, Tarleton ordered forward the battalion of the 71st Regiment of Highlanders waiting in reserve, 150 yards behind the main line. They quickly advanced to flank the Americans' third line on its right, the British left.[22] As they did, Captain Andrew Wallace of Virginia, commanding the right-most company, ordered his men to refuse their right flank—that is, swing like a door backward so they would not be enfiladed by the muskets of the 71st firing perpendicularly down the third line. This was a difficult maneuver for any unit under fire to perform, and somehow the Virginia Militia fired a volley, about-faced, and then began marching away instead of swinging on the hinge of the unit to their left. As they marched away, they exposed the company next to them to fire, and so its commander ordered a volley be delivered, and then about-faced and followed Wallace; and then the next, and then the next. Howard in the center then ordered the rest of the third line to fire a volley and follow the example of the other retreating companies.[23]

Seeing a retreat that he most certainly had not ordered, Morgan left off re-forming the militia with Pickens and raced his horse to the scene. Finding John Eager Howard, Morgan expressed what Graham described as "feelings of astonishment and alarm"—perhaps one of the most carefully phrased understatements in the entire historiography of the American Revolution. Howard responded, with a gesture to his steadily marching regulars and riflemen, that "men were not beaten who retreated in that order." A moment of consideration was all Morgan needed to agree. He ordered Howard to spread the word to his officers to face about and fire when the command was given—and then he rode quickly ahead to pick a spot suitable for that purpose.[24]

At that moment, more or less, Washington sent Howard a messenger to tell him, "They are coming on like a mob; give them a fire and I will charge them." As the infantry began an ascent of the opposite side of the swale from where they had begun, Morgan rode along the rear of their ranks, pointing out to each captain where he wanted them to halt and make their stand. "Face about boys! Given them one good fire, and the victory is ours!" He rode along behind the line, bellowing this, as Howard's and Triplett's men turned and began to fire by company, a wave of tearing, ripping volleys that tore the guts out of the disordered green-and-red-coated soldiers pursuing them. Then Howard ordered a bayonet charge, and the Americans lowered their weapons and assaulted the British—man bites dog.

The British broke, but behind them now were Washington and the cavalry. They rode through the fleeing British—particularly the detachment of the 7th Regiment of Foot (the Fusiliers) and the infantry of the British Legion—wheeled their horses, and then charged through them yet again. For the first time on an American battlefield, cavalry were used in the devastating way that would have thrilled the heart of a Prussian general. Men of the Fusiliers threw themselves to the ground to avoid the sabers of the troopers and began to shout that they surrendered. Some of the Americans began to shout in response, "Tarleton's quarter! Tarleton's quarter!," meaning no quarter at all. But Morgan put a stop to that, preventing a massacre. Simultaneously, Kirkwood and his Delaware company—who had suffered 25 percent casualties during the toe-to-toe gunfight with the British light infantry—broke through the British line and attacked Tarleton's two cannon, running pell-mell at them. One officer, racing another to the guns, pole vaulted on his spontoon to be the first to clamber atop one. The slaughter was immense, the artillerymen resisting until they were all killed or wounded. Then Howard led the remainder of his soldiers toward the right to assist Pickens and his militia in their attack on the Highlanders.[25]

As the third line began to reach the site of its final stand, Pickens had his men back in hand and was urging them forward, sweeping around the right of the third line. There they formed just in time to confront the 71st Regiment as it came up to the line. Major McArthur's battalion was driven back, but it refused to break. Instead it fell back steadily, looking for safety at the bottom of the field.

Tarleton was, in the meantime, doing what he could to use his cavalry to cover the Scots. But the cavalry of his legion refused to charge—"above two hundred dragoons forsook their leader, and left the field of battle." Only the forty troopers of 17th Dragoons followed him, along with their fourteen officers, and these were too few to rescue Fraser's Highlanders.[26]

As Tarleton attempted to find some way of rescuing his army, Howard brought up his regulars, wheeling them to block the escape of the 71st Regiment. Pickens's militia then charged into the Scots, and all became hand-to-hand combat. Major James Jackson of Georgia—born in England twenty-four years before, immigrated as a child, later to be senator and governor of the state—attempted to seize the regimental colors but was driven back. He compromised by taking Major McArthur prisoner.[27]

All was lost for Tarleton's infantry, but he was determined to preserve some honor by recapturing his guns. With his fifty-four troopers of the 17th Dragoons, he charged back up the field, but they were intercepted by Washington's dragoons. Americans were convinced that the day had ended with a thrilling duel between William Washington and Banastre Tarleton. "Tarleton and two of his officers charged Col. Washington," Morgan told Ed Snickers. "Tarleton fired both his pistols at Washington, and wounded his horse . . . before two of Washington's men came up & cut the two Officers very much—Tarleton cleared himself by the swiftness of his Horse." Whoever the British officer was that Washington fought, it was probably not Tarleton. But regardless, these were the last reported shots of the day on the Cowpens. Tarleton and his surviving cavalry rode off down the Green River Road toward their baggage, justifying the infantry's perennial belief that few people had ever seen a dead cavalryman.[28]

THE battle was over, and Morgan knew exactly what he had done; there was no moment of dazed coming to awareness of victory for him. One story has him picking up the Marylanders' nine-year-old drummer boy and kissing him on both cheeks. Howard describes clutching seven swords, given to him by surrendering British officers, when Morgan rode up to him. "You have done well," said Morgan, "for you have been successful; had you failed, I would have shot you."

"Had I failed," said Howard, with the insouciance of the Maryland aristocrat, "there would have been no need of shooting me."[29]

He had, Morgan said, given Tarleton a "devil of a whipping, a more compleat victory never was obtained." He was not wrong; the numbers show he wasn't even bragging. Tarleton had lost 110 men killed and 701 captured, 229 of whom were wounded. He had additionally left behind on the field two small cannon, the colors of the 7th Regiment (they still hang in the West Point Chapel), eight hundred muskets, thirty-five wagons, one hundred horses, and perhaps most important of all, his reputation in the South for invincibility. The Americans also seized seventy African Americans who had been working as officers' servants, all of whom had certainly escaped from enslavement. Now they were put back in that condition. Two of them, Nat and Toby, would be enslaved by Morgan for the rest of his life.[30]

Major James Jackson later reminded Morgan of another episode that occurred after the final shots. Among the plunder left by Tarleton was a store of wine, over which Morgan had promptly placed a guard—the last thing he needed was incapable soldiers when he meant to soon be on the road for North Carolina. When Jackson asked for some wine to give to the wounded, the sergeant commanding the guard refused. "You came very angrey," Jackson recalled years later, "and I expected you would have struck me. . . [F]eeling myself injured, I explained to you the conduct of the Fellow, and could not help adding that my conduct had deserved a better return. . . . [I]t was then you made the sergeant beg my pardon on his knees."[31]

The battle must have been over by 9:00 or 10:00 AM at the latest. Morgan gave orders to Washington to pursue Tarleton with his dragoons and some mounted militia. He set the remainder of the infantry to collecting their trophies and getting the prisoners ready to march. At noon they stepped out, heading north.[32]

When Morgan and the army marched away, William Washington and his troopers were still in pursuit of the fleeing Tarleton, accompanied by the indomitable Captain Robert Kirkwood and his equally resilient Delawareans, along with some Virginia militia. Kirkwood's company had just fought a battle in which it had taken 25 percent casualties; nevertheless, it still marched twelve miles in three hours, took a lunch break, linked up with Washington, and then marched back to the battlefield. It began to rain. But that night, reported one of their sergeants, they "lay amongst the Dead & Wounded very well pleased with our days Work."[33]

THE Old Wagoner had indeed cracked his whip over Tarleton and destroyed his little army. But victories in battle do not determine victory in war. Generations of military historians have noted with an odd sort of pique that Nathanael Greene never won a battle outright yet nevertheless in about nine months confined the British to Charleston and its immediate environs. If battles are what win wars, then Greene's campaign of 1780–1781 seems like a dirty trick. But a different way of reading events would indicate what is seemingly unthinkable for some, that wars are not won by adding up the win-loss record of battles. It is not enough, then, to focus on the tactical perfection of Morgan's victory. The consequences of Cowpens were not determined solely on the battlefield. Morgan had removed nearly all of Cornwallis's light troops, those best suited for fighting the partisan war in the South, as completely as a chess player takes an opponents' queen off the board. But to preserve that victory, Morgan now had to run.

There were, of course, other consequences of Cowpens. Just as Morgan had first by happenstance drawn Tarleton into a logistical trap, and then by careful intent into a tactical trap on the battlefield itself, now his race north would in time lure Cornwallis into another logistical trap. But more important was the effect that Cowpens had on the Carolina backcountry. Greene had sent Morgan to give heart to the Patriot cause. Now, just a few miles from the site of the great Patriot victory at King's Mountain, Morgan had doomed the Loyalist cause. There would be raids and counterraids, reprisals and massacres still to come. But there would be no more Fergusons, no more Tarletons, who could give aid and comfort to the internal enemy. There would be no Loyalist uprising on behalf of the king, no ranks of rifle-carrying Loyalists to join the royal cause. If the southern strategy was already, by December 30, 1780, a dead man walking, then at Cowpens it was Morgan, the militia of Georgia, the Carolinas, and the Continentals of Maryland and Delaware who had cut off its head.

Chapter Fifteen

RACE FOR
THE DAN

S OMETIME on January 23, 1781, Edward Giles and Baron de
Glaubeck rode into Greene's camp near the settlement of
Cheraws on the Pee Dee River in northeastern South Carolina, bearing Morgan's dispatch from the battlefield. Everyone
went slightly mad with joy. "We have had a *feu de joie*," wrote
Otho Williams, "drunk your healths, swore you were the finest fellows on earth, and love you, if possible, more than ever. The General has, I think, made his compliments in very handsome terms.
Enclosed is a copy of his orders. It was written immediately after
we received the news and during the operation of some cherry
bounce."[1]

Greene might have been tipsy with alcohol and joy, but it did not
damage his thinking. He concluded almost immediately that this
news would draw Cornwallis after Morgan, and consequently he
feared for the safety of the Flying Army, which could fly no more
with so many prisoners to drag along after it. He began to meditate
on the possibilities open to him if he could draw Cornwallis after

the American army deep into North Carolina, perhaps even to Virginia. Orders began to blizzard out from him and his adjutant general, Williams: Brigadier General Isaac Huger was, in Greene's absence, to break camp and begin a march to Salisbury; the magazines at Salisbury and Hillsborough were to be prepared for evacuation north; and boats were to be collected on the Catawba, Yadkin, and Dan Rivers. Then, on the twenty-sixth, Greene took off cross-country to find Morgan, accompanied only by a small cavalry escort.[2]

Cornwallis was indeed already in motion. When Tarleton dismounted on the evening of the seventeenth at Winnsborough to inform his commander of his defeat, Cornwallis was leaning on his sword. As he listened, he pressed it so hard that it finally snapped. It was a perfect metaphor for what Morgan had done to the noble lord's army by depriving it of nearly all his light troops.[3]

The day after Tarleton returned, Brigadier General Alexander Leslie finally arrived with his substantial reinforcement from Charleston. On the nineteenth, Cornwallis broke camp and marched toward Cowpens. Tarleton rode ahead to scout the Cowpens battlefield, accompanied by his remaining cavalry and German riflemen. They returned with the report that only wounded were there and that Morgan was long gone. Cornwallis quickly decided Morgan would be establishing a defensive position north of the Broad River. He pointed his army toward King's Mountain and headed after Morgan.[4]

Morgan ran. He was in a race from the very moment he sent Kirkwood to snap up any of Tarleton's straggling survivors. The first lap was against the moment when news of Tarleton's defeat reached Cornwallis; then a second lap, against the moment of Cornwallis's start after him; and then the final lap as each army sought to cross the Catawba River. Gaining an advantage in the first two laps would see his men to safety. To gain that advantage, he had to above all things move his army as fast as it could possibly go; but he also needed intelligence of Cornwallis, and to prevent intelligence from reaching Cornwallis.

To secure the intelligence he dispatched men to watch Cornwallis's camp and then follow him, with reports to be carried daily to Morgan. For security against that same kind of news of his own movements reaching Cornwallis, Morgan sent out other units to intimidate Tories and keep them home rather than riding to inform the British.[5]

For greater speed and latitude, he sent off the prisoners by a separate way, over the western fords of the Broad, with directions to keep to the western fords of all the Piedmont rivers, close to the foothills of the Blue Ridge. The prisoners were accompanied by militia returning to North Carolina and Virginia at the ends of their enlistments. Morgan took fords lower down the rivers, in between the prisoner escorts and the pursuing British. But he also separated them from his army because the prisoners were valuable resources. Not only were they Cornwallis's veteran light infantry, unable to be replaced, but they were bargaining chips. Should they be gotten safely away to camps in the Shenandoah Valley, or in Maryland and Pennsylvania, then they could be used to trade for those American prisoners dying in the prison hulks floating in Charleston Harbor.[6]

As Cornwallis pushed toward the northwest and King's Mountain, Morgan was moving east. On the evening of the nineteenth, after a laborious march with tired and overburdened troops, he crossed the Little Broad; during the march that day he sent his two aides with his dispatch notifying Greene of the victory. By the twenty-first he was at Ramsour's Mill, and on the twenty-third he reached Sherald's Ford on the Catawba River, the day before Cornwallis finally arrived at Ramsour's Mill. The Flying Army was now over twenty miles ahead of its pursuer and on the other side of the Catawba.

A look at the map—real, or the one that had been carefully drawn in his mind—convinced Morgan that he needed to stay on the north bank of the Catawba to resist any further moves by Cornwallis. Should he instead begin to march for the fords over the Yadkin, the next major river in North Carolina, then Cornwallis might be able to catch up with him before he made the safety of the other side, or he might turn west and free the prisoners. Morgan had to buy some time on the Catawba, if only he could get sufficient militia to support him.

He had the assistance of Brigadier General William Lee Davidson, a fellow veteran of Valley Forge where Davidson had commanded the 5th North Carolina Regiment. Now Davidson commanded the Salisbury District of the North Carolina Militia. He had approximately five hundred men under arms, but Morgan believed 250 of them had no flints for their guns. To bring more men into camp, Davidson was promising them with credit for three months' service if they would only stay in the field six weeks.[7] Those who responded to the incentive collected boats from the south side of the Catawba away from where Cornwallis might be able to use them and worked to block the numerous fords across the Catawba by digging into the banks to ruin the paths up out of the water and piling up abatis where paths emerged from the fords, with breastworks behind the abatis.[8]

From Sherald's Ford, Morgan sent a stream of letters to Greene. Of Cornwallis, he assured Greene, "I have got men that is watching his movements, and will give you the earliest accounts, but I think they will be this way, if the strok we gave Tarlton dont check him." He took other measures as well, including sending a party of militia to kill draft horses that Cornwallis might otherwise use.[9]

Then the next day, Morgan sent in his notice. It had been, he told Greene, his "sanguine expectation to do something clever this campaign." Now he manifestly had, and now he "must inform you that I shall be oblig'd to give over the persuite." The old agony had returned, the "pain in the hip." For three weeks it had been troubling him, but now "on geting wet the other day" he had it strike hard, so that "at times when I am walking or standing still am obliged to set down in the place it takes me, as quick as if I were shot." Nothing could cure this, Morgan concluded, other than rest. He would have to leave, for attempting to go through the winter campaign would "totally disable me from further service."[10]

Indeed, Morgan had been so disabled by sciatica, or whatever it was, that he had been forced to spend time in his tent on his back; in addition to the awful pain, he also had a fever. On the twenty-ninth there were rumors that Cornwallis was near, ready to attack, and Morgan dragged himself up from his bed and into the saddle. There, on the other side of the river, he could see the first elements of Cornwallis's force. But during the day, the Catawba started to rise from the rains in the mountain and the Piedmont. By the thirtieth it could only be crossed by boat, and there were none left on the south side of the river.

In the course of his pursuit of Morgan, Cornwallis had done some hard thinking. It seemed to him that his entire grip over South Carolina and Georgia, and his plans for taking North Carolina and Virginia, depended on bringing Morgan to battle and destroying him. Before Cowpens, this would have been more easily accomplished. His cavalry and light troops would rapidly precede him, make contact with the enemy, and fix the enemy in place. Then his "heavy" infantry, accompanied by artillery and baggage wagons, would arrive, and the enemy would be set up for smashing. But now he no longer had that capability; so he decided to make all his army into a Flying Army.

He did that by burning his baggage train. This meant he destroyed all of his wagons except for those that carried ammunition and a few empty ones to act as ambulances when the time came. Provisions would be what could be gotten along the way, and instructions were given regarding the processing and consumption of the mysterious staple of the Americans, corn. Everything else—all the luxuries that officers carried on campaign, tents, provisions, even the British soldier's precious rum—was destroyed. Cornwallis set an example by being the first to light the fires, burning his own equipment in front of the eyes of his soldiers, including his tent (for the rest of the campaign, he rolled himself up in a blanket and slept as did his soldiers). Then he got back on the road after Morgan. His load lightened, he quickly arrived at the Catawba, only to be stopped by its floodwaters.[11]

Then, on January 31, Nathanael Greene rode into Morgan's camp.

Immediately after his arrival, he and Morgan, accompanied by William Washington and Brigadier General Davidson, held a conference on a log outside of camp. Greene did not know all the details of what Cornwallis had done when he arrived at Sherald's Ford, but his imagination and logic were impeccable enough so as to make the discussion decisive. They decided that the negatives on the tactical ledger were too great to give battle to Cornwallis when he crossed the river: the Catawba could not, of course, remain a barrier forever; when its waters relented, there were too many fords to defend. Also, the militia had not assembled in the numbers needed, and there were only three hundred Continentals in Morgan's Flying Army to serve as a core for what militia there were. All these things pointed to Morgan's retreating for Salisbury and the crossings of the Yadkin. This would be made possible by Davidson delaying Cornwallis's crossing for as long as possible before melting away into the countryside to fight another day. Making things even worse, not only were they opposed by Cornwallis in front of them, but there was now a British force behind them. Morgan's old commander and friend Benedict Arnold had in September defected to the British. Now he was a British brigadier general leading an invasion of Virginia. Greene was certain that Arnold's invasion was coordinated with Cornwallis, designed to trap the Southern Army between two forces. But for the moment, Cornwallis was the greater threat.[12]

Morgan's men were on the road early the next morning, but not before he had a chance to write Governor Jefferson an impassioned letter. He gave Jefferson his opinion that Cornwallis would attempt a crossing that morning, that it was doubtful any militia could oppose him, and that it was impossible for his force to do so, or for even a reunited Southern Army to do so. Therefore, "I am of opinion that Lord cornwallis fully intends to make a push through this state In order to make a junction on the roan oak [Roanoke River] or els whares, nor do I see what is to hinder him."

"Great god what is the reason we cant Have more men in the field," he continued, with "so many men in the country Nearby idle for want of employment. How distressing it must be to an anxious mind to see the country over Run and destroyed for want of assistance which I am realy afraid will be the case if proper exertion are not made use of." He had done his part at the Cowpens, and now he was "entirely emmaciated" by his labors that winter, "so that shant be of much use in the field this winter-if [e]ver I am, but as I have been broke down in the services of my country shall bear the infirmitys of old age with more satisfaction."[13]

That day Morgan and his army marched thirty miles in mud and rain. Behind them, not long after they had set out, Cornwallis forced a crossing of the Catawba. The militia under Davidson were covering four different fords. Quite by accident, the British advance guard took the wrong turn in the middle of the floodwaters, and rather than being confronted by the strongest of the fortifications, it ended up coming up out of the river at the ford that was least guarded.[14] By another accident, Davidson had just ridden to that crossing to check up on things, and he was killed by a bullet from a Loyalist's rifle. Later that day, other militia finally gathering to support Davidson were surprised by Tarleton and the troopers of his legion, who charged into them screaming, "Remember the Cowpens!"[15] Now Cornwallis set after Morgan at full speed to catch him before he reached the Yadkin River.

But Morgan reached Trading Ford on the Yadkin on the evening of February 2. There he met Tadeusz Kosciuszko, who had gathered boats from up and down the river. That night the Flying Army was ferried to safety on the north bank. Once more it was separated from Cornwallis by a river rough from wind and flood. As the last parties made it across, a British advance party arrived on the other side and threw some shots across the roiling water. The next day the British brought up a battery of artillery and pestered the American camp in view on the other side. Legendarily, one cannonball passed through the roof of the cabin in which Greene was writing without his even bothering to look up.

In another, less-conspicuous shelter, Morgan lay on a bed of leaves, covered with a blanket, "rheumatic from head to foot." Yet later that evening he was down by the river, questioning returning scouting parties. For Morgan, the whole campaign must have consisted of rounds of incapacity and pain from which he was able to free himself occasionally by force of his enormous will.[16]

What he learned from his scouts was that the British were now out of provisions and had to take time to forage across the country. After four days of waiting for the waters to subside and contemplating a frontal assault across the Yadkin, Cornwallis instead marched northwest toward the upper fords of the river. He was certain that Morgan and Greene would now be heading toward the upper fords of the Dan, the next major river running west to east, the last barrier before Virginia. Now Cornwallis would be able to intercept them.

Morgan, in fact, began to march north, paralleling Cornwallis's path. But then he swung to the east, covering forty-seven miles in two days. He was headed toward Guilford Courthouse, a hamlet of just a few cabins on the Carolina Road; Greene followed. On February 5, Morgan arrived there, now also suffering from "piles"—hemorrhoids— such that he could barely ride. Nevertheless, he dealt with such administrative matters as he could in Greene's absence. The prisoners were pushed ahead, across the Dan and into Virginia; he made attempts to secure provisions and forage; he directed the repair of a six-pounder cannon's carriage; and he sent out baggage wagons to collect what they could in the surrounding countryside.[17]

Huger arrived with the other half of the Southern Army at 4:00 PM on February 7, and on the ninth, Greene held a formal council of war, an unusual activity for one who boasted that he never called them. Just four men were there: Greene, Morgan, Huger, and Williams, in his capacity as Greene's adjutant general. Its purpose was almost certainly political, to affirm what Greene already knew, that he did not have strength enough to oppose Cornwallis. Given that there were just 1,426 infantry in Greene's army, "exclusive" of six hundred militia, the council agreed they could not oppose Cornwallis, who they estimated had "twenty five hundred or three thousand men." Therefore, "it was determined unanimously that we ought to avoid a general action at all Events, and that the Army ought to retreat immediately over the Roanoke River."[18]

While Morgan had made his intention of leaving the army clear over two weeks before, Greene and other officers still attempted to inveigle him into staying. Lieutenant Colonel Henry Lee, according to his recollections of years later, was particularly insistent. Lee was a cousin of Richard Henry Lee's, the Virginian who was so proud of his colony's riflemen. Rising in the ranks of the Continental cavalry, Lee, by 1781, commanded a partisan legion, the American equivalent of Tarleton's British Legion, right down to the green jackets both units wore. A graduate of Princeton, Lee seemed to be a natural soldier, as flamboyant and aggressive as cavalrymen traditionally were, and yet shrewd.

That shrewdness was employed in trying to shame Morgan into staying. Lee suggested that some might think Morgan was afraid of the army's failure, that he was running from a fight. It is perhaps a measure of Morgan's illness that while—according to Lee—he wavered for a moment, ultimately he did not rise to Lee's bait.[19]

Greene's attempt at persuasion had an even greater incentive. He reorganized the Flying Army into an even more formidable force than it had been at Cowpens, adding to it Harry Lee's 2nd Partisan Corps, a combined force of light infantry and dragoons, as well as sixty Virginia riflemen, a total of about seven hundred men. Its goal was to act as interference for the rest of the army, remaining just ahead of Cornwallis, and "harassing the enemy in their advance." It was just the sort of force and task that Morgan loved.[20]

But Morgan was used up; there were no more reserves of strength left for him to draw on. Otho Williams, clerk turned rifleman turned dependable adjutant general, took command of the new light corps. On February 10, Nathanael Greene wrote out Daniel Morgan a leave of absence, to take effect "untill he gathers his health."[21] That same day Morgan headed back to the Valley, riding in a carriage. All told, he had spent no more than five months in the Carolinas. It had been time well spent.

MORGAN's journey home was extraordinarily slow and agonizing; the carriage he rode in did not seem to improve matters much. In addition to his constant pain, he now had a fever every day. Because of this, he made multiple stops. The first was for several days at the house of Brigadier General Robert Lawson, whom Morgan had known as a major in the 4th Virginia Regiment and who now commanded a brigade in the Virginia Militia.

A few days later, Morgan was at Carter Harrison's plantation, his health not improving; in fact, he was feeling sicker. But such was Morgan's anxiety for Greene and his army that when he had gotten to Lawson's, despite the pain and fever, he picked up a pen and scratched out what hard-earned advice he could.

"I expect Lord Cornwallis will push you until you are obliged to fight him," he wrote, "on which much will depend." From what Morgan had seen on the roads during his trip north, and talking with Lawson and others, he thought Greene would soon have a "great number of militia" joining him. The conclusion Morgan made was simple: "if [the militia] fight you'll beat Cornwallis, if not, he will beat you and perhaps cut your regulars to pieces, which will be losing all our hopes."

Greene could choose, then, between fighting a battle like Cowpens or one like Camden. To ensure a victory like Cowpens, the Old Wagoner gave him careful advice: First separate out from the rest of the militia those who had seen Continental service and riflemen. These former Continentals should then be grouped in detachments that would be placed in the same line as the Continentals, effectively multiplying the number of Greene's regular troops. Riflemen, he advised, should be placed under "enterprising officers" (good partisan leaders, in other words) on the flanks of the army to enfilade the British ranks as they advanced. Then came one of the more cold-blooded pieces of tactical advice in the Revolutionary War: place "the remainder of the Militia in the centre with some picked troops in their rear with orders to shoot down the first man that runs."[22]

It is hard to imagine Charles Lee or Horatio Gates giving that advice. Unlike them, Morgan did not believe that a natural passion for liberty would hold citizen-soldiers in line to do their duty. Where there was no passion, and no training, and no Morgan to motivate them, then threats must do the job. Morgan succeeded at Cowpens with his militia not because he trusted militia as a group but because he believed in them as individuals. Perhaps it is an example of a kind of dual-consciousness. Morgan had been a militia ensign, after all, and a laborer, a wagoner, and a farmer—he had been one of them. But now he was a general, a member of an ever-higher level of Virginia gentry. And yet, he was not quite one or the other. Like so many of the men now emerging in American society, he had risen far in the swirling, bubbling, creative ferment of colonial America. But now the revolutionary moment was refining and distilling him into something that even colonial America could not have imagined. It would take those with the cultural mentality shaped by the old order some time to get used to these new men in this new world; it would take Morgan some time to get used to himself. Perhaps he never did.

Chapter Sixteen

ENDINGS

ARS do not end with triumphal parades that escort each and every victorious soldier back to his or her garden gate. Nor do they finish with every sailor kissing a nurse in Times Square. Once the guns are silent, soldiers and sailors experience the months, weeks, and days until peace or their demobilization as a series of sometimes-unconnected episodes. There is no longer a narrative arc of combat and fellowship. Instead they straggle offstage in a series of choppy scenes that no competent playwright or experienced director would allow.

The end of Morgan's war was no different. He was never retired, never dismissed from the army, but simply on leave for most of the time. The episodes making up the last years of the war and of his military life are like passing slides projected against a wall. By collecting those impressions, we can understand the end of one of Morgan's revolutions, and the beginnings of his next.

APRIL 1781
Soldier's Rest, Frederick County, Virginia
Morgan was away from home on April 10, one of the first days since he returned that he had ridden out. For what remained of Feb-

ruary and all of March, he did not leave the house, such was the severity of his condition. The only way he had found of relieving the pain was cold baths. He took a lot of them. By April the "ciatick" pain in his hip had left him, but by then he suffered from a pain in his head that he reported "Makes me blind as a bat two or three times a day."[1]

But on this day he was at long last away, when it happened that a trooper of Harry Lee's 2nd Partisan Corps arrived at Soldier's Rest bringing good medicine: a British flag taken at Cowpens, bound north to be delivered to Congress. The trooper also bore a letter from Greene describing the Battle of Guilford Courthouse, with particular attention to how Greene had imitated Morgan's disposition of forces at Cowpens. "The enemy are now retiring from us," Greene wrote Morgan, and "we shall follow them immediately with a determination for another touch." His commander concluded by informing him that Lafayette was headed south with a small army of light infantry to oppose the invasion of Virginia still being led by their old friend: "Arnold must fall."[2]

Morgan responded to Greene with his usual directness of emotion and sentiment. "I have been particularly happy in my connections with the army, and am happy to tell you, sir, you are among the number I esteem. . . .You perhaps will call this a flattering letter," Morgan wrote, "but it has always given me pleasure to give every one his due; and I think it right, or where is the grand stimulus that pushes men on to great actions?" Characteristically, he added, "On the other hand, I am as willing to give a person his demerits, if the person be worthy of notice."[3]

Now Daniel Morgan was a person worthy of notice. He knew that his mere presence could bring more people to join an army, would give courage to the soldiers; and he knew he could win crushing victories as well. As his health improved, he began to plan on rejoining Greene in South Carolina to finish the job. He seems to have envisioned re-creating the Flying Army and bringing it south. That would be a fine thing: not only to return to Greene's army, but return with trained and equipped reinforcements.

JUNE 1781

The Appalachian Mountains

Once more Morgan was leading men out of Winchester to fight for the cause of the Revolution. This time he was at the head of about four hundred men, rather than the ninety-eight he had led to Boston, and he was a brigadier general. It did his heart good to be accompanied by Colonel Christian Febiger; "Old Denmark" had moved to Frederick County and was thinking of settling there with his young bride. It was like old times, only better—except that Morgan was not heading south to join Greene, or east to assist Lafayette against Cornwallis's invasion of Virginia, but west to the Lost River region in Hampshire County, beyond the first ranges of the Appalachians. His enemies this time were Virginians, seemingly in rebellion against the government of Virginia.

In the western regions of the commonwealth, where there was the largest free white population, the citizens had an ever-increasing resentment of the cost of a war that had been prolonged for six years and gave no sign of ending. Ever higher taxes, impressments of provisions and forage, the endless drafts on militia—these had all increased disaffection toward the Revolutionary government. This did not mean their affections were any warmer toward the royal government, but the Revolutionary governments did not always see this distinction.[4]

Morgan had been worried about this sentiment since he returned to Frederick County to recuperate. He had returned to find his fellow citizens "in a ferment about the Taxes." When some said they would not pay, he wrote Governor Jefferson, "I endeavoured to convince them of the danger of such a step, and threatened them should they attempt to fly in the face of the Law, since which the matter is silenced." (As always where Morgan is concerned, one can only imagine what actual words this understatement conceals.) The incident had persuaded Morgan that "a small force ought to be kept up in each county as well to inforce the Laws is to defend the States, for had great Britton it in her power to send ever so many men in the field against us, I should still be in hopes to repel them, but when ever I see the Laws trampled on with Impunity I shall begin to despair."[5]

That trampling had begun in Hampshire County, where a mob set upon a Virginia official who was attempting to recruit militia and round up the cattle with which to feed them. He was driven out, and the rioters, suddenly discovering they were a movement, elected John Claypool (or Claypole; spellings vary) their leader. Then they drank, toasting the king, and perhaps under that influence threatened that they would join Cornwallis's army. Governor Jefferson and the state legislature were certain this could be no accident; surely the rebellion must be occurring because of some sort of preexisting treasonous correspondence with the British army. However, their most immediate concern was not to prevent Claypool and the rebels from joining Cornwallis with their supposed strength of one thousand men, but to make certain other disaffected Virginians, particularly those in the Valley, did not follow Hampshire County's example. Urgent letters were sent to Frederick County requesting that a force be sent to suppress the rebellious Virginians, with the understanding that Morgan was to lead it—his presence would be the "only sure remeddy."[6]

Morgan took two days to march his militia to the Lost River. His name proved to be more powerful than the force that accompanied him: Claypool and other leaders of the riot fled before him. A few shots were exchanged and a few Loyalists captured. Then Morgan selected the farm of the richest of the would-be rebels, which conveniently came with its own distillery, camped his men there, and ate the man's cattle and drank his whiskey barrels dry. Like Queen Elizabeth I, Morgan knew that the best way to suppress a potential rebellion was to spend some time as houseguest of the chief rebel. After even a short visit, the rebel's heart might be readier for rebellion than it had ever been, but its capital would be unable to support it.

All in all, it was an excellent training exercise, and the best news of all for Morgan was that he continued to feel fine; there were no relapses. He left Old Denmark in command, to herd the militia back home, and hurried back to Winchester in order to complete his preparations for joining the Southern Army.

JULY 6, 1781
The American Camp near Jamestown Island
For months, Morgan had been creating a new force with which to join the Southern Army. His first intention was to join Greene. Finally, after the sideshow of Claypool's rebellion, he was able to

focus his attention on that task. But now his aim was to join not Greene but the Marquis de Lafayette.

Lafayette had come to Virginia with a cobbled-together unit of light infantry, intending to oppose Benedict Arnold's occupation of Norfolk and his raids up the James River and throughout the Tidewater region. On his arrival, Lafayette found that Arnold had been reinforced by two thousand men under Sir William Phillips, and he fell back before their combined strength. Then in May, just a week after Phillips's sudden death, Cornwallis arrived with his army. Before this overwhelming force, Lafayette could only imitate Greene's tactics prior to the Battle of Guilford Courthouse. He retreated to the north, Cornwallis in pursuit. Throughout the spring, Cornwallis and Lafayette marched and countermarched, with Tarleton and other experienced British partisans raiding the hitherto untouched Virginia countryside. Lafayette all the while pleaded for reinforcements, to Washington, to the government of Virginia, and to Daniel Morgan.

In response, Morgan had put together the kind of combined arms unit at which he was now the acknowledged master, a collection this time of riflemen supported by cavalry. The horsemen were mounted, due to Morgan's horse buying (and seizing) in the lower Valley, but lacked uniforms, weapons, and "every other requisite of the dragoon."[7] His riflemen often were without rifles, and all lacked the ammunition necessary to carry out a campaign.

In the meantime, the civilian authorities of Virginia were going slightly insane with impatience. Cornwallis's invasion and Tarleton's raid on Charlottesville had stretched civil government almost to its breaking point. Removed to the safety of Staunton in the Valley, Thomas Nelson had been elected governor by the legislature and immediately took executive authority that in time led to charges of dictatorship. Indeed, by the new year, one legislative committee was investigating Thomas Jefferson for inadequately exercising his executive power to oppose the British invasion, while another investigated Thomas Nelson for exercising too much of it.

But fortunately, Nelson did not know this in advance, or would not have cared if he did. He was impatient that Morgan move to Lafayette's assistance and not let details like finance and supply detain him. At his urging, Morgan sent his cavalry to Lafayette—who badly wanted mounted troops—with the hope that swords and necessary accoutrements would be available elsewhere in Virginia. He eventually marched south with his riflemen in the same expectation.

Morgan finally arrived at Lafayette's camp the day after a battle at Greenspring Plantation. There, while crossing the James River near Jamestown Island, Cornwallis had lured the American general into a trap. In the end, only Anthony Wayne's Pennsylvania Brigade entered it, and then fought its way clear. But it was another indication of how necessary Morgan and his accompanying cavalry and light troops were. Lafayette promptly put Morgan in command of the special light corps, composed of riflemen, militia, Continentals, and cavalry, including those he had sent forward from Winchester and a group of Maryland gentlemen who had showed up on horseback eager to serve.

Yet on the very night of his arrival, Morgan suffered a relapse of his "sciatical complaint." After the excursion to Hampshire County, the pressure of raising his troops, and bringing them down the breadth of the state—now, just as he arrived in proximity with the enemy, he was struck by the familiar agony.[8]

The pains continued for the next month. During that time, Cornwallis dispatched Tarleton on a raid west to Prince Edward and Bedford Counties, two hundred miles away, to destroy supplies intended for Greene's army. Lafayette in turn sent Morgan and Wayne to intercept him. Unfortunately for Morgan, who eagerly sought a reencounter with his old enemy, Tarleton's small force was able to slip around the blocking positions that Wayne and Morgan had assumed. Despite that misadventure, Cornwallis's lingering at Portsmouth, and his continual pain, Morgan still dreamed of going south to rejoin Greene. Just a week or so before he left Lafayette and his last command in the Continental army, Morgan wrote that he hoped to soon be on the march south to join Greene and "all the old heroes." But a few sentences later he bleakly and simply said, "I am afraid I am broke down."[9]

By the time Morgan received Greene's reply, he was once more in Frederick County, preparing to go to Bath Springs for a water cure. Hopefully the words of his old commander were something of a balm for his troubled spirit. "Great generals are scarce," wrote Greene, "there are few Morgans to be found."[10]

SEPTEMBER 20, 1781

Morgan was home, precisely where he did not want to be. His body had not regained its strength, and his spirit was troubled. Now he was writing a letter to George Washington, expressing the latter.

On August 14, news had reached Washington that the Comte de Grasse would be sailing to Chesapeake Bay. By the nineteenth, Washington had the French and American armies near New York on the road marching south to Virginia, there to join with de Grasse and Lafayette in cornering Cornwallis. On September 14, Washington reached Williamsburg and Lafayette's army.

For Morgan it was almost inexpressibly bitter that Washington had returned to their home state to win a great victory and that he would not be present. He had fought for the glorious cause as far north as any Continental soldier had fought for it, and he had gone farther south to fight than most. Altogether he had marched and fought in eleven colonies. But now, when the moment of decision came to his own Virginia, he would not be present. Now he poured his feelings into a fervent letter to his old commander as best as he could. He even drafted it first, before writing a clean copy.

"Such has been my peculiar fate," Morgan wrote, "that during the whole course of the present war I have never on any important event had the honor of serving particularly under your excellency. It is a misfortune I have ever sincearly lamented[.] there is nothing on earth would have given more real pleasure than to have made this campaign under your excellancys' Eye to have sheared the danger, and let me add the glory too, which I am almost confident will be acquired."[11]

Whatever the depths of Washington's reserve and the power of his self-control—and both were considerable—his heart could not have failed to be slightly warmed by this evidence that he had conquered Morgan's affections.

DECEMBER 1781

In this month, and again sometime in 1782—probably in July—Morgan had two very different dinners, with two different Europeans.

The first was with Captain Joseph Graham, a British officer captured at Yorktown and marched to Winchester for internment. He

and his fellow prisoners had marched through the Virginia countryside, to the great satisfaction of its inhabitants watching them
pass by. Reaching Winchester, they found that there were no lodg-
ings for the enlisted men and it was already mid-November, with
the promise of a winter soon to come. Some of Graham's men were
placed in a church in town, at least until Morgan got wind of it. He
quickly wrote bidding Graham to vacate the church at once. Graham protested that there was no other place available. By this time
there was snow on the ground, and the British had no tools available to them.

Morgan was unsympathetic. "I received your letter . . . and am
really surprised at the purport of it," he wrote back. "Two or three
days before Christmas our army began to hut at Middlebrook, Jersey, and nothing to keep off the inclemency of the weather too hot
for me. You have time enough, the snow won't last long, it will be
going directly, if your men don't know how to work they must
learn; we did not send them to come among us, neither can we work
for them to build them houses." He reminded Graham that he had
himself been a prisoner for "five month and twelve days; six and
30 officers and their servants in one room, consider this and you
have nothing to grumble at."

He concluded, "I have wrote this letter in a plain, rough stile,
that you might know what you had to depend on, at which I hope
youl not take umbrage." Characteristically Morgan: defiant, bash-
ful, courteous, all at the same time.

Graham did not take umbrage. In fact, curious to meet Morgan,
he invited him to dinner at the house where he was lodging with
two other officers—the home of Frederick County's colonel of militia. Morgan told him the story of his flogging, of his receiving only
499 out of 500 lashes—he knew these men understood what the incident showed about his character. He also talked about Saratoga,
describing how he had taken the height on the British right during
the Battle of Bemis Heights and ordered one of his men to shoot the
officer on the grey horse who had proved to be Brigadier General
Simon Fraser. All in all, Graham thought that Morgan spoke more
with "volubility" than "good taste."[12]

The Marquis de Chastellux was a different sort of dinner companion. Major General François Jean de Beauvoir, Marquis de

Chastellux, was a soldier with decades of service as well as a member of the *Académie Française,* an author of books and plays, and deeply interested in any natural phenomena or geological formation he encountered. A friend of Voltaire's, he embodied that strand of the "conservative" French Enlightenment. Where Voltaire and his generation had seen England as the embodiment of all that France might be, de Chastellux was one of the first to translate that vision to the shores of America.

Therefore Morgan fascinated him. Here was an embodiment of American manhood, the commander of riflemen. De Chastellux had not read Hector St. John Crevecouer's tribute to the new man, the American, but he already believed it. It intrigued him that greatness could come from such unrefined soil.

As a soldier, de Chastellux was further fascinated that this unlettered man had achieved something close to Hannibal's victory at Cannae, that double envelopment that every young military cadet and armchair general dreams of duplicating. Before he had a chance to meet Morgan, the French general was already interrogating any of the Virginian veterans of Cowpens that he encountered for details of the battle.

When he finally met Morgan, that fascination was joined with charm. Following the defeat of Cornwallis, Washington immediately dispersed his army, sending Wayne and a Pennsylvania brigade to join Greene in the South and marching the rest back to their customary position in and around West Point on the Hudson. But Rochambeau's French army had remained in Yorktown and Williamsburg for that winter, and it was not until summer 1782 that they finally set out for the North. Rochambeau had ridden ahead to Philadelphia to consult with the French ambassador, leaving the Marquis de Chastellux in charge of the march.

The French army was crossing the Occoquan Creek at Colchester, Virginia, close to where it enters the Potomac, when Morgan encountered the wagons and artillery going through a ford upstream of the main body. De Chastellux records that "finding the carters did not understand their business, he stopped, and showed them how they ought to drive." Finally, "having put every thing in order, he alighted at the Marquis', and dined with him." Not surprisingly, the Marquis described him as being "tall, and of a very martial appearance." Also as one might expect of a French *philosophe* who, if not a follower of Rousseau breathed the same air, he found that Morgan "called to mind the ancient Gallic and German chiefs, who, when in peace with the Romans, came to visit and offer them assistance." Morgan, as the French general describes him, seems a natural man, almost a natural child, who ingenuously "admired our troops, and never ceased looking at them; often repeating, that the greatest pleasure of his life would be, to serve in numerous and brilliant armies."[13]

So, on the one hand an American version of a Shakespearean clown, perhaps a Toby Belch, mixing humor, cunning, and boasting together. And on the other, a Gallic chieftain, a child of nature and of war. Yet in both accounts, still recognizably the same man.

FEBRUARY 1782

Morgan had many things on his mind: the failure of Congress to pay him, his need of money for a horse, his gold medal, moving into his new mansion of Saratoga, wondering how he would pay for it or for its furnishings. But in the midst of all this, he took time to write a letter to Thomas Nelson, governor of Virginia, asking for leniency toward a Loyalist.

This Loyalist was none other than John Claypool, the pseudo-leader of the faux rebellion that Morgan had suppressed the previous May. Having surrendered, Claypool was threatened with death for his treason. He had appealed to Morgan to plead his case, and now Morgan was doing so.[14] It was, said Morgan, "the first time I ever spoke in favour of a Tory, or ever wished their lives spared them—but Humanity as well as policy urges me to say something in favour of Claypool, and wish he may obtain forgiveness. . . . Humanity asks for forgiveness on the basis of Claypool's wife and fourteen children who need him to support them," Morgan argued; but policy demanded it because the people of his region listened to him, and a penitent Claypool could prevent another revolt by encouraging his neighbors to submit to Virginia's government.[15]

So one of Morgan's last acts as a military leader of the Revolution was asking that mercy be extended to a former enemy who would soon be a fellow countryman.

FEBRUARY 1783

Another year, another February, and Morgan was once again writing a letter demanding what he saw as rightfully his own. This one was directed to Benjamin Lincoln, once a Continental army general, now the secretary of war under the Confederation's government.

He had been promised, Morgan reminded him, a gold medal from Congress in honor of his victory at Cowpens. Surely, he wondered, there had been time enough to make one? Frequently had he enquired after it, and he had been told "that nothing prevented it being sent to me but the low Situation of Finances." Surely now Congress had sufficient money for such an expenditure. "I not only wish you to expedite the making of it," Morgan wrote, "but that you may also pay some attention to the Mannor in which it may be done and with devices purposely imblematical of the Affair."

Soldiers in the modern age often claim that no one fights for medals, that no soldier much cares if he gets one or not, that having one is no great thing. When a medal is pinned on them, they say something to the effect that it is not they who are being rewarded but all of the fellow soldiers in their unit. Morgan did not share that perspective. He wanted that medal, he wanted it for himself, and he wanted it to look good. He did not want it for the cash value of the gold that composed it or for the artistry that created "devices purposely imblematical." It could be in bronze and he would still crave it. What he wanted was an object that was the physical manifestation of "his Country's Applause to his conduct," a material "acknowledgement of my Country's Approbation."[16]

To have that was gratifying in and of itself. It also gave him a status that few if any could achieve. The modern man might say he was the same person before he had the medal, that he did not need the medal to be proud of himself. Dan Morgan might agree, but also patiently—or, more likely, impatiently—explain that it was necessary to have a Congressional Gold Medal in order for others to understand who he was.

APRIL 1790

Morgan finally received a heavy little package from George Washington, president of the United States. A short note informed him of the pleasure at being finally able to send the enclosed to him.[17]

Within was the long-awaited reward. America, depicted in the customary form of an Indian woman, was placing a wreath on the head of a man identified as "Daniell Morgan Duci Exercitus." The obverse side showed a somewhat realistic image of Morgan commanding his little Flying Army, on horseback, leading his Continentals in their bayonet charge against the British.

Morgan's war ends, not with a final shot but with him holding a gold medal in his hands, examining the gilded scene of eternally silent combat, and remembering.

PART FOUR

Away, You Rolling River

Chapter Seventeen

HAPPINESS

Oh Shenandoah,
I long to see you,
Away, you rolling river . . .
—*Oh Shenandoah*

B Y the time peace was announced in 1783, Morgan was already a man transformed. Twenty years before he had been a teamster with a common law wife. Ten years after that he had been a yeomen with his own lands, a few enslaved people, and some of the lower offices possible in the Virginia hierarchy. Had it ended there, he still would have done very well for himself considering how he had begun.

On September 3, 1784, Morgan was having his dinner with George Washington, who was staying at his brother Charles's home, Happy Retreat, on the outskirts of the eponymous Charles Town. He and his former commander were joined by other friends, relatives, and local luminaries: cousin Warner Washington, Ralph Wormeley, Edward Snickers, and "many other gentlemen" of the surrounding area in Berkeley and Frederick Counties. Yet it is his conversation with Morgan that Washington records in his diary of the trip.

Among other objectives of his trip, Washington was interested in establishing a route for a Potomac-Ohio Canal and doing whatever else he could to encourage the "Inland Navigation of the Potomack." It was his dream that ships would one day arrive at Alexandria or Georgetown, and there load a cargo brought by canal from the Ohio valley. He found Morgan as enthusiastic for such improvements as himself. Morgan told him that "a plan was in contemplation to extend a road from Winchester to the Western Waters, to avoid if possible an interference with any other State but," added Washington ruefully, "I could not discover that Either himself, or others, were able to point it out with precision."

While Morgan could not "point . . . out with precision" the best route a road or canal connecting the Potomac and Ohio should take, he was convinced such a route should exist. He also told Washington that Frederick, Berkeley, and Hampshire Counties "would contribute freely towards the extension of the Navigation of the Potomack." Like Washington, Morgan was now eager for internal improvements, not just on the Potomac but on the Shenandoah and the Ohio; not only roads, but canals.[1]

This shared passion for commerce and transport would, in time, make Washington and Morgan political allies. But there were, first, problems of character and reputation to be overcome. These were part of the tension between Morgan the continual striver and the new Morgan: the general, the hero of America, the winner of a gold medal from Congress. Such a tension was inevitable for anyone like Morgan who still sought to climb further up the social pyramid. And such tensions inevitably led to contradictions and defeats. One could not simply be all things to all people all the time. Morgan was certainly not. Like other former generals and officers, he discovered that "the acquisition of great property required an agressive, secretive cunning that was at odds with the other attributes of gentility, especially a reputation."[2]

Morgan was now a public figure, not merely a retired general, but a retired general who had won a great victory—not many American generals could say that in 1784. His was now a name that had made insurgents flee before him, its reputation great enough that those who knew him only by it would plead for him to lead them.

This meant he now faced the greatest task of his life, creating a peacetime life that was worthy of his wartime record. To do that, he had to find ways to maximize his independence, such that he was able to maintain the reputation he had had in wartime. He would, as befitted a Virginia patriarch, have to provide for his heirs—and first he had to see both of them married. And that required property, as well as other, less tangible means of achieving and keeping status in Shenandoah, Virginia, and early American society.

Not all his friends and peers managed to do this. Nathanael Greene died unexpectedly in 1786, compromised by immense debts. So too were von Steuben, Anthony Wayne, and Henry Lee, to name just a few. Others, like Horatio Gates, never recovered their reputation or standing. Therefore, to be not only solvent but prosperous was challenge enough; to continue to also enjoy a reputation befitting that of a distinguished character of the Revolution was doubly difficult.

As a good Virginian, Morgan knew the first thing to do in establishing himself was to establish his family. By "family" Virginians meant their entire household, both its people and its worldly goods—including enslaved people who before the law were both. During a man's lifetime—or during that of a widow who refused to remarry—a family had to be maintained in a way suitable to their station in the Virginia hierarchy. That was one of the pressures that led Morgan to take his furlough from the army in 1779 and that kept men like George Mason on their plantations for long periods in between occasional acts of governmental service.[3]

Responsibility to the family by the patriarch continued after his death. To leave one's family impoverished after death was a mark of disgrace. They must be provided for in a suitable way, else one's reputation would be buried with the body.

To do that, a Virginian had to build up capital. This meant purchasing things that gained value over time. There were four ways to do this. The two that remain familiar to us were purchasing land and financial instruments—though the types of both were very different than what we are used to. The other two means of increasing capital were the purchase or acquisition of animals and people, both of which had the possibility of multiplying. Morgan built his wealth in all four ways.

THE first manifestation of Morgan's new status was his equally new home, which he tellingly named Saratoga, placed between the villages of Boyce and Millwood. Building required, in the first place, a loan from Charles Mynn Thruston, and in the second place, the labor of Hessian prisoners of war held in Winchester. This Hessian contribution is not found in any records but is part of a long local tradition. That Hessian prisoners would be used for its construction is not a very great surprise. Prisoners of war in Lancaster, Pennsylvania, for example, were much sought after on the local labor market. They offered local farmers and businessmen labor that was missing because so many other men who would otherwise have been unskilled labor were serving in the Continental army or had been drafted into militia service.

Morgan, from as early as 1779, headed some of his letters "Saratoga." So perhaps work was under way as early as that point, or there was an earlier home on the site. Certainly the Saratoga that now stands was ready for the Morgan family in spring 1782. It was built like many other fine homes in the Valley, western Maryland, and Pennsylvania. Constructed from local stone, it was two stories, with a central passage on the ground floor, the pattern that would one day be described as a Shenandoah I-house.

Its owner furnished it in the style to which his family needed to be accustomed. To it he added seven feather beds, three carpets, seven mirrors, two tea tables, twelve mahogany chairs, a sideboard, and a desk.[4] This was a fine, even grand, display. Morgan's near neighbor, Lord Fairfax, also had twelve mahogany chairs, but only two mirrors.[5] Such possessions placed Morgan at the very top of Virginia society.

MARRIAGES were another way to reinforce and display social status for Morgan and other Virginians. Far more important than building a house and furnishing it was finding families for his daughters. In this Morgan also succeeded. Perhaps not too surprisingly, Nancy and Betsey Morgan married officers of the Continental army. Both marriages also exposed their father—in his person, his fortune, and his reputation—to hazards domestic and political. Marriage, like any other way of increasing a family's fortune, involved risk.[6]

In the early 1780s, Nancy Morgan married Presley Neville, the son of Morgan's friend John Neville, who had commanded the 4th Virginia Regiment. The connection to the Neville family must have been very gratifying to Morgan for many reasons. It was a case of the daughter marrying the son of a good friend, which is at the very least gratifying for the friends. Presley was well educated, a graduate of the College of Pennsylvania in Philadelphia, and with sufficient knowledge of French that he had been selected as Lafayette's American aide. Like his father, Presley settled in southwest Pennsylvania, and after their marriage, he and Nancy moved into a home in Pittsburgh. They and their many children (Nancy eventually gave birth to fifteen children; not surprisingly, Presley was often concerned for her health) often visited Frederick County during their parents' lifetimes. If Morgan's letters to Presley are any indication, he maintained a very friendly relationship with his son-in-law. Indeed, Presley was the nearest thing in the next generation Morgan had to a confidant.[7]

Betsey's marriage was less fortunate. She married James Heard, an officer from New Jersey. He had supposedly known Morgan during the war and, like him, emigrated from New Jersey to the Valley. Whether he did that explicitly to meet Betsey Morgan is unknown, but he married her and they settled in Winchester. During the war, Heard was wounded in the leg, and it never healed. This must have resulted in a considerable amount of pain for the rest of his long life. Whether it was the pain that caused it, he was also what eighteenth-century observers might refer to as a choleric personality, though if they did they would have been overindulging in politeness. Heard spent money quickly, and he got drunk. One court case against him alleged that when drunk at the Martinsburg races, Heard horsewhipped someone who gave him rum in a tumbler rather than a mug. How to provide for Betsey and her children after his death, without putting money intended for them into Heard's control, became one of the preoccupations of Morgan's last years.[8]

By the mid-1780s at the latest, Morgan's family also contained a secret member, never mentioned by Morgan in any surviving documents, including his will. This was an illegitimate son of Daniel

Morgan named Willoughby. It is most probable that his mother was a resident of Winchester, but it is uncertain who she was. At an early age, Willoughby was sent to Kentucky—or to South Carolina—where he lived his early years. Yet he continued to maintain contacts to Winchester and Frederick County for the rest of his life, and by 1811 was a Winchester resident.[9]

What Abigail knew, what Nancy or Betsey or any of the family knew—that is unknown. Whether Willoughby's mother was one of any conquests or a sudden and unrepeated dalliance is also impossible to know. But Willoughby, in many ways, turned out to be very much his father's son.

Morgan's family also contained slaves. Their numbers changed over the years. In 1789, he had two, a man named James and a young woman named Tenor. We know this because on September 3, 1789, he advertised in the Alexandria newspaper that they had run away, offering twenty dollars for their return or information leading to their return. James, Morgan wrote, is "of a yellow cast, his hair remarkably long for a Negro." He took with him a number of clothes, including "a good pair of leather breeches . . . osnaburg shirts, overalls, good shoes." Tenor also took "several sorts of clothing, so that it is uncertain what she may wear."[10]

How many slaves Morgan had at any one time is difficult to say because, like his other property, the best record we have of them comes at his death. Otherwise they remain elusive traces in the record, appearing like that advertisement momentarily, not emerging again. So we know he took as spoils of war two young men from the battlefield at Cowpens; we know James and Tenor freed themselves from him and that there were plenty of clothes about the place for them to take; and we know how, as death approached, he distributed those people he owned. And that is all we know, and very likely all that can be known.

AT the close of the war, Morgan owned several hundred acres in the Valley. But following the war he began to amass landholdings in the west. This began with the property he received for his Revolutionary service as well as for his service in Lord Dunmore's War—the former an amusingly precise 11,666 2/3 acres in Kentucky. By 1795, he had one hundred thousand acres in the far western regions of Virginia. At his death he owned—in Virginia, Ohio, Kentucky, and Tennessee—a staggering two hundred fifty thousand acres.[11]

That he was land rich but cash poor almost goes without saying—the same could be said of nearly every member of the Virginia gentry, among whom the rarest of birds was someone both land rich and cash rich. Owning two hundred fifty thousand acres of land was a hopeful investment in the future promise of America. But it was in the present almost always a tangled complication of squatters angry that someone should own land and not improve it, and of land agents who, if of virtuous and good character, managed to conceal it. That western land was, though, a promise to his family, for his grandchildren and great-grandchildren. It was a way to secure their future prosperity in his present.

But there were other ways of doing that, using some of the few financial instruments at hand. At some point in 1782, Morgan began to buy debt certificates from Virginia soldiers. This became a point of contention and blight on his reputation over the next decade, possibly to the end of his life. It might also have been how he established the fortune with which he died.

Debt certificates or soldiers' certificates were terms used for what were simply state-sanctioned IOUs. Without any money to pay their soldiers, individual states issued certificates to those who had served or were serving stating the amount they were owed at the end of their service. These would be signed by the treasurer of Virginia, for example, but there was nothing in the treasury with which to pay them. By 1786, these certificates were selling for 10 percent of their dollar value on the Philadelphia market. While this was about the low point of their value, even on their issuing they were judged to be less valuable than their stated amount.[12]

Soldiers with these certificates were unlikely to hold onto them. They required some immediate money, sometimes to make their way home or to start farming again, or perhaps to buy a small amount of acreage on which to farm. They could not wait until the certificates regained their value. A trade, therefore, grew up in which these certificates were purchased at their current market value, which was of course far less than the stated value on the paper.

Certificates often were used as one of the only possible forms of currency, even though they were accepted in an act of hope that they would eventually be redeemed—a hope that at times in the 1780s did not seem justified. Yet that such purchases came to be seen—or were then seen—as somewhat morally compromised is evident from George Washington's attitude toward them. In a decades-long effort to settle a debt owed to him by the estate of John Mercer of Fredericksburg, in 1786 he was offered payment in either enslaved people or in soldiers' certificates. As far as Washington was concerned, this was rather like being asked to choose between being punched in the face with a dumbbell or a concrete block. "I never mean," Washington wrote, "to possess another slave by purchase." Yet, likewise, "I never did, nor never intend to purchase a military certificate."[13] In a later letter, he wrote, "I profess an entire ignorance of the real difference between military Certificates & specie . . . never having had inclination or intention to deal in them."[14] Ignorance was in this case apparently a kind of security. Ultimately, military certificates being more acceptable than enslaved people to Washington, he accepted them at a four-to-one ratio (£2,000 in Virginia military certificates to cover £500 of debt in Virginia currency).

Washington may well have been an outlier in his distaste for dealing in certificates. Horatio Gates in 1791 notified no less a person than Treasury Secretary Alexander Hamilton of a transfer of certificates totaling $14,037.52.[15] This was a substantial sum; Gates, and many others, found certificates to be a source of financial security. The settling of estates in Virginia over the next twenty years often involved the redemption of soldiers' certificates. In a cash-free society, in which a debt from Dan Morgan to his tailor could be signed over to a third party as a form of payment, certificates were a more-than-acceptable substitute for specie.

Yet Washington's wariness of even admitting knowledge of what the going rate for certificates was, let alone accepting certificates in payment, shows there was another dimension to certificates. As Morgan biographer William Graham explained it decades after the fact, soldiers selling their certificates attracted speculators "who, intent upon making money, no matter how, saw in the occasion nothing but the advantageous opening which afforded them for a profitable investment." In his telling, Morgan was indignant at the low rates these speculators offered to soldiers for the certificates and urged soldiers to hold onto their certificates at all costs. But if there were men "who would be obliged to make every sacrifice to obtain money," he offered to pay twice the amount offered by the speculators. "Contrary to Morgan's expectations," numerous soldiers then asked him to make good this offer, and "he was thus induced to receive as many of their certificates as the amount of funds he had on hand enabled him to accept."[16]

Putting aside all of Graham's suggestions about Morgan's good intentions, the simple story is that Morgan bought certificates, and probably a great many of them. Moreover, considering what Gates and many others were able to receive for them after the establishment of the federal government's credit, it is very likely that for Morgan it was an excellent financial investment.

However, it was not a very good investment in his public reputation. There was, in the word that spread abroad, always a hint that something improper had been done—perhaps the simple purchasing of the certificates, perhaps (contra Graham's version of the story) at paying far too little for them. It lingered as a persistent blemish on Morgan's honor for at least a decade. And it rankled, enough that he confronted some of those who gossiped about him, who, as Graham puts it, "had been luckless enough to throw themselves in his way."[17] To be sure, no resulting suits for assault appear in the Frederick County court records. Perhaps Morgan confined himself to bruising them with strong language.

"Why will you contend with people so much below you?" Charles Thruston counseled him. "You are placed now on an eminence, and should suffer the little people to pass by you in silence. . . . For, let me tell you sir, your situation is much altered. Your reputation, fortune, and present station in life, demand of you to conduct yourself with greater complacency, affability, and condescension to all, in the same proportion that these have increased and improved."[18] Sound advice, yet how difficult for a man to follow who had been fighting and scrapping, in one way or another, his whole life.

IN addition to his financial investments, his farming, and his contending for his public reputation, there was yet another enterprise on Morgan's roster of activities, a means by which he could finally secure hard cash. This was the construction and running of a mill complex just down the road from Saratoga, in a crossroads community now appropriately christened Millwood. Carter Burwell had inherited from his grandfather King Carter a considerable amount of land in eastern Frederick County. He was one of the first of many Tidewater aristocrats to shift their residences from their played-out tobacco lands along the eastern rivers to the Shenandoah. There he built a suitable replacement for his showplace near Williamsburg, Carter's Grove, a vast mansion he rather unimaginatively christened Carter's Hall. Nearby he established a store, and across the road he and Morgan joined to build what is now called the Burwell-Morgan Mill.[19]

There were already numerous mills in the Shenandoah, and wherever colonial Americans lived. Flour was the essential food commodity, so in settled areas, any resident was probably within six or so miles of a mill. These were custom mills, which milled grains for an individual farmer's use. Burwell and Morgan built a merchant mill, designed to mill flour that would be sold outside the valley, in Potomac or Rappahannock ports. They could do that by transporting their barrels of flour just a mile or so down the road to the banks of the Shenandoah and loading it onto boats. Or they could put it on wagons, about which Morgan knew everything, and ship it to his old friends and business contacts in Falmouth and Fredericksburg. To these old Tidewater connections Morgan now added Christian Febiger, the Danish rolling stone who had finally come to rest in Philadelphia and opened a merchant enterprise.[20]

THESE many enterprises and commercial concerns meant that as early as 1784, Morgan was a proto-Federalist, both a nationalist and an enthusiast for the glorious benefits of commerce. His life as a teamster had prepared him to be one. It had focused him on commercial connections, transportation, and the problems of credit long before he turned to cultivating the land for himself. Now his land investments focused him on the west, just as Washington had been so focused. His investment in the merchant mill made him eager for further improvements—roads, a Shenandoah free from rocks, canals reaching from the Potomac to the Ohio—that benefit not just himself and other investors but, as he saw it, the whole nation.

Democratic-Republicanism in any form, particularly the one advocated by Thomas Jefferson, never had a chance with Morgan. A philosophy of the enlightenment possible for yeomen farmers was not of particular interest to the homeless boy turned stump grubber. Perhaps this was because he had no time for philosophy, perhaps because he saw no great nobility in small farming, or perhaps because he had always seen the importance of connections, of networks, of transport and movement. After all, roads had allowed him to walk far from home. Now they, whether on land or water, could allow him and others to grow rich.

So by the late 1780s, Morgan had made it to a much higher plane of existence than he could have imagined when he walked into Winchester in 1753. He possessed a mansion, business interests, and his ever-increasing acreage. Both his daughters were married. He was at the center of affairs in his area and determined that his area be the center of a nationwide transportation network. Really there was little more to hope for or to do in life.

But Morgan wanted more. He desired to have a good reputation, and he wanted it from the source he regarded as the highest: George Washington. He remained the committed Washingtonian he had been since 1778. But Washington's approbation was not easy to gain, and Morgan did not have it. This was nowhere clearer than in the months following the battle known as St. Clair's Defeat, the greatest victory ever won by Native Americans against the United States.

St. Clair's Defeat is a mild name for what was the systematic destruction of an American army. Commanded by Major General Arthur St. Clair, it was essentially the entire field force of the US Army, excluding the small garrison forces along the Eastern Seaboard. On the modern Ohio-Indiana border, it encountered an-

other army, a larger and better-trained one of Indian warriors commanded by Little Turtle of the Miami and Blue Jacket of the
Shawnee. This Indian army attacked St. Clair's one thousand men
just as they had stacked their guns and lined up to get their morning
meal.

Morgan had numerous old comrades and friends in the fight.
Chief among them was Richard Butler, the Pennsylvanian who had
been his second in command in the Jerseys, at Saratoga, and in the
fighting around Philadelphia. So was Thomas Butler, Richard's
brother; and William Darke of Virginia—who once brawled with
Morgan at Battletown—as well as Darke's son Joseph. Robert Kirkwood—who, with his surviving soldiers of Delaware, had been in
line with Howard at Cowpens—was also there. Kirkwood was now
a resident of Ohio with two hundred acres in Jefferson County, and
he had once more taken service in the US Army. He was thirty-five
years old, the veteran of thirty-two battles during the Revolution,
and still a captain.

The fighting was savage. With the pickets driven in, the attackers
surrounded the camp. St. Clair's army was in a killing zone. Numerous attempts were made to break out. William Darke led two
unsuccessful bayonet charges against the attacking Indians; his son
was badly wounded in the second of these. Richard Butler was also
severely wounded. When after three hours St. Clair ordered a retreat, Butler was propped up against some backpacks in the center
of camp, given a pistol, and left behind. Robert Kirkwood, who had
passed through all his battles and skirmishes without any wound
whatsoever, had been killed. "He died as he lived," wrote Harry
Lee, "the brave, meritorious, unrewarded Kirkwood."[21]

Based on the ratios of casualties suffered by a force, it was the
worst defeat the US Army has ever suffered. The casualty rate for
officers was 88 percent, for enlisted and noncommissioned soldiers,
97.4 percent. Six hundred seventy-one were dead and two hundred
seventy-one wounded; only twenty-four left the battlefield un-
harmed. The wounded included only those capable of leaving the
battlefield; all those left behind were executed, including Richard
Butler.[22]

Not only had an army been destroyed, but for a moment the entire vision of westward expansion seemed to teeter on the verge of

falling and smashing. If, with British support, sufficient Indians could be brought together to oppose the settlement of the Ohio valley, then all of Washington's hopes for the future would be for naught. The small settlements that continued to exist west of the Alleghenies would, because of the necessities of geography, look north to British Canada or south to Spanish Louisiana for support. They would ship their goods back and forth to New Orleans rather than by new roads and canals to Philadelphia or the Federal City on the Potomac. And if by some freak of the ongoing European wars Britain should take Louisiana, then it would dominate the rest of the continent and confine the United States to a rim of settlement on the western edge of the Atlantic.

WHEN the news came to Washington of St. Clair's disaster, he was probably at one of his wife's Friday receptions. He held his countenance until it was concluded before erupting in a rage carefully described by his secretary Tobias Lear. "To suffer that army to be cut to pieces hacked, butchered, tomahawked, by a surprise, the very thing I guarded him against! O God, O God, he's worse than a murderer! How can he answer to his country!"[23]

The fit of anger was soon suppressed, and in the following months Washington strove to finally settle the problem of an ineffective army in the Northwest Territory. As part of this effort, on March 9, 1792, he drafted a memorandum on potential general officers to lead the new army of the United States. "The following list," Washington wrote (or dictated) "contain the names of all the General Officers now living, & in this Country, as low as actual Brigadiers inclusively. Except those who it is conjectured would not, from age, want of health, & other circumstances come forward by any inducements that could be offered to them—& such as ought not to be named for the important trust of Commander in Chief."

He surveyed the surviving general officers of the Continental army, weighed them in the balance, and found all of them wanting. Each of them was considered for failings of drink (George Weedon of Fredericksburg, Virginia, sometimes tavern owner—"no enemy it is said to the bottle") and of debt (Major General Anthony Wayne—"No œconomist it is feared").Their past service was considered; their last rank, their willingness to be superseded, and their emotional equilibrium were all taken into account (Friedrich Baron von Steuben—"High in his ideas of Subordination—impetuous in his temper."). When Washington was unfamiliar with their battle-field behavior, when they had fought successfully yet he was not a witness to it, it almost seemed to count against them.

Washington's notations on Morgan were as:

> Brigadier General Morgan. Has been fortunate, & has met with *eclat*. Yet there are different opinions with respect to his abilities as an Officer. He is accused of using improper means to obtain certificates from the Soldiers. It is said he has been (if the case is not so now) intemperate; that he is troubled with a palpitation which often lays him up. And it is not denied that he is illiterate.[24]

In the end, the command went to Anthony Wayne, despite Washington's considered view that Wayne was "more active & enterprizing than judicious & cautious. . . . Open to flattery—vain—easily imposed upon—and liable to be drawn into scrapes." It turned out to be an excellent choice, for Wayne showed an ability to train and supply an army that he had not displayed in the previous war, an ability of such a high degree that it is doubtful anyone else on the list could have surpassed him.[25]

Morgan was offered command as one of Wayne's brigadiers, as was Otho Williams. Both refused because of reasons of health— Williams was now as inveterate a traveler to the various Virginia springs as was Morgan. Yet that note indicates that Morgan had blotted his copybook with Washington. In Jefferson's notes of a lengthy cabinet conversation, Washington refers to Morgan first of all proposed general officers with simply, "No head. Health gone. Speculator." At least one of those was true.[26]

It was not that Morgan had done wrong, necessarily, but that there was the appearance of wrongdoing. In developing his family's fortune, Morgan had run afoul of public perception. He was a cut-corners kind of man now, just the sort of person Washington could not tolerate. So what Morgan desired perhaps almost as much as that fortune, the good opinion of George Washington, seemed to be unattainable.

Chapter Eighteen

LIBERTY

ONCE more Daniel Morgan was leading a light corps of an American army on an arduous march against a threat to the Revolution. Yet this time, November 1, 1794, Morgan was a major general, his troops were all Virginia militia, and his commander was Virginia governor Harry Lee, formerly the very young commander of the 2nd Partisan Corps. Morgan's corps was slogging its way through the mud of the Appalachian Mountains. The threat was from other Americans who saw themselves as following the precepts of the Revolution, just as Morgan saw them as rebels against the new order that the Revolution created. His objective was Pittsburgh, now under what Morgan alternatively believed to be either anarchy or rebel government. Most alarmingly of all, his daughter Nancy was in Pittsburgh, along with his growing brood of grandchildren.

One Virginia militiaman, impressed with the arduousness of his service, compared the march through the Alleghenies to Hannibal's crossing the Alps. Morgan's view on such hardships is unknown. Certainly it was not the Maine wilderness, not even a camp at Grindal's Shoals on the Pacolet River, with the forage and supplies decreasing in quantity every day. Now supplies were in relative abundance. The militia even had uniforms and shoes.[1]

Despite the many differences, Morgan in other ways seemed very much the same man he had always been, when in loincloth and leggings he led his men in hauling their bateaux mile after painful mile. He demonstrated this one night at Parkinson's Ferry on the Monongahela as he supervised the river crossing of the Light Division. Here was Morgan, somewhere in his late 50s, frequently bedridden over the last two or so years, a constant visitor to the health-giving hot springs of Virginia, yet now well enough to personally confront a tavern keeper selling whiskey to his boys at the exorbitant price of $1 per gallon. When confronted, the man "began to treat me with indignity," Morgan reports to Governor Lee, "and I broke his mouth, which closed the business." No doubt. While "the people look very sour at us," Morgan continued, "I will bring them to by good treatment; the rebuff I gave the tavern-keeper will assist me, as it will show them they must not be too impertinent."[2]

MORGAN was drawn into the party conflicts of the 1790s in much the same way as other national and local leaders. He had of course been a nationalist since his service in the army, and he endorsed measures as early as the 1780s that would become those of the Federalist Party—and that thirty years later would become planks of the Whig Party platform. By 1793, Morgan, like other Federalists, feared anarchy above all things. He did not like the French Revolution, and if possible, he liked Jeffersonian enthusiasm for it even less. He thought opposition to Washington's measures wrong, in part because he had come to see opposition to anything Washington did as wrong but also because he saw it as a threat to national unity. Like others of the nascent Federalist faction, he believed he was above party because he supported Washington and his government.

The republican rage against the excise tax on whiskey was, as far as Morgan was concerned, another proof of their anarchic tendencies. Searching about for a tax to impose internally, Secretary of the Treasury Alexander Hamilton had hit upon a tax on spirits. This was, as far as Hamilton was concerned, a luxury tax—note that he did not tax beer or cider, the most common drinks in popular use. It affected not just whiskey but also New England rum.

Yet it was disproportionately harsh on those small farmers who also maintained a distillery. Commercial enterprises could tolerate a tax of eight cents a gallon; the yeoman farmer with a still, Jefferson's philosophical ideal and his political support, was less able to sustain it. They saw it as a means of bankrupting them by a powerful government; national Jeffersonians saw it as a conspiracy by Hamilton and the arch-Federalists to target their party.

Three years after the imposition of the tax, resistance in western Pennsylvania to the excise became violent. For Morgan, it threatened what he loved the most.

Favoring old soldiers as he did for federal positions, Washington appointed John Neville commissioner of excise for western Pennsylvania. In summer 1794, a group of about thirty men made a first unsuccessful assault on Neville's Virginiaesque plantation, Bower Hill. Beaten off by rapid rifle fire, they increased their ranks to as many as six hundred and tried once more. After a gun battle, the detachment of US Army soldiers who had come to defend Bower Hill surrendered, and the house and outbuildings were burned. Neville had already been sent to safety; riding to his father's assistance, Morgan's son-in-law Presley Neville was apprehended by the rebels along with the federal marshal for Pittsburgh, David Lenox.[3]

Most western Pennsylvanians were against the unfairness of the excise tax, but some were more against it than others. The most radical among them began to prepare for a wider resistance. On July 26, they stopped the mail for Philadelphia and read through it to see who supported and who opposed them. One of the letters they read was from Presley Neville to Morgan, denouncing those who had attacked and burned his father's plantation and detained him. Presley, fearing reprisals, fled east with a group of "exiles," leaving behind him Nancy Morgan Neville and their children.

Washington's response was as swift as the events. In early August, he sent three commissioners to Pittsburgh to negotiate with the rebels while simultaneously seeking and gaining a Supreme Court finding that western Pennsylvania was beyond the help of local law enforcement. That finding in hand, he issued a proclamation calling for militia and ordering the rebels to disperse by September 1. Then he set about calling up an army of twelve thousand five hundred men, drawn from the militias of New Jersey, Pennsylvania, and Virginia. He did not wish to wait for negotiations to drag on into autumn and winter, delaying the possibility of forceful action.[4]

Morgan was now a major general of the Virginia Militia, in command of the state's northern district. So he was in effect going into the field to effect his daughter's rescue. He assured Harry Lee, who as governor of Virginia was determined to lead his state's troops personally, that he was fit and ready for the field despite the last few years of illness. "I feel as Hearty as I ever was—and am convinced I could undergo the fatigues of two or three campaigns."[5] While he would prefer to fight foreign invaders rather than fellow citizens, he also thought that the rebels needed to be suppressed as an example to others who might be so tempted.

IT was not until the first week of October that Morgan's troops began the march to Fort Cumberland, where they were to rendezvous with other Virginia and the Maryland Militia. Morgan himself left with a detachment on October 6. Other detachments followed as soon as they were properly officered and organized. After Morgan's arrival, and President Washington's visit, Lee, at Washington's recommendation, gave Morgan his old command of the light troops, to travel without baggage in advance of the left wing of the army, composed of the Maryland and Virginia Militias, moving quickly to get first to the objective. He marched north for Pittsburgh on October 21.

Following the crossing at Parkinson's Ferry, and busting the mouth of the tavern keeper, Morgan led his troops into Washington County, Pennsylvania, camping near the county courthouse—the center of the population that had supported the rebellion.[6] Nevertheless, Morgan assessed the population as unthreatening and decided to leave the majority of his command there and ride swiftly to Pittsburgh with a detachment of soldiers and a provost marshal's unit, as well as Treasury Secretary Hamilton and a number of the "exiles," including John and Presley Neville.

In Pittsburgh, he and the Nevilles found Nancy and her children safe.[7] When they had heard news of the advancing federal army, the leaders of the insurrection had fled down the Ohio into Spanish territory. That night, while Morgan and the Neville family were at dinner in the Neville home, a messenger came running to the door. He told Morgan that some of his soldiers had decided to make an example of Henry Brackenridge, an attorney and one of the leading citizens of Pittsburgh, whom the Nevilles suspected of being one of the forces behind the rebellion. Brackenridge lived close by. Morgan and John Neville got up from the table and, without even putting on their hats (a tremendous breach of decorum, manners, and custom prior to 1963 or so), ran out to the street and to the rescue, "declaring that the ruffians must pass over their bodies before they could perpetrate the deed."[8]

Brackenridge was not particularly grateful for the intervention, blaming the soldiers' attack on incitement by angry talk against him by the "Neville interest." Indeed, the Nevilles seem to have been eager for Brackenridge to be punished severely for what they believed to be his secret manipulations of the rebellion—manipulations so secret they could not be proved, which only served to show how secret and dangerous they were.[9] Morgan certainly believed in Brackenridge's guilt to the very end of his service in western Pennsylvania. Yet he never took action on his suspicions.

WITHIN three days of the troops' arrival, it was determined that the bulk of them could march home, there being no further need for them. However, Harry Lee directed that the detachments from Frederick and Berkeley Counties should remain in Pittsburgh under Morgan's command. They would stay until soldiers could be enlisted for nine months' service, at which point Morgan would remain in command.[10] So Morgan's last military service was to become the commander of an army of occupation in his own country, in effect the military governor of western Pennsylvania.

By December he could write a garrulous report to Washington, which while partly supporting Washington's opinion that Morgan was semiliterate, was also far more informative than many a letter the president typically received. Morgan explained that recruiting for the nine-months detachment was going slowly but that he did not think he really required the regiment of infantry, four troops of cavalry, and battery of artillery Governor Lee—in his role of commander of the federal army—had ordered him to raise before departing for Virginia. "My own opinion," Morgan wrote, "is that a great maney men will be unnecessary for this service—as the alarm that these people have Experienced is so great that thay will Never forget it so far as to fly in the face of the law again."

He continued:

> I am Dealing very Gently with them and am becoming very popular for which I am very Happy—as it has been my opinion from the first of this business that we ought to make these people our friends if we could Do so without lessening the Dignity of government which in my opinion ought to be supported at any Risque—several of the out lyers have come in within a few Days & Deliverd themselves to me; I have let them on parol with orders to come to me when called for I Expect this Kind of treatment will bring in the whol Except Bradford the Tinker and one or two others.[11]

Morgan could engage in this kind of policy because he knew he and Washington were in perfect agreement on the goal, "the Dignity of government."

By December he had removed his little command from Pittsburgh and encamped at McFarland's Ferry, several miles up the Monongahela River from the town. (About two miles upstream from modern Elizabeth, Pennsylvania.)[12] There he had his men build log huts for themselves, an activity at which he was a past master.

Throughout that winter, he continued with his policy of winning converts and friends to the federal government. One of the men who waylaid a stagecoach with the US mail, John Mitchell, turned himself in to Morgan. But according to one of Morgan's local political opponents, one opposed to the Neville interest, when Mitchell was apprehended and examined, Morgan could not at first believe this was the man accused of the crime. This was apparently because of his "evident simplicity," referring either to his manner and bearing or perhaps his being simple headed. Yet Mitchell insisted he had done the deed, and Morgan "instead of confining him, he gave him a pass to go to Philadelphia, thereby putting it in his power to reflect on his situation, and make his escape."[13] Whether or not Morgan so intended, he certainly did not see any reason to punish Mitchell, any more than he had seen reason to punish John Claypool for his rebellion against the state of Virginia in 1781. "He is like most others who have been led astray, weak—ignorant and unthinking," wrote Morgan to his president. "Considering therefore the man, and that he was merely the agent of others in this odious transaction I feel myself constrained to recommend him as an object of mercy. Were those who first fomented these disturbances brought to condign punishment I should rejoice; but when the poor and illiterate are brought forward as perpetrators of crimes, pland by the dark designing incendiary, my regard to strict justice gives way to compassion." In the end, Mitchell did go to trial and was one of only two people sentenced to death before being pardoned by the president.[14]

The only discernible influence of the Neville interest on Morgan's rule as military governor of western Pennsylvania was his enduring enmity toward Henry Brackenridge. Morgan's poor opinion of him was not improved by Brackenridge's insistence on representing numerous rebels in court. He persisted in seeing Brackenridge as the puppet master behind the rebellion and perhaps a continuing instigator of plots against the federal government. Nevertheless, he never acted on those suspicions, and Breckenridge remained a free man.[15]

Military occupations always create victims in the civilian population around them. During Morgan's absence in March 1795 from the army as he campaigned for Congress in the lower Valley, discipline lapsed and the soldiers took advantage of that relaxation. Morgan returned to find claims against them that he found dubious but seem in retrospect to be well founded.

Yet all in all, Morgan was a highly effective military governor, acting with genial moderation to further the goals of the administration—particularly considering that his old friend John Neville looked to him to give him his total revenge.[16] It is an interesting insight into his character that a man whom Washington regarded as semiliterate should have behaved with such justice, moderation, and deep political savvy. The Old Wagoner was probably a much more subtle personality then even his letters and the anecdotes about him reveal. Certainly whatever his IQ, he must have had an abundance of what some refer to as emotional intelligence. Even more impressive, though, was his ability to turn that intelligence into action and policy.

GIVEN his activities, it is not surprising that Morgan now decided to run for Congress, something he had contemplated doing for a few years. But now, confronting disunion in Pennsylvania, he increasingly began to fear that disunion would next manifest itself in Virginia. For him, disunion simply meant the growth of party structures opposed to the measures of the federal government. These were now widespread in Virginia, behind the increasingly powerful triumvirate of Jefferson, Madison, and Monroe.

Besides that, he did not care for Robert Rutherford (Robin, to his friends, and "old Robin" to his enemies), the current incumbent of the First Congressional District of Virginia. Morgan had, he told Isaac Zane, "a hearty contempt for the character that now serves us."[17]

Rutherford and Morgan were roughly contemporaries. When Morgan was an ensign in Jack Ashby's company of rangers, Rutherford was captain of his own ranger company, one notably better organized and staffed than Ashby's. Rutherford became a political supporter of Washington's, and in 1766 took the seat from Frederick County that Washington had occupied when the latter was elected from Fairfax County. During the Revolution, he had been a delegate to the Virginia conventions and served in the Virginia Senate. In the contest between Rutherford and Morgan, Rutherford was part of the established elite and Morgan was the chippy new-money contender.[18]

What else might have angered Morgan about Rutherford? He was Scottish, but some of Morgan's best friends were Scottish—one was even Danish, so surely it was not foreignness that irritated Morgan. Rutherford, according to local Frederick County lore, dressed with studied informality—possibly irritating for a man who enjoyed socks and tailoring as much as Morgan.[19] Rutherford, especially when compared to Morgan, was insufferably prolix; a letter from Rutherford to either an adversary or friend was like receiving a written harangue.[20]

But neither the differences of class nor of personal style explains Morgan's contempt for Rutherford, which was uncordially returned. Only the new politics of the 1790s can explain it. It was not just that Rutherford dressed like a tramp, it was that he saw virtue in so doing and preened himself on his republican simplicity. It was not his social position that explains it but the fact that he voted with Madison in Congress thirty-eight out of forty-two times.[21] It was not his Scottishness that inspired Morgan's contempt but his republicanism, which the former homeless boy increasingly saw as akin to anarchism, or, to use a term he and fellow Federalists would employ, Jacobonism. Rutherford and fellow Jeffersonians were conflated in Morgan's mind with the guillotine, Tom Paine's atheism, and insurrection in western Pennsylvania. And there, perhaps, was the center of Morgan's anger and political engagement. Jacobins in western Pennsylvania had threatened the lives and property of those he loved. That was more than enough to make them enemies.

Not surprisingly, the Neville interest was squarely behind Morgan in his race against Robin Rutherford. "You are about to Engage in as difficult or worse piece of business than the engagement with Tarleton," John Neville told him. "Tomorrow morning old Robin takes up his line of march to meet you in the field of election," Presley Neville wrote him from Philadelphia. "For God's sake defeat him, you have been used to conquest, and don't let such a raccoon get the better of you, he speaks with the most insulting confidence on the occasion, use all your address, influence, and Execution and let us know your prospects."[22]

Electioneering had to be done in part by proxy, as Morgan was at his post above Pittsburgh. Isaac Zane and others harangued on his behalf; Morgan sent a letter to the electors and then, in early March, took leave, rode home, and spoke publicly as much as he could. But to no success, for on March 16, 1794, Rutherford won again. He triumphantly proclaimed to Madison that on that day he "secured my reelection, against every artifice & misrepresentation, that could be engendered in the lowest walks of Society, together with inflaming weak fantastical minds to a pitch of real ferosity, as all these were to mount the war Horse and ride triumphant to Military honours, under the banners of this mighty son of Mars." ("War Horse," "Military honours," "mighty son of Mars"—it is not very hard to see what it was about Morgan that Rutherford resented.) Morgan and his supporters, Rutherford alleged, had left "No fraud . . . untryed—one Sharper it is said Voted Eight times under feigned names, & out of about 500. Votes listed to this champion I am well assured, there is not 200 legal."[23]

It was in effect the opening battle of a contest that would be waged until the election of 1800, and it opened a vein pulsing with vitriol and rage. Morgan and his allies might have seen Rutherford as a "raccoon" and a Jacobin; Rutherford and his allies saw them as "the monyed interest, Certificate mongers and Stock Jobbers alarmed when ever the people Speak out about abuses"—and who could doubt he was referring to Morgan himself with that triple-barreled description?[24] Given such a characterization of a political opponent, it seemed there could be no compromise, only total political victory for one and total defeat for the other.

WITH his military service over and his first campaign lost, Morgan continued in his intent to support Washington and the government against the now emergent Democratic-Republican opposition. His energies were focused on the Jay Treaty and its passage.

Chief Justice John Jay had been sent by Washington to negotiate an outcome with Great Britain that would benefit American territorial expansion and overseas trade while also avoiding war, for there was a distinct possibility the United States would be drawn into the European-wide war that began in 1793. The result was a treaty that Jay believed was the best that could be gotten in the circumstances. Essentially it was both a declaration of pro-British neutrality and a "repudiation of the Franco American alliance of 1778."[25] It submitted various claims of American merchants and appointments to arbitration and delayed British evacuation of forts that were clearly on territory recognized as American in the Treaty of Paris signed in 1783.

Whatever long-term advantages the Jay Treaty possessed—and they were substantial—they were invisible to the overwhelming majority of Americans. Washington's house in Philadelphia was besieged by angry mobs. John Jay himself joked that the United States was illuminated each night by the numerous effigies of him being burned by protesters. To its opponents, which included seemingly most Americans regardless of political inclination, the treaty seemed a betrayal of the Revolution by the man who had led the nation to victory.

Washington and those who followed him were far from unaware of that aspect of the treaty. One anecdote, stemming from Aaron Burr, has it that Morgan opposed the Jay Treaty until he heard that Washington was for it—and then, he said, "I shut my pan." That is not impossible to believe, despite the source.[26] For one thing, Washington himself was undecided about signing the Jay Treaty even after it had been approved by the Senate. What eventually persuaded him to do so were two things: his strategic vision and his capacity for taking offense. Strategic vision enabled him to realize that war with Britain or any other European power ought to be postponed until the United States was more powerful and stable. Because America was a maritime trading power without a navy, it was forced to depend on the British navy to ensure the tranquility of its trade. Washington therefore placed his money on Britain to win.

He took offense at Jefferson and Madison turning the argument over Jay's Treaty into a constitutional question with overtones of personal attack. They suggested that ultimately questions of foreign policy must be decided not simply by the executive with the approval of the Senate but also with the concurrence of the House of Representatives. In effect this suggested that Washington did not remember, or did not care to remember, both the actual letter of the Constitution and the substance of the debates in the Constitutional Convention over which he had presided. This enraged him, as they ought to have anticipated. Once his two fellow Virginians had thrown that gauntlet down in front of him, he was bound to pick it up and throw it back in their faces.

Madison thereby learned the "cardinal principle of American politics in the 1790s: whoever went face-to-face against Washington was destined to lose."[27] Washington signed the treaty and, much to the disgust of his opponents, in two years the majority of Americans had no more objections to it.

Morgan, in his way, did what he could to change the popular perception of the treaty in the Valley. Indeed, he built his next campaign for Congress around support for it. He engaged in a campaign along with other leading citizens in the Valley and in the Northern Neck to publish public letters and petitions in support of peace with England. As the campaign of 1796 drew closer, he stumped Frederick and Berkeley Counties in support of the Jay Treaty, Washington, Adams, and his own election to Congress. Morgan was, therefore, a foot soldier in what Jefferson termed the conspiracy of bankers, speculators, federal officeholders (whose ranks were filled with former officers of the Continental army), and all those alienated from agrarian society. Morgan combined several of those attributes yet could hardly be said to have rejected the farming life. This must have made Morgan particularly offensive to Jefferson and his followers; the Sage of Monticello had never grubbed stumps. Morgan was precisely the sort of person who should have been allied with their conception of American society yet he was powerful in the opposition, putting the Democratic-Republican interest in danger.[28]

In the election of March 20, 1797, Morgan was victorious. Rutherford appealed to the House Committee on Privileges and Elections, protesting what he saw as fraudulent conduct in Winchester. He listed three offenses: Morgan had brought voters to the polls in wagons, men from other congressional districts had cast votes for Morgan, and the crowd enjoying drinks provided by Morgan after voting had been so boisterous it discouraged Rutherford's supporters from going to the polls. These accusations seem to have been just a way to delay Morgan's taking his seat, as two of three of the activities were part of the accepted and traditional behavior of politicians and voters in Virginia—the exception being people voting outside their own district. An investigation over the summer led Rutherford to end his protest—or, as Morgan wrote to Washington rather more colorfully, "old Robin my old opponant have been Draging me about the Destrict by Notifications taking Depositions for five weeks past. but I believe the old man conceives himself Defeated."[29]

Morgan's first time in Congress was at a special session called for May 1797, and he took no part in the debates. Republicans believed him to be a moderate Federalist, able to be wooed away from the developing High Federalist faction coalescing around Alexander Hamilton, who was out of government and personally at odds with President John Adams. The special session was, from the Republican perspective, designed to begin a war with France; from a moderate Federalist perspective, it was simply a prudent means of improving national defense in a time of potential war. (High Federalists would have agreed with the Republicans and seen nothing much wrong with that.)

Yet while he may have had a reputation as a moderate, Morgan took actions that summer that much more reflected a High Federalist perspective. In his capacity as major general of militia commanding the Northern District of Virginia, he issued public orders to his subordinates to conduct patrols through their districts to guard against the possibility of a slave revolt. While pronouncing himself in favor of gradual abolition, he ominously suggested that enslaved people in northern Virginia were increasingly restless for their freedom because of the influence of "different self-created societies," a reference to the Democratic-Republican societies that Federalists saw at the bottom of every civil disturbance. (This same language would be used by Democratic-Republicans after the discovery of "Gabriel's Rebellion" in 1802.) It seems that Morgan intended his patrols to intimidate not enslaved Virginians but Jeffersonian Virginians, and possibly to even use his militia as an internal security force—or at least threaten to do so.[30]

In a way, Morgan's measures in Virginia anticipated the debate that began in October when he and his fellow congressmen returned to Philadelphia. There, in spring 1798, they received word of the failed attempt by the three American commissioners to negotiate a better state of affairs with France, stymied by a demand for a bribe before any meeting could occur with the French foreign minister. This news enraged Federalists, dismayed Democratic-Republicans, and led to a series of sweeping bills for external and internal security. Money flowed into the Navy Department; a "New Army" was created, its initial size to be ten thousand, commanded by Washington reluctantly emerging from retirement, able to oppose any French attack on the continent; trade agreements and all previous treaties with France were ended; attacks on French ships were authorized; and the Sedition Act was passed to suppress any attempts at obstructing these policies. To Morgan and other Virginia Federalists, these were sensible defensive measures to preserve the independence and trade of the United States. As for the Alien and Sedition Acts, nothing in them was foreign to precedent or common law.[31]

For Morgan, the passage of this legislation was the "consolation for my long stay at Congress," for it meant nothing less than that "the independence of America had been secured for a long time," he wrote Presley Neville. "We have in our struggles the last session gained a great victory over the Democrats," he exulted, "and I intend to follow up the advantage till I see them crush'd to atoms." He wrote that the Jeffersonians "at this time look like a parcel of egg sucking dogs that have been caught breaking up hen's nests." (A rustic metaphor even for rustics.) The laws would "stop the mouths of the demogoguing Jacobins."[32]

So while subsequent generations of historians have at best tut-tutted the Alien and Sedition Acts, or wrung their hands, or attributed them to the vindictiveness of Abigail Adams, we see here the Old Wagoner convinced that they were necessary for the survival of the republic. Morgan was seeking to prevail in what he clearly saw as the early stages of a civil war, beginning with the origins of the Whiskey Rebellion and now culminating in a war against the Jacobinism that had infected the United States.

Suffering an onset of illness, and fearing the yellow fever that had swept through Philadelphia in previous summers of the 1790s, Morgan left Congress without voting on the Sedition Act or bidding a personal farewell to President Adams. "I believe this is my last Journey to Phila," he wrote. "Tis probable I may never have the honor to see you again, I wish you health and happiness, and that your Merits and Virtues may be rewarded in this world & the next—I beg the honor, when you see Mrs. Adams that you mention to her the sincere respect of an old Soldier."[33]

Chapter Nineteen

DEATH

ORGAN returned not to Saratoga but to Soldier's Rest, his first home near Battletown. Sometime in the late 1790s, with the Nevilles restored to their home in Pittsburgh and the Heards also moved out of Saratoga, his dream home was too big for him. Like so many Americans since, he built that big house he had always wanted just before he no longer had need of it.

Now back at Soldier's Rest, even that more-modest establishment was too large for him, and he was unable to superintend the enterprises of farm and mill. The expression "if I was the man I was" appears several times in his letters and recollections. That applied to his landholdings in Kentucky, managed by an agent he believed to be a "damned ragged Raskel. . . . [I]f I were ten year younger," he wrote Presley Neville, "I would ride all the way to Kentucky in order to whip him from south post to gun firing. You must do as well as you can with them lands as I wish to have nothing more to do with them as I suppose in a very few years at furthest a much smaller quantity will serve me—had you any chance to sell—I suppose not however I do expect they will sell pritty well by and by (that so) what you don't want to keep."[1]

What gave him as much worry in his last years, possibly even more than Thomas Jefferson and Democratic-Republican societies, was the fate of his daughter Betsey and her children. "The lands on this side of the Ohio River I intend to appropriate to Betseys family," he wrote Presley Neville, "and how to do it I am at a loss to know as I shall be too unwieldy to pay attention to them myself, and if I trust them to Major Heard He will make sad havock with them I fear." Morgan no longer thought of Heard as one of Betsey's family; he was simply an obstacle to the happiness of Morgan's daughter and grandchildren.

In his funeral sermon for Morgan, William Hill said that "while he retained any recollection, the welfare of his country was his topic, and appeared to absorb his whole soul." But there was another concern that perhaps surpassed that one, the welfare of Morgan's family after he was gone: that all the fighting and scrabbling and doing since he first came to the Valley should not be lost; that some posterity should live after him.

ONE of the most precious of all the achievements of Morgan's last years must have been finally receiving the open regard of George Washington, the reciprocation of his own devotion. As Alexander Hamilton began creating the new army designed to defend the United States against a French invasion, it had a secondary objective of serving to intimidate the internal Jacobin enemy. Morgan might be infirm, might no longer be able to travel to advise Washington, the commander in chief, but he was still able to write him with the names of Virginians he judged suitable candidates to be officers in the new army. They would need to be not only promising military material but without any compromising republican tendencies. Morgan showed no hesitation in creating a federalist officer corps.

Thus in June 1799, responding to a request from Washington to nominate officers to the "New Army," Morgan sent Washington (and Secretary of War James McHenry) a list of those candidates very much like the one Washington had made of potential general officers in 1793. "I should have answered your letter sooner, but wished to inform myself of such characters as would best fit the Army," Morgan wrote. "I find but few of the old Officers that are altogether fit for the Service, from different causes (Vizt) some too old and infirm; others incumbered with large families, and some too much in the habit of drinking which I always view as a very great misfortune to mankind, should any in future offer of superior talents, I will transmit you a list of their names." Also very important, Morgan added, was that such officers were "firmly attached to Government."[2]

When he had begun this work of assessment and recommendation, he wrote a note to Washington recommending a man whose "virtues as a man are such as give him universal estimation among those who know how to appreciate merit"—a description he might have chosen for himself. Acknowledging the receipt of Morgan's note, Washington added:

"I assure you, my dear Sir, it gave me not a little pleasure to find the account of your death in the newspapers was not founded in fact—and I sincerely pray that many years may elapse before that event takes place, and that in the meantime, you may be restored to the full enjoyment of your health, and to your usefulness in Society, being, with very great regard Your sincere friend & servt."[3]

That was, for Washington, an effusive salutation; terming himself "sincere friend and servant" was the closest Washingtonian equivalent to a hug. A later letter assured Morgan that Washington had complete "confidence in your knowledge of characters (especially of the old & meritorious Officers of the Virginia line)—of your patriotism, and willingness to form a respectable Corps of Officers for our native State." For Morgan, those were precious words.[4]

By the end of that year, 1799, Washington was dead, and Morgan continued on. He was becoming a relic of a previous age. All of his intimate friends had moved on, down the rivers into the west or across the last river of all. John Neville, long before, and Betsey and her Presley, of course. But Horatio Gates, now an ardent Democratic-Republican, had left Berkeley County for New York City and a wealthy widow. Peter Bruin had pulled up stakes and was now living on the banks of the Mississippi, north of Natchez.

And then there were those who had gone into the dominion of the "Grim King," the term Washington often used to refer to death. Greene had gone first, before the Constitution had even been framed, killed by heatstroke in 1786. Otho Williams was gone, died in summer 1794, his wound and mistreatment as prisoner finally killing him on a journey to the soothing waters of a Virginian hot spring. Isaac Zane, that curious Quaker, had died in 1795. Old Denmark, Christian Febiger, had ended his life as treasurer of the Commonwealth of Pennsylvania, dying in Philadelphia in 1796.

All of them had been younger than Morgan, had seen less of life than he had, been less beat up by life than he had, yet all were now gone. The Grim King still waited to claim Morgan, and it could not be very much longer before he did.

HARRY LEE excelled at brief capsule obituaries—they are scattered throughout his *Memoirs*, which were chiefly dedicated to recalling and celebrating the southern campaigns of which he had been so important an actor, partly intended to settle a few scores (as memoirs generally are), and also intended as a monument to his generation of Revolutionary heroes. He saw his country in the first decade of the new century as enjoying a liberty without considering its source. The *Memoirs* were a call for America to both recognize its heroes and place himself in that pantheon.[5]

Well educated in the classics at home and at the College of New Jersey by John Witherspoon, Lee knew how to write a death scene—Plutarch, one of his favorite literary and historical models, provided him with excellent templates. As in Plutarch, Lee's death scenes conveyed a life and a life's philosophy. Thus the death of Robert Kirkwood at St. Clair's Defeat conveyed the heroism, the tragedy, the irony, of a veteran soldier dying forgotten and alone after surviving so many other battles.

To this program of memorialization Lee brought a philosophical perspective. Fellow classmates at Princeton like Philip Fithian and Andrew Hunter had been Presbyterian ministers in the making. Others, like James Madison a few years before him, had not become either ministers or Presbyterians but had seriously contemplated Christian theology. But Lee was a serious philosophical Deist, a would-be Stoic who did not have much use if any for the piety of his fellow Virginians or that of his second wife, Anne Carter Lee. The enthusiasms of the increasingly evangelical United States at the turn of the nineteenth century were, for him, mere enthusiasms. In a curious way this made the elderly Morgan the innovator and young Lee the reactionary, a throwback to the earlier decades of the eighteenth century in Virginia when "enthusiastic" was one of the most damning things that could be said of a man, and enthusiasm was the sort of a behavior one could expect from a woman.[6]

So Lee was perhaps writing more in sorrow than in contempt when he noted that "General Morgan, like thousands of mortals when nearly worn out by the hand of time, resorted for comfort to the solace of religion."[7] He was referring to Morgan becoming a Presbyterian.

Morgan might have put things slightly differently. One crony, James Mackin, after hearing Morgan describe how he had prayed before the assault on Quebec, said to him, "I expect you prayed like a man I once knew, who led a very wicked life" and when driven to pray concluded, "If thou wilt help me now, and extricate me out of my present difficulties, I promise not to trouble thee again for a long time." Morgan was not amused. "No, Mr. Mackin," he said, "I never used mockery . . . nor ever treated religion disrespectfully. I always believed in the truth and importance of religion, and knew that I was a great sinner for neglecting my duty to my God. If I ever prayed in earnest it was on that occasion."[8] In this way of thinking, or of presentation, his new religious sensibility was the result of a long progression.

Certainly Morgan could articulate what he believed. Miles Fisher, one of the Quakers who had been interned in Winchester over winter 1777–1778, wrote to him twenty years later, reminding him of their meeting and inquiring as to his religious beliefs—which Fisher indicated he expected were Deism of some kind. Morgan was, again, not amused. He was not, he responded tartly, of "Tom Pain's creed." Instead:

I believe in one God, the first and great cause of all goodness. I also believe in Jesus christ the redeemer of the world. I also believe in the Holy gost the comforter—here perhaps we may Differ a little as I believe Jesus christ was from eternity and a part of the godhead—was Detached by the Father to Do a certain piece of service which was to take on Human Nature, which Human Nature was to suffer Death for the redemption

of Mankind and who after that service was completely ful-
filled that he returned to and was consolidated with the Godhead.

He continued on in that vein, eventually apologizing for having
said "more than I intended," then indicating that perhaps it was the
party conflict of the 1790s that also had influenced his turn to
Christianity. "I alwaise wished to support it as I alwaise thought it
the first streng[th] and best support to good government whare you
have no religion you are true to have no government for as religion
Disappears anarchy takes place and fixes a compleat Hell upon
Earth, till religion returns." He concluded darkly, "So it is and will
be in France How long we Don't know & I wish it may not come
Here for I think I Discover its approaches." As Jefferson faced
Adams in the election of 1800, Morgan, like many others, must
have been convinced that that moment was indeed imminent.[9]

So Morgan became a Christian, and a Presbyterian, as consolation in old age; because of a lifelong feeling for the divine, or of
being hunted by the divine; because of the party politics of the
1790s; or perhaps, as Graham suggests, because of the urging of
the long-suffering Abigail Morgan. But friendship had something
to do with it, as one might expect from this friendable man. A
young minister had come to the new congregation in Winchester,
and Morgan took a great liking to him.

They must have been an odd couple. William Hill was over thirty
years younger than Morgan, born in 1769. He had graduated from
Hampden-Sydney in 1785, when that college and seminary was just
ten years old, founded by a Princetonian student of John Witherspoon's, Samuel Stanhope Smith. Ordained, Hill was installed as
the pastor of the Winchester Presbyterian Church in 1800.[10] He was
one of the many young pastors that began to fan out across the
South planting new Presbyterian churches where before the Revolution there had been an established church. At this moment,
Presybterians were keenly interested in cooperation with other
Protestant sects, even with quasi-religious sects such as the Masons,
in order to cement the moral order of the new republic. Hill seems
to have shared this nationalist passion, which would have made
Morgan fascinating to him personally and would have made his
message congenial to Morgan.[11]

Either that year or just before Hill's arrival, Morgan had joined the Presbyterian Church and been communed—an important point made by Virginians at the time and easily missed, as many church members did not take communion (George Washington, for instance). Now, in 1800, the Morgans moved from Berryville to Winchester, where they lived in the house of Betsey and the wastrel Major Heard.[12]

There Morgan and Hill were convenient to one another, and Hill seems to have spent numerous hours with Morgan. In his last two years of life, Morgan seems to have been mostly confined to bed. Hill helped him up to the chamber pot, saw to his needs, talked with him, and listened. Story after story came out, and Hill wrote them down—without which James Graham's eventual biography would have been impossible, as well as every subsequent biography.

THERE in his sickroom, Morgan managed to achieve a solution to the problem of Major Heard. On March 16, 1801, he established three deeds with the courts of Frederick County. The most substantive of these was in effect a trust for Betsey. To Presley Neville and Lawrence Butler—another veteran officer of the Virginia line during the Revolution—Morgan sold all of his enumerated property for $1. This included sixteen enslaved people, as well as 24 horses, 64 sheep, 114 hogs, and "51 head of horned cattle." This property was to be managed and held for "the sale and separate disposal of his daughter Betsey Heard . . . without interference, molestation, or claim of her said husband with or to the said property or the use or profits thereof." Under Virginia law, so long as Major Heard was married to Betsey the rule of coverture meant that what was given to her was now his. But not now. The officers of the trust could only act on Betsey's own directions, until the death of her husband, at which point the property "with its increase" would be conveyed to her. Should Betsey predecease Major Heard, then the property would be conveyed to her children. Morgan's last victory was to give his daughter some power and authority in a bad marriage.

He also gave other gifts. Because of the "natural love and affection which I have and bear unto my beloved granddaughters Matilda Heard and Nancy Heard," Morgan pronounced in his other deed of

March 16, 1801, "I give Matilda a girl slave named Kitty about fifteen years of age" and to Nancy "one girl slave about thirteen years of age." Four months later, he deeded a handsome bequest to the children of the Smith family of Rockingham County. Into the care of the trustees were placed not only a dark bay horse, a bay mare and colt, three cows, and three calves, but also "one Negroe man named Toney" and a "Negroe woman named Hartwell." All these were "to be preserved for the infants until they were of age."[13]

While Morgan might have thought of himself as a friend of gradual abolition, as he had once proclaimed in a newspaper announcement, at the end of his life he showed no indication of being an actor or initiator of it. He was a member of the Virginian elite, and therefore, like most of them, he took slavery as a simple fact of life. Ultimately, the continuing security of his family was of more importance to him.

For all his life, Morgan had been a man of action, and a doer, but now there was nothing to be done. A man who had grubbed stumps and guided Conestoga wagons could now not even get himself to a chamber pot, or from his bed to his easy chair. The indignities of his body, which he had suffered for so long, seemed to be culminating.

Yet even now there were moments when he seemed reluctant to finally go. One traditional Winchester story has it that when his doctor finally told him he would soon die, Morgan was incredulous.

"You don't mean that I will continue on for some years?"

"No, General, I do not expect that you will last the week."

"Doctor," said Morgan, "if I could be the man I was when I was 21, I would be willing to be stripped stark naked on the top of the Allegheny Mountain, to run for my life with a pack of dogs at my heels."[14]

This fits with Harry Lee's stoic telling of Morgan's death. Morgan had, said Lee, often expressed the desire "to pass his life as a galley slave rather than exchange this world for that unknown."[15] Yet anyone who has read *The Odyssey* must be at least a little suspicious of this recollection. In Book 10, Odysseus sails to the edge of the world and the Kingdom of the Dead, seeking knowledge from the ghosts who inhabit that land. There he lures the shades to him by offering a bowl of warm blood, freshly drained from a dead sheep. Among them is Achilles, hero of the Greeks at Troy, greatest of warriors, Odysseus's old comrade, now King of the Dead. With his usual ready line of glib chatter, Odysseus marvels that not only was Achilles the greatest warrior in the world of the living, even in the afterlife he has made it to the top. "No winning words about death to me, shining Odysseus!" replies Achilles, "By god, I'd rather slave on earth for another man—some dirt-poor tenant farmer who scrapes to keep alive—than rule down here over all the breathless dead"—I would rather be most menial of the menial in all the living world than be the most powerful of those who live no longer.[16] Life is everything; slavery is better than death.

Odysseus and Achilles are themselves archetypes for all those who have suffered in combat, and—in Odysseus's case—returned home with physical wounds healed but spiritual wounds forever bleeding. Perhaps Harry Lee was saying that Morgan was the Achilles of the Revolution. Or perhaps he was making the point that the greatest glories of life are those of life, not to be found in the mysterious unknown that lies before us. Or perhaps he was doing both, or neither.

Not surprisingly, William Hill—who was Lee's informant for Morgan's last years as he is for the rest of us—took a different lesson from Morgan's death. In his funeral sermon he observed that Morgan's character improved over his life, "as he was in his last days brought to see the impropriety and folly of these things, and sincerely repent of the same." Against Lee's deistic pessimism, fueled by the despair of Lee's own last years of financial debt, Hill presented Christian hope.[17] Morgan's death became, in a small way, a kind of intellectual battleground at a key moment in the shift of American and Southern sensibility.

Contemporaries could take other lessons from Morgan's life and death. Colonial and Revolutionary Americans did not, despite their praise of reason, see emotion as reason's opposite. Instead they believed the two were necessary companions in emotional and intellectual life. Disordered emotions and passions were, of course, to be restrained; and they must have a laudable goal. But they were not to be erased from one's consciousness.[18]

Morgan was, in his way, an exemplar of authentic passion, perhaps a bit rough at times, but for the best possible of republican ends. His movement in life from brawler to soldier was an indication of that, and of what other citizens might achieve. From a man of ungoverned passion, he had become one who could direct those passions for the common good. He might threaten a soldier with a stick of firewood, but it was for the good of the army. He might punch out a tavern owner, but it was because he was gouging Morgan's soldiers. Morgan remained authentic, to use a term he would not recognize, yet he was simultaneously directed toward both the goods of the republic and, ultimately, the divine. In this Morgan was something of a foretaste of the Romantic hero, and of the ideal of the American democratic citizen.

Daniel Morgan died on July 6, 1802. The greatest crowd in the history of Winchester came to his funeral and interment. Morgan had been one of them since he had walked into the little town. His death brought an end to the community's first half-century of existence. Among the soldiers who fired a salute over his grave were seven men carrying rifles, the remaining members of the ninety men who had followed him out of Winchester to Boston and to Quebec.[19]

EPILOGUE

A FTER Daniel Morgan's death, Nancy and Presley Neville continued to live in Pittsburgh, where Presley continued as a civic leader. They had, all told, fifteen children. Through the years, Presley amassed greater and greater debts, until in 1816 he was forced to sell his Pittsburgh properties and move down the Ohio to a tract of land along the river near Cincinnati, given to him for his service in the Revolution. There he created a little village he named Neville, where he and Nancy lived in a log cabin until he died two years later.

Betsey and Major Heard eventually separated, sometime after they moved to Logan County, Kentucky, along the Tennessee border. Heard returned to New Jersey, where he lived in poverty. His appeal for a military pension in 1817 contained an endorsement by his old commander Harry Lee, himself now in poverty and self-imposed exile. One of Betsey's daughters, Matilda Heard, married a second cousin, a former Marine Corps officer named Presley Neville O'Bannon. During the American war against Tripoli, O'Bannon led the Marine detachment in a little army of mercenaries commanded by William Eaton, which marched from the Nile across the northern Sahara to seize Derna in Libya in 1805. Abigail Curry Morgan died in the O'Bannon home on May 20, 1816.[1]

By 1812, Morgan's son Willoughby was living in Winchester. It was from there that, like his father before him, he left with a company of men to fight the British. During the War of 1812, he showed himself to be an officer of considerable usefulness and intelligence, and he accepted a commission in the regular army. The rest of his

life was spent in frontier outposts along the Mississippi, often at
Jefferson Barracks in St. Louis. When Colonel Willoughby Morgan
died in 1832, he was commandant of Fort Crawford in Prairie du
Chien, Wisconsin. An inventory of his possessions would have made
his father proud, for he had a rich library that included not only
poetry of Walter Scott but William Paley's *Theology*, John Bunyan's
Pilgrim's Progress, the *Federalist,* and an Old Testament in Hebrew.
The son had gone into regions of the mind where the father had not
been able to travel. But Willoughby demonstrated that in a small
way, he was his father's son: the final sale of his belongings revealed
that he shared Daniel Morgan's fondness for fancy clothes. In
Willoughby's wardrobe were no fewer than twenty-three "fancy
handkerchiefs," twenty-one waistcoats, and thirty-seven pairs of
socks.[2]

AT Morgan's funeral, William Hill observed to the assembled multitude, "When we consider the obscurity from which he arose; the
honour and power to which he ascended; and the great services
which he has rendered his country—we may say he had very few
equals."[3] It had indeed been an ascent, but not a serene and gradual
one. Each step had been sharp and sometimes severe, requiring immense effort—certainly Hill was correct to also say that Morgan's
"successes are not attributable only to a fortunate occurrence of circumstances." Yet it was not only effort that enabled Morgan to succeed. His feet could have been crushed by a falling stump or by a
wagon wheel; he could have lost a hand in the sawmill where he
was foreman; the scars of the flogging might have gotten infected;
the Indian's shot might have gone two inches to the left—the list of
fortunate circumstances in Morgan's life is a long one.

But in addition to the perennial argument between talent and
luck, there is an almost equally contentious dispute over leadership
in the American Revolution and the culture that made it possible.
On one side of this long-standing argument in early American history is the contention—traceable to John Adams and others of the
Revolutionary generation—that the founders and their society were
created by the crisis of the Revolution. The opposing view is that
colonial America was already an "altogether more open, mobile,

expansive, dynamic, flexible, and participatory" society and culture than it is popularly believed to have been.[4] America was, therefore, already a nursery of competent talent before the Revolution.

Morgan's life shows that it is necessary to achieve some halfway point between these two schools of thought. Not because truth is always halfway between two points, but because both of them can be demonstrated by different phases of his life. If colonial Virginia had been the "backward-looking and confining" place of both popular and scholarly imagination, then it is impossible to see how a man like Morgan could have ascended as he did.[5] But in fact there were means of advancement and ways to succeed even in what was arguably the most hierarchical and traditional of the American colonies.

Yet it is also impossible to imagine Morgan without the Revolution. John Adams seemed to be making a simple observation, not stating a sociological law, when he wrote, "when society gets disturbed, men of great abilities and good talents are *always* found or made." Previous cultural institutions and personal experiences made Morgan and many others, but the disturbance of the Revolution elevated them to positions they could not have anticipated.[6] Morgan was a creation of the dynamic society of colonial America; he was given a role of national importance when the Revolution summoned forth his talents. In this he was not alone, but one of thousands, even tens of thousands.

Morgan should, to this day, be a representative of those thousands less well attested than he who also lived revolutionary lives. But the reality is very different. Soon after Morgan's coffin was lowered into the obscurity of his grave, his reputation sank with equal speed into even deeper darkness. Today, while Morgan remains obscure at best, other men like Daniel Boone and Davy Crockett occupy the space in the popular imagination that was once Morgan's, relegating the Old Wagoner to the dim dark at the back of the historical stage. This continuing obscurity came about for three reasons—one an accident of technology and timing, two because of Morgan's countercultural choices.

The accident first. Both Boone and Crockett lived long enough to be lionized and mythicized by the new American publishing industry; Crockett benefited from that industry's production of cheap novels, campaign biographies, and instant autobiographies. On a wave of pulp, the reputations of Boone and Crockett rose into the stratosphere of the archetypal. It was Crockett's further great fortune to rise even higher with the advent of broadcast TV, a success so total that the demand among young boys for coonskin hats sent raccoon tails into shortage. Morgan, always lucky while he was alive, did not enjoy such cosmic luck in death.

Morgan also made a mistake or two in establishing a post-mortem reputation because he was out of step with the people. The first was choosing as his political home the Federalist Party, which put him on the losing side in Virginia and national politics. Had he chosen to join the Jeffersonians, he would have been hailed and memorialized as a great American hero in ways he never was. He would have been the Democratic-Republican frontier hero in a hunting shirt. Instead he was the Valley Federalist who advocated canals, roads, a standing army with only loyal Federalists as officers, and the Alien and Sedition Acts.

Perhaps most important of all, Morgan ran against the grain of American culture. Daniel Boone had moved from North Carolina to Kentucky, and in later years kept moving farther and farther west until he became simultaneously a subject of the King of Spain and an American archetypal hero. Davy Crockett, when he picked the wrong faction in the Democratic Party and lost his election, also did what Morgan did not do. "You may go to Hell and I shall go to Texas," he told his Tennessee constituents, and that western journey to death at the Alamo forever established him as an icon of American culture.

But Morgan stayed put. Perhaps, had his health been better, he too would have moved west. Certainly all of his extended family did: his wife, his daughters, his son, all died west of the Appalachians. Charles Mynn Thruston, the one-time Anglican pastor and Virginia colonel, traveled off down the rivers, ending his life in the Mississippi Territory near Natchez; so too did Peter Bruin, who had ridden south with Morgan in September 1781. If he could have, perhaps Morgan would gone searching for a place to settle on the edge of the frontier.

In all likelihood, however, he would have remained where he had been since he first crossed the Potomac. He had after all passed up plenty of chances to move during the 1760s. It seems deeply ironic that a man who experienced so many social, political, and personal revolutions should have been so resolutely attached to a particular place. But it was instead his particular calling to build a place, to be one of those who created a community in the lower Shenandoah. He did not move west in a search for evermore virginal land but chose to nourish what he owned; he did not engage in the perpetual search for a new Eden, because he had found his own Eden when he was eighteen and never saw any reason to abandon it. This sort of mission, unfortunately, has never been prized by Americans as part of their mythic self-image. Fortunately for the development of our culture and civilization, it is practiced nonetheless.

So Dan Morgan remained in the place he loved, and as is often the case, that place did not always return that love. Just as no one can be a hero to his valet, and no prophet is honored in his hometown, so too was Morgan curiously forgotten in Winchester and the lower Valley. Plenty of Winchester's citizens preserved memories of Morgan the brawler and roisterer, Morgan the drunkard and profligate, which sat uneasily with the hero of Cowpens and the Congressional Gold Medal, not to mention with his membership in Dr. Hill's Presbyterian congregation. The traumas of secession and the Civil War seem to have overlaid Morgan's memory with other concerns—until his remains suffered a curious threat.

In August 1951, a group of South Carolinians arrived in Winchester to remove Morgan's body to the Cowpens Battlefield. They were armed with the approval of Morgan's great-great-great-granddaughter and an overwhelming sense of righteousness. Planning ahead for their campaign with care and attention that would have impressed the meticulous Nathanael Greene, they included in their number an attorney and an undertaker. The attorney, one J. Manning Poliakoff, charged that only one of forty people in Winchester could even identify Morgan. On the other hand South Carolinians, by Poliakoff's account, learned of Morgan in school, regarded him as a hero, and considered him an exemplar for all of their actions. "What would Morgan do?" was apparently a question always in the foremost thoughts of citizens of South Carolina.

This sudden South Carolinian attack prompted a defensive response by those who had forgotten who Morgan was. Winchester defenders of the general's mortal remains quickly brought suit in court, while the southern eminences of James F. Byrnes of South Carolina and Harry Flood Byrd of Virginia (and Winchester) championed the claims of their respective states. As one observer noted, Morgan himself might well have mourned the fact that in the end, the entire dispute was settled in court (the South Carolinians lost and paid court costs), never reaching the point of "downright fighting." How satisfying it would have been had they settled their differences with a hard-fought brawl over the grave of the Old Wagoner. He would have loved it.[7]

The actions of those gentlemen from South Carolina would have been instantly familiar to a host of medieval European monks: the gentlemen were stealing relics. Like monks who poached a bone of a saint and spirited it away to their own abbey, the South Carolina boosters wanted to steal away Morgan's relics to their soil, and with it something else more ethereal and mysterious—call it presence, call it mana, call it honor—that they wished to place in close juxtaposition with the memory of his greatest military achievement.

But Morgan cannot be found on his battlefields. He spent less than a day at Cowpens, just around a month in South Carolina; perhaps four months at most in both the Carolinas. The Saratoga Campaign—including the journeys to and from the battlefields—took at most three months. His battlefields are not his greatest legacy. He did harsh and necessary work there, as he saw it, but he did not love them; he loved the lower Valley of the Shenandoah, and he was one of the thousands who created it and called it home.

In turn, the lower Shenandoah created him. Morgan was not his own creation; no one really is their own creation. Self-fashioning is not only an academic but a popular concept in part because the self-made person is a concept that appeals to Americans of all times, all places, and all ideologies. We are, we like to believe, precisely who we make ourselves. But this is not quite so. We are also made by everything around us: society, culture, landscape, good fortune, providence. All these things grind at us, goad us, form us, mold us, direct us, however much we kick and bite against them. You will not find Morgan's presence beneath the walls of Quebec, or at Freeman's farm, not even at Cowpens. But if you stop for a while in the lower Valley, perhaps by the sign post that gives White Post its name; by the rocky waters of the Shenandoah; or the road that runs in front of Saratoga's long drive; on the lawn of Soldier's Rest; or by the stream as it runs past Burwell and Morgan's mill, there you can still look about you and see what he made, and what made him.

NOTES

PROLOGUE

1. William Henry Herndon and Jesse William Weik, *Herndon's Lincoln: The True Story of a Great Man*, vol. 2 (Springfield, IL: Herndon's Lincoln Publishing, 1921), 375.
2. Edmund S. Morgan, *The Meaning of Independence: John Adams, Thomas Jefferson, George Washington* (New York: W.W. Norton, 1978), 4.
3. Personal communication with the author, June 30, 2018.

CHAPTER I: HOME

1. At the time Morgan arrived, the county courthouse—or county seat, as everyone outside of Virginia terms it—of Frederick County was called Frederick Town. To simplify matters, and to distinguish it from Frederick Town, Maryland (Frederick the Prince of Wales was popular in the colonies), I call it Winchester even though it was not until a few years later that it was so named.
2. James Graham, *The Life of General Daniel Morgan [. . .] with Portions of His Correspondence, Etc.* (New York: Derby & Jackson, 1856), 20; Don Higginbotham, *Daniel Morgan: Revolutionary Rifleman*, 1st ed. (Chapel Hill: University of North Carolina Press, 1961), 1; Benjamin Berry, "Notes, Concerning Daniel Morgan," Virginia Historical Society, Richmond.
3. Warren R. Hofstra and Karl B. Raitz, eds., *The Great Valley Road of Virginia: Shenandoah Landscapes from Prehistory to the Present* (Charlottesville: University of Virginia Press, 2010), 80.
4. Bruce Catton, *A Stillness at Appomattox* (Garden City, NY: Doubleday, 1962), 307.
5. Warren R. Hofstra, *The Planting of New Virginia: Settlement and Landscape in the Shenandoah Valley,* Creating the North American Landscape (Baltimore: Johns Hopkins University Press, 2004), 60. The Valley and its pre-Virginian settler past is discussed in Michael N. McConnell, "Before the Great Road: Indian Travelers on the Great Warriors' Path," in *Great Valley Road,* ed. Hofstra and Raitz, 57–78.
6. Hofstra, *Planting,* 56–57, 61.
7. Ibid., 127, 131; John Fontaine, *The Journal of John Fontaine: An Irish Huguenot Son in Spain and Virginia, 1710–1719* (Williamsburg, VA: Colonial Williamsburg Foundation, 1972), 90–100.

8. For a discussion of the geography and geology of the Shenandoah, see Karl Raitz, "The Lay of the Land," in *Great Valley Road*, ed. Hofstra and Raitz, 17–56; Robert D. Mitchell, "'Over the Hills and Far Away': George Washington and the Changing Virginia Backcountry," 72, in *George Washington and the Virginia Backcountry*, 1st ed., ed. Warren R. Hofstra (Madison, WI: Madison House, 1998).

9. Hofstra, *Planting*, 84.

10. Ibid., 66–67.

11. For "King" Carter see Louis B. Wright and Lessing J. Rosenwald, *Letters of Robert Carter, 1720–1727: The Commercial Interests of a Virginia Gentleman* (San Marino, CA: Huntington Library Publications, 1940), vii-xiii; Louis Morton, *Robert Carter of Nomini Hall: A Virginia Tobacco Planter of the Eighteenth Century* (Charlottesville: University Press of Virginia, 1969), 10–23.

12. Pierre Marambaud, *William Byrd of Westover, 1674–1744* (Charlottesville: University Press of Virginia, 1971), 51, 250.

13. Warren R. Hofstra, *A Separate Place: The Formation of Clarke County, Virginia* (White Post, VA: Clarke County Sesquicentennial Committee, 1986), 3.

14. Hofstra, *Planting*, 223–224.

15. Mitchell, "'Over the Hills,'" 72.

16. Ibid.

17. Graham, *Life of Morgan*, 18.

18. Ibid., 17.

19. Higginbotham, *Daniel Morgan*, 2. Examples of this speculation can be found salted throughout in North Callahan, *Daniel Morgan, Ranger of the Revolution*, 1st ed. (New York: Holt, Rinehart and Winston, 1961).

20. Berry, "Notes"; Graham, *Life of Morgan*, 19.

21. Graham, *Life of Morgan*, 19–20.

22. Berry, "Notes"; Graham, *Life of Morgan*, 20–21; for Lord Fairfax, see Stuart E. Brown, *Virginia Baron: The Story of Thomas, 6th Lord Fairfax* (Berryville, VA: Chesapeake, 1965).

23. Douglas Southall Freeman, *George Washington, a Biography* (New York: Scribner, 1948), 1:195–198; John E. Ferling, *The Ascent of George Washington: The Hidden Political Genius of an American Icon*, 1st US ed. (New York: Bloomsbury Press, 2009), 9–13.

24. Philander Chase, "A Stake in the West: George Washington as Backcountry Surveyor and Landholder," 177, in Hofstra, *George Washington and the Virginia Backcountry*.

25. T.J. Jackson Lears, *Something for Nothing: Luck in America* (New York: Viking, 2003), 22.

26. Thomas Young, "Memoir of Major Thomas Young," *Orion* 3 (1843): 84–88, 100–105.

27. For more on the Allason firm and its international reach, see Robert William Spoede, "William Allason, Merchant in an Emerging Nation," PhD diss., College of William and Mary, 1973. The classic study is Miles S. Malone, "Falmouth and the Shenandoah: Trade before the Revolution," *American Historical Review* 40, no. 4 (1935): 693–703.

28. George Shumway and Howard C. Frey, *Conestoga Wagon, 1750–1850: Freight*

Carrier for 100 Years of America's Westward Expansion, 3rd ed. (York, PA: G. Shumway, 1968), 11–12.
29. Barry Carozzi, "Historic Roads of Virginia," Idiom 46, no. 3 (2010): 30.
30. Arthur L. Reist, Conestoga Wagon, Masterpiece of the Blacksmith (Lancaster, PA: Forry and Hacker, 1975), 10; Shumway and Frey, Conestoga Wagon, 11.
31. Reist, Conestoga Wagon, 11.
32. T. Triplett Russell and John K. Gott, Fauquier County in the Revolution (Warrenton, VA: Fauquier County American Bicentennial Commission, 1976), 69.

CHAPTER 2: WAR

1. David L. Preston, Braddock's Defeat: The Battle of the Monongahela and the Road to Revolution, Pivotal Moments in American History (Oxford: Oxford University Press, 2015), 37.
2. Ibid., 90. For this rate see the accounts of Joseph Coombs and Daniel Morgan in the Shenandoah Store Ledger B, October 1762–September 1763, Library of Virginia, Richmond.
3. Preston, Braddock's Defeat, 90.
4. Fred Anderson, Crucible of War: The Seven Years' War and the Fate of Empire in British North America, 1754–1766, 1st Vintage Books ed. (New York: Vintage Books, 2001), 93–94; Preston, Braddock's Defeat, 38.
5. Preston, Braddock's Defeat, 83–84.
6. Graham located the punishment at Fort Chiswell, in the New River valley of southwestern Virginia, based on Rev. William Hill's inquiries. Graham, Life of Morgan, 28–30. But both Higginbotham and Preston have argued that the best estimate of when it occurred seems to be during some phase of Braddock's march. Higginbotham, Daniel Morgan, 5n7; Preston, Braddock's Defeat, 83.
7. Colonial Office Series 5, vol. 717, nos. 19, 19i, and vol. 721, no. 10, PRO, London. "November 14, 1710. Petition of Ann Pauley to the Queen on behalf of Charles Arabella, master of a sloop, a subject of the Duke of Florence and now a prisoner near Chester River in Maryland at Virginia. He was condemned for blasphemy and fined 20 pounds, bored three times thro' the tongue, and sentenced to six months imprisonment. Being unable to pay, he has continued above a year in prison."; John Briggs, Christopher Harrison, Angus McInnes, and David Vincent, Crime and Punishment in England: An Introductory History (London: Routledge, 2005), 61–73.
8. Stephen Brumwell, Redcoats: The British Soldier and the War in the Americas, 1755–1763 (Cambridge: Cambridge University Press, 2002),100–112; Matthew C. Ward, Breaking the Backcountry: The Seven Years' War in Virginia and Pennsylvania, 1754–1765 (Pittsburgh: University of Pittsburgh Press, 2003), 112–113.
9. Alexander V. Campbell, The Royal American Regiment: An Atlantic Microcosm, 1755–1772. (Norman: University of Oklahoma Press, 2014) 138; Gwenda Morgan and Peter Rushton, Rogues, Thieves, and the Rule of Law: The Problem of Law Enforcement in North-East England, 1718–1800 (London: UCL Press, 1998), 132–138; Sylvia R. Frey, The British Soldier in America: A Social History of Military Life in the Revolutionary Period (Austin: University of Texas Press, 1981), 90–92; Brumwell, Redcoats, 101.
10. James Titus, The Old Dominion at War: Society, Politics, and Warfare in Late Colonial Virginia, American Military History (Columbia: University of South Car-

olina Press, 1991), 104; Adam Stephen to George Washington, 25 July 1756, *Founders Online*, National Archives, last modified June 13, 2018, http://founders.archives.gov/documents/Washington/02-03-02-0267, original source: *The Papers of George Washington*, Colonial Series, vol. 3, *16 April 1756–9 November 1756*, ed. W.W. Abbot (Charlottesville: University Press of Virginia, 1984), 294–296. Adam Stephen was a Scotsman, a graduate of the University of Aberdeen and of the noted three-year course in medicine at the University of Edinburgh. He was neither a backcountry yokel nor a chinless aristocrat.

11. Peter Burroughs, "Crime and Punishment in the British Army, 1815–1870," *English Historical Review* 100, no. 396 (1985): 545–571; Brumwell, *Redcoats*, 100–106.

12. Graham, *Life of Morgan*, 30; Samuel Graham, *Memoir of General Graham, with Notices of the Campaigns in Which He Was Engaged from 1779 to 1801*, ed. J.J. Graham (Edinburgh: privately printed, 1862), 70. See also Preston's comments in *Braddock's Defeat*, 99–100.

13. Graham, *Life of Morgan*, 29.

14. Preston, *Braddock's Defeat*, 65, 41, 121.

15. Titus, *Old Dominion*, 1–3.

16. Ibid., 77.

17. Ibid., 76.

18. Ibid., 75; Warren Hofstra, "'A Parcel of Barbarians and an Uncouth Set of People,'" in Hofstra, *George Washington and the Virginia Backcountry*, 95.

19. Hofstra, "Parcel of Barbarians," 103–109.

20. Ward, *Breaking the Backcountry*, 60–62.

21. Titus, *Old Dominion*, 94.

22. Glenn F. Williams, *Dunmore's War: The Last Conflict of America's Colonial Era* (Yardley, PA: Westholme, 2017), 129–130; Titus, *Old Dominion*, 79. Nearly every colony in America employed rangers of some sort at some point in its history. The traditional account is John K. Mahon, "Anglo-American Methods of Indian Warfare, 1676–1794," *Mississippi Valley Historical Review* 45, no. 2 (1958): 254–275; Brumwell, *Redcoats*, 211–215, discusses the creation of units of rangers during the Seven Years' War. Incidental information can also be found in Brian D. Carroll, "'Savages' in the Service of Empire: Native American Soldiers in Gorham's Rangers, 1744–1762," *New England Quarterly* 85, no. 3 (2012): 383–429.

23. George Washington to William Cocks and John Ashby, 10 October 1755, *Founders Online*, National Archives, last modified June 13, 2018, http://founders.archives.gov/documents/Washington/02-02-02-0087, original source: *The Papers of George Washington*, Colonial Series, vol. 2, *14 August 1755–15 April 1756*, ed. W.W. Abbot (Charlottesville: University Press of Virginia, 1983), 90–92n4.

24. George Washington to John Ashby, 14 October 1755, *Founders Online*, National Archives, last modified June 13, 2018, http://founders.archives.gov/documents/Washington/02-02-02-0105, original source: *Papers of George Washington*, Colonial Series, vol. 2, 111–112.

25. Nor was Fort Ashby the only post on the frontier to be rendered helpless by rum; cf. Ward, *Breaking the Backcountry*, 110.

26. Ibid., 68.

27. George Washington to William Stark, 20 April 1756, *Founders Online*, National Archives, last modified June 13, 2018, http://founders.archives.gov/documents/Washington/02-03-02-0020, original source: *Papers of George Washington*, Colonial Series, vol. 3, 23–24. Fort Edwards, or "Joseph Edwards' Fort," as Washington referred to it in some letters, was in today's Capon Bridge, West Virginia, twenty miles west of Winchester.

28. George Washington to Robert Dinwiddie, 19 April 1756, *Founders Online*, National Archives, last modified June 13, 2018, http://founders.archives.gov/documents/Washington/02-03-02-0015, original source: *Papers of George Washington*, Colonial Series, vol. 3, 20–21.

29. Graham, *Life of Morgan*, 33; John Fenton Mercer to George Washington, 17 April 1756, *Founders Online*, National Archives, last modified June 13, 2018, http://founders.archives.gov/documents/Washington/02-03-02-0007, original source: *Papers of George Washington*, Colonial Series, vol. 3, 11.

30. Graham, *Life of Morgan*, 33–34.

31. Mercer to Washington, 17 April 1756, *Founders Online*.

32. Daniel Morgan to Miles Fisher, Philadelphia, 11 January 1798, letter, Historical Society of Pennsylvania, Philadelphia.

CHAPTER 3: BUSTING LOOSE

1. Hofstra, *Planting*, 384n30.

2. Higginbotham cites the Charles Carter Lee Papers as evidence of this, but I have found no such reference in these papers; cf. Higginbotham, *Daniel Morgan*, 8n12.

3. Graham, *Life of Morgan*, 41.

4. Hofstra, *Planting*, 245; Mitchell, "'Over the Hills,'" 77–78.

5. Hofstra, *Planting*, 247–248,

6. Ibid., 255.

7. Ibid., 252.

8. Mitchell, "'Over the Hills,'" 78.

9. Mitchell, "'Over the Hills,'" 77.

10. Malone, "Falmouth and the Shenandoah," 693–703.

11. Shenandoah Store Ledgers A and B, 1761–1763, Library of Virginia, Richmond.

12. Frederick County Virginia Order Book, vol. 9, Orders of the Frederick County Court, 1760–1761, Frederick County Clerk of the Circuit Court, Winchester, VA.

13. Frederick County Virginia Order Book, vol. 11, Orders of the Frederick County Court, 1763, Frederick County Clerk of the Circuit Court, 89.

14. Frederick County Virginia Order Book, vol. 10, Orders of the Frederick County Court, 1762, Frederick County Clerk of the Circuit Court, 404.

15. As Higginbotham originally speculated. *Daniel Morgan*, 10.

16. Berry, "Notes"; Graham, *Life of Morgan*, 38.

17. Graham, *Life of Morgan*, 37–38.

18. Jane Carson, *Colonial Virginians at Play* (Williamsburg, VA: Colonial Williamsburg Foundation, 1989), 164–165; Rhys Isaac, *The Transformation of Virginia, 1740–1790* (Chapel Hill: published for the Institute of Early American History and Culture by the University of North Carolina Press, 1982), 96; Thomas Anburey, *Travels through the Interior Parts of America in a Series of Letters,* vol. 2 (London: Printed for William Lane, 1791), 217–218.

19. Berry, "Notes."

20. Higginbotham, *Daniel Morgan*, 9.

21. Carson, *Colonial Virginians*, 167.

22. Isaac, *Transformation*, 119.

23. Freeman, *Washington*, 3:293.

24. See Erin Skye Mackie, *Rakes, Highwaymen, and Pirates: The Making of the Modern Gentleman in the Eighteenth Century* (Baltimore: Johns Hopkins University Press, 2009), a study of the popular literature focused on the incorrigible and irresistible heroes of the eighteenth century.

25. Shenandoah Store Ledgers A and B, 1761–1763, Library of Virginia, Richmond.

26. For more on courtship and marriage in colonial America, see Ellen K. Rothman, *Hands and Hearts: A History of Courtship in America* (Cambridge, MA: Harvard University Press, 1987).

27. Higginbotham, *Daniel Morgan*, 13.

28. Ibid., 14.

29. T.H. Breen, *Tobacco Culture: The Mentality of the Great Tidewater Planters on the Eve of Revolution* (Princeton, NJ: Princeton University Press, 1985), 105–106.

CHAPTER 4: MAKING IT

1. The "governor" was almost always a lieutenant governor. For example, from 1751–1758, the 2nd Earl of Albemarle was the actual governor of Virginia. Rather than go to Virginia himself, he was content to secure the majority of the income the position provided and have Robert Dinwiddie function in his place. Not until 1768 was Virginia's actual governor in residence in Virginia itself.

2. Brent Tarter, *The Grandees of Government: The Origins and Persistence of Undemocratic Politics in Virginia* (Charlottesville: University of Virginia Press, 2013), 87–89.

3. Ibid., 90.

4. Daniel Morgan to Henry Lee [November 6, 1794?], in Henry Lee, *The Campaign of 1781 in the Carolinas: With Remarks, Historical and Critical, on Johnson's Life of Greene. To Which Is Added an Appendix of Original Documents, Relating to the History of the Revolution* (Philadelphia: E. Littell, 1824), appendix, xxvi-xxvii.

5. Higginbotham, *Daniel Morgan*, 12n20.

6. Graham, *Life of Morgan*, 38; Higginbotham, *Daniel Morgan*, 13.

7. Freeman Hansford Hart, *The Valley of Virginia in the American Revolution, 1763-1789* (Chapel Hill: University of North Carolina Press, 1942), 4–5.

8. Higginbotham, *Daniel Morgan*, 12; Hart, *Valley of Virginia*, 8–9; Frederick County Virginia Order Book, vol. 14, Frederick County Clerk of the Circuit Court.

9. Shenandoah Store Ledgers A and B, 1761–1763, Library of Virginia, Richmond; Frederick County Virginia Order Book, vol. 16, 1767, Frederick County Clerk of the Circuit Court, 218.

10. Marriage Bond, Daniel Morgan Collection, William L. Clements Library, University of Michigan, Ann Arbor.

11. Roger W. Moss, "Isaac Zane, Jr., a 'Quaker for the Times,'" *Virginia Magazine of History and Biography* 77, no. 3 (1969): 291–306; Frederick County Virginia Order Book, vol. 16, 218.

12. Promise of Payment, 4 August, 1764, Daniel Morgan Collection, Clements Library, University of Michigan, Ann Arbor.

13. "Letter to Francis Triplett [1769?]," Daniel Morgan Papers, Library of Virginia, Richmond. Higginbotham suggested that this letter might have been misdated by a later archivist or collector, given that it concerns payment for Soldier's Rest, whose deed was not recorded until 1772 in the county records. *Daniel Morgan*, 13.

14. Joseph F. Kett, *The Pursuit of Knowledge under Difficulties: From Self-Improvement to Adult Education in America, 1750–1990* (Stanford, CA: Stanford University Press, 1994), 6; "Edmund Burke, Speech on Conciliation with the Colonies," Fundamental Documents, The Founders' Constitution, University of Chicago Press, accessed March 20, 2018, http://press-pubs.uchicago.edu/founders/documents/v1ch1s2.html. See also Philip A. Cusick, *A Passion for Learning: The Education of Seven Eminent Americans* (New York: Teachers College Press, 2005), 155–160. Cusick emphasizes the purpose of education (whether directed by oneself or by another teacher), and particularly the communal setting in which it occurred and toward which it was directed.

15. Kett, *Pursuit of Knowledge*, 15.

16. John Neville to General Morgan, letter, Haverstraw, NY, November 9, 1779, Theodorus Bailey Myers Collection, ser. 5, Papers of General Daniel Morgan, New York Public Library, http://digitalcollections.nypl.org/items/06a54590-42cf-0133-a1de-00505686d14e; Memorandum on General Officers, 9 March 1792, *Founders Online*, National Archives, last modified June 13, 2018, http://founders.archives.gov/documents/Washington/05-10-02-0040, original source: *The Papers of George Washington*, Presidential Series, vol. 10, *1 March 1792–15 August 1792*, ed. Robert F. Haggard and Mark A. Mastromarino (Charlottesville: University of Virginia Press, 2002), 74–79.

17. Kett, *Pursuit of Knowledge*, 16.

18. Williams, *Dunmore's War*, 105.

19. William Waller Hening, ed., *The Statutes at Large; Being a Collection of All the Laws of Virginia, from the First Session of the Legislature in the Year 1619* (Charlottesville, VA: published for the Jamestown Foundation of the Commonwealth of Virginia by the University Press of Virginia, 1969), 4:475–476; Frederick County Virginia Order Book, vol. 13, Orders of the Frederick County Court, 1774, Frederick County Clerk of the Circuit Court, 19.

20. Hening, *Statutes*, 6:64–69, 370.

21. Ibid., 6:64–69.

22. Frederick County Virginia Order Book, vol. 15, 1774, Orders of the Frederick County Court, Frederick County Clerk of the Circuit Court, 211.

23. See Williams, *Dunmore's War*, 65–74, for a detailed description and dissection of these events; and Patrick Griffin in *American Leviathan: Empire, Nation, and Revolutionary Frontier*, 1st ed. (New York: Hill and Wang, 2007), 98–108.

24. James Corbett David, *Dunmore's New World: The Extraordinary Life of a Royal Governor in Revolutionary America—with Jacobites, Counterfeiters, Land*

Schemes, Shipwrecks, Scalping, Indian Politics, Runaway Slaves, and Two Illegal Royal Weddings, Early American Histories (Charlottesville: University of Virginia Press, 2013), 57, 59. A very different interpretation of Dunmore and his policy is provided in Griffin, *American Leviathan*, 98–108.

25. Max M. Mintz, *The Generals of Saratoga: John Burgoyne & Horatio Gates* (New Haven, CT: Yale University Press, 1990), 75–77; Williams, *Dunmore's War*, 225. Gates was radical enough that he would write in 1775, "I am ready to risque my Life to preserve the Liberty of the Western World," which, as one of his biographers observes, "was a remark that few colonials would have dared assert." Paul David Nelson, *General Horatio Gates: A Biography* (Baton Rouge: Louisiana State University Press, 1976), 37.

26. Williams, *Dunmore's War*, 106.

27. Colonel Charles Mynn Thruston to George Washington, 14 March 1777, *Founders Online*, National Archives, accessed December 19, 2017, http://founders.archives.gov/documents/Washington/03-08-02-0612, n2; Williams, *Dunmore's War*, 68.

28. Col. Angus McDonald to Captain Daniel Morgan, letter, June 11, 1774, Myers Collection, http://digitalcollections.nypl.org/items/696e01a0-4074-0133-c329-00505686a51c.

29. Ibid.; Williams, *Dunmore's War*, 108.

30. William Crawford to George Washington, 8 June 1774, *Founders Online*, National Archives, last modified June 13, 2018, http://founders.archives.gov/documents/Washington/02-10-02-0066, original source: *The Papers of George Washington*, Colonial Series, vol. 10, *21 March 1774–15 June 1775*, ed. W.W. Abbot and Dorothy Twohig (Charlottesville: University Press of Virginia, 1995), 93–94.

31. Much of the discussion in the next few pages is based on Williams, *Dunmore's War*, 152, 184–193, and 308.

32. Harry M. Ward argues that the resolves were most likely the product of university-trained Adam Stephen; while that is possible or perhaps even probable, it cannot be certain. See Harry M. Ward, *Major General Adam Stephen and the Cause of American Liberty* (Charlottesville: University Press of Virginia, 1989), 111–112; Williams, *Dunmore's War*, 303.

33. "Resolutions Adopted at a Meeting of the Officers under the Command of Lord Dunmore, Convened at Fort Gower," American Archives: Documents of the American Revolutionary Period, 1774–1776, Digital Collections and Collaborative Projects, University Libraries, Northern Illinois University, accessed August 8, 2017, http://amarch.lib.niu.edu/islandora/object/niu-amarch%3A99267.

34. Daniel Morgan, "Letter to Miles Fisher from Daniel Morgan," Philadelphia, January 11, 1798, Historical Society of Pennsylvania, Philadelphia. See also Jim Glanville, "The Fort Gower Resolves and Daniel Morgan's Role," *Winchester-Frederick County Historical Society Journal* 23 (2012): 1–22.

35. David Lowenthal, *The Past Is a Foreign Country* (Cambridge: Cambridge University Press, 1985), 210.

36. "Address of the Freeholders of Fincastle County, Virginia, to Lord Dunmore," American Archives, accessed August 9, 2017, http://amarch.lib.niu.edu/islandora/object/niu-amarch%3A102502.

37. John E. Selby, *The Revolution in Virginia, 1775–1783* (Williamsburg, VA: Colonial Williamsburg Foundation, distributed by University Press of Virginia, 1988), 18.

38. Ibid., 1–2.

CHAPTER 5: REBELLION

1. Henry Lee, *The Revolutionary War Memoirs of General Henry Lee,* 1st Da Capo Press ed. (New York: Da Capo, 1998), 174; John Joseph Henry, "Campaign against Quebec," in Kenneth Lewis Roberts, ed., *March to Quebec: Journals of the Members of Arnold's Expedition* (New York: Doubleday, Doran, 1940), 327; David Meschutt, "Portraits of Daniel Morgan, Revolutionary War General," *American Art Journal* 17, no. 3 (1985): 35–43.

2. Receipt from Captain Daniel Morgan to David Prenpain, January 1772–January 1773, Daniel Morgan Collection, Clements Library, University of Michigan, Ann Arbor.

3. With "backcountry" understood as all that area "back of" Tidewater, or, the land on the other side of the fall line, which was that geographical boundary where eastern rivers descended over falls or rapids into the coastal plain.

4. The divisions and struggles that did occur are examined in Michael A. McDonnell, *The Politics of War: Race, Class, and Conflict in Revolutionary Virginia* (Chapel Hill: published for the Omohundro Institute of Early American History and Culture by the University of North Carolina Press, 2007).

5. Tarter, *Grandees*, 93–94; Alonzo Thomas Dill, "Sectional Conflict in Colonial Virginia," *Virginia Magazine of History and Biography* 87, no. 3 (1979): 300–315.

6. "Meeting of the Freeholders and other Inhabitants of the County of Frederick, in Virginia, and Gentlemen practising at the Bar, held in Winchester," 8 June 1774, American Archives, accessed August 24, 2018, http://amarch.lib.niu.edu/islandora/object/niu-amarch%3A80483.

7. Charles Royster, *A Revolutionary People at War: The Continental Army and American Character, 1775–1783* (Chapel Hill: published for the Institute of Early American History and Culture, Williamsburg, Virginia, by the University of North Carolina Press, 1979), 31.

8. Richard Henry Lee, to Arthur Lee [Feb. 24, 1775], in *The Letters of Richard Henry Lee,* ed. James Curtis Ballagh (New York: Macmillan, 1911), 130.

9. Jeff Cooper, *The Art of the Rifle* (Boulder, CO: Paladin Press, 1997), 1.

10. Brumwell, *Redcoats*, 249–250.

11. Patrick Hornberger and Joe Kindig III, *Masterpieces of the American Longrifle: The Joe Kindig, Jr. Collection,* 1st ed. (Trappe, MD: Eastwind, 2015), 23–24; Joseph K. Kindig III, *Artistic Ingredients of the Longrifle* (York, PA: George Shumway, 1989), 101. See also Henry J. Kauffman, *The Pennsylvania-Kentucky Rifle* (Harrisburg, PA: Stackpole, 1960).

12. Joe Kindig, *Thoughts on the Kentucky Rifle in Its Golden Age,* ed. Mary Ann Cresswell (Wilmington, DE: George N. Hyatt, 1960), 3.

13. This individualism, and the idea of marksmanship, would have reverberations throughout the history of the military culture of the United States and, arguably, in popular culture. For a glimpse of a later stage of this, following the American

Civil War, see Russell Gilmore, "'The New Courage': Rifles and Soldier Individualism, 1876–1918," *Military Affairs* 40, no. 3 (1976): 97–102.

14. James Madison to William Bradford, 19 June 1775, *Founders Online*, National Archives, last modified June 13, 2018, http://founders.archives.gov/documents/Madison/01-01-02-0047, original source: *The Papers of James Madison*, vol. 1, *16 March 1751–16 December 1779*, ed. William T. Hutchinson and William M. E. Rachal (Chicago: University of Chicago Press, 1962), 151–154.

15. "Frederick County (Virginia) Committee, June 19, 1775." American Archives, accessed November 2, 2017, http://amarch.lib.niu.edu/islandora/object/niu-amarch%3A85392.

16. John Adams to Abigail Adams, 11 June 1775, *Founders Online*, National Archives, last modified June 13, 2018, http://founders.archives.gov/documents/Adams/04-01-02-0146, original source: *The Adams Papers*, Adams Family Correspondence, vol. 1, *December 1761–May 1776*, ed. Lyman H. Butterfield (Cambridge, MA: Harvard University Press, 1963), 215–217. New England's lack of the rifle is partly explained in Edward Pierce Hamilton, "Colonial Warfare in North America," *Proceedings of the Massachusetts Historical Society* 80 (1968): 3–15.

17. John Robert Sellers, "The Virginia Continental Line, 1775–1780," PhD diss., Tulane University, 1968, 5.

18. Ibid., 6; "Committee of Observation for Frederick County, Maryland." American Archives, accessed November 2, 2017, http://amarch.lib.niu.edu/islandora/object/niu-amarch%3A79234.

19. Sellers, "Virginia Continental Line," 7.

20. Henry, "Campaign against Quebec," 396.

21. Samuel Kercheval, *A History of the Valley of Virginia,* 3rd ed., rev. and extended (Woodstock, VA: W.N. Grabill, 1902), 225–227.

22. For examples of powder horns and their appurtenances, see James R. Johnston, *Accouterments* (Ashley, OH: Golden Age Arms, 1990). The subject of hunting shirts is ably discussed by Neal Hurst in "A 'Kind of Armour, Being Peculiar to America': The American Hunting Shirt," (undergraduate honors thesis, College of William and Mary, June 12, 2013), https://publish.wm.edu/honorstheses/572. Further information can be found in Byron C. Smith, "White Savages in Hunting Shirts: The Rifleman's Costume of National Identity and Rebellion in the American Revolution" (master's thesis, University of Richmond, 2000). Simon Harrison suggests that the use of the hunting shirt, the appropriation of certain native items like the tomahawk, and "cross-dressing," such as the wearing of leggings and loincloth, might have freed the wearer "from some of the formalities and constraints of conventional European war." Simon Harrison, *Dark Trophies: Hunting and the Enemy Body in Modern War* (New York: Berghahn Books, 2012), 42.

23. "Letter from a Gentleman in Fredericktown, Maryland, to His Friend in Baltimore. Reception There of Captain Morgan's Company of Riflemen, from Virginia, on Their Way to Boston." American Archives, accessed October 24, 2016, about:reader?url=http%3A%2F%2Famarch.lib.niu.edu%2Fislandora%2Fobject%2Fniu-amarch%253A78690.

24. Myers Collection, http://digitalcollections.nypl.org/items/932a9940-55af-0133-88d7-00505686a51c.

25. John Esten Cooke and William Garrott Brown, *Virginia: A History of the People* (New York: Houghton, Mifflin, 1883), 450.

CHAPTER 6: THE MARCH UPCOUNTRY

1. Henry, "Campaign against Quebec," 326–327.

2. Ibid., 302.

3. Ron Chernow, *Washington: A Life* (New York: Penguin, 2010), 200.

4. James Warren to John Adams, 11 September 1775, *Founders Online*, National Archives, last modified June 13, 2018, http://founders.archives.gov/documents/ Adams/06-03-02-0075, original source: *The Adams Papers*, Papers of John Adams, vol. 3, *May 1775–January 1776*, ed. Robert J. Taylor (Cambridge, MA: Harvard University Press, 1979), 131–134.

5. Brigadier General Nathanael Greene to George Washington, 10 September 1775, *Founders Online*, National Archives, last modified June 13, 2018, http://founders.archives.gov/documents/Washington/03-01-02-0341, original source: *Papers of George Washington*, Revolutionary War Series, 1:445–446n1.

6. George Washington to Samuel Washington, 30 September 1775, *Founders Online*, National Archives, last modified June 13, 2018, http://founders.archives. gov/documents/Washington/03-02-02-0067, original source: *Papers of George Washington*, Revolutionary War Series, 2:72–74.

7. Artemas Ward to John Adams, 23 October 1775, *Founders Online*, National Archives, last modified June 13, 2018, http://founders.archives.gov/documents/ Adams/06-03-02-0120, original source: *Adams Papers*, Papers of John Adams, 3:234–236.

8. Mark R. Anderson, *The Battle for the Fourteenth Colony: America's War of Liberation in Canada, 1774–1776* (Hanover, NH: University Press of New England, 2013), 353.

9. The best biography of Arnold is James Kirby Martin's *Benedict Arnold, Revolutionary Hero: An American Warrior Reconsidered* (New York: New York University Press, 1997).

10. Ibid., 64–79, 106–107.

11. George Washington to Major General Philip Schuyler, 20 August 1775, *Founders Online*, National Archives, last modified June 13, 2018, http://founders.archives.gov/documents/Washington/03-01-02-0233, original source: *Papers of George Washington*, Revolutionary War Series, 1:331–334.

12. Martin, *Benedict Arnold*, 113.

13. George Washington to Colonel Benedict Arnold, 14 September 1775, *Founders Online*, National Archives, last modified June 13, 2018, http://founders.archives. gov/documents/Washington/03-01-02-0355, original source: *Papers of George Washington*, Revolutionary War Series, 1:455–456.

14. Martin, *Benedict Arnold*, 124.

15. "General Orders, 5 September 1775," *Founders Online*, National Archives, last modified June 13, 2018, http://founders.archives.gov/documents/Washington/ 03-01-02-0308, original source: *Papers of George Washington*, Revolutionary War Series, 1:414–416.

16. Martin, *Benedict Arnold*, 119; Jon Butler, *Awash in a Sea of Faith: Christianizing the American People*. Studies in Cultural History (Cambridge, MA: Harvard University Press, 1990), 188.

17. Colonel Benedict Arnold to George Washington, 25–27 September 1775, *Founders Online,* National Archives, last modified June 13, 2018, http://founders.archives.gov/documents/Washington/03-02-02-0038, original source: *Papers of George Washington,* Revolutionary War Series, 2:40–44; Martin, *Benedict Arnold,* 123.

18. Martin, *Benedict Arnold,* 121–122.

19. George Washington to Captain Daniel Morgan, 4 October 1775, *Founders Online,* National Archives, last modified June 13, 2018, http://founders.archives.gov/documents/Washington/03-02-02-0091, original source: *Papers of George Washington,* Revolutionary War Series, 2:93.

20. Martin, *Benedict Arnold,* 107, 121–124.

21. Ibid., 124–125.

22. Henry Dearborn, "Journal of Quebec Expedition," in Roberts, *March to Quebec,* 136.

23. Ibid.,134; Higginbotham, *Daniel Morgan,* 30.

24. Henry, "Campaign against Quebec," 329.

25. Higginbotham, *Daniel Morgan,* 32. Smith was one of the "Paxton Boys" who in 1763 had massacred Susquehannock Indians in supposed retaliation for Pontiac's uprising. Thomas A. Desjardin, *Through a Howling Wilderness: Benedict Arnold's March to Quebec, 1775,* 1st ed. (New York: St. Martin's Press, 2006), 29. His idea of command seems to have been that he was first among equals in a gang of vigilantes.

26. Henry, "Campaign against Quebec," 331.

27. Martin, *Benedict Arnold,* 127.

28. Modern re-creations of eighteenth-century bateaux weigh 417 pounds; https://maineboats.com/print/issue-150/quebec-bateau.

29. Henry, "Campaign against Quebec," 336.

30. Henry, "Campaign against Quebec," 338; Martin, *Benedict Arnold,* 137.

31. Abner Stocking, "Journal," in Roberts, *March to Quebec,* 555.

32. Henry, "Campaign against Quebec," 338.

33. Higginbotham, *Daniel Morgan,* 35.

34. Stocking, "Journal," 556.

35. Martin, *Benedict Arnold,* 139.

36. Isaac Senter, "Journal," in Roberts, *March to Quebec,* 222.

37. Stocking, "Journal," 558.

38. John Phillips Resch, *Suffering Soldiers: Revolutionary War Veterans, Moral Sentiment, and Political Culture in the Early Republic* (Amherst: University of Massachusetts Press, 1999), 65–66.

39. Richard Godbeer, *The Overflowing of Friendship: Love between Men and the Creation of the American Republic* (Baltimore: Johns Hopkins University Press, 2009), 119–154.

CHAPTER 7: QUEBEC

1. Anderson, *Crucible of War,* 344–349.

2. Graham, *Morgan,* 79.

3. Martin, *Benedict Arnold,* 143–145.

4. Ibid., 145.

5. Ibid., 146.

6. Henry, "Campaign against Quebec," 353; George Francis Gillman Stanley, *Canada Invaded, 1775–1776,* Canadian War Museum, Historical Publications, no. 8 (Toronto: Hakkert, 1973), 78.

7. Henry, "Campaign against Quebec," 453; Martin, *Benedict Arnold,* 147.

8. Anderson, *Battle for the Fourteenth Colony,* 144, 151.

9. Henry, "Campaign against Quebec," 360–361.

10. Martin, *Benedict Arnold,* 161; Anderson, *Battle for the Fourteenth Colony,* 166.

11. Henry, "Campaign against Quebec," 363; John Pierce, "Journal," in Roberts, *March to Quebec,* 688.

12. Simeon Thayer, "Journal," in Roberts, *March to Quebec,* 270; George Morison, "Journal," in Roberts, *March to Quebec,* 534.

13. Benedict Arnold, "Journal," in Roberts, *March to Quebec,* 102; Stanley, *Canada Invaded,* 93–94.

14. Graham, *Life of Morgan,* 447.

15. Stocking, "Journal," 564; Morison, "Journal," 536; Martin, *Benedict Arnold,* 168.

16. Martin, *Benedict Arnold,* 176.

17. Daniel Morgan, "[Morgan's Autobiography for 1774–1776]," Myers Collection, http://digitalcollections.nypl.org/items/932a9940-55af-0133-88d7-00505686a51c.

18. Martin, *Benedict Arnold,* 176; Higginbotham, *Daniel Morgan,* 45.

19. Morgan, "[Morgan's Autobiography?]"; Higginbotham, *Daniel Morgan,* 45.

20. Higginbotham, 46; Martin, *Benedict Arnold,* 176.

21. Morgan, "[Morgan's Autobiography]"; Martin, *Benedict Arnold,* 177.

22. Stocking, "Journal," 565; Martin, *Benedict Arnold,* 177.

23. Morison, "Journal," 537.

24. Henry, "Campaign against Quebec," 237; Morison, "Journal," 536–537.

25. Henry, "Campaign against Quebec," 379.

26. Ibid., 378.

27. Morison, "Journal," 538.

28. Graham, *Life of Morgan,* 103.

29. Ibid., 104. Graham's numbers seem derived in part from Henry's memoirs; they are supported by the three lists of members of Morgan's company of 1775, and by the rates of attrition, particularly due to disease, in other companies in Arnold's army.

CHAPTER 8: MORGAN'S RIFLEMEN

1. Arnold, "Journal," 102–103; Martin, *Benedict Arnold,* 172–173.

2. Henry, "Campaign against Quebec," 389.

3. Graham, *Life of Morgan,* 112.

4. Thomas J. Fleming, *Now We Are Enemies: The Story of Bunker Hill* (New York: St. Martin's Press, 1960), 209.

5. Martin, *Benedict Arnold,* 191, 189.

6. Ibid., 192–193; Arnold, "Journal," 111–112.

7. Henry, "Campaign against Quebec," 397–409; Graham, *Life of Morgan,* 110–111; Martin, *Benedict Arnold,* 192–196.

8. Martin, *Benedict Arnold*, 208–209.

9. Joseph A. Waddell, "Diary of a Prisoner of War at Quebec, 1776," *Virginia Magazine of History and Biography 9*, no. 2 (1901): 144–152.

10. Ibid.; Higginbotham, *Daniel Morgan*, 52–53.

11. Letter from Christopher Greene and 33 Others to Guy Carleton, Seminary, Quebec city, June 7, 1776, Myers Collection, http://digitalcollections.nypl.org /items/f7946d80-3f9f-0133-e8b8-00505686a51c.

12. Henry, "Campaign against Quebec," 427.

13. George Washington to John Hancock, 28 September 1776, *Founders Online*, National Archives, last modified June 13, 2018, http://founders.archives. gov/documents/Washington/03-06-02-0324, original source: *The Papers of George Washington*, Revolutionary War Series, vol. 6, *13 August 1776–20 October 1776*, ed. Philander D. Chase and Frank E. Grizzard Jr. (Charlottesville: University Press of Virginia, 1994), 421–422.

14. Betsy Knight, "Prisoner Exchange and Parole in the American Revolution," *William and Mary Quarterly* 48, no. 2 (1991): 201–222, https://doi.org/10.2307/ 2938068.

15. Jeremy Black, *Plotting Power: Strategy in the Eighteenth Century* (Bloomington: Indiana University Press, 2017), 208–209.

16. Hew Strachan, *European Armies and the Conduct of War* (London: Allen & Unwin, 1983), 27.

17. John S. Pancake, *1777: The Year of the Hangman* (Tuscaloosa: University of Alabama Press, 1977), 53, 112.

18. Patrick Henry to Morgan, March 15, 1777, Williamsburg, VA, Myers Collection, http://digitalcollections.nypl.org/items/48ca94e0-3fa8-0133-c12e-005056 86d14e.

19. Colonel Charles Mynn Thruston to George Washington, 14 March 1777, *Founders Online*, National Archives, last modified June 13, 2018, http://founders.archives.gov/documents/Washington/03-08-02-0612, original source: *The Papers of George Washington*, Revolutionary War Series, vol. 8, *6 January 1777–27 March 1777*, ed. Frank E. Grizzard Jr. (Charlottesville: University Press of Virginia, 1998), 574–575.

20. Brigadier General Peter Muhlenberg to George Washington, 23 February 1777, *Founders Online*, National Archives, last modified June 13, 2018, http://founders.archives.gov/documents/Washington/03-08-02-0457, original source: *Papers of George Washington*, Revolutionary War Series, 8:428–429.

21. Colonel Charles Mynn Thruston to George Washington, 2 June 1777, *Founders Online*, National Archives, last modified June 13, 2018, http://founders.archives.gov/documents/Washington/03-09-02-0594, original source: *The Papers of George Washington*, Revolutionary War Series, vol. 9, *28 March 1777–10 June 1777*, ed. Philander D. Chase (Charlottesville: University Press of Virginia, 1999), 596.

22. Elizabeth A. Fenn, *Pox Americana: The Great Smallpox Epidemic of 1775–82*, 1st ed. (New York: Hill and Wang, 2010), 88–98; Lieutenant Colonel Christian Febiger to George Washington, 6 March 1777, *Founders Online*, National Archives, last modified June 13, 2018, http://founders.archives.gov/documents/ Washington/03-08-02-0547, original source: *Papers of George Washington*, Revolutionary War Series, 8:520–522.

23. Muhlenberg to Washington, 23 February 1777, *Founders Online.*

24. "General Orders, 1 June 1777," *Founders Online,* National Archives, last modified June 13, 2018, http://founders.archives.gov/documents/Washington/03-09-02-0571, original source: *Papers of George Washington,* Revolutionary War Series, 9:577–578.

25. "General Orders, 13 June 1777," *Founders Online,* National Archives, last modified June 13, 2018, http://founders.archives.gov/documents/Washington/03-10-02-0020, original source: *The Papers of George Washington,* Revolutionary War Series, vol. 10, *11 June 1777–18 August 1777,* ed. Frank E. Grizzard Jr. (Charlottesville: University Press of Virginia, 2000), 19–20.

26. There may also have been North Carolinians in the Provisional Rifle Corps, but this remains to be determined; if so, they were lumped into companies of Virginians.

27. Nathanael Greene to Benjamin Lincoln, 9 June 1777, *The Papers of General Nathanael Greene,* ed. Richard K. Showman, Dennis Michael Conrad, and Roger N. Parks (Chapel Hill: published for the Rhode Island Historical Society by the University of North Carolina Press, 1976), 2:105.

28. Thomas J. McGuire, *The Philadelphia Campaign: Brandywine and the Fall of Philadelphia,* 1st ed., vol. 1 (Mechanicsburg, PA: Stackpole, 2006), 41.

29. Richard Kidder Meade [to Morgan], letter, headquarters [location unspecified], June 15, 1777, Myers Collection, http://digitalcollections.nypl.org/items/ 9e3fbc70-405c-0133-2841-00505686a51c.

30. John Adams to Abigail Adams, 18 June 1777, *Founders Online,* National Archives, last modified June 13, 2018, http://founders.archives.gov/documents/ Adams/04-02-02-0210, original source: *The Adams Papers,* Adams Family Correspondence, vol. 2, *June 1776–March 1778,* ed. L. H. Butterfield (Cambridge, MA: Harvard University Press, 1963), 267–268.

31. McGuire, *Philadelphia Campaign,* 1:42.

32. George Washington to Colonel Charles Armand, 11 June 1777, *Founders Online,* National Archives, last modified June 13, 2018, http://founders.archives.gov/documents/Hamilton/01-01-02-0186, original source: *The Papers of Alexander Hamilton,* vol. 1, *1768–1778,* ed. Harold C. Syrett (New York: Columbia University Press, 1961), 270.

33. McGuire, *Philadelphia Campaign,* 1:50–52.

34. Joseph Ward to John Adams, 28 June 1777, *Founders Online,* National Archives, last modified June 13, 2018, http://founders.archives.gov/documents/ Adams/06-05-02-0142, original source: *The Adams Papers,* Papers of John Adams, vol. 5, *August 1776–March 1778,* ed. Robert J. Taylor (Cambridge, MA: Harvard University Press, 2006), 234–235.

35. Ibid.; Harry M. Ward, *General William Maxwell and the New Jersey Continentals,* Contributions in Military Studies No. 168 (Westport, CT.: Greenwood Press, 1997), 62.

36. McGuire, *Philadelphia Campaign,* 1:54.

37. Colonel Daniel Morgan to George Washington, 19 July 1777, *Founders Online,* National Archives, last modified June 13, 2018, http://founders.archives.gov/ documents/Washington/03-10-02-0332, original source: *Papers of George Washington,* Revolutionary War Series, 10:339–341; Fitzgerald's response is in note 1.

38. Colonel Daniel Morgan to George Washington, 24 July 1777, *Founders Online*, National Archives, last modified June 13, 2018, http://founders.archives.gov/documents/Washington/03-10-02-0381, original source: *Papers of George Washington*, Revolutionary War Series, 10:390–391.

39. George Washington to Colonel Daniel Morgan, 24 July 1777, *Founders Online*, National Archives, last modified June 13, 2018, http://founders.archives.gov/documents/Washington/03-10-02-0380, original source: *Papers of George Washington*, Revolutionary War Series, 10:390.

40. George Washington to Colonel Daniel Morgan, 16 August 1777, *Founders Online*, National Archives, last modified June 13, 2018, http://founders.archives.gov/documents/Washington/03-10-02-0624, original source: *Papers of George Washington*, Revolutionary War Series, 10:641.

CHAPTER 9: SARATOGA

1. The Continental army's organization can be confusing; it was so at the time because it was an ad hoc structure, changing and shifting according to circumstance. Washington was the commander in chief, and his was the "Main Army" after spring 1776, focused on the British army in New York and New Jersey. The "Northern Army" was the army of the "Northern Department," centered on northern New York, designed at first to attack Canada and later to defend against attacks from Canada on the Mohawk and Hudson valleys. Its commander from July 1775 to July 1777 was Major General Philip Schuyler, a wealthy Albany merchant and landowner.

2. John R. Bratten, *The Gondola Philadelphia and the Battle of Lake Champlain* (College Station: Texas A&M University Press, 2002), 35–44.

3. Douglas Cubbison, *The American Northern Theater Army in 1776: The Ruin and Reconstruction of the Continental Force* (Jefferson, NC: McFarland, 2010), 265–266.

4. John F. Luzader, *Saratoga: A Military History of the Decisive Campaign of the American Revolution*, 1st paperback ed. (New York: Savas Beatie, 2010), 33–35.

5. Luzader, *Saratoga*, 55.

6. Pancake, *1777*, 122.

7. Ibid.; Luzader, *Saratoga*, 80–82.

8. Pancake, *1777*, 154.

9. Dean R. Snow, *1777: Tipping Point at Saratoga* (New York: Oxford University Press, 2016), 62.

10. Ibid., 42. Theodore Roosevelt on James Wilkinson: "In all our history, there is no more despicable character." Theodore Roosevelt, *The Works of Theodore Roosevelt: Volume 11, The Winning of the West* (New York: C. Scribner's Sons, 1923), 143. Frederick Jackson Turner called Wilkinson "the most consummate artist in treason that the nation ever possessed." Frederick J. Turner, "The Origin of Genet's Projected Attack on Louisiana and the Floridas," *American Historical Review* 3, no. 4 (1898): 653.

11. Luzader, *Saratoga*, 216–217.

12. James Wilkinson, *Memoirs of My Own Times* (Philadelphia: printed by Abraham Small, 1816) mentions Morgan's turkey call. For light infantry signaling procedures, see Matthew H. Spring, *With Zeal and with Bayonets Only: The British*

Army on Campaign in North America, 1775–1783, Campaigns and Commanders, vol. 19 (Norman: University of Oklahoma Press, 2008), 247.

13. For Freeman, settlement patterns in the area, and the loyalties of tenants, see Theodore Corbett, *No Turning Point: The Saratoga Campaign in Perspective,* Campaigns and Commanders, vol. 32 (Norman: University of Oklahoma Press, 2012), ch. 1, and Luzader, *Saratoga,* 221–222.

14. For more about Van Swearingen, see George Washington to Captain Van Swearingen, 18 August 1777, *Founders Online,* National Archives, last modified June 13, 2018, http://founders.archives.gov/documents/Washington/03-10-02-0646, original source: *Papers of George Washington,* Revolutionary War Series, 10:661–662. The editors report that Swearingen was captured later in the Saratoga Campaign, but one British source reports that he was taken in Forbes's counterattack on Morris's precipitate attack; cf. Anburey, *Travels,* 364–365.

15. Wilkinson, *Memoirs,* 238; Luzader, *Saratoga,* 236.

16. Friedrich Riedesel, *Memoirs and Letters of Major General Riedesel* (Albany, NY: J. Munsell, 1868), 1:148.

17. Luzader, *Saratoga,* 243–246.

18. Riedesel, *Memoirs,* 148–149; Pancake, *1777,* 160; Snow, *1777,* 130–131.

19. Riedesel, *Memoirs,* 154.

20. Ibid., 155; Snow, *1777,* 165, 172.

21. Riedesel, *Memoirs,* 155–156.

22. Snow, *1777,* 178, 181, 188, 195–196.

23. Eric H. Schnitzer, "Tactics of the Battle of Saratoga," in *The Saratoga Campaign: Uncovering an Embattled Landscape,* ed. William A. Griswold and Donald W. Linebaugh (Hanover, NH: University Press of New England, 2016), 39–81; Corbett, *No Turning Point,* 60.

24. Wilkinson, *Memoirs,* 254; Martin, *Benedict Arnold,* 385–391; Luzader, *Saratoga,* 244–246; Pancake, *1777,* 182.

25. The concept of OODA—Observe-Orient-Decide-Act—is best described in Grant Hammond's *The Mind of War: John Boyd and American Security* (Washington, DC: Smithsonian Institution Press, 2001), particularly 152–153.

26. Henry Dearborn, *Revolutionary War Journals of Henry Dearborn, 1775–1783,* ed. Lloyd A. Brown, Howard Henry Peckham, and Hermon Dunlap Smith (New York: Da Capo Press, 1971),108.

27. Snow, *1777,* 243–244.

28. Wilkinson, *Memoirs,* 268.

29. Luzader, *Saratoga,* 284; Snow, *1777,* 245–246.

30. Snow, *1777,* 251–252.

31. Ibid., 246.

32. Snow, *1777,* 248; Luzader, *Saratoga,* 285.

33. Samuel Graham, *Memoir of General Graham, with Notices of the Campaigns in Which He Was Engaged from 1779 to 1801,* ed. J.J. Graham (Edinburgh: privately printed, 1862), 70; Snow, *1777,* 259–261.

34. Snow, *1777,* 262–263.

35. Wilkinson, *Memoirs,* 270; Snow, *1777,* 263.

36. Snow, *1777,* 265.

37. Schnitzer, "Tactics," 64.

38. Pancake, *1777*, 186–187.
39. Schnitzer, "Tactics," 65.
40. Snow, *1777*, 272.
41. Graham, *Life of Morgan*, 165. Graham bases this on an anecdote related by Morgan to Rev. William Hill.
42. Snow, *1777*, 277, 293–294, 304.
43. Wilkinson, *Memoirs*, 286; Riedesel, *Memoirs*, 171; Pancake, *1777*, 188–189; Luzader, *Saratoga*, 309–310.
44. Mintz, *Generals of Saratoga*, 18; Luzader, *Saratoga*, 335.
45. Graham, *Life of Morgan*, 174.
46. Luzader, *Saratoga*, 338.
47. Boyd did not write his theory down but contained it in a presentation. A PowerPoint version can be found courtesy of the Project on Governmental Oversight at http://www.dnipogo.org/boyd/patterns_ppt.pdf. The applications of Boyd's ideas to infantry combat are described and theorized by Captain Aaron Bazin in "Boyd's O-O-D-A Loop and the Infantry Company Commander," *Infantry* 1, no. 1 (February 2005): 18. For a biography of Boyd, see Robert Coram, *Boyd: The Fighter Pilot Who Changed the Art of War*, 1st ed. (Boston: Little, Brown, 2002).
48. Roger Lamb, *Memoir of His Own Life* (Dublin: J. Jones, 1811), 204–206.

CHAPTER 10: THE WASHINGTONIAN

1. George Washington to Alexander Hamilton, 30 October 1777, *Founders Online*, National Archives, last modified June 13, 2018, http://founders.archives.gov/documents/Hamilton/01-01-02-0331, original source: *Papers of Alexander Hamilton*, 1:347–349.
2. Luzader, *Saratoga*, 338.
3. Ibid.
4. The standard account of the Battle of Brandywine is found in McGuire, *Philadelphia Campaign*, 1:ch. 4.
5. William Heth, "On Our March 25 Miles from Philadelphia," to Morgan, letter, September 20, 1777, Myers Collection, http://digitalcollections.nypl.org/items/3a391140-3fa8-0133-751b-00505686d14e.
6. For an evaluation of Maxwell's performance in New Jersey in spring 1777, see Mark V. Kwasny, *Washington's Partisan War, 1775–1783* (Kent, OH: Kent State University Press, 1996), 115–116, and David Hackett Fischer, *Washington's Crossing* (New York: Oxford University Press, 2004), 348–349.
7. "To George Washington from Major John Clark, Jr., 4 November 1777," *Founders Online*, National Archives, last modified June 13, 2018, http://founders.archives.gov/documents/Washington/03-12-02-0102, original source: *The Papers of George Washington*, Revolutionary War Series, vol. 12, *26 October 1777–25 December 1777*, ed. Frank E. Grizzard Jr. and David R. Hoth (Charlottesville: University Press of Virginia, 2002), 114–116.
8. "To George Washington from Major John Clark, Jr., 16 November 1777," *Founders Online*, National Archives, last modified June 13, 2018, http://founders.archives.gov/documents/Washington/03-12-02-0265, original source: *Papers of George Washington*, Revolutionary War Series, vol. 12, 276; Thomas J. McGuire, *The Philadelphia Campaign: Germantown and the Roads to Valley Forge*, 1st ed., vol. 2. (Mechanicsburg, PA: Stackpole, 2006), 211.

9. Brigadier General George Weedon was formerly a Fredericksburg, Virginia, tavern owner, a bon vivant who endeared himself to his fellow officers; it is highly probable that Morgan knew him before the war, but there is no written proof of that.

10. Harry M. Ward, *Charles Scott and the "Spirit of '76"* (Charlottesville: University Press of Virginia, 1988), 41.

11. Major General Nathanael Greene to George Washington, 21 November 1777, *Founders Online*, National Archives, last modified June 13, 2018, http://founders.archives.gov/documents/Washington/03-12-02-0338, original source: *Papers of George Washington*, Revolutionary War Series, 12:340–341.

12. George Washington to Major General Nathanael Greene, 22 November 1777, *Founders Online*, National Archives, last modified June 13, 2018, http://founders.archives.gov/documents/Washington/03-12-02-0345, original source: *Papers of George Washington*, Revolutionary War Series, 12:349–350n2.

13. Major General Nathanael Greene to George Washington, 22 November 1777, *Founders Online*, National Archives, last modified June 13, 2018, http://founders.archives.gov/documents/Washington/03-12-02-0346, original source: *Papers of George Washington*, Revolutionary War Series, 12:350–351.

14. McGuire, *The Philadelphia Campaign,* 2:223.

15. Ibid., 241–243.

16. Unless otherwise noted, information on Whitemarsh comes from Stephen R. Taaffe, *The Philadelphia Campaign, 1777–1778,* Modern War Studies (Lawrence: University Press of Kansas, 2003), 145–147, and McGuire, *Philadelphia Campaign*, 2:237–255.

17. Major John Clark Jr., to George Washington, 3 December 1777, *Founders Online*, National Archives, last modified June 13, 2018, http://founders.archives.gov/documents/Washington/03-12-02-0481, original source: *Papers of George Washington*, Revolutionary War Series, 12:511–513.

18. McGuire, *Philadelphia Campaign*, 2:251–252.

19. Joseph Plumb Martin, *Ordinary Courage: The Revolutionary War Adventures of Joseph Plumb Martin* (New York: John Wiley & Sons, 2012), 67.

20. Wayne K. Bodle, *The Valley Forge Winter: Civilians and Soldiers in War* (University Park: Pennsylvania State University Press, 2002), 1–5.

21. Major John Clark Jr. to George Washington, 20 December 1777, *Founders Online*, National Archives, last modified June 13, 2018, http://founders.archives.gov/documents/Washington/03-12-02-0586, original source: *Papers of George Washington*, Revolutionary War Series, 12:644–645.

22. Colonel Daniel Morgan to George Washington, 23 December 1777, *Founders Online*, National Archives, last modified June 13, 2018, http://founders.archives.gov/documents/Washington/03-12-02-0632, original source: *Papers of George Washington*, Revolutionary War Series, 12:690–691; Bodle, *Valley Forge*, 104, 109.

23. Ibid.

24. Colonel Daniel Morgan to George Washington, 24 December 1777, *Founders Online*, National Archives, last modified June 13, 2018, http://founders.archives.gov/documents/Washington/03-12-02-0640, original source: *Papers of George Washington*, Revolutionary War Series, 12:694–695.

25. The first debunking of the mythology of the Conway Cabal was executed by Jared Sparks in the 1830s; its modern debunker was Bernhard Knollenberg in his *Washington and the Revolution: A Reappraisal; Gates, Conway, and the Continental Congress* (New York: Macmillan, 1940). It is time for a critical reappraisal of the episode, which was of the utmost importance to those who were involved in what they believed to be a civil-military conflict.
26. Daniel Morgan to George Washington, 20 September 1781, *Founders Online*, National Archives, last modified June 13, 2018, http://founders.archives.gov/documents/Washington/99-01-02-06989.
27. L. Scott Philyaw, "George Washington, Daniel Morgan, and the Ideal of Service," in *Sons of the Father: George Washington and His Protégés*, ed. Robert M.S. McDonald, Jeffersonian America (Charlottesville: University of Virginia Press, 2013), 47.
28. Isaac Zane to Colonel Morgan, Marlboro Iron Works, Frederick County, VA, April 8, 1778, Myers Collection, http://digitalcollections.nypl.org/items/d25cd4f0-55ad-0133-5cb9-00505686a51c.
29. Quakers Exiled in Virginia collection (MC.950.153), Quaker & Special Collections, Haverford College, Haverford, PA; Moss, "Isaac Zane, Jr."; Arthur J. Mekeel, *The Relation of the Quakers to the American Revolution* (Washington, DC: University Press of America, 1979), 173–184.
30. Daniel Morgan to Miles Fisher, 11 January 1798, letter, Historical Society of Pennsylvania.
31. Graham, *Life of Morgan*, 189.

CHAPTER 11: MONMOUTH

1. This would have been, when attached to its parent regiment, Company B of the 1st Pennsylvania Regiment, raised predominantly from Northumberland County in the Lehigh Valley; cf. John B.B. Trussell and Charles C. Dallas, *The Pennsylvania Line: Regimental Organization and Operations, 1776–1783* (Harrisburg: Pennsylvania Historical and Museum Commission, 1977), 27.
2. Alexander Hamilton to Colonel Daniel Morgan [17 May 1778], *Founders Online*, National Archives, last modified June 13, 2018, http://founders.archives.gov/documents/Hamilton/01-01-02-0457, original source: *Papers of Alexander Hamilton*, 1:488–489.
3. George Washington to Colonel Daniel Morgan, 18 June 1778, *Founders Online*, National Archives, last modified June 13, 2018, http://founders.archives.gov/documents/Washington/03-15-02-0471, original source: *The Papers of George Washington*, Revolutionary War Series, vol. 15, *May–June 1778*, ed. Edward G. Lengel (Charlottesville: University of Virginia Press, 2006), 459.
4. "General Orders, 22 June 1778," ibid., 492–495. The most complete account of Washington's guard is the ancient monograph by Carlos E. Godfrey, *The Commander-in-Chief's Guard: Revolutionary War* (Washington, DC: Stevenson-Smith, 1904), 60–61, which includes pension records indicating which of the guard fought at Monmouth.
5. *Flank companies* referred to the position of these units when a battalion deployed its constituent companies into a long line, each company two or three ranks deep. As the oldest of elite troops, a grenadier company took the position of honor

on the far right of a battalion's ranks; light infantry, not instituted until 1772 and thus junior to the grenadiers, took the position on the far left of the line.

6. George Washington to Colonel Daniel Morgan, 23 June 1778, *Founders Online,* National Archives, last modified June 13, 2018, http://founders.archives.gov/documents/Washington/03-15-02-0539, original source: *Papers of George Washington*, Revolutionary War Series, 15:518.

7. Karl von Clausewitz, *On War* (New York: Knopf, 1993), 138.

8. Major General Philemon Dickinson to George Washington, 25 June 1778, *Founders Online,* National Archives, last modified June 13, 2018, http://founders.archives.gov/documents/Washington/03-15-02-0568, original source: *Papers of George Washington*, Revolutionary War Series, 15:537.

9. Colonel Daniel Morgan to George Washington, 25 June 1778, *Founders Online,* National Archives, last modified June 13, 2018, http://founders.archives.gov/documents/Washington/03-15-02-0578, original source: *Papers of George Washington*, Revolutionary War Series, 15:544.

10. Mark Edward Lender and Garry Wheeler Stone, *Fatal Sunday: George Washington, the Monmouth Campaign, and the Politics of Battle*, Campaigns and Commanders, vol. 54 (Norman: University of Oklahoma Press, 2016), 167.

11. Alexander Hamilton to Elias Boudinot, [5 July 1778], *Founders Online,* National Archives, last modified June 13, 2018, http://founders.archives.gov/documents/Hamilton/01-01-02-0499, original source: *Papers of Alexander Hamilton*, 1:510–514.

12. Nathanael Greene to George Washington, 24 June 1778, Greene Papers, 2:447.

13. Lender and Stone, *Fatal Sunday,* 175, 190.

14. Ibid., 208.

15. Ibid., 211. It should be noted that this anecdote is taken from the reminiscences of the often-unreliable George Washington Parke Custis, Washington's step-grandson.

16. Graham, *Life of Morgan*, 206.

17. Alexander Hamilton to Brigadier General Charles Scott, [27 June 1778], *Founders Online,* National Archives, last modified June 13, 2018, http://founders.archives.gov/documents/Hamilton/01-01-02-0495, original source: *Papers of Alexander Hamilton*, 1:507.

18. George Washington to Colonel Daniel Morgan, 28 June 1778, *Founders Online,* National Archives, last modified February 1, 2018, http://founders.archives.gov/documents/Washington/03-15-02-0626, original source: *Papers of George Washington*, Revolutionary War Series, 15:580.

19. Lender and Stone, *Fatal Sunday,* 349.

20. Colonel Daniel Morgan to George Washington, 30 June 1778, *Founders Online,* National Archives, last modified June 13, 2018, http://founders.archives.gov/documents/Washington/03-15-02-0656, original source: *Papers of George Washington*, Revolutionary War Series, 15:598–599.

CHAPTER 12: HONOR

1. For more on Du Bouchet, see "To George Washington from Major General William Heath, 5 May 1777," *Founders Online*, National Archives, accessed Au-

gust 13, 2017, http://founders.archives.gov/documents/Washington/03-09-02-0336; for more on Kermorvan, see George Washington to John Hancock, 21 June 1776, *Founders Online*, National Archives, accessed November 16, 2017, http://founders.archives.gov/documents/Washington/03-05-02-0039; for the congressional controversy over Glaubeck's fraud against Greene and his estate, see "Memorandum from Oliver Wolcott, Junior, [November 1791]," *Founders Online*, National Archives, accessed December 6, 2017, http://founders.archives.gov/documents/Hamilton/01-09-02-0408.

2. Examples of Febiger's administrative efficiency can be found particularly in his later service in Virginia from 1781 and 1782 as he supported Greene's Southern Army. Christian Febiger, "Febiger Papers, 1777–1782," ed. Bruce Lancaster (Cambridge, MA: Harvard College Library, 1947).

3. "To George Washington from Colonel Daniel Morgan, 24 November 1778," *Founders Online*, National Archives, last modified June 13, 2018, http://founders.archives.gov/documents/Washington/03-18-02-0295, original source: *The Papers of George Washington*, Revolutionary War Series, vol. 18, *1 November 1778–14 January 1779*, ed. Edward G. Lengel (Charlottesville: University of Virginia Press, 2008), 282–283; Higginbotham, *Daniel Morgan*, 94.

4. This stripping away of the Provisional Rifle Corps' constitutive elements in July and August can be seen sequentially through this series of letters: George Washington to Major General Philip Schuyler, 22 July 1778, *Founders Online*, National Archives, accessed May 14, 2018, http://founders.archives.gov/documents/Washington/03-16-02-0146; Brigadier General John Stark to George Washington, 29 July 1778, *Founders Online*, National Archives, accessed May 14, 2018, http://founders.archives.gov/documents/Washington/03-16-02-0215; George Washington to Jonathan Trumbull, Sr., 6 September 1778, *Founders Online*, National Archives, accessed May 14, 2018, http://founders.archives.gov/documents/ Washington/03-16-02-0570.

5. Neil L. York, "Pennsylvania Rifle: Revolutionary Weapon in a Conventional War?" *Pennsylvania Magazine of History and Biography* 103, no. 3 (1979): 302–324.

6. Ibid., 303.

7. The Regiment of Rifles, activated in 1808, was essentially a re-creation of Morgan's riflemen. They even wore hunting shirts. Yet during the War of 1812, they were deployed only in company-sized units. Even more curiously, Henry Dearborn, as Thomas Jefferson's secretary of war, had been deeply involved in the design of the elegant Harpers Ferry Rifle of 1803, yet he made no provision in the design for a bayonet attachment.

8. John W. Wright, "The Corps of Light Infantry in the Continental Army," *American Historical Review* 31, no. 3 (1926): 454–461, https://doi.org/10.2307/1840985.

9. Paul David Nelson, *Anthony Wayne: Soldier of the Early Republic* (Bloomington: Indiana University Press, 1985), 53–59. The entire Paoli affair is fully treated in Thomas J. McGuire, *Battle of Paoli: The Revolutionary War "Massacre" Near Philadelphia, September 1777* (Mechanicsburg, PA: Stackpole, 2015).

10. George Washington to John Jay, 30 June 1779, *Founders Online,* National Archives, last modified June 13, 2018, http://founders.archives.gov/documents/

Washington/03-21-02-0256, original source: *The Papers of George Washington,* Revolutionary War Series, vol. 21, *1 June–31 July 1779*, ed. William M. Ferraro (Charlottesville: University of Virginia Press, 2012), 306–307.

11. Joseph Jones to George Washington, 18 July 1780, *Founders Online,* National Archives, last modified June 13, 2018, http://founders.archives.gov/documents/Washington/99-01-02-02544. This is an Early Access document from *The Papers of George Washington.* It is not an authoritative final version; George Washington to Joseph Jones, 22 July 1780, *Founders Online,* National Archives, last modified June 13, 2018, http://founders.archives.gov/ documents /Washington/99-01-02-02623. This is an Early Access document from *The Papers of George Washington.* It is not an authoritative final version.

12. George Washington to John Jay, 30 June 1779, *Founders Online,* National Archives, last modified June 13, 2018, http://founders.archives.gov/documents/ Washington/03-21-02-0256, original source: *The Papers of George Washington,* Revolutionary War Series, 21, 306–307.

13. Ibid.

14. Bertram Wyatt-Brown, *Southern Honor: Ethics and Behavior in the Old South* (Oxford: Oxford University Press, 1982), 3–24.

15. John Adams to Nathanael Greene, 9 March 1777, *Founders Online,* National Archives, accessed May 14, 2018, http://founders.archives.gov/documents/ Adams/06-05-02-0058.

16. Murray Milner, *Status and Sacredness: A General Theory of Status Relations and an Analysis of Indian Culture* (New York: Oxford University Press, 1994), 23; Caroline Cox, *A Proper Sense of Honor: Service and Sacrifice in George Washington's Army* (Chapel Hill: University of North Carolina Press, 2004), 64.

17. Lorri Glover, *Founders as Fathers: The Private Lives and Politics of the American Revolutionaries* (New Haven: Yale University Press, 2014). For example, while Thomas Jefferson was a member of the Virginia legislature during the Revolution, he attended only 25 percent of its sessions. George Mason of Virginia, a widower with several young children, nearly always resisted pleas for him to come to either Congress or the Virginia legislature. Washington is the great counterexample; in this he was, as in other things, unusual.

18. Higginbotham, *Daniel Morgan,* 101–102.

19. Carl P. Borick, *A Gallant Defense: The Siege of Charleston, 1780* (Columbia: University of South Carolina Press, 2003), 229–235.

20. John Buchanan, *The Road to Guilford Courthouse: The American Revolution in the Carolinas* (New York: John Wiley, 1999), 106–112, 120–121.

21. Graham, *Life of Morgan,* 233–234.

22. Higginbotham, *Daniel Morgan,* 102.

23. Ibid., 103.

24. Otho Williams, "A Narrative of the Campaign of 1780," in William Johnson, *Sketches of the Life and Correspondence of Nathanael Greene: Major General of the Armies of the United States, in the War of the Revolution,* vol. 1 (Charleston, SC: Printed for the author by A.E. Milner, 1822), app. B, 494.

25. "Letter from Thomas Pinckney to William Johnson, 27 July 1822," *Historical Magazine* 10, no. 8 (August 1886): 244–253; Buchanan, *Road to Guilford Courthouse,* 156.

26. Williams, "Narrative," 494–495.

27. Ibid., 495.

28. Alexander Hamilton to James Duane, 6 September 1780, *Founders Online,* National Archives, last modified June 13, 2018, http://founders.archives. gov/documents/Hamilton/01-02-02-0842, original source: *The Papers of Alexander Hamilton,* vol. 2, *1779–1781,* ed. Harold C. Syrett (New York: Columbia University Press, 1961), 420–421.

29. Pension application of Guilford Dudley, W8681, Revolutionary War Pension and Bounty-Land Warrant Application files, RG 15, National Archives.

CHAPTER 13: SOUTH

1. Pension application of Peter Bruin, S42092, Revolutionary War Pension and Bounty-Land Warrant Application files, RG 15, National Archives; Peter [Bruin?] to General Morgan, Guilford Court House, Myers Collection, accessed December 17, 2017, http://digitalcollections.nypl.org/items/b48c4ff0-3e18-0133-82b6-00505686d14e.

2. Graham, *Life of Morgan,* 237.

3. Williams, "Narrative," 507.

4. Buchanan, *Road to Guilford Courthouse,* 186–191.

5. John W. Gordon, *South Carolina and the American Revolution: A Battlefield History* (Columbia: University of South Carolina Press, 2003), 112–114.

6. Lee, *Memoirs,* 87; Gordon, *South Carolina,* 104–106.

7. Williams, "Narrative," 488.

8. Higginbotham, *Daniel Morgan,* 108; Walter Clark, ed. *The State Records of North Carolina,* vol. 14 (Goldsboro, NC: Nash Brothers: 1896), 397, 400.

9. For William Washington's biography, see Daniel Kevin Murphy, *William Washington, American Light Dragoon: A Continental Cavalry Leader in the War of Independence* (Yardley, PA: Westholme, 2014).

10. "'A Gentleman of Maryland': The Short Life of Edward Giles," *History Hermann* (blog), June 21, 2017, accessed May 13, 2018, https://histhermann.wordpress.com/2017/06/21/a-gentleman-of-maryland-the-short-life-of-edward-giles/.

11. John Parke Custis to George Washington, 17 February 1778, *Founders Online,* National Archives, last modified November 26, 2017, http://founders. archives.gov/documents/Washington/03-13-02-0480, original source: *The Papers of George Washington,* Revolutionary War Series, vol. 13, *26 December 1777–28 February 1778,* ed. Edward G. Lengel (Charlottesville: University of Virginia Press, 2003), 565.

12. Higginbotham, *Daniel Morgan,* 110.

13. Daniel Morgan to [Horatio Gates], Salisbury, NC, New York Public Library, Digital Collections, accessed December 1, 2017, http://digitalcollections.nypl.org/items/4c0244c0-406b-0133-8ac3-00505686d14e.

14. Higginbotham, *Daniel Morgan,* 113.

15. Graham, *Life of Morgan,* 248; Williams, "Narrative," 509.

16. Higginbotham, *Daniel Morgan,* 117–118.

17. Ibid., 119.

18. Williams, "Narrative," 510.

19. "To George Washington from Major General Nathanael Greene, 31 May 1779," *Founders Online,* National Archives, last modified June 13, 2018, http://

founders.archives.gov/documents/Washington/03-20-02-0650, original source: *The Papers of George Washington*, Revolutionary War Series, vol. 20, *8 April–31 May 1779*, ed. Edward G. Lengel (Charlottesville: University of Virginia Press, 2010), 705–708.

20. Robert Middlekauff, *The Glorious Cause: The American Revolution, 1763–1789*, rev. and expanded (Oxford: Oxford University Press, 2005), 469.

21. Nathanael Greene to Daniel Morgan, 16 December 1780, Greene Papers, 6: 589–590.

22. Black, *Plotting Power*, 208.

23. Daniel Morgan to Nathanael Greene, 15 January 1781, Greene Papers, 7:128.

24. Ibid.,127; Daniel Morgan to Nathanael Greene, 24 January, 1781, Greene Papers, 7:192.

25. Daniel Morgan to Nathanael Greene, 4 January 1781, Greene Papers, 7:50–51.

26. Buchanan, *Road to Guilford Courthouse*, 299; Daniel Morgan to Nathanael Greene, 15 January, 1781, Greene Papers, 7:128; the definitive biography of Pickens is Rod Andrew, *The Life and Times of General Andrew Pickens: Revolutionary War Hero, American Founder* (Chapel Hill: University of North Carolina Press, 2017).

27. Daniel Morgan to Nathanael Greene, 15 January, 1781, Greene Papers, 7:128.

28. Ibid.

29. Robert Stansbury Lambert, *South Carolina Loyalists in the American Revolution*, 1st ed. (Columbia: University of South Carolina Press, 1987), 166.

30. For Tarleton's biography, see Robert D. Bass, *The Green Dragoon: The Lives of Banastre Tarleton* (Orangeburg, SC: Sandlapper Press, 2003). Now dated, Bass's biography deserves a replacement.

31. Lawrence E. Babits, *A Devil of a Whipping: The Battle of Cowpens*, rev. ed. (Chapel Hill: University of North Carolina Press, 2001), 46. Tarleton, like Patrick Ferguson and John Simcoe, commander of the Queen's Rangers, was a consistent advocate for the greater involvement of Loyalist troops in full-scale counterinsurgency. Like them, he seems to have had an emotional attachment to the Americans he led. I.F.W. Beckett, *Modern Insurgencies and Counter-Insurgencies: Guerrillas and Their Opponents Since 1750* (London: Routledge, 2001), 4.

32. Banastre Tarleton, *A History of the Campaigns of 1780 and 1781 in the Southern Provinces of North America* (New York: New York Times, 1968), 20, 28, 29, 108.

33. Andrew Jackson O'Shaughnessy, *The Men Who Lost America: British Leadership, the American Revolution, and the Fate of the Empire* (New Haven: Yale University Press, 2013), 266; Gordon, *South Carolina*, 103–104.

34. Earl Cornwallis to Lt. Col. Tarleton, 2 January 1781, in Tarleton, *History of the Campaigns*, 108.

CHAPTER 14: COWPENS

1. George White, *Statistics of the State of Georgia: Including an Account of Its Natural, Civil, and Ecclesiastical History; Together with a Particular Description of Each County, Notices of the Manners and Customs of Its Aboriginal Tribes, and a Correct Map of the State* (Savannah: W. Thorne Williams, 1849), 438.

2. Daniel Morgan to Nathanael Greene, 5 January, 1781, Greene Papers, 7:51.

3. Daniel Morgan to Nathanael Greene, 15 January, 1781, Greene Papers, 7:127–128.

4. Wayne E. Lee, *Crowds and Soldiers in Revolutionary North Carolina: The Culture of Violence in Riot and War* (Gainesville: University Press of Florida, 2001), 176–181.

5. Tarleton, *History of the Campaigns*, 211.

6. Babits, *Devil of a Whipping*, 47.

7. Tarleton, *History of the Campaigns*, 214.

8. Pension application of Dennis Trammell, R10672, Revolutionary War Pension and Bounty-Land Warrant Application files, RG 15, National Archives.

9. Daniel Morgan to Edward Snickers, January 26, 1781, Horatio Gates Papers, New York Historical Society.

10. Tarleton, *History of the Campaigns*, 215, 221; Charles Stedman, *The History of the Origin, Progress, and Termination of the American War* (London: printed for the author, 1794), 2:321.

11. Morgan to Snickers, January 26, 1781, Gates Papers; Middlekauff, *Glorious Cause*, 471, 475.

12. These dispositions have been carefully reconstructed by Lawrence Babits in *Devil of a Whipping*, 40–42, 79.

13. Young, "Memoir," 84–88, 100–105.

14. Pension application of Lawrence Everheart, S25068, Revolutionary War Pension and Bounty-Land Warrant Application files, RG 15, National Archives.

15. Tarleton, *History of the Campaigns*, 215, 221; Babits, *Devil of a Whipping*, 81–83.

16. Babits, *Devil of a Whipping*, 84; Stedman, *History*, 321; Tarleton, *History of the Campaigns*, 216.

17. Graham, *Life of Morgan*, 298–299; Higginbotham, *Daniel Morgan*, 136.

18. Young, "Memoir," 84–88, 100–105.

19. James Potter Collins and John M. Roberts, *Autobiography of a Revolutionary Soldier* (Clinton, LA: Feliciana Democrat, 1859), 57.

20. Tarleton, *History of the Campaigns*, 216.

21. Babits, *Devil of a Whipping*, 103.

22. Tarleton, *History of the Campaigns*, 217.

23. Babits, *Devil of a Whipping*, 111.

24. Graham, *Life of Morgan*, 303; Babits, *Devil of a Whipping*, 112.

25. Babits, *Devil of a Whipping*, 113, 117, 120.

26. Tarleton, *History of the Campaigns*, 218.

27. James Jackson to General Morgan, letter, Philadelphia, February 9, 1795, Myers Collection, http://digitalcollections.nypl.org/items/6632d400-3fa9-0133-0c04-00505686d14e.

28. Higginbotham, *Daniel Morgan*, 141; Babits, *Devil of a Whipping*, 126.

29. Babits, *Devil of a Whipping*, 137–138.

30. Higginbotham, *Daniel Morgan* 142; Babits, *Devil of a Whipping*, 137–138. Tarleton could not resist the temptation to claim that "the loss was almost equally shared" and that only four hundred prisoners were taken. Tarleton, *History of the Campaigns*, 218.

31. Jackson to Morgan, February 9, 1795.

32. Daniel Morgan to Nathanael Greene, 19 January, 1781, Greene Papers, 7:154.

33. Babits, *Devil of a Whipping*, 133–134.

CHAPTER 15: RACE FOR THE DAN

1. Graham, *Life of Morgan,* 323.

2. Greene Papers, 2:209n4.

3. Franklin B. Wickwire, *Cornwallis and the War of Independence* (London: Faber & Faber, 1971), 269.

4. Wickwire, *Cornwallis*, 274.

5. Babits, *Devil of a Whipping,*141.

6. Wickwire, Cornwallis, 269.

7. Daniel Morgan to Nathanael Greene, 28 January 1781, Greene Papers, 7:211; Higginbotham, *Daniel Morgan,* 148.

8. Daniel Morgan to Nathanael Greene, 28 January 1781, Greene Papers 7: 211.

9. Daniel Morgan to Nathanael Greene, 23 January 1781, Greene Papers, 7:178.

10. Daniel Morgan to Nathanael Greene, 24 January 1781, Greene Papers, 7:190–191.

11. O'Shaughnessy, *Men Who Lost America*, 267.

12. "To Isaac Huger, 30 January 1781," Greene Papers 7:219–221.

13. Daniel Morgan to Thomas Jefferson, 1 February 1781, *Founders Online*, National Archives, last modified June 13, 2018, http://founders.archives.gov/documents/Jefferson/01-04-02-0608, original source: *The Papers of Thomas Jefferson*, vol. 4, *1 October 1780–24 February 1781*, ed. Julian P. Boyd (Princeton, NJ: Princeton University Press, 1951), 495–496.

14. Buchanan, *Road to Guilford Courthouse*, 349.

15. Higginbotham, *Daniel Morgan,* 152.

16. Buchanan, *Road to Guilford Courthouse*, 350.

17. Greene Papers 7:254, 256.

18. Ibid., 7:261–262.

19. Lee, *Revolutionary War Memoirs*, 174.

20. Greene Papers 7:268.

21. Nathanael Greene to General Morgan, camp at Guilford Court House, February 10, 1781, Myers Collection, http://digitalcollections.nypl.org/items/99a81330-3fa1-0133-72ae-00505686a51c.

22. Greene Papers, 7:324–325; for Greene's modifications of Morgan's advice, see Lawrence Edward Babits and Joshua B. Howard, *Long, Obstinate, and Bloody: The Battle of Guilford Courthouse* (Chapel Hill: University of North Carolina Press, 2009), ch. 1.

CHAPTER 16: ENDINGS

1. Graham, *Life of Morgan,* 373–374.

2. Nathanael Greene to General Daniel Morgan, 20 March 1781. Greene Papers 7:455-456.

3. Graham, *Life of Morgan,* 373–374.

4. For more on these discontents, see McDonnell, *Politics of War*, ch. 12.

5. Daniel Morgan to Thomas Jefferson, 23 March 1781, *Founders Online*, National Archives, last modified June 13, 2018, http://founders.archives.gov/docu-

ments/Jefferson/01-05-02-0292, original source: *The Papers of Thomas Jefferson*, vol. 5, *25 February 1781–20 May 1781*, ed. Julian P. Boyd (Princeton, NJ: Princeton University Press, 1952), 218–219.

6. "Claypool's Rebellion: Paston to County Lieutenant of Frederick," West Virginia Division of Culture and History, http://www.wvculture.org/history/revwar/claypool04.html, accessed December 18, 2017; McDonnell, *Politics of War*, 455–456.

7. Graham, *Life of Morgan*, 384.

8. Graham, *Life of Morgan*, 395.

9. Anthony Wayne to Daniel Morgan, Camp of Goods Bridge, VA, July 29, 1781, Myers Collection, http://digitalcollections.nypl.org/items/938e5f20-55ab-0133-ae70-00505686d14e; Graham, *Life of Morgan*, 395.

10. Graham, *Life of Morgan*, 395.

11. Daniel Morgan to George Washington, 20 September 1781, *Founders Online*, National Archives, last modified November 26, 2017, http://founders.archives.gov/documents/Washington/99-01-02-06989. This is an Early Access document from *The Papers of George Washington*. It is not an authoritative final version.

12. Graham, *Memoir*, 68–70, 71.

13. François Jean Chastellux, *Travels in North America: In the Years 1780, 1781, and 1782* (Chapel Hill: published for the Institute of Early American History and Culture at Williamsburg, VA, by the University of North Carolina Press, 1963), 239.

14. John Claypool to General Morgan, Lost River, 1781, Myers Collection, http://digitalcollections.nypl.org/items/35aae190-3e1a-0133-a6a6-00505686d14e.

15. "Daniel Morgan to Governor Benjamin Harrison, 10 February 1782," in *Calendar of Virginia State Papers*, ed. William Palmer (Richmond: 1875–1893), 3:57–58.

16. Daniel Morgan to General Lincoln and John Mercer, Saratoga, February 6, 1783, Myers Collection, http://digitalcollections.nypl.org/items/1fe12830-405b-0133-2891-00505686d14e.

17. Graham, *Life of Morgan*, 414.

CHAPTER 17: HAPPINESS

1. George Washington diary entry, September 1784, *Founders Online*, National Archives, last modified November 26, 2017, http://founders.archives.gov/documents/Washington/01-04-02-0001-0001, original source: *The Diaries of George Washington*, vol. 4, *1 September 1784–30 June 1786*, ed. Donald Jackson and Dorothy Twohig (Charlottesville: University Press of Virginia, 1978), 1–54.

2. Alan Taylor, "Political Personae in the Early Republic," in *Federalists Reconsidered*, ed. Doron S. Ben-Atar and Barbara B. Oberg (Charlottesville: University Press of Virginia, 1998), 233.

3. Glover, *Founders*, 3.

4. Higginbotham, *Daniel Morgan*, 173; Frederick County Superior Court Deed Book 4, Frederick County Clerk of the Circuit Court, Winchester, VA, 20, 22.

5. Thomas, Lord Fairfax, Frederick County, VA, Will Book 4, pt 2, 589–595. Given that the probate of Lord Fairfax's estate was taken on April 1, 1782, one is inclined to wonder if Morgan did not acquire a few things from his near-neighbor's estate sale.

6. Glover, *Founders*, 24–25.

7. J. Bernard Hogg, "Presley Neville," *Western Pennsylvania Historical Magazine* 19, no. 1 (March 1936): 17–26.

8. Higginbotham, *Daniel Morgan*,182; pension application of James Heard, s.540, Revolutionary War Pension and Bounty-Land Warrant Application files, RG 15, National Archives; Daniel Morgan to Presley Neville, Soldier's Rest, 1798, Myers Collection, https://digitalcollections.nypl.org/items/ae9eadc0-406f-0133-f363-00505686d14e#/?uuid=ae9eadc0-406f-0133-f363-00505686d14e.

9. Higginbotham, *Daniel Morgan*, 183; for the persistent Winchester gossip surrounding Willoughby's maternity even into the twenty-first century, see Nancy S. Schaefer, "Abigail Morgan: Wife of the 'Old Waggoner'" (master's thesis, University of Oklahoma, 2004).

10. *Virginia Gazette and Alexandria Advertiser* (Alexandria, VA), Sept. 3, 1789, 4.

11. Graham, *Life of Morgan*, 412–413; Higginbotham, *Daniel Morgan*, 213.

12. The best discussion of the controversy over debt certificates is in Woody Holton, *Unruly Americans and the Origins of the Constitution* (New York: Hill and Wang, 2007), 90.

13. George Washington to John Francis Mercer, 9 September 1786, *Founders Online*, National Archives, last modified June 13, 2018, http://founders.archives.gov/documents/Washington/04-04-02-0232, original source: *The Papers of George Washington*, Confederation Series, vol. 4, *2 April 1786–31 January 1787*, ed. W. W. Abbot (Charlottesville: University Press of Virginia, 1995), 243–244. For the contempt held toward those who purchased soldiers' certificates, see Holton, *Unruly Americans*, 260.

14. George Washington to John Francis Mercer, 24 November 1786, *Founders Online*, National Archives, last modified June 13, 2018, http://founders.archives.gov/documents/Washington/04-04-02-0353, original source: *Papers of George Washington*, Confederation Series, 4:393–395.

15. Horatio Gates to Alexander Hamilton [23 October 1791], *Founders Online*, National Archives, last modified June 13, 2018, http://founders.archives.gov/documents/Hamilton/01-09-02-0298, original source: *The Papers of Alexander Hamilton*, vol. 9, *August 1791–December 1791*, ed. Harold C. Syrett (New York: Columbia University Press, 1965), 413–414.

16. Graham, *Life of Morgan*, 408–409.

17. Ibid.

18. Ibid., 411.

19. For this transition from Tidewater to Valley, see Christopher Michael Curtis, *Jefferson's Freeholders and the Politics of Ownership in the Old Dominion*, Cambridge Studies on the American South (New York: Cambridge University Press, 2012), particularly 90–91. Burwell-Morgan Mill is now maintained by the Clarke County Historical Society; more can be found about it at http://www.burwellmorganmill.org.

20. Higginbotham, *Daniel Morgan*, 177–178; Warren Hofstra and Clarence R. Geier, "Farm to Mill to Market: Historical Archaeology of an Emerging Grain Economy in the Shenandoah Valley," in *After the Backcountry: Rural Life in the Great Valley of Virginia, 1800–1900*, 1st ed., ed. Kenneth E. Koons and Warren R. Hofstra (Knoxville: University of Tennessee Press, 2000), 58–59.

21. William Darke to George Washington, 9–10 November 1791, *Founders Online*, National Archives, last modified June 13, 2018, http://founders.archives. gov/documents/Washington/05-09-02-0094, original source: *Papers of George Washington*, Presidential Series, 9:158–168; Lee, *Memoirs*, 185.

22. Colin G. Calloway, *The Victory with No Name: The Native American Defeat of the First American Army* (Oxford: Oxford University Press, 2015), 116–122.

23. Ibid., 130.

24. "Memorandum on General Officers, 9 March 1792," *Founders Online*, National Archives, last modified June 13, 2018, http://founders.archives.gov/documents/Washington/05-10-02-0040, original source: *Papers of George Washington*, Presidential Series, 10:74–79.

25. Ibid.; Alan D. Gaff, *Bayonets in the Wilderness: Anthony Wayne's Legion in the Old Northwest* (Norman: University of Oklahoma Press, 2004), particularly chapter five, for examples of Wayne's attention to detail. See also Andrew J. Birtle, "The Origins of the Legion of the United States," *Journal of Military History* 67, no. 4 (2003): 1249–1261.

26. "Memorandum of Consultation on Indian Policy, 9 March 1792," *Founders Online*, National Archives, accessed May 22, 2018, http://founders.archives.gov/documents/Jefferson/01-23-02-0205.

CHAPTER 18: LIBERTY

1. Higginbotham, *Daniel Morgan*, 191

2. Lee, *Campaign of 1781*, xxvi-xxvii.

3. Thomas P. Slaughter, *The Whiskey Rebellion: Frontier Epilogue to the American Revolution* (New York: Oxford University Press, 1986), 179–180; William Hogeland, *The Whiskey Rebellion: George Washington, Alexander Hamilton, and the Frontier Rebels Who Challenged America's Newfound Sovereignty* (New York: Scribner, 2006), 154–157.

4. Slaughter, *Whiskey Rebellion*, 199.

5. Higginbotham, *Daniel Morgan*, 189. Virginia had a particular interest in the Whiskey Rebellion, since at the time it adjoined southwestern Pennsylvania and it was suspected that many western Virginians shared the rebels' sentiments; some "riots" occurred in those counties. See Kevin T. Barksdale, "Our Rebellious Neighbors: Virginia's Border Counties during Pennsylvania's Whiskey Rebellion," *Virginia Magazine of History and Biography* 111, no. 1 (2003): 5–32, particularly 16–18.

6. William Findley, *History of the Insurrection in the Four Western Counties of Pennsylvania in the Year MDCCXCIV: With a Recital of the Circumstances Specially Connected Therewith, and an Historical Review of the Previous Situation of the Country* (Philadelphia: printed by Samuel Harrison Smith, 1796), 98.

7. Graham, *Life of Morgan*, 430.

8. Hugh Henry Brackenridge, *History of the Western Insurrection in Pennsylvania, Commonly Called the Whiskey Insurrection, 1794* (Pittsburgh: W.S. Haven, 1859), 291.

9. Hogeland, *Whiskey Rebellion*, 157.

10. Graham, *Life of Morgan*, 432; Leland D. Baldwin, ed., "Orders Issued by General Henry Lee during the Campaign against the Whiskey Insurrectionists," *Western Pennsylvania Historical Magazine* 19 (June 1936): 79–111.

11. Daniel Morgan to George Washington, December 1794, *Founders Online*, National Archives, last modified June 13, 2018, http://founders.archives.gov/documents/Washington/05-17-02-0236, original source: *The Papers of George Washington*, Presidential Series, vol. 17, *1 October 1794–31 March 1795*, ed. David R. Hoth and Carol S. Ebel (Charlottesville: University of Virginia Press, 2013), 348–350.

12. Zadok Cramer, *The Ohio and Mississippi Navigator Comprising an Ample Account of Those Beautiful Rivers, from the Head of the Former, to the Mouth of the Latter,* . . . 11th ed. (Pittsburgh: Cramer and Spear, 1821), 38.

13. Findley, *History of the Insurrection*, 213.

14. Daniel Morgan to George Washington, 19 January 1795," *Founders Online*, National Archives, last modified June 13, 2018, http://founders.archives.gov/documents/Washington/05-17-02-0272, original source: *Papers of George Washington*, Presidential Series, 17:413–414.

15. Daniel Morgan to George Washington, 9 April 1795, *Founders Online*, National Archives, last modified June 13, 2018, http://founders.archives.gov/documents/Washington/05-18-02-0020, original source: *The Papers of George Washington*, Presidential Series, vol. 18, *1 April–30 September 1795*, ed. Carol S. Ebel (Charlottesville: University of Virginia Press, 2015), 26–28.

16. John Neville to General Morgan, letter, Pittsburgh, November 28, 1794, Myers Collection, http://digitalcollections.nypl.org/items/5ae59e50-42cf-0133-3275-00505686d14e; John Neville to General Morgan, letter, Pittsburgh, January 28, 1795, Myers Collection, http://digitalcollections.nypl.org/items/d023c820-42cf-0133-3181-00505686d14e.

17. Higginbotham, *Daniel Morgan*, 195.

18. Robert Rutherford to George Washington, 15 December 1790, *Founders Online*, National Archives, last modified June 13, 2018, http://founders.archives.gov/documents/Washington/05-07-02-0046, original source: *The Papers of George Washington*, Presidential Series, vol. 7, *1 December 1790–21 March 1791*, ed. Jack D. Warren Jr. (Charlottesville: University Press of Virginia, 1998), 86–89.

19. Winchester-Frederick County Historical Society, *Men and Events of the Revolution in Winchester and Frederick County, Virginia* (Winchester, VA: Winchester-Frederick County Historical Society, 1975), 25–27.

20. For examples of Rutherford's style, see his letters to Washington and to Madison: Robert Rutherford to George Washington, 4 March 1795, *Founders Online*, National Archives, last modified June 13, 2018, http://founders.archives.gov/documents/Washington/05-17-02-0417, original source: *Papers of George Washington*, Presidential Series, 17:613–617, and Robert Rutherford to James Madison, 30 March 1795, *Founders Online*, National Archives, last modified June 13, 2018, http://founders.archives.gov/documents/Madison/01-15-02-0410, original source: *The Papers of James Madison*, vol. 15, *24 March 1793–20 April 1795*, ed. Thomas A. Mason, Robert A. Rutland, and Jeanne K. Sisson (Charlottesville: University Press of Virginia, 1985), 501–503.

21. Higginbotham, *Daniel Morgan*, 196.

22. John Neville to Daniel Morgan, letter, Pittsburgh, 28 January, 1795, Myers Collection, http://digitalcollections.nypl.org/items/d023c820-42cf-0133-3181-00505686d14e; Presley Neville to Daniel Morgan, letter, Philadelphia, 3 March

1795, Myers Collection, http://digitalcollections.nypl.org/items/a801c6c0-4078-0133-6e7a-00505686d14e.
23. Rutherford to Madison, 30 March 1795, *Founders Online*. The classic description of Virginia elections is Charles S. Sydnor, *Gentlemen Freeholders: Political Practices in Washington's Virginia* (Chapel Hill: published for the Institute of Early American History and Culture at Williamsburg, VA, by the University of North Carolina Press, 1952). It has been supplanted by John Kolp, *Gentlemen and Freeholders: Electoral Politics in Colonial Virginia* (Baltimore: Johns Hopkins University Press, 1998).
24. Ibid.
25. Joseph Ellis, "The Farewell," in *George Washington Reconsidered*, ed. Don Higginbotham (Charlottesville: University Press of Virginia, 2001), 212–249.
26. Higginbotham, *Daniel Morgan*, 199.
27. Ibid., 228.
28. Joseph Jones to James Madison, 23 March 1797, *Founders Online*, National Archives, last modified June 13, 2018, http://founders.archives.gov/documents/Madison/01-16-02-0381, original source: *The Papers of James Madison*, vol. 16, *27 April 1795–27 March 1797*, ed. J. C. A. Stagg, Thomas A. Mason, and Jeanne K. Sisson (Charlottesville: University Press of Virginia, 1989), 502–503.
29. Daniel Morgan to George Washington, 30 October 1797, *Founders Online*, National Archives, last modified June 13, 2018, http://founders.archives.gov/documents/Washington/06-01-02-0393, original source: *The Papers of George Washington*, Retirement Series, vol. 1, *4 March 1797–30 December 1797*, ed. W. W. Abbot (Charlottesville: University Press of Virginia, 1998), 440–441.
30. Daniel Morgan, "General Morgan's Division Orders," *Alexandria (VA) Advertiser*, Sept. 11, 1797, 3; Philanthropos, "Communication," *Alexandria (VA) Advertiser*, Sept. 12, 1797, 3.
31. [Henry Lee], *Address of the Minority in the Virginia Legislature to the People*, Richmond, VA, 1798, Virginia Historical Society, Richmond.
32. Daniel Morgan to Presley Neville, Soldier's Rest, 1798, Myers Collection, https://digitalcollections.nypl.org/items/ae9eadc0-406f-0133-f363-00505686d14e#/?uuid=ae9eadc0-406f-0133-f363-00505686d14e.
33. Daniel Morgan to John Adams, 3 March 1799, *Founders Online*, National Archives, last modified June 13, 2018, http://founders.archives.gov/documents/Adams/99-02-02-3368. This is an Early Access document from *The Adams Papers*. It is not an authoritative final version.

CHAPTER 19: DEATH

1. Daniel Morgan to Presley Neville, Soldier's Rest, 1798, Myers Collection, https://digitalcollections.nypl.org/items/ae9eadc0-406f-0133-f363-00505686d14e#/?uuid=ae9eadc0-406f-0133-f363-00505686d14e.
2. George Washington to Daniel Morgan, 10 April 1799, *Founders Online*, National Archives, last modified June 13, 2018, http://founders.archives.gov/documents/Washington/06-03-02-0367, original source: *The Papers of George Washington*, Retirement Series, vol. 3, *16 September 1798–19 April 1799*, ed. W. W. Abbot and Edward G. Lengel (Charlottesville: University Press of Virginia, 1999), 477–478n1.

3. George Washington to Daniel Morgan, 10 April 1799, *Founders Online*, National Archives, last modified June 13, 2018, http://founders.archives.gov/documents/Washington/06-03-02-0367, original source: *The Papers of George Washington*, Retirement Series, vol. 3, 477–478.

4. For a discussion of the nuance of Washington's salutations, see Peter Henriques, "The Great Collaboration : The Increasingly Close Relationship between George Washington and Alexander Hamilton," in McDonald, *Sons of the Father*, 204.

5. Charles Royster, *Light-Horse Harry Lee and the Legacy of the American Revolution*, 1st ed. (New York: Knopf, 1981), 197–199.

6. Graham, *Life of Morgan*, 447.

7. Lee, *Memoirs*, 584.

8. Graham, *Life of Morgan*, 447.

9. Daniel Morgan, "Letter to Miles Fisher from Daniel Morgan," Philadelphia, January 11, 1798, Historical Society of Pennsylvania, Philadelphia.

10. James R. Graham, *The Planting of the Presbyterian Church in Northern Virginia: Prior to the Organization of Winchester Presbytery, December 4, 1794* (Winchester, VA: Geo. F. Norton, 1904), 101.

11. See William Harrison Taylor, *Unity in Christ and Country: American Presbyterians in the Revolutionary Era, 1758–1801* (Tuscaloosa: University of Alabama Press, 2017), 98–103, for examples of what he terms "interdenominational nationalism" among southern Presbyterians.

12. Graham, *Life of Morgan*, 448.

13. Deeds entered March 16 and July 9, 1801, Frederick County Superior Court Deed Book, vol. 4.

14. David Conrad, "Early History of Winchester," in *Annual Papers of Winchester Virginia Historical Society* 1 (1931): 172.

15. Lee, *Memoirs*, 584.

16. Homer, *The Odyssey*, tr. Robert Fagles (New York: Penguin, 1997), bk. 11, lines 555–557.

17.William Hill, "Sermon, 1802, Concerning Daniel Morgan," Virginia Historical Society, Richmond.

18. Nicole Eustace, *Passion Is the Gale: Emotion, Power, and the Coming of the American Revolution* (Chapel Hill: published for the Omohundro Institute of Early American History and Culture by the University of North Carolina Press, 2008), 4–6.

19. Graham, *Life of Morgan*, 448; L. N. Barton, "List of the members of Daniel Morgan's Rifle Company and of the 'Dutch Mess,'" in *Men and Events of the Revolution in Winchester and Frederick County, Virginia* (Winchester, VA: Winchester-Frederick County Historical Society, 1975).

EPILOGUE

1. Pension application of James Heard. Lee's endorsement is dated September 25, 1812. O'Bannon's actions are described in many histories, for example, Frank Lambert, *The Barbary Wars: American Independence in the Atlantic World* (New York: Farrar, Straus and Giroux, 2007).

2. "Books Belonging to Willoughby Morgan" and "Account of Sales at Fort Crawford, WI...," [1831], Daniel Morgan Collection, Clements Library.

3. William Hill. "Sermon, 1802, Concerning Daniel Morgan."
4. Jack Greene, "Afterword," in McDonald, *Sons of the Father*, 266.
5. Ibid.
6. Ibid., 258.
7. *Life*, Sept 3, 1951, "Who Gets the General's Body?"; *Smithsonian*, May 1980, "Our Old Patriots' Remains Don't Get to Rest in Peace."

BIBLIOGRAPHY

American Archives. Digital Collections and Collaborative Projects. University Libraries. Northern Illinois University. http://amarch.lib.niu.edu/.

Anburey, Thomas. *Travels through the Interior Parts of America in a Series of Letters.* Vols. 1 and 2. London: Printed for William Lane, 1791.

Anderson, Fred. *Crucible of War: The Seven Years' War and the Fate of Empire in British North America, 1754–1766.* 1st Vintage Books ed. New York: Vintage Books, 2001.

Anderson, Mark R. *The Battle for the Fourteenth Colony: America's War of Liberation in Canada, 1774–1776.* Hanover, NH: University Press of New England, 2013.

Andrew, Rod. *The Life and Times of General Andrew Pickens: Revolutionary War Hero, American Founder.* Chapel Hill: University of North Carolina Press, 2017.

Arnold, Benedict. "Journal," In Kenneth Lewis Roberts, ed. *March to Quebec; Journals of the Members of Arnold's Expedition.* New York: Doubleday, Doran, 1940.

Babits, Lawrence E. *A Devil of a Whipping: The Battle of Cowpens.* Rev. ed. Chapel Hill: University of North Carolina Press, 2001.

Babits, Lawrence Edward, and Joshua B. Howard. *Long, Obstinate, and Bloody: The Battle of Guilford Courthouse.* Chapel Hill: University of North Carolina Press, 2009.

Baldwin, Leland D., ed. "Orders Issued by General Henry Lee during the Campaign against the Whiskey Insurrectionists." *Western Pennsylvania Historical Magazine* 19 (June 1936).

Barksdale, Kevin T. "Our Rebellious Neighbors: Virginia's Border Counties during Pennsylvania's Whiskey Rebellion." *Virginia Magazine of History and Biography* 111, no. 1 (2003): 5–32.

Barton, L. N. "List of the members of Daniel Morgan's Rifle Company and of the 'Dutch Mess.'" In *Men and Events of the Revolution in Winchester and Frederick County, Virginia.* Winchester, VA: Winchester-Frederick County Historical Society, 1975.

Bazin, Capt. Aaron. "Boyd's O-O-D-A Loop and the Infantry Company Commander." *Infantry* 1, no. 1 (February 2005): 3.

Beckett, I.F.W. *Modern Insurgencies and Counter-Insurgencies: Guerrillas and Their Opponents Since 1750.* London: Routledge, 2001.

Ben-Atar, Doron S., and Barbara B. Oberg, eds. *Federalists Reconsidered.* Charlottesville: University Press of Virginia, 1998.

Berry, Benjamin. "Notes, Concerning Daniel Morgan." Virginia Historical Society. Richmond.

Birtle, Andrew J. "The Origins of the Legion of the United States." *Journal of Military History* 67, no. 4 (2003): 1249–61.

Black, Jeremy. *Plotting Power: Strategy in the Eighteenth Century.* Bloomington: Indiana University Press, 2017.

Bodle, Wayne K. *The Valley Forge Winter: Civilians and Soldiers in War.* University Park: Pennsylvania State University Press, 2002.

Borick, Carl P. *A Gallant Defense: The Siege of Charleston, 1780.* Columbia: University of South Carolina Press, 2003.

Brackenridge, Hugh Henry. *History of the Western Insurrection in Pennsylvania, Commonly Called the Whiskey Insurrection, 1794.* Pittsburgh: W.S. Haven, 1859.

Bratten, John R. *The Gondola Philadelphia and the Battle of Lake Champlain.* College Station: Texas A&M University Press, 2002.

Breen, T.H. *Tobacco Culture: The Mentality of the Great Tidewater Planters on the Eve of Revolution.* Princeton, NJ: Princeton University Press, 1985.

Briggs, John, Christopher Harrison, Angus McInnes, and David Vincent. *Crime and Punishment in England: An Introductory History.* London: Routledge, 2005.

Brown, Stuart E. *Virginia Baron: The Story of Thomas, 6th Lord Fairfax.* Berryville, VA: Chesapeake, 1965.

Brumwell, Stephen. *Redcoats: The British Soldier and War in the Americas, 1755–1763.* Cambridge: Cambridge University Press, 2002.

Buchanan, John. *The Road to Guilford Courthouse: The American Revolution in the Carolinas.* New York: Wiley, 1999.

Burroughs, Peter. "Crime and Punishment in the British Army, 1815–1870." *English Historical Review* 100, no. 396 (1985): 545–71.

Butler, Jon. *Awash in a Sea of Faith: Christianizing the American People.* Studies in Cultural History. Cambridge, MA: Harvard University Press, 1990.

Callahan, North. *Daniel Morgan, Ranger of the Revolution.* 1st ed. New York: Holt, Rinehart and Winston, 1961.

Calloway, Colin G. *The Victory with No Name: The Native American Defeat of the First American Army*. Oxford: Oxford University Press, 2015.

Campbell, Alexander V. *The Royal American Regiment: An Atlantic Microcosm, 1755–1772*. Norman: University of Oklahoma Press, 2014.

Carozzi, Barry. "Historic Roads of Virginia." *Idiom* 46, no. 3 (2010): 30.

Carson, Jane. *Colonial Virginians at Play*. Williamsburg, VA: Colonial Williamsburg Foundation, 1989.

Catton, Bruce. *A Stillness at Appomattox*. Garden City, NY: Doubleday, 1962.

Chastellux, François Jean. *Travels in North America: In the Years 1780, 1781, and 1782*. Chapel Hill: published for the Institute of Early American History and Culture at Williamsburg, VA, by the University of North Carolina Press, 1963.

Chernow, Ron. *Washington: A Life*. New York: Penguin, 2010.

Clark, Walter, ed. *The State Records of North Carolina*, vol. 14. Goldsboro, NC: Nash Brothers, 1896.

Clausewitz, Karl von. *On War*. New York: Knopf, 1993.

Collins, James Potter, and John M. Roberts. *Autobiography of a Revolutionary Soldier*. Clinton, LA: Feliciana Democrat, 1859.

Conrad, David. "Early History of Winchester." *Annual Papers of Winchester Virginia Historical Society* 1 (1931).

Cooke, John Esten, and William Garrott Brown. *Virginia: A History of the People*. New York: Houghton, Mifflin, 1883.

Cooper, Jeff. *The Art of the Rifle*. Boulder, CO: Paladin Press, 1997.

Corbett, Theodore. *No Turning Point: The Saratoga Campaign in Perspective*. Campaigns and Commanders, vol. 32. Norman: University of Oklahoma Press, 2012.

Cox, Caroline. *A Proper Sense of Honor: Service and Sacrifice in George Washington's Army*. Chapel Hill: University of North Carolina Press, 2004.

Cramer, Zadok. *The Ohio and Mississippi Navigator Comprising an Ample Account of Those Beautiful Rivers, from the Head of the Former, to the Mouth of the Latter, . . .* 11th ed. Pittsburgh: Cramer and Spear, 1821.

Cubbison, Douglas. *The American Northern Theater Army in 1776: The Ruin and Reconstruction of the Continental Force*. Jefferson, NC: McFarland, 2010.

Curtis, Christopher Michael. *Jefferson's Freeholders and the Politics of Ownership in the Old Dominion*. Cambridge Studies on the American South. New York: Cambridge University Press, 2012.

Cusick, Philip A. *A Passion for Learning: The Education of Seven Eminent Americans*. New York: Teachers College Press, 2005.

Daniel Morgan Collection. William L. Clements Library. University of Michigan, Ann Arbor.

David, James Corbett. *Dunmore's New World: The Extraordinary Life of a Royal Governor in Revolutionary America—with Jacobites, Counterfeiters, Land Schemes, Shipwrecks, Scalping, Indian Politics, Runaway Slaves, and Two Illegal Royal Weddings*. Early American Histories. Charlottesville: University of Virginia Press, 2013.

Dearborn, Henry. "Journal of Quebec Expedition." In Kenneth Lewis Roberts, ed. *March to Quebec; Journals of the Members of Arnold's Expedition*. New York: Doubleday, Doran, 1940.

———. *Revolutionary War Journals of Henry Dearborn, 1775–1783*. Edited by Lloyd A. Brown, Howard Henry Peckham, and Hermon Dunlap Smith. New York: Da Capo Press, 1971.

Desjardin, Thomas A. *Through a Howling Wilderness: Benedict Arnold's March to Quebec, 1775*. 1st ed. New York: St. Martin's Press, 2006.

Dill, Alonzo Thomas. "Sectional Conflict in Colonial Virginia." *Virginia Magazine of History and Biography* 87, no. 3 (1979): 300–315.

Ellis, Joseph. "The Farewell." In *George Washington Reconsidered*, edited by Don Higginbotham. Charlottesville: University Press of Virginia, 2001.

Eustace, Nicole. *Passion Is the Gale: Emotion, Power, and the Coming of the American Revolution*. Chapel Hill: published for the Omohundro Institute of Early American History and Culture by the University of North Carolina Press, 2008.

Febiger, Christian. "Febiger Papers, 1777–1782." Edited by Bruce Lancaster. Cambridge, MA: Harvard College Library, 1947.

Fenn, Elizabeth A. *Pox Americana: The Great Smallpox Epidemic of 1775–82*, 1st ed. New York: Hill and Wang, 2010.

Ferling, John E. *The Ascent of George Washington: The Hidden Political Genius of an American Icon*. 1st US ed. New York: Bloomsbury Press, 2009.

Findley, William. *History of the Insurrection in the Four Western Counties of Pennsylvania in the Year MDCCXCIV: With a Recital of the Circumstances Specially Connected Therewith, and an Historical Review of the Previous Situation of the Country*. Philadelphia: printed by Samuel Harrison Smith, 1796.

Fischer, David Hackett. *Washington's Crossing*. New York: Oxford University Press, 2004.

Fleming, Thomas J. *Now We Are Enemies: The Story of Bunker Hill*. New York: St. Martin's Press, 1960.

Fontaine, John. *The Journal of John Fontaine: An Irish Huguenot Son in Spain and Virginia, 1710–1719* (Williamsburg, VA: Colonial Williamsburg Foundation, 1972), 90–100.

Founders Online, National Archives. https://founders.archives.gov.

Frederick County Superior Court Deed Book. Vol. 4, 1801. Frederick County Clerk of the Circuit Court, Winchester, VA.

Frederick County Virginia Order Books. Vols. 9–16. Frederick County Clerk of the Circuit Court, Winchester, VA.

Freeman, Douglas Southall. *George Washington, a Biography*. New York: Scribner, 1948.

Frey, Sylvia R. *The British Soldier in America: A Social History of Military Life in the Revolutionary Period*. Austin: University of Texas Press, 1981.

Gaff, Alan D. *Bayonets in the Wilderness: Anthony Wayne's Legion in the Old Northwest*. Norman: University of Oklahoma Press, 2004.

Gilmore, Russell. "'The New Courage': Rifles and Soldier Individualism, 1876–1918." *Military Affairs* 40, no. 3 (1976): 97–102.

Glanville, Jim. "The Fort Gower Resolves and Daniel Morgan's Role." *Winchester-Frederick County Historical Society Journal* 23 (2012): 1–22.

Glover, Lorri. *Founders as Fathers: The Private Lives and Politics of the American Revolutionaries*. New Haven: Yale University Press, 2014.

Godbeer, Richard. *The Overflowing of Friendship: Love between Men and the Creation of the American Republic*. Baltimore: Johns Hopkins University Press, 2009.

Godfrey, Carlos E. *The Commander-in-Chief's Guard: Revolutionary War*. Washington, DC: Stevenson-Smith, 1904.

Gordon, John W. *South Carolina and the American Revolution: A Battlefield History*. Columbia: University of South Carolina Press, 2003.

Graham, James. *The Life of General Daniel Morgan, with Portions of His Correspondence, Etc.* New York: Derby & Jackson, 1856.

Graham, James R. *The Planting of the Presbyterian Church in Northern Virginia: Prior to the Organization of Winchester Presbytery, December 4, 1794*. Winchester, VA: Geo. F. Norton, 1904.

Graham, Samuel. *Memoir of General Graham, with Notices of the Campaigns in Which He Was Engaged from 1779 to 1801*. Edited by J.J. Graham. Edinburgh: privately printed, 1862.

Greene, Jack. "Afterword," in *Sons of the Father: George Washington and His Protégés*, edited by Robert M.S. McDonald. Jeffersonian America. Charlottesville: University of Virginia Press, 2013.

Greene, Nathanael. *The Papers of General Nathanael Greene*, vols. 1–13. Edited by Richard K. Showman, Dennis Michael Conrad, and Roger N. Parks. Chapel Hill: published for the Rhode Island Historical Society by the University of North Carolina Press, 1976.

Griffin, Patrick. *American Leviathan: Empire, Nation, and Revolutionary Frontier.* 1st ed. New York: Hill and Wang, 2007.

Hamilton, Edward Pierce. "Colonial Warfare in North America." *Proceedings of the Massachusetts Historical Society* 80 (1968): 3–15.

Hammond, Grant Tedrick. *The Mind of War: John Boyd and American Security.* Washington, DC: Smithsonian Institution Press, 2001.

Harrison, Simon. *Dark Trophies: Hunting and the Enemy Body in Modern War.* New York: Berghahn Books, 2012.

Hart, Freeman Hansford. *The Valley of Virginia in the American Revolution, 1763–1789.* Chapel Hill: University of North Carolina Press, 1942.

Hening, William Waller, ed., *The Statutes at Large; Being a Collection of All the Laws of Virginia, from the First Session of the Legislature in the Year 1619.* Vol. 4. Charlottesville, VA: published for the Jamestown Foundation of the Commonwealth of Virginia by the University Press of Virginia, 1969.

Henriques, Peter. "The Great Collaboration: The Increasingly Close Relationship between George Washington and Alexander Hamilton." In *Sons of the Father: George Washington and His Protégés,* edited by Robert M.S. McDonald. Jeffersonian America. Charlottesville: University of Virginia Press, 2013.

Henry, John Joseph. "Campaign against Quebec." In Kenneth Lewis Roberts, ed. *March to Quebec; Journals of the Members of Arnold's Expedition.* New York: Doubleday, Doran, 1940.

Herndon, William Henry, and Jesse William Weik. *Herndon's Lincoln: The True Story of a Great Man.* Vol 2. Springfield, IL: Herndon's Lincoln Publishing, 1921.

Higginbotham, Don. *Daniel Morgan: Revolutionary Rifleman.* 1st ed. Chapel Hill: University of North Carolina Press, 1961.

Hill, William. "Sermon, 1802, Concerning Daniel Morgan." Richmond: Virginia Historical Society.

Hofstra, Warren R., ed. *George Washington and the Virginia Backcountry.* 1st ed. Madison, WI: Madison House, 1998.

———. *The Planting of New Virginia: Settlement and Landscape in the Shenandoah Valley.* Creating the North American Landscape. Baltimore: Johns Hopkins University Press, 2004.

———. *A Separate Place: The Formation of Clarke County, Virginia.* Clarke County Sesquicentennial ed. White Post, VA: Clarke County Sesquicentennial Committee, 1986.

Hofstra, Warren, and Clarence R. Geier. "Farm to Mill to Market: Historical Archaeology of an Emerging Grain Economy in the Shenandoah Valley." In *After the Backcountry: Rural Life in the Great Valley of Virginia, 1800–1900*, edited by Kenneth E. Koons and Warren R. Hofstra. 1st ed. Knoxville: University of Tennessee Press, 2000.

Hofstra, Warren R., and Karl B. Raitz, eds. *The Great Valley Road of Virginia: Shenandoah Landscapes from Prehistory to the Present.* Charlottesville: University of Virginia Press, 2010.

Hogeland, William. *The Whiskey Rebellion: George Washington, Alexander Hamilton, and the Frontier Rebels Who Challenged America's Newfound Sovereignty.* New York: Scribner, 2006.

Hogg, J. Bernard. "Presley Neville." *Western Pennsylvania Historical Magazine* 19, no. 1 (March 1936): 17–26.

Holton, Woody. *Unruly Americans and the Origins of the Constitution.* New York: Hill and Wang, 2007.

Homer. *The Odyssey.* Translated by Robert Fagles. New York: Penguin, 1997.

Horatio Gates Papers. New York Historical Society.

Hornberger, Patrick, and Joe Kindig III. *Masterpieces of the American Longrifle: The Joe Kindig, Jr. Collection.* 1st ed. Trappe, MD: Eastwind Publishing, 2015.

Isaac, Rhys. *The Transformation of Virginia, 1740–1790.* Chapel Hill: published for the Institute of Early American History and Culture by the University of North Carolina Press, 1982.

Johnson, William. *Sketches of the Life and Correspondence of Nathanael Greene: Major General of the Armies of the United States, in the War of the Revolution*, vols. 1-2. Charleston, SC: Printed for the Author by A.E. Milner, 1822.

Kauffman, Henry J. *The Pennsylvania-Kentucky Rifle.* Harrisburg, PA: Stackpole, 1960.

Kercheval, Samuel. *A History of the Valley of Virginia.* 3rd ed., rev. and extended. Woodstock, VA: W.N. Grabill, 1902.

Kett, Joseph F. *The Pursuit of Knowledge under Difficulties: From Self-Improvement to Adult Education in America, 1750–1990.* Stanford, CA: Stanford University Press, 1994.

Kindig, Joe. *Thoughts on the Kentucky Rifle in Its Golden Age.* Edited by Mary Ann Cresswell. Wilmington, DE: George N. Hyatt, 1960.

Kindig, Joseph K., III. *Artistic Ingredients of the Longrifle.* York, PA: George Shumway, 1989.

Knight, Betsy. "Prisoner Exchange and Parole in the American Revolution." *William and Mary Quarterly* 48, no. 2 (1991): 201–22.

Knollenberg, Bernhard. *Washington and the Revolution: A Reappraisal; Gates, Conway, and the Continental Congress.* New York: Macmillan, 1940.

Koons, Kenneth E., and Warren R. Hofstra, eds. *After the Backcountry: Rural Life in the Great Valley of Virginia, 1800–1900.* 1st ed. Knoxville: University of Tennessee Press, 2000.

Kwasny, Mark V. *Washington's Partisan War, 1775–1783*. Kent, OH: Kent State University Press, 1996.

Lamb, Roger. *Memoir of His Own Life*. Dublin: J. Jones, 1811.

Lambert, Robert Stansbury. *South Carolina Loyalists in the American Revolution*, 1st ed. Columbia: University of South Carolina Press, 1987.

Lears, T. J. Jackson. *Something for Nothing: Luck in America*. New York: Viking, 2003.

Lee, Henry. *The Campaign of 1781 in the Carolinas: With Remarks, Historical and Critical, on Johnson's Life of Greene. To Which Is Added an Appendix of Original Documents, Relating to the History of the Revolution*. Philadelphia: E. Littell, 1824.

———. *The Revolutionary War Memoirs of General Henry Lee*. 1st Da Capo Press ed. New York: Da Capo, 1998.

Lee, Richard Henry. *The Letters of Richard Henry Lee*. Edited by James Curtis Ballagh. New York: Macmillan, 1911.

Lee, Wayne E. *Crowds and Soldiers in Revolutionary North Carolina: The Culture of Violence in Riot and War*. Gainesville: University Press of Florida, 2001.

Lender, Mark Edward, and Garry Wheeler Stone. *Fatal Sunday: George Washington, the Monmouth Campaign, and the Politics of Battle*. Campaigns and Commanders, vol. 54. Norman: University of Oklahoma Press, 2016.

Lowenthal, David. *The Past Is a Foreign Country*. Cambridge: Cambridge University Press, 1985.

Luzader, John F. *Saratoga: A Military History of the Decisive Campaign of the American Revolution*. 1st paperback ed. New York: Savas Beatie, 2010.

Mahon, John K. "Anglo-American Methods of Indian Warfare, 1676–1794." *Mississippi Valley Historical Review* 45, no. 2 (1958): 254–75. https://doi.org/10.2307/1902929.

Malone, Miles S. "Falmouth and the Shenandoah: Trade before the Revolution." *American Historical Review* 40, no. 4 (1935): 693–703.

Marambaud, Pierre. *William Byrd of Westover, 1674–1744*. Charlottesville: University Press of Virginia, 1971.

Martin, James Kirby. *Benedict Arnold, Revolutionary Hero: An American Warrior Reconsidered*. New York: New York University Press, 1997.

Martin, Joseph Plumb. *Ordinary Courage: The Revolutionary War Adventures of Joseph Plumb Martin*. New York: John Wiley & Sons, 2012.

McDonald, Robert M.S., ed. *Sons of the Father: George Washington and His Protégés*. Jeffersonian America. Charlottesville: University of Virginia Press, 2013.

McDonnell, Michael A. *The Politics of War: Race, Class, and Conflict in Revolutionary Virginia*. Chapel Hill: published for the Omohundro Institute of Early American History and Culture by the University of North Carolina Press, 2007.

McGuire, Thomas J. *The Battle of Paoli: The Revolutionary War "Massacre" Near Philadelphia, September 1777*. Mechanicsburg, PA: Stackpole, 2015.

———.*The Philadelphia Campaign: Brandywine and the Fall of Philadelphia*. 1st ed., vol. 1. Mechanicsburg, PA: Stackpole, 2006.

———.*The Philadelphia Campaign: Germantown to Valley Forge*, vol. 2. Mechanicsburg, PA: Stackpole, 2006.

Mekeel, Arthur J. *The Relation of the Quakers to the American Revolution*. Washington, DC: University Press of America, 1979.

Meschutt, David. "Portraits of Daniel Morgan, Revolutionary War General." *American Art Journal* 17, no. 3 (1985): 35–43.

Middlekauff, Robert. *The Glorious Cause: The American Revolution, 1763–1789*. Rev. and expanded. Oxford: Oxford University Press, 2005.

Milner, Murray. *Status and Sacredness: A General Theory of Status Relations and an Analysis of Indian Culture*. New York: Oxford University Press, 1994.

Mintz, Max M. *The Generals of Saratoga: John Burgoyne & Horatio Gates*. New Haven, CT: Yale University Press, 1990.

Morgan, Daniel. "Letter to Miles Fisher from Daniel Morgan." Philadelphia, January 11, 1798. Historical Society of Pennsylvania, Philadelphia.

———. Papers of General Daniel Morgan. Theodorus Bailey Myers Collection. Series 5. New York Public Library. https://digitalcollections.nypl.org/collections/theodorus-bailey-myers-collection#/?tab=navigation&roots=4:ec482a70-2e58-0133-e1a5-58d385a7b928.

Morgan, Edmund S. *The Meaning of Independence: John Adams, Thomas Jefferson, George Washington*. New York: W.W. Norton, 1978.

Morgan, Gwenda, and Peter Rushton. *Rogues, Thieves, and the Rule of Law: The Problem of Law Enforcement in North-East England, 1718-1800*. London: UCL Press, 1998.

Morison, George. "Journal." In Kenneth Lewis Roberts, ed. *March to Quebec; Journals of the Members of Arnold's Expedition*. New York: Doubleday, Doran, 1940.

Morton, Louis. *Robert Carter of Nomini Hall: A Virginia Tobacco Planter of the Eighteenth Century*. Charlottesville: University Press of Virginia, 1969.

Moss, Roger W. "Isaac Zane, Jr., a 'Quaker for the Times.'" *Virginia Magazine of History and Biography* 77, no. 3 (1969): 291–306.

Murphy, Daniel Kevin. *William Washington, American Light Dragoon: A Continental Cavalry Leader in the War of Independence.* Yardley, PA: Westholme, 2014.

Nelson, Paul David. *Anthony Wayne, Soldier of the Early Republic.* Bloomington: Indiana University Press, 1985.

———. *General Horatio Gates: A Biography.* Baton Rouge: Louisiana State University Press, 1976.

O'Shaughnessy, Andrew Jackson. *The Men Who Lost America: British Leadership, the American Revolution, and the Fate of the Empire.* New Haven: Yale University Press, 2013.

Palmer, William, ed. *Calendar of Virginia State Papers.* Richmond: 1875–1893.

Pancake, John S. *1777: The Year of the Hangman.* Tuscaloosa: University of Alabama Press, 1977.

Philyaw, L. Scott. "George Washington, Daniel Morgan, and the Ideal of Service." In *Sons of the Father: George Washington and His Protégés,* edited by Robert M.S. McDonald. Jeffersonian America. Charlottesville: University of Virginia Press, 2013.

Pierce, John. "Journal." In Kenneth Lewis Roberts, ed. *March to Quebec; Journals of the Members of Arnold's Expedition.* New York: Doubleday, Doran, 1940.

Preston, David L. *Braddock's Defeat: The Battle of the Monongahela and the Road to Revolution.* Pivotal Moments in American History. Oxford: Oxford University Press, 2015.

Reist, Arthur L. *Conestoga Wagon, Masterpiece of the Blacksmith.* Lancaster, PA: Forry and Hacker, 1975.

Resch, John Phillips. *Suffering Soldiers: Revolutionary War Veterans, Moral Sentiment, and Political Culture in the Early Republic.* Amherst: University of Massachusetts Press, 1999.

Riedesel, Friedrich. *Memoirs and Letters of Major General Riedesel.* Vol. 1. Albany, NY: J. Munsell, 1868.

Roberts, Kenneth Lewis, ed. *March to Quebec; Journals of the Members of Arnold's Expedition.* New York: Doubleday, Doran, 1940.

Rothman, Ellen K. *Hands and Hearts: A History of Courtship in America.* Cambridge, MA: Harvard University Press, 1987.

Royster, Charles. *Light-Horse Harry Lee and the Legacy of the American Revolution.* 1st ed. New York: Knopf, 1981.

———. *A Revolutionary People at War: The Continental Army and American Character, 1775–1783.* Chapel Hill: published for the Institute of Early American History and Culture, Williamsburg, VA, by the University of North Carolina Press, 1979.

Russell, T. Triplett, and John K. Gott. *Fauquier County in the Revolution*. Warrenton, VA: Fauquier County American Bicentennial Commission, 1976.

Schnitzer, Eric H. "Tactics of the Battle of Saratoga." In *The Saratoga Campaign: Uncovering an Embattled Landscape,* edited by William A. Griswold and Donald W. Linebaugh, 39–81. Hanover, NH: University Press of New England, 2016.

Selby, John E. *The Revolution in Virginia, 1775–1783*. Williamsburg, VA: Colonial Williamsburg Foundation, distributed by University Press of Virginia, 1988.

Sellers, John Robert. "The Virginia Continental Line, 1775–1780." PhD diss., Tulane University, 1968.

Senter, Isaac. "Journal." In Kenneth Lewis Roberts, ed. *March to Quebec; Journals of the Members of Arnold's Expedition*. New York: Doubleday, Doran, 1940.

Shenandoah Store Ledgers A and B. Library of Virginia, Richmond.

Shumway, George, and Howard C. Frey. *Conestoga Wagon, 1750–1850: Freight Carrier for 100 Years of America's Westward Expansion*. 3rd ed. York, PA: G. Shumway, 1968.

Slaughter, Thomas P. *The Whiskey Rebellion: Frontier Epilogue to the American Revolution*. New York: Oxford University Press, 1986.

Snow, Dean R. *1777: Tipping Point at Saratoga*. New York: Oxford University Press, 2016.

Spoede, Robert William. "William Allason, Merchant in an Emerging Nation," PhD diss., College of William and Mary, 1973.

Stanley, George Francis Gillman. *Canada Invaded, 1775–1776*. Canadian War Museum, Historical Publications, no. 8. Toronto: Hakkert, 1973.

Stedman, Charles. *The History of the Origin, Progress, and Termination of the American War*. London: printed for the author, 1794.

Stocking, Abner. "Journal." In Kenneth Lewis Roberts, ed. *March to Quebec; Journals of the Members of Arnold's Expedition*. New York: Doubleday, Doran, 1940.

Strachan, Hew. *European Armies and the Conduct of War*. London: Allen & Unwin, 1983.

Sydnor, Charles S. *Gentlemen Freeholders: Political Practices in Washington's Virginia*. Chapel Hill: published for the Institute of Early American History and Culture at Williamsburg, VA, by the University of North Carolina Press, 1952.

Taaffe, Stephen R. *The Philadelphia Campaign, 1777–1778*. Modern War Studies. Lawrence: University Press of Kansas, 2003.

Tarleton, Banastre. *A History of the Campaigns of 1780 and 1781 in the Southern Provinces of North America*. New York: New York Times, 1968.

Tarter, Brent. *The Grandees of Government: The Origins and Persistence of Undemocratic Politics in Virginia.* Charlottesville: University of Virginia Press, 2013.

Taylor, Alan. "Political Personae in the Early Republic." In *Federalists Reconsidered,* edited by Doron S. Ben-Atar and Barbara B. Oberg. Charlottesville: University Press of Virginia, 1998.

Taylor, William Harrison. *Unity in Christ and Country: American Presbyterians in the Revolutionary Era, 1758–1801.* Tuscaloosa: University of Alabama Press, 2017.

Thayer, Simeon. "Journal." In Kenneth Lewis Roberts, ed. *March to Quebec; Journals of the Members of Arnold's Expedition.* New York: Doubleday, Doran, 1940.

Titus, James. *The Old Dominion at War: Society, Politics, and Warfare in Late Colonial Virginia.* American Military History. Columbia: University of South Carolina Press, 1991.

Waddell, Joseph A. "Diary of a Prisoner of War at Quebec, 1776." *Virginia Magazine of History and Biography* 9, no. 2 (1901): 144–52.

Ward, Harry M. *Charles Scott and the "Spirit of '76."* Charlottesville: University Press of Virginia, 1988.

———. *General William Maxwell and the New Jersey Continentals.* Contributions in Military Studies No. 168. Westport, CT: Greenwood Press, 1997.

———. *Major General Adam Stephen and the Cause of American Liberty.* Charlottesville: University Press of Virginia, 1989.

Ward, Matthew C. *Breaking the Backcountry: The Seven Years' War in Virginia and Pennsylvania, 1754–1765.* Pittsburgh: University of Pittsburgh Press, 2003.

White, George. *Statistics of the State of Georgia: Including an Account of Its Natural, Civil, and Ecclesiastical History; Together with a Particular Description of Each County, Notices of the Manners and Customs of Its Aboriginal Tribes, and a Correct Map of the State.* Savannah: W. Thorne Williams, 1849.

Wickwire, Franklin B. *Cornwallis and the War of Independence.* London: Faber & Faber, 1971.

Wilkinson, James. *Memoirs of My Own Times.* Philadelphia: printed by Abraham Small, 1816.

Williams, Glenn F. *Dunmore's War: The Last Conflict of America's Colonial Era.* Yardley, PA: Westholme, 2017.

Winchester-Frederick County Historical Society. *Men and Events of the Revolution in Winchester and Frederick County, Virginia.* Winchester, VA: Winchester-Frederick County Historical Society, 1975.

Wright, John W. "The Corps of Light Infantry in the Continental Army." *American Historical Review* 31, no. 3 (1926): 454–61.

Wright, Louis B., and Lessing J. Rosenwald. *Letters of Robert Carter, 1720–1727: The Commercial Interests of a Virginia Gentleman.* San Marino, CA: Huntington Library Publications, 1940.

Wyatt-Brown, Bertram. *Southern Honor: Ethics and Behavior in the Old South.* Oxford: Oxford University Press, 1982.

York, Neil L. "Pennsylvania Rifle: Revolutionary Weapon in a Conventional War?" *Pennsylvania Magazine of History and Biography* 103, no. 3 (1979): 302–24.

Young, Thomas. "Memoir of Major Thomas Young." *Orion* 3 (1843): 84–88, 100–105.

ACKNOWLEGMENTS

I BEGAN this book with a quote from *King Lear*, and now I end it with one: "Nothing can be made out of nothing" (Act 1.1). So it is with books, which are the result not only of reading and thinking, but ideally of conversation and even of the smallest and seemingly most insignificant remarks.

Without the work of Warren Hofstra, this new biography of Daniel Morgan could not have been written. Brent Tarter was, as always, my guide through the intricacies of Virginia's history. Richard Sullivan advised me on colonial Virginia rifles with the considerable authority of a Colonial Williamsburg gunsmith. The bulk of this biography was written during the early morning before going to work at the Advanced Studies in Culture Foundation in Charlottesville, Virginia. There I benefited from the friendship, advice, and encouragement of Murray Milner, Jackson Lears, and Jay Tolson. Joseph Davis was kind enough to bring me in for an "Emerging Ideas" seminar, allowing a historian to perform before sociologists. John Arpin and Andrus Ashoo carefully and patiently read the manuscript, and they offered thoughtful insight during the editing process.

As an independent historian, I could not have done this work without the benefits of new digital collections such as Founder's Online—perhaps the National Archives' greatest achievement since preserving the Declaration of Independence and the Constitution in argon gas. But thankfully, for those of us who love the detective work, research in physical archives is still necessary. As always, I benefited from the collections and staff of the Rockefeller Library of the Colonial Williamsburg Foundation; the Library of Virginia; the Stewart Bell Jr. Archives at the magnificent Handley Library in Winchester, VA; and the staff of the manuscript collections at the Library of Congress. I must also give particular thanks to Dr. Paula Skreslet, reference and archives librarian at Union Presbyterian Seminary in Richmond, VA; Terese Austin, Jayne Ptolemy, and Jakob Dopp at the William L. Clements Library of the University of Michigan; Ellen Clark and Michele Silverman at the library of the Society of the Cincinnati; and John McClure, Matthew Guillen, Emily Bradford, and Anne McCrery, who superintend my home away from home, the library of the Virginia Museum of History and Culture.

My thanks also to Bruce H. Franklin of Westholme for taking a chance on a novice author. His care and attention to detail have been admirably enabled by the copyediting of Ron Silverman, the maps of Tracy Dungan, and the brilliant design of Trudi Gershenov. Work on this book began when my agent Roger Williams asked if I'd like to write a biography of Daniel Morgan. He could not know that my enthusiastic *yes* was thanks in part to my aunt, Mary Louise Zambone Martin, who took me, annually, to Valley Forge, and bought me my first-ever scholarly book on the Revolution—Don Higginbotham's *Daniel Morgan, Revolutionary Rifleman*. My wife, Beth, has welcomed Daniel's presence over the past few years, and perhaps even came to like him a little bit; I thank her for her love, curiosity about the strange world of Virginia, and careful editorial work. My sister, Jennifer, encouraged and questioned me in turn; I thank her for her many gifts, good sense, and life-long friendship. I dedicate this book to my parents, Candus Dorothea and Albert Stephen, who are the foundation of this book: they encouraged my questions; supplied me with many books; let me wander in the woods; and took me to the places Daniel Morgan went.

INDEX

learning to read and write, 49
letter to Washington and, 260,
   287-288, 298-299
losing respect for Lord Dunmore
   and, 60
march to Quebec and, 80-81
marriage to Abigail Curry and, 42-
   43
partisan warfare and, 119-120,
   126, 135, 141, 143, 158, 165,
   172, 181, 209, 212, 216, 221,
   242, 251-253, 255, 283
Pontiac's War and, 34-35
replacing Stephenson and, 115-116
slave population in lower Valley
   and, 8-9
Soldier's Rest and, xv, 33, 47, 55,
   170, 201, 254-255, 297, 313,
   321n13, 343n8, 346n32
supporting Washington against the
   Conway Cabal and, 168
taking command of Woodford's
   Virginia brigade and, 186
Morgan, Nancy, 42, 47, 272-274,
   283, 285-286, 303-304, 307
Morgan's Rifles, 122-123
Morgan, Willoughby, 307-308
Morris, Joseph, 123, 149, 161
Mount Defiance, 133
Mount Holly, 160-161
Mount Vernon, 13, 41, 196
Muhlenberg, John Peter Gabriel,
   121-123, 160, 211, 328n20
Münchausen, Friedrich von, 124
Murray, Robert, 55
Muskingum River, 57-58

Nagel, George, 81
Narragansett Bay, 215
Native Americans, 54, 74, 82, 119-
   120, 132, 135, 278-279, 283
Navy Department, 295
Neally's Fort, 31
Nelson, Horatio, 195
Nelson, Thomas, 258, 263
Neville, John, 48, 172, 273, 285-
   289, 291, 299, 321n16,
   346n22

Neville, Presley, 152, 172, 273, 285-
   286, 296-299, 303, 307,
   343n8, 346n22
New Haven Green, 83
New Jersey Brigade, 158, 174
New Jersey Loyalist infantry, 208
New Jersey militia, 117, 119, 125,
   174, 181
New Spain, 94
New York Harbor, 114, 116, 128,
   181
Nielsen Farm, 135
Ninth Regiment of Foot, 137-138,
   155
Norridgewalk Falls, 88
North Carolina Brigade, 174
North Carolina militia, 219, 228,
   230-231, 243, 247
Northern Neck, 7, 15, 41, 211, 293
North River, 116
Nova Scotia, 25

O'Bannon, Presley Neville, 307
Occoquan Creek, 262
The Odyssey, 304
Ogden, Matt, 87
Ohio River, 18, 21, 25, 34, 52-54,
   58, 76, 279, 286, 298, 307
Old Chapel, 51
Oneidas, 142, 154, 173
OODA loops, 153-154
Opequon Creek, 3, 6, 9, 31, 108
Ottendorf, Nicholas Baron von, 126
Ottoman Empire, 59
"Overmountain Men", 208

Pacolet River, 219, 225, 283
Paine, Thomas, 291, 301
Paley, William, 308
Paoli massacre, 191
Paramus, 129
Parkinson's Ferry, 284, 286
Parliament, 54, 78, 82
Parr, James, 173
The Partisan (De Jeney), 118
partisan warfare, 117-120, 126, 135,
   141, 143, 158, 165, 172, 181,